# CLIFF

PATRICK DONCASTER & TONY JASPER

# CLIFF

SIDGWICK & JACKSON
LONDON

First published 1981 by Sidgwick & Jackson Limited

This edition published 1992 by Sidgwick & Jackson Limited
a division of Pan Macmillan Publishers Limited
Cavaye Place London SW10 9PG
and Basingstoke

Associated companies throughout the world

ISBN 0-283-06134-0

3 5 7 9 8 6 4

A CIP catalogue record for this book is available from
the British Library

Phototypeset by Parker Typesetting Service, Leicester
Printed and bound in Great Britain by Mackays of Chatham PLC, Chatham, Kent

To

PETER AND BARBARA SHARROCKS
WINN AND ROY JEWELL
JACK AND ELSIE MARY ELLIOTT
MANUEL, DANIEL, LUISA AND JULIA

# CONTENTS

# ACKNOWLEDGEMENTS

Special mention must be made of Diana Brinton, Christine Whitehead, Anton Husmann, Harry De Louw, Mary Posner, Takao Horie, Helen Gummer and those credited in the 1981 edition of this book, not forgetting Cliff and those associated with him.

Major mention must be made of the late Pat Doncaster, with whom the original work was written.

# INTRODUCTION

The Cliff Richard story is an ongoing affair. Since Pat Doncaster and I chronicled his career in the 1981 edition of this book, he has had a success at least comparable with his supposed heyday, from the late 1950s to the Beatles period in the following decade. The process of bringing up-to-date most artists who have had major acclaim generally entails some 'padding' to give the impression that a new edition is more than an exercise to find a way for an author and publisher to make some money. However, an update on Cliff is a major affair. So many things have happened, and for most of any year, except for holidays, he is active somewhere in the world.

I find the 1980s Cliff, with the exception of 'We Don't Talk Anymore', which appeared in the months immediately preceding the 1980s, and the 1974 album *The 31st of February Street*, far more interesting than the Cliff of the 1960s and 1970s. One could almost wish that era might be allowed to take a back seat, perhaps to be wheeled out on special occasions. I would ban 'Bachelor Boy' – and the like – not because it isn't a good pop record, along with many others of its period, but simply because it has held Cliff back from maturing as a performer. Taking into account *The 31st of February Street*, one can see how he can still walk and sing with some of the best performers in popular music, and probably tower over most, but that's hardly likely to happen when his repertoire must always include the old numbers that are so easy when it comes to vocalizing and presenting. Cliff is one of the few professionals around who knows the studio situation backwards and who on stage surpasses almost any current performer and, unlike Madonna, however entertaining she may be at times, doesn't have to flirt with the small ideas of tatty decadence.

The years after 1981 form the bulk of this hopefully weighty addition to a book that was a national top ten hardback chart hit, and is still borrowed frequently from public libraries (as witnessed in my PLR return).

Sifting through the vast collection of Cliff material that I possess, speaking with people involved in his career, hearing again some of the music, watching videos, recalling concerts, pawing through many interviews with Cliff (and a few with Bill Latham, his great buddy) it is clear that the 1980s has enough material in itself for a book, for even with the increased number of pages in this new edition, masses and masses of material can only gain a passing reference.

There is something very British about our unwillingness to recognize our own. Cliff would enjoy vastly greater respect if he was an American or, God forbid, if he died tomorrow – then, and perhaps only then, would something approaching a true assessment be made. Equally, there is something in human nature that makes us take a few facts on board, and then stay with them, irrespective of whatever else might change or enlarge the established scenario. Hence my earlier remark about Cliff and 'Bachelor Boy'; even now, producers of major events and even, dare I say, some fans, cannot get beyond this. They leave Cliff floundering in times gone. And while some are stuck with the 1960s Cliff, others are quite oblivious of the seventies. And, more alarmingly, since religion is such a strong factor in Cliff's life and he cannot now be understood without reference to it, there are Christians who somehow fail, or do not wish to see, the colossal work he has done in direct and indirect evangelism. Sometimes his contribution is treated as some kind of minor addendum; if this is so, it's simply because a great deal of Christian witness doesn't come within shouting distance of meeting some of the people Cliff has affected with his faith. Cliff's contribution towers over any other from someone with faith in a pop culture. I don't think he is interested in being 'foremost' but the simple fact is that he is just that. Yet I am not sure if the various Christian, mostly mainstream bodies with whom I have had dealings, really see him as part of an overall mission. That, some might say, is life. And it is sad.

This new edition of *Cliff* does not offer so-called answers to familiar Cliff questions, such as: is he gay? (People say to me 'you must know' but even if I did, which I don't, I wouldn't answer. I confess that my real care would be that he is happy, whatever he chooses.) Nor is there an answer to the perennial question: why is he not married?, save to reply with the question: why should he be? This comes up in the new text only because his involvement with Sue Barker became national news. That saga tells one thing, among others: it is hard to be a major star, and it is even harder for someone like Cliff to attempt a relationship with *anyone*, when even a mere sighting of him with them can mean column inches and speculation.

This book aims simply to tell his story as it has been set out publicly, although perhaps with more comment and observation in the new edition compared with the previous one. My impression of Cliff is of a relatively uncomplicated person with enormous strength and energy, of extraordinary talent and musical ability that is only, even now, partially unfurled. Here is a man who can talk anyone into silence and who has a quick, and often very amusing, sense of humour. I admire him as a Christian, and I am irritated by the apparent indifference of some so-called musical experts who, in their own arrogance, dismiss him, as they search for a new short-lived trend-setter, complete with fancy phrases, quirky sounds and banal, forced image. What Cliff does with his time is his own business, except that he has never asked me to play tennis against him, and once I did rather well in that field . . .

# CHAPTER ONE

# OVERTURE
# AND BEGINNERS

On an autumn evening in 1957 a beefy lad named John Foster and some of his pals walked into the Five Horseshoes pub at Hoddesdon, Hertfordshire, for a pint or two.

They were in Teddy Boy rig – long drape coats and drainpipe trousers that might have been moulded to their legs.

John was eighteen, tall and big-chested, and earned his drinking money driving a dumper truck and tractor at a local sewage works. He ordered a pint of black and tan, a mixture of brown ale and light beer.

'It was a kind of long public bar that doubled as a hall,' John recalls, although he can't remember the exact date or whether or not it was a Saturday night.

'I don't think it was,' he says, 'because it wasn't all that busy, but I was a bit of a Teddy Boy in those days and got dressed up at weekends. There was nothing posh about the place and there was this group playing at the end of the bar. Three young lads. They had no lead guitar, just two rhythm guitars and drums and this dark-haired kid doing an Elvis act.

'They didn't have much of a repertoire and were just there to play a few songs. All done in three chords.

'There was something about the youngster who was singing and playing guitar, something that was sort of magic.

'I knew nothing about show business. My one claim was that twice I'd been up to the 2 i's coffee bar in Soho, where the rock 'n' rollers played. It was only twenty-five miles to London from where I lived in the village of Hertford Heath, but it was big-time to go to London in those days.

'Anyway, I said to my mates, "I'm going to manage that kid." They thought I was barmy.

'I went up to him and said, "Hello, my name's John Foster – do you want a manager?"

'His name was Harry Webb and he was about seventeen, a year younger than me. Anyway, Harry agreed. I told him to ring me, because I was on the phone and he wasn't. He lived in a council house at Cheshunt, not very far away . . .'

It was the start of something not only big but sensational.

Within twelve short months Harry Webb would become Cliff Richard; cut a smash hit record for a major label; make his debut on television and tour the land with a variety bill headed by American singing stars, the Kalin Twins.

In no time at all he would become a film star, top the bill at the hallowed London Palladium and be a name as well known as soap powder in millions of homes.

John Foster smiles and says: 'I lost my job at the sewage works. They fired me for taking too much time off.'

# CHAPTER TWO

# BIRTH OF AN AGE GROUP

Harry Rodger Webb – 'both my father and I spelled Rodger with a d,' he says – was thirteen and a half the day the revolution began; a normal, healthy schoolboy who had failed the dreaded eleven-plus examination that would have gained him a place in a grammar school. Now he was plodding on towards a future that promised little other than a job behind a desk somewhere and a workaday, possibly middle-class life with each new day following much the same monotonous pattern as the previous one.

But . . . came the revolution.

The date was 12 April 1954, and no one knew at that time that it would turn out to be a historic day – least of all one William John Haley, a plumpish twenty-seven-year-old American with family links in Lancashire (his mother's father had been a baker in Ulverston which was, coincidentally, the birthplace of Stan Laurel).

On that April day Bill Haley, who played reasonable guitar, and six colleagues who traded with him as a lively band called the Comets, gathered before the microphones in New York City to record a modest number entitled 'Rock Around The Clock'.

It was like lighting a slow-burning fuse. The song would take its time to travel. In 1956 it would explode with a gigantic roar. Rock 'n' roll would break from its bondage, a lusty offshoot of the black man's music hitherto confined to the ghettos and a few rebellious white youngsters.

In earlier years it had been frowned upon (as was New Orleans jazz in the beginning) and had been generally discarded as 'race music'. More knowledgeable folk called it rhythm and blues.

The usually simple lyrics were strong on two words – rock and roll – although they were rarely linked. The singer was gonna

3

rock his baby. They were also gonna roll. They were words that pictured movement and the movement was definitely sexual, lyrics that would at some stage be labelled by a reprimanding *Variety*, America's show business bible, as *leer-ics* . . .

It was a white disc jockey named Alan Freed who first thought of tying the two words together and giving race music a more acceptable – to whites – description. Rock 'n' roll, he called it. Thus rock 'n' roll it became right across the world. In the end people, being people, would axe it to the one word, rock.

Till then rock, at least in Britain, had been a minty pink stick with the name of a seaside town running through it, or something a ship smashed into on a dirty night at sea. Or, as a dictionary defined it – a swaying to and fro.

Freed, then in his late twenties, had entered music accidentally in the early fifties when he was working in Akron, Ohio, as a sportscaster. A disc jockey went sick and Freed took his place, spinning tunes that were middle of the road and intended for all ears, parents and young people alike, sung by balladeers such as Crosby, Nat King Cole, Perry Como, Rosemary Clooney and Sinatra. The family then used to listen together. The Teen Age had not yet dawned, when it would become accepted that sons and daughters would have a record-player of their own and play their *own* music in their own dens or bedrooms. They had no music to call their own until Haley and Freed came along – unless you count nursery rhymes.

Freed moved on to Cleveland, where one day a call from Leo Mintz, boss of the big city's largest record store, led him to the three words that would echo around the globe and at the same time bring him a fortune – and catch the ears of Harry Webb.

White kids, said the store chief breathlessly, were now suddenly going for rhythm and blues records by black artists. The old cliché was never more true – they were 'selling like hot cakes'.

Alan Freed was not a man to let a trend skip past him. He started to play R&B, as the term had now been abbreviated, and his listening figures were boosted by a new age group – teenagers.

Then R&B was dropped to make way for his new description: rock 'n' roll. It was the dawn of a new era, both musically and economically. He claimed no copyright on the phrase, but at the outset some disc companies *did* pay a fee to him so that they could use the term.

Freed, who punctuated his shows with excited cries and howls, using such exhortations as 'Go-man-go!', detached himself from the microphone to promote dances and rock 'n' roll concerts, eventually being wooed to New York in 1954 – the year of 'Rock Around The Clock' – to air his adopted music on station WINS. Rock was arriving, although the artists were still mainly black.

Bill Haley, despite the softness of his looks and the absurd trademark of a kiss curl plastered to his broad forehead, was shrewd enough to notice this youthful rebellion at about the same time as Freed.

In the early fifties, Haley was leading a country and western band – not far from Freed in Ohio – around the adjoining state of Pennsylvania. They called themselves the Saddlemen and, in retrospect, looked and sounded rather square, as the saying then went.

As early as 1951 Haley had begun to record songs with the word rock in the title. One was 'Rock The Joint', which sounded very much like the godfather of 'Rock Around The Clock'. By 1953 he had recorded 'Shake, Rattle and Roll' – still, it is noticeable, not stringing the two all-important words together.

The Saddlemen were renamed the Comets, but his success was for some time purely local. Rock 'n' roll had to wait for 'Rock Around The Clock' for its first white star and acclaimed king.

The song was first heard in the film *The Blackboard Jungle*, which dealt with the new-found movement of youthful protest, this time against the background of school.

It was released early in 1955 but still 'Rock Around The Clock' had a long way to go before it became the battle hymn of the new teenage group and the symbol of rebellion.

A cheap, scrappy movie production made in 1956 did the trick. It was entitled *Rock Around The Clock* and it brought together at last Alan Freed and Bill Haley, the first King of Rock. It was a blockbuster of a hit. The Haley disc was reissued and in Britain alone that year sold a million – a then undreamed-of figure.

It was quite a year. The third giant of rock 'n' roll, already waiting in the wings, was unleashed on the world with a song called 'Heartbreak Hotel'. The singer was a truck driver named Elvis Aaron Presley, born one of twins (the other died) and destined soon to oust Haley from his throne.

All three* were to be immense influences on the life and times

* Not one of the trio survives. Alan Freed died of uremia in January 1965. He was forty-two. Presley died in August 1977, also aged forty-two. Haley died in February 1981, at fifty-five the oldest survivor.

of Harry Rodger Webb: Alan Freed for giving the world the three immortal words that would describe Harry's eventual trade; Haley for giving them life and soul; and Presley for a new young image with which Harry could identify – a gyrating sexual image with dyed, greasy black hair and sideburns, along with a mean moody scowl.

Here for the youth of the world, like a long-awaited messiah, was the real symbol to go along with the music. Presley was twenty-one in that break-out year of rock 'n' roll. He was the rage of the year.

Now the young had built for themselves a solid foundation for the new age group. The word 'teen' began to dominate headlines and crept into song titles. Magazines appeared aimed solely at the teens, along with fashions and movies. It was a rebellion against parents, against authority, against all forms of rules and regulations, nuclear weapons, fuddy-duddyism, the Church in all its varied branches – against anything, in fact, that wasn't young. It was a movement that would grow and grow and lead eventually to such anti-heroes as the Rolling Stones and the numerous protesters who wallowed in their wake.

Not that the new, emergent age group found revolution to be a smooth ride in the mid-fifties. Authority started a rebellion of its own, while parents looked on with grave suspicion.

First Alan Freed and Bill Haley took most of the stick, until Elvis the Pelvis, as he was quickly dubbed, became the figurehead of the Big Beat, which some people in the media, endeavouring to ditch the rock label were now calling the music. Both Haley and Freed were accused across the States – and later in Britain – of fermenting rock riots. Freed, booming with his sell-out concerts, was getting pins stuck in him by city fathers and mayors who sagely nodded their heads and decided to ban him from appearing in their cities. Commented Freed: 'It's a shame that ninety-seven per cent of the country's youngsters must suffer because of the three per cent hoodlum element.'

At the same time in Britain a minority of troublemaking Teddy Boys – a group that adopted rock 'n' roll as their very own – danced in the aisles and ripped up cinema seats in several areas when *Rock Around The Clock* was shown. Said Haley: 'I don't see why some people get so hot under the collar. Some folks hate to see kids happy. I can tell you honestly – I've never seen a riot . . .'

Which was true, it seems. When he invaded Britain early in 1957 with his Comets, his stage act of around thirty minutes was a harmless, run of the mill presentation that was about as sexual as a team of performing seals. The Comets looked like a bunch of oldies desperately trying to hang on to a youthful image by falling around and playing their instruments in unorthodox positions. Rudy Pompilli blew his saxophone standing on his head. Bill Williamson, lying on his back, plucked away at his bass fiddle held aloft. It was laughable.

But there was no denying the music. It did something to people. It made then get out of their seats and want to dance in the aisles or swarm towards the stage while Haley mouthed the banal lyrics.

Harry Webb, still at school in Cheshunt in Hertfordshire, was swept up in it all. The inoffensive Haley, now at thirty an old man in the eyes of the teens, was unknowingly responsible for getting Harry one of his few black marks in life.

Harry played truant one day, getting up at five to take himself off to Kilburn, in northwest London, to join the throng scrambling for tickets to see Haley and his Comets in action at the vast 4,000-seater Gaumont State cinema. Next day the school took Harry's prefect badge away for this evil deed. With a hint of rebellion Harry protested to the headmaster: 'If we'd been to see the Bolshoi Ballet you'd have given us a pat on the back.'

He also promised, tongue in cheek it seems, never to skip school again 'unless Elvis is coming'.

His English teacher, Mrs Jay Norris, was kinder. 'In ten years' time, Harry,' she said, 'I'll bet you won't even remember the name Bill Haley.'

'I'll bet you a box of chocolates I will, miss,' Harry said.

Ten years later he was as good as his word . . .

But Elvis was to be his greater hero and responsible for the enormous eruption in his life that would culminate in Harry Webb becoming Cliff Richard, international rock 'n' roll star.

Harry joined the teen movement along with millions of others. Before Freed, Haley and Presley they had been simply young people, youngsters, youth, in-betweens or kids, and had frequently been dismissed as being at the awkward age.

Not any more.

Now Harry's hero Elvis was finding knives in his back. Some American critics were crying that he was obscene. One complained that he was just 'a male burlesque dancer'.

In New York for one of his early coast-to-coast TV appearances, Elvis had his guitar taken away for the performance and was seen

7

on screen only from the waist up – in case he offended anyone. Elvis without movement was like Hardy without Laurel.

Neither Elvis nor his astute manager Tom Parker, the self-styled Colonel, sought out a dark corner of the studio to weep in. Instead they pocketed £17,000 (a fortune a quarter of a century ago) for this one innocuous stint on the nationwide box.

Away from television Elvis was also being accused of incitement to riot and causing teenage misbehaviour. He said innocently, and no doubt with a prod from the Colonel, 'If I thought my rock 'n' roll singing was causing juvenile delinquency, I would go back to driving a truck. I don't love money that much . . .'

Nevertheless, a worried pastor in the Deep South held a prayer service that Elvis might 'be granted salvation'. And in St Louis a black disc jockey named James Dillon Burks described rock 'n' roll as 'an ignorant type of music.'

Haley's record company started to show a little concern about the music's image as well, issuing a disc with one side entitled 'Teenager's Mother', whose lyric protested that rock wasn't sinful and 'can't be bad if it makes you glad'. The whole idea went sour. The A-side was called 'Rip It Up'!

A rather bemused Bill Haley sailed into Britain with the Comets for the first time in the old Cunarder *Queen Elizabeth* on 5 February 1957 for a tour that took in London, Manchester, Birmingham, Leeds, Newcastle, Liverpool, Cardiff and Plymouth.

Earlier, on Wednesday 23 January, the *Daily Mirror* had astonished the rest of Fleet Street and no doubt millions of its readers by devoting the whole front page to announcing its 'big plans' to welcome 'the King of Rock 'n' Roll'. Haley loomed large on the page with his guitar.

The only other story on page one, dwarfed by the bold black type surrounding Haley, disclosed that Prince Charles and Princess Anne had been inoculated against polio, which had been claiming many young victims up and down the country.

Despite the wave of criticism rock 'n' roll was now attracting, the *Mirror* was not only sponsoring the Haley tour but also extending a big hand. It gave away seats at the concerts and Haley discs in simple competitions and also hired a train – a Rock 'n' Roll Special – to greet him at Southampton and escort him in triumph to London.

*Mirror* columnist Noel Whitcomb was despatched to the United States to join Haley at his home in Chester, Pennsylvania, to ghost a daily column by Haley as he journeyed to New York to embark aboard the *Queen Elizabeth* and as the liner sailed the Atlantic.

All the Comets were married men and, like Haley, brought along their wives – the whole party travelling tourist class.

At Waterloo Station in London, 3,000 fans besieged the baffled Haley as he tried to enter his limousine. Hundreds of girls lost their shoes in the great scuffle and some were injured. The New Battle of Waterloo, screamed the headlines.

Haley didn't know what hit him. 'Fantabulous!' he kept mouthing, a new word to go with the new music. 'My feet didn't touch the ground for fifty yards,' he said. 'I lost my gloves, the buttons off my overcoat and a case with my overnight gear in it.'

Thus rock 'n' roll, to which Harry Webb had now sworn his devotion, had arrived and now seemed about to achieve its first acknowledgement of respectability in Britain.

The *Mirror* had done its homework. Some months before deciding to sponsor Haley it hosted a small rock 'n' roll party in a suite at the Waldorf Hotel in London's Aldwych to find out what the music did or could do to people.

Disc columnist Patrick Doncaster and writer Tony Miles (later to become chairman of Mirror Group Newspapers) took along several attractive secretaries from the office, the Rev. John Hornby, an East End vicar, and a tame psychologist.

Keith Waterhouse, creator of *Billy Liar* and then a *Mirror* feature writer, scoured parts of London in a cab and plucked a handful of likely lads off the streets to be guinea pigs – with some difficulty, it must be said, because they were all a little suspicious of a character who suddenly halted a taxi at the kerb to invite them to a rock party!

Haley and Presley records were played for more than two hours to the assembled participants in what was seen at the time as a bold experiment. But there was no mini riot, no horseplay, no rave-up. Just some honest to goodness unsexy dancing which consisted mainly of the girls being twirled until their skirts ballooned. The Rev. Hornby managed a twirl or two himself. He summed up rock 'n' roll thus: 'It's exciting rhythm, enormous fun. It's a red herring to blame it for the bad behaviour of Teddy Boys.'

The psychologist had this to say: 'This is music stripped bare – a persistent, insistent beat. A perfectly good outlet for the exuberance of youth. But,' he added as a possible warning, 'the impact depends on the person . . .'

This, then, was the way it was in Britain as Harry Webb steered his course towards the world of rock, taking in one of the *Mirror's* Haley concerts at Kilburn late in February 1957 (the one that cost him his prefecture).

There were still the fors and againsts, for the movement was swelling. Already Britain had someone who had been heralded as the nation's answer to Presley – a tousle-headed blond merchant seaman with a wide, toothy grin, a Cockney from Bermondsey born Tommy Hicks but now renamed Tommy Steele.

He had been launched into Discland in September 1956, the first of many, after discovery in the 2 i's coffee bar in Soho – a location that would become a Mecca for the pilgrims and hopefuls of rock 'n' roll.

But Presley? 'I hate him!' Tommy had said, all of nineteen years and ready to set the world alight.

Honestly?

'Well, I don't really hate him. I just don't like his style.'

His own style, however, was little removed from Presley's. When told by one critic that he sounded something like Elvis he retorted: 'I was singing like this *before* Presley . . . Bill Haley's my man . . .'

That September week of Tommy's launch in 1956 with a British-made song, 'Rock With The Caveman' on the Decca label, founding father Haley had *five* records in the Top Twenty chart (early charts were limited to twenty placings but grew with the industry until the weekly lists took in fifty and then seventy-five).

One of the writers of 'Rock With The Caveman' was to be found at the 2 i's coffee bar, an unassuming East-Ender with a lot of ambition but at that time a silk-screen printer and a dab hand at décor.

In fact he decorated the tiny cellar beneath the little café – barely roomy enough to swing a guitar – and incorporated two large eyes. The cellar was where the music blasted forth and when this Cockney wasn't splashing paint around he sat in with the various hopefuls and groups, strumming his fingers up and down a washboard in rhythm.

His name: Lionel Bart. Even then he was dreaming of writing a musical based on Dickens' *Oliver Twist* and had roughed out a first act in a Woolworth's sixpenny lined notepad. When someone pointed out loftily that no producer would ever look at a first act with something like fourteen scene changes, Bart was undaunted and forged on.

He was to figure large in the life of Harry Webb, write a song that would be a turning point in his life and his career when he became Cliff Richard, and help mould him into someone above the average rock 'n' roller who swivelled his hips and curled a lip, exuding rebellion. Someone a little nicer . . .

The 2 i's would also be for ever a landmark in the life of Harry Webb. Like a magnet, it would draw him as it did thousands of others, including one Terry Nelhams, from Acton way, who would become Adam Faith.

Literally thousands would fall by the wayside and go back to their jobs or the dole. Only Steele and Cliff Richard would emerge as giants, go forward into manhood and still be names that could fill a theatre thirty years later.

# CHAPTER THREE

# INDIAN SUNSET

The long trek to the 2 i's in Soho and fame as a rock 'n' roller extraordinary began for Harry Rodger Webb halfway across the world in India, where he was born on 14 October 1940 in Lucknow.

Britain was at war with Germany and Italy, standing alone, fighting for survival and her freedom. The Battle of Britain had been won – just, but enough for Hitler to call off Operation Sealion, his much-trumpeted and feared invasion of England set for 15 September, a month before baby Harry weighed in at Lucknow. The Battle of Britain was the first German defeat of the Second World War and America had yet to play its hand.

For Harry's parents, Rodger and Dorothy Webb, England was still the homeland, although neither of them had ever seen it. Both had relatives braving it out in bomb-battered Britain. He had been born of English parents in Burma and was now an area manager employed by the well-known catering firm of Kellner. His wife Dorothy had been born of English parents in India, her father a British regular soldier. They married within six months of meeting.

India was then British India and for exiles the bonds were close. They were, however, peaceful days in the Indian empire while Britain still felt the lash of nightly air raids and Mr Churchill stalked the ruins in a steel helmet next morning. Japan would be the obvious threat to India and invasion was always a possibility, although it wasn't until late 1941, when Harry was fourteen months old, that Japan attacked neighbouring Burma. Ironically, it would be the Indians who ran the Webb family out of their home and livelihood in the end, after partition in 1947 . . .

When Harry was born, Lucknow was a garrison town of some half million souls and the home base of a celebrated Indian division which was fighting for Britain in the western desert.

Father Rodger was thirty-five when his first-born arrived. His wife was some fifteen years his junior, small, with the dark eyes that Harry would inherit.

They found Lucknow a pleasant town, situated on the Gumti River, a tributary of the Ganges, 303 miles southwest of Delhi and a little over 600 miles northwest of Calcutta, where the Webbs would later settle. Lucknow boasted spacious parks and traditional industry, being noted for its *Chikan* work of fine hand embroidery. It also produced gold and silver thread work, cotton fabrics and perfumes.

From Lucknow, where Harry had his first lessons in paddling in the Gumti, the family moved on to Cawnpore and Jaipur before taking up their final residence in a company flat in Calcutta. The Webbs were now five, with the addition of Donella, more fondly known as Donna, and Jacqueline – two sisters to annoy Harry, who at least on one occasion demonstrated that he was the eldest and therefore the boss.

His mother has said, 'Of course they squabbled, like all children do. But my husband always drummed it into Harry that a gentleman never hits a lady. Donella, who is two years younger, sometimes took advantage of this and teased him terribly. One day he got really mad at her and chased her with a rolled-up newspaper. But he said it was all right – it was the newspaper that did the hitting!' Dad ordered him to count up to ten before ever thinking of doing it again.

Young Harry accompanied his father on fishing trips and found kite flying, Indian style, great fun as well as something of a challenge. Kite-fliers indulged in air battles, trying desperately to sever each other's slender controlling threads and put the kite out of order. It was a deadly serious sport, with some fliers coating their threads with particles of glass to slice through an 'enemy' kite and thus bring it down or send it soaring into the heavens on the breeze.

In India it was the good life for the Webbs, with four servants and a style of living far beyond the dreams of the majority of the population.

Thus, after India gained independence, British families were targets of retaliation for the have-nots of the British Raj days. There were riots, Britons were pelted with stones and other missiles, and to stay on in such conditions seemed decidedly dangerous. 'Why don't you go home to your own country?' an angry demonstrator yelled at Mrs Webb.

The Webbs uprooted and, after debating whether to pick up the pieces in England or Australia, sailed for Britain in the autumn of 1948 in the SS *Ranghi*. Harry, his eighth birthday not very far away, was unable to cope with the rock 'n' roll of the ocean during the three-week voyage to Tilbury and spent a lot of the time in his quarters with the sea's most dreaded malady.

England, still punch-drunk from the war that had ended only three years earlier, was as yet no land fit for heroes and certainly no attraction for a family of five bent on making a new life. Mr Webb set foot on British soil for the first time with only £5 in his pocket. The prospects were anything but hopeful.

Britain was in a shabby state. Food was still rationed and the transition from war to peace was still painfully slow. Men returned from the forces were still gloomily waiting for somewhere to live, with homes being allocated on a points system. Clement Attlee was Labour Prime Minister and, with president Truman of the United States, was finding that peace was not an easy road.

Life for the Webbs, after the comparative luxury of India, was indeed spartan when they settled in one room in Carshalton, Surrey, alongside one of Harry's grandmothers. They ate, slept and lived in that one room, all five of them.

For Harry there was his first British school, Stanley Park Road Primary, where he was to discover how merciless childish tongues could be. His skin had been burned dark by the Indian sun and he spoke English with a trace of the accent much parodied by Peter Sellers. 'Nigger!' the kids taunted Harry. And 'Indie-bum!' when they found out that he had been born in India. He had to learn how to defend himself in frequent playground battles.

One misguided teacher goaded him one day by saying: 'Come on, Webb, you can't run off to your wigwam any more!'

England was definitely hostile and he didn't like it one little bit in those early days.

There was little improvement in the Webbs' living standards when later an aunt took them into her home at Waltham Cross, Hertfordshire. Again it was one room, with everyone getting in each other's way, and life threatened to become increasingly difficult when Mrs Webb was expecting a fourth child.

Their plight resulted in the allocation of a council house in Hargreaves Close at nearby Cheshunt. Joan, a third sister for Harry, was born just prior to the move.

By now father was working as a clerk at Atlas Lamps, part of the Ferguson complex at Enfield in Middlesex, on the A10 route into Hertfordshire and Cambridge. But the going was still hard and conditions still in sharp contrast to those they had enjoyed in India. There was no money to lavish on furniture and Mr Webb even had to make some of it, fashioning sturdy chairs from packing cases which he bought for a few pence. They lasted for years.

Mrs Webb, her hands already full coping with four children, went out to work part-time in the evenings at a paint-brush factory at Broxbourne, cycling to and fro to save pennies. She recalls that Harry 'was marvellous. He always gave his sisters their tea and put them to bed for me'.

He remembers seeing his mother in tears at times when the pressures became just too heavy for her.

For Harry there was another primary school at Waltham Cross, where he swotted for the eleven-plus examination that he felt sure he would pass but didn't. It was a sad blow.

By this time he was completely anglicized and the harsh British winters had worn away any traces of the Indian tan.

He moved on to Cheshunt's secondary modern school for the formative years and, without being brilliant, proved himself an adept pupil, becoming a prefect and something of a sportsman. At soccer he was a reliable right back and was good enough to be chosen for a place in the county's under-fourteen side. He swam, played badminton and basketball and was a fair hand with the javelin, setting a school record that wasn't broken for many years.

To raise a few shillings he occasionally caddied at a local golf course. One day, as his mother's birthday came around, he went there with swimming gear beneath his jeans, stripped off and plunged into the stream that ran through the course to retrieve lost golf balls, which he sold. For mother there were two pound notes to help make it a happy birthday.

He played in school theatrical productions, putting his all into the title role of *Toad of Toad Hall* and Bob Cratchit in Dickens' *A Christmas Carol*.

At fifteen he could have left school to go to work but, encouraged by his parents, he stayed on for another eighteen months to take O levels, achieving a pass in English.

In the world of pop music the revolution that would engulf Harry Webb was beginning to take hold with skiffle and rock 'n' roll.

Skiffle worked itself up into a national craze. All across the nation youngsters were banding themselves together with hastily learned guitars and a do-it-yourself bass which conjured a deep twang from a tea chest by means of string and broom handle.

Harry was still only fifteen when along came Elvis, who would be his idol and responsible for a giant upheaval in his life.

Thus far, however, Harry had given only a slight indication of where his future path might lie by being part of a boy and girl vocal group, calling themselves the Quintones, which made its first public appearance at a Youth Fellowship dance in Cheshunt.

The transition to rock 'n' roll was to be as slow as Presley's take-off in Britain. Elvis was certainly no overnight sensation when he was launched here on record in the first week of March 1956, with his first major disc on the powerful American RCA label – 'Heartbreak Hotel' and 'I Was The One' (issued here under the HMV banner).

Strangely, it seems in retrospect, the publicity material that came with the record said nothing about his being a foremost exponent of rock 'n' roll and revealed instead that American teenagers were hailing him as the King of Western Bop, an odd linking of two musical styles – country and western and bebop, a jazz phase of the early forties.

The *Daily Mirror* critic, introducing Elvis to Britain discophiles, posed the question, 'Will British girls fall for him?' And supplied his own answer, 'I think it's likely – in time.'

He was partly right. The record moved incredibly slowly, but was a smashing great hit by summer. Young Harry Webb, along with sister Donna, was an early devotee.

Around this time his father had spent a fiver on a guitar that both of them played. Dad used to strum a banjo in India with a traditional jazz outfit and could also play guitar. He gave Harry his first lesson, teaching him the simple three-chord trick that was sufficient for struggling skifflers and early rockers.

As Presley zoomed to fame with 'Heartbreak Hotel', Harry's worship of him grew. He tried to look like Elvis, growing sideburns, greasing his hair, imitating his scowl in front of a mirror at home, the same curl of the lip that was taken to be some demonstration of protest or defiance. And he began to try to sing like him, giving an Elvis impression when he appeared with the Quintones.

'He was my idol,' he has said frequently over the years.

Yet it was skiffle rather than rock that put Harry Webb on the glory trail.

He had left school when it happened and had become a £4 15s a week credit control clerk at Atlas Lamps, working in the same large office as his father, the pair of them cycling the dreary miles from Cheshunt to Enfield daily.

Word came via a schoolfriend that a local outfit called the Dick Teague Skiffle Group was in need of a singer. Harry went into his act at an audition for Teague, passed and was at last on his way.

On drums in the Teague group was one Terry Smart whose leanings, like those of Harry, were towards the more vital rock 'n' roll. Within a short time both broke away from Teague and set up their own rock group, the Drifters, along with a third member – Norman Mitham, a schoolmate of Harry's.

They met nightly to practise this new art in the Webb council house. The incessant racket brought down the wrath of the neighbours and the housing authority, after investigating complaints, decreed that the music would have to cease by ten o'clock. But the Drifters were now an entity and treading the path to fame as Harry Webb and the Drifters, belting out rock at local dances and youth venues.

The road would lead one evening to the Five Horseshoes at Hoddesdon, where their pay was measured in pieces of silver, and to the encounter with John Foster, the sturdy Teddy Boy from the sewage works.

To this day John doesn't know exactly what prompted him to ask Harry Webb if he could be his manager.

'It was just this magic,' John says now, shaking his head slightly in bewilderment, 'and he certainly aroused a lot of excitement with the girls.

'I was just doing a funny little ordinary job at the sewage works and knew absolutely nothing about show business, but I had a feeling that this boy could be a star.

'I went over to Cheshunt to the Webbs' council house home and met his mum and dad. His father wasn't interested and just didn't want to know, but then we were all pretty young and naive and, after all, I was only a year older than Harry.

'Anyway, I believed in this lad and my mother and father put together the money to make a private recording of the Drifters. How much was it, Mum?' he asked her as we talked in the little house where Harry and the Drifters used to practise, as well as sleep occasionally in those primitive days.

'Ten pounds,' she said as if it were only yesterday.

'That's right,' John said. 'They recorded two songs, "Lawdy Miss Clawdy" and "Breathless".

'I slapped around with our tape, trying to get people interested in Harry Webb and the Drifters, but no one was terribly impressed,' John remembered.

'One of the people I went to was Ian Bevan, Tommy Steele's agent. Tommy was making it big by this time. Anyway, Mr Bevan did listen to the tape. Afterwards he said, "I like rock 'n' roll – it's great thing, but if I was you I'd tell this fellow not to give up his day job!"

'A long time later when I met Bevan he recalled the occasion and asked me, "How'd that boy do?"

' "He's Cliff Richard now!" I told him.'

Nothing could sway John Foster in his early enthusiasm for Harry Webb and his great belief that he had discovered a star. He thought there might be more interest in his charges down at the 2 i's in Soho.

So Foster sallied forth to London once more by Green Line bus.

Surely there was someone who would give a break to Harry Webb, star in waiting.

# CHAPTER FOUR

# IN DARKEST SOHO

It was a different Soho in the fifties, abounding in coffee bars and characters, a cosmopolitan colourful quarter where you could smell the cheeses and salami on the evening air.

There were no porn shops, no marital aid stores or erotic cinemas proclaiming 'Hard Core Porno Films Now Showing' or warnings that 'persons under eighteen are not admitted to these premises'. Striptease was in its infancy and mostly inoffensive.

Soho, however, was still a honeyed invitation from a doorway. It was still an ugly white scar down a mobster's cheek, for the habitués included a fair proportion of tarts and gangsters and their protection heavies. Yet somehow the atmosphere was more *Guys and Dolls* vintage than sleazy and sinister.

Thousands of ordinary citizens – at that time the majority of them teenagers – were able to trek there to drink coffee and listen to music, in coffee bars or jazz clubs, without being coaxed to sample the pleasures of sex.

The 2 i's was at the Wardour Street end of Old Compton Street, sandwiched between a delicatessen and another neon-signed coffee lounge called Heaven and Hell.

Heaven and Hell was as harmless as a fairground ghost train ride, offering nothing more exciting than coffee and music from a jukebox. Heaven was simply the ground floor. Hell was the basement. It was hot all right, because of lack of ventilation, and lit only by red-eyed devil masks on the walls and the jukebox.

'Everybody wants to go to hell,' the then proprietor said. 'We had a parson in the other night. He started up in Heaven on the ground floor, but after a while said, "I must see what it's like down there." He found Hell quite pleasant . . .'

The 2 i's didn't try to be clever at all. It was a rather plain little establishment, no larger than an ordinary high street café, which it closely resembled. There was a bar with stools, a jukebox and a gleaming espresso machine – then the newest thing. Along with your coffee you could munch a hot dog.

The big attraction was the basement, where young people could belt out their revolutionary music and hope for instant fame.

Two brothers with the surname Irani had been the first proprietors. Thus the 2 i's. The original hand-painted sign spelt it with a small i – although a neon sign proclaimed 2 I's with a capital. The hand-painted sign described the establishment as a coffee bar. A small neon sign called it a café. It kept its name when it was taken over by two young all-in wrestlers. The one most in evidence at night was Paul Lincoln, a stocky Australian then in his early twenties – a man who nursed a dark secret. He was, in fact, the celebrated mystery figure known as Doctor Death, who fought countless bouts in the ring wearing a black mask.

Nobody – certainly not the newspapers or the hopefuls who descended on the coffee bar from many parts of Britain – had any idea that this cheerful chap who encouraged rock 'n' rollers to come and play for him was the much-feared Doctor Death. He kept his secret until he retired from the wrestling ring several years later.

Said Mr Lincoln, as most of us knew him, 'There are bags of kids these days who have talent but don't get the opportunity of showing what they can do. We try to give them a chance.'

Not everybody who appeared at the 2 i's received payment. It was principally a showcase, but there were those willing to toil away nightly for something like ten shillings (50 pence now). They included Harry Webb and the Drifters . . .

But there was the excitement of it all: being on display at the 2 i's, where the elusive talent scout might be the man leaning against the wall in the shadows, waiting to dispense a fat recording contract and put your name up in lights.

It had happened to Tommy Steele. It had happened to the skiffling Vipers group and briefly to a lad named Terry Dene.

Terry had been eighteen, came from London's Elephant and Castle district and worked as a packer by day – packing records in HMV's Oxford Street store, where Harry Webb made his demonstration recording!

One night Terry, determined to be heard and seen, jumped on to the stage at the 2 i's while a perspiring group took a break, and sang to his own guitar accompaniment. Paul Lincoln listened, became his manager and Dene's enterprise won him an immediate week in cabaret and a contract with a major recording label, Decca – sworn rivals of his HMV employers.

The up and coming boss of the Parlophone company was the man to watch for, a slim ex-Fleet Air Arm flier named George Martin. 'I make a regular visit to Soho,' he said at the time. 'It has become a breeding ground for talent. Six months ago I wouldn't have dreamed of going there.'

It was George who signed the successful Vipers but passed up Tommy Steele, who was singing with them. He never made another mistake like that. Within a few years he would be the only recording manager to open his door to a struggling foursome calling themselves the Beatles when everyone else was slamming them shut in their faces . . .

Thus there was much excitement in the Drifters' camp when John Foster managed to book them into the 2 i's for a week's engagement. This, at last, could be it. But that week proved a great disappointment for Harry Webb and his colleagues, Terry Smart and Norman Mitham.

There were no show business moguls in Teddy Bear overcoats, smoking long cigars, waiting to make them famous.

There was no George Martin waiting for the right singer to come along to compensate for having missed out on Tommy Steele.

There was no Lionel Bart, whom Harry had dreamed of meeting; of having Bart force a song on him and spin him headlong into stardom. 'I was really disgruntled with the 2 i's,' Cliff says today. 'Nothing seemed to happen and it was a great letdown at the time.'

Even Paul Lincoln wasn't much impressed with the Drifters – although years later he estimated that he had kissed more than a million pounds goodbye through not having involved himself in the golden-lined futures of Tommy Steele, Adam Faith and Harry Webb.

At that time Lincoln was attracting the attention of 5,000 teenagers a year, he estimated, all seeking discovery either in person or by writing to him. 'Most of these kids wanted to throw up their jobs, come to town and work for almost nothing. I told them how tough it was, to stick to their jobs and try to make a go of it part-time.'

For Harry Webb the nightly journey to the bright lights held little fascination. As John Foster remembers: 'We used to get the

Green Line into London – number 715a, Hertford to Oxford Street – and Cliff was always sick on the bus.

'But it used to take us past the old Finsbury Park Empire, a famous variety theatre at that time, and one night I pointed it out to Cliff as we went past and said, "Some day your name will be up there in lights . . .'

Cliff still recalls John Foster's words fondly. 'We used to have a giggle and laugh as well on the old 715a bus,' he says.

Despite the overall disappointment, the 2 i's would turn up some trumps for him. It was there that he met a young red-haired RAF man named Ian Samwell, nearing the completion of his two-year national service and popularly known as Sammy.

Samwell, a Londoner, was a regular pilgrim to Soho on off-duty nights, with a hankering to be up there as one of the boys making music. He had learned piano when younger and had recently taken up the guitar when Harry Webb and the two Drifters came into his life.

Sammy, like John Foster, sensed the magic in this dark-eyed, chubby lad; a magic that cried out to be set free on a far wider public. He also noticed that there was something not quite all there about the Drifters: they had no lead guitar.

He saw his chance. When the music stopped he sought out Harry, pointed out the deficiency and asked him if he needed a lead guitar. 'I just went up to the stage and asked – it was as easy as that,' he recalls today at the age of forty-three.

There was no hesitation on Harry's part and so Samwell became the third Drifter whenever the Royal Air Force let him out for a night. Within a short space of time Ian Samwell would have a leading part to play in the transformation of Harry Webb into Cliff Richard . . .

Says John Foster, 'While we were at the 2 i's a promoter – I believe his name was Bob Greatorex – came in one night and took an interest in what the Drifters were offering. In fact he was so keen he couldn't wait to book us for a one-night stand at a dance hall in Ripley, Derbyshire.

'We all adjourned to The Swiss pub, a few doors down from the 2 i's in Old Compton Street, to talk the deal over.

'Bob asked us what we called the lead singer. "Harry Webb," we said. Bob didn't like it; it didn't sound exciting enough, he said, and he asked us to think of another name. And he wanted it quickly because he had to get the bills printed for the dance hall show and there wasn't much time left.

'It wasn't easy. We threw around a lot of names and agreed eventually that Cliff sounded pretty good as a first name. We got as far as Cliff Bussard – why Bussard I don't know – but it didn't sound quite right. Then I came up with Cliff Richards. "That sounds all right," this Bob fellow said.

'Then Sammy Samwell had a bright idea. "Why don't we leave the "s" off the end? A lot of people would get it wrong and call him Richards, but having to correct them would get the name known and talked about."'

So it was farewell Harry Webb! Long live Cliff Richard!

The dropping of the 's' gave great publicity value in those fledgling days. Even now some people who ought to know better still refer to him as Cliff Richards . . .

As far as John Foster can remember, the fee for the Ripley gig was about ten pounds.

'I know there was nothing left after we had paid all our expenses. Even so we couldn't afford the cheapest of digs. After the show that night we slept in the dance hall! But it was all experience.'

It was on a night at the 2 i's that John Foster was alerted by a poster advertising a talent contest to take place on a Saturday morning at the Gaumont Cinema on the green at Shepherd's Bush. Conducting this free-for-all was a Canadian radio personality named Carroll Levis who, like Hughie Green, roamed the country searching for new names with his discovery shows.

Cliff's mother had already written for an audition with the Hughie Green setup, but thus far the negotiations had only reached the form-filling stage. Earlier, Cliff had entered a talent contest at the Trocadero Cinema at the Elephant and Castle, only to have his amplification gear fail, forcing him to retire from the competition extremely hurt and near to tears.

Now there was another talent contest. Foster, still not out of his teens and the man to whom Cliff and the Drifters were looking for miracles, dreamed up one of his inspired super-moves.

Why should they enter some crummy talent show and run the risk of coming nowhere? They were a going concern, starring, albeit practically for nothing, at the famous 2 i's.

Why shouldn't they go along to the Gaumont and offer their services free – provided the management would let them top the bill as an attraction? Not just as miserable contestants.

Full of enthusiasm, John Foster put it to them. 'They fell for it,' he smiles now. 'They thought they were getting something for nothing, I suppose, even though the Drifters were still a little bit raw and sounded thin without a bass guitar.'

It was felt at this time, too, that perhaps the Drifters and their star turn, now officially Cliff Richard, might make more progress if they had an agent.

'It shows you just how much I knew about show business,' John Foster says. 'I went along to see an agent named George Ganjou and asked him if he'd come along to Shepherd's Bush to take a look at Cliff and the boys.'

Ian Samwell told me that he had picked out Ganjou's name and address in *The Stage*, the theatrical weekly, and had made the same plea to him earlier.

The world of agent Ganjou was as far removed from the new world of rock as an Eskimo from a palm-fringed beach, but there were few agents devoting themselves to rock 'n' roll at this period. He was then coming up to sixty and had been a member of a celebrated variety and cabaret act called the Ganjou Brothers and Juanita. They were billed as an adagio dance presentation, with the three brothers bewigged and magnificently attired like French courtiers in silk breeches. They tossed Juanita gracefully around the stage, sweeping high and sweeping low in poetic motion, a beautiful act that needed no words and which they performed with immense success right across the world.

George, who has now died – 'I was born on the first day of the century' – said Juanita must have flown more than a thousand miles through the air via his brothers Serge and Bob and himself.

He was born in Warsaw of a Russian father and Polish mother and in his teens played second flute in a Warsaw symphony orchestra. He also played piccolo: 'I was no James Galway but I leaned towards classical music from those days.'

The brothers left a Europe in turmoil after the end of the First World War and settled and worked in America, arriving in Britain with their adagio act in 1933 to 'join the Crazy Gang at the London Palladium', George remembered.

'We finished our career appearing on television in *Sunday Night at the London Palladium* in 1957 – a year before I was aware of Cliff Richard.'

George had started his variety agency business three years before in 1954 and now began to devote all his time to it.

'Speciality acts were my forte,' he said, and he covered the world in search of them. When Cliff and the Drifters intruded into his life he had also become the sole agent for entertainment at the Butlin holiday camps.

He appeared to have complete recall of the advent of Cliff Richard and even remembered that it was a Friday afternoon in July 1958 when an insistent caller came knocking at his door.

'It was John Foster,' he said, 'and John told me that he had this young man appearing in the morning at the Gaumont at Shepherd's Bush and how great he was and that I should see him.

'I tossed a coin to see whether I should play golf on that Saturday morning or try to do some business. The coin came down business, so I went along.

'I was not a rock 'n' roll expert. I didn't care for it, to be truthful, but I sat back in the stalls as I usually did. Then came the band with Cliff Richard. They started to do their gyrations and music and everybody went absolutely mad about Cliff. The audience screamed and yelled and Cliff gave what I thought was a very clever performance.

'He was something new. I liked his looks, his behaviour, his personality. I could see that he had great potential. It was music that lots of other people would like even if it wasn't my type of music.

'He was not a Caruso, but as far as crooning was concerned he had something which appealed to girls and women. Vocal and visual – that's what he was. I knew then that he would become a star, although he was dressed a bit peculiarly.'

John Foster says he had decked Cliff out in something like Teddy Boy rig. The drape jacket was pink, with pink day-glo socks to match, burning brightly like neon signs. The pants were black along with the shirt. The obligatory suede shoes were grey.

'Cliff was a very beautiful young man,' George mused as we talked in his flat on the Chelsea Embankment, 'and he looked too nice to be a Teddy Boy.'

George wasted no time after witnessing the explosion caused by Cliff and the Drifters at the Gaumont. 'Next day – Sunday – I took the tape of Cliff and his band to Norrie Paramor, a friend of mine.'

Norrie was a soft-spoken, sparse-haired ex-pianist who had led his first band at the remarkable age of fifteen. He had been with an RAF orchestra during the war and later with a lively outfit called Harry Gold and his Pieces of Eight, frequently heard on radio.

In the summer of 1958 he was artistes and repertoire manager of the Columbia label, part of the EMI recording complex. He had been having considerable success with an Irish thrush from Belfast named Ruby Murray who sang four hits at a time into the then Top Twenty; with golden trumpeter Eddie Calvert, a million-seller with 'Oh Mein Papa', and Michael Holliday, a big-band singer who sounded like Bing Crosby.

Mr Paramor had yet to catch up with rock 'n' roll.

Said George Ganjou, 'Norrie was neither here nor there about Cliff's tape, but he did say he would like to meet him and have another go with him and his boys in the EMI studios. Then Norrie went off on holiday for two weeks.'

Those two weeks bothered Mr Ganjou who, although he was no rock 'n' roll fan, was increasingly convinced that he had a winner, although so far no contract had been signed. 'During those two weeks, if they had known,' said George, 'anybody could have had Cliff Richard!'

Nobody did.

Along with the Cliff Richard tape, George left another for Norrie's consideration made by a singer named Tino Valdi. 'He was Ukrainian,' George said, 'and a wonderful singer of opera.'

When George rang Norrie on his return from holiday it was to enquire first about Tino Valdi – not the good-looking kid who belted out rock 'n' roll in the style of the now-unstoppable Elvis.

'But Valdi was not Norrie's type,' George said, 'though he *was* interested in Cliff. We went to the studios at Abbey Road to audition and that was the start of it all. Norrie said afterwards: "I think we've got something here!"

'I signed Cliff to a sole agency agreement, guaranteeing him that he would be earning a thousand pounds a week within six months. I was really sticking my neck out! I started by booking him into Butlin's at Clacton for three weeks for thirty pounds a week and my first wife, Adela, who had been a dancer, began to advise him on his appearance. He would not look up enough with those dark eyes, for one thing.'

It was an all-happening July for Cliff Richard and the Drifters, as they were labelled on their debut disc. It was recorded at Abbey Road during that month with the added help of two seasoned session musicians – professionals who backed various artists and remained anonymous.

Ian Samwell recalls today that Columbia really didn't want the Drifters on the disc at all – 'only Cliff. I got a seven pound fee for playing guitar on it in the end!'

The two titles were 'Schoolboy Crush' and 'Move It' and the release date was set for 29 August 1958.

With little subtlety, the recording industry was intent on snaring the early teens or the Nellies, as were called the hordes of screaming girls now worshipping idols of their own age.

Already a fourteen-year-old black American rocker named Frankie Lymon had topped the bill for a fortnight at the London Palladium with his group the Teenagers (what else?) – a visit simply inspired by the fact that his record 'Why Do Fools Fall in Love?' had been a smash hit in Britain (he died of a drug overdose by the time he was twenty-five).

Therefore the trend showed that a title with *teen* or some young-orientated word such as *schoolboy* in it might well hit the bell in a big way. So 'Schoolboy Crush' was made the A-side, or main side, of Cliff's first record.

This song had been brought to Norrie Paramor by singer/music publisher Franklyn Boyd ... another name that would have some bearing on the early career of Cliff Richard.

'Move It', the B-side, was a home-grown effort, conjured up by Ian Samwell and given its title by John Foster. 'He wrote it on top of a bus,' says John, 'and it was on top of a bus that I said why not call it "Move It"? Lots of things seemed to happen to us on buses,' John smiles.

Samwell recalls: 'It was a London–Colney/Cheshunt bus. I was stationed in the RAF at this time at Hendon but lived at home in St Albans on compassionate grounds because my mother was ill.'

The lyric, he says, was based on recurring reports that rock 'n' roll was beginning to fade and included a line that said 'they say it's going to die'.

True, there had been something of a lull after the earlier explosions of Haley and Presley in 1956. Cliff was, in fact, two years late coming to the scene, but rock 'n' roll continued to produce new names and new songs, many of which made only a fleeting impression on the recording scene – songs, for instance, such as 'The Teen Commandments', which qualified for a bad-taste award at the end of 1958. Alongside this 'Schoolboy Crush' sounded almost distinguished.

But again, like the initial stint at the 2 i's, Cliff's first record did not make any immediate waves. There was no star-overnight sensation, no rags-to-riches-all-in-a-week story. Cliff Richard was as yet just another new boy on the treadmill and it would be up to the Nellies, with their spending power, either to make or break him.

Norrie Paramor felt confident in his new find and refused to join in the pessimism about the future of rock 'n' roll. 'I just can't see the kids giving up these personalities with a beat,' he said, interviewed for Patrick Doncaster's column in the *Daily Mirror* on 31 July 1958.

Paramor had given him a sneak preview of Cliff's record a month before it was due for release and the *Mirror* devoted the whole top of page ten to the dawn of Cliff Richard. NEW RECRUIT FOR THE DISC WAR was the bold black heading alongside a two-column picture of the lad, looking mean, moody – and chubby, it must be said – in an open-necked shirt, a gold cross on a chain around his neck.

He was seen as an ace up the sleeve of Columbia when the record companies would do battle for the annual autumn sales boom that followed the end of the summer holidays.

The story told how Norrie had done his homework via his daughter Carolyn, who was then nearly fourteen. He had taken home a test pressing – a metal disc thinly coated with shellac and not meant to last more than a few spins, perhaps as few as thirty.

Carolyn's copy was worn out in a few days.

The *Mirror* column summed up that Cliff Richard's personality shone through the grooves and decided that he could succeed in Discland. It also disclosed that his favourite artist was Elvis and that his ambitions were to win a gold record for a million sales and to meet Elvis.

This was the first-ever mention of Cliff Richard in a national newspaper. Within a year the cutting libraries in every Fleet Street office would have a considerable section devoted to him.

Around the end of July our new recruit for the disc war gave up his job as a credit control clerk with Atlas Lamps where, he was told on parting, it had been realized that he had never been cut out for it.

So he joined the Discland militants, became officially a professional artist on 9 August and began to look and present himself even more like his idol, Presley.

Off went the Drifters to Butlin's at Clacton where Cliff, the Discland rookie, soldiered on resolutely, wondering when or if his first record would ever achieve one of those elusive little lines of type in the hit chart – one line that could really bring sudden fame and put up your money, along with your name in lights.

The group had travelled without original Drifter, Norman Mitham. 'He dropped out when we became professional,' Cliff explains. 'It was all amicable. Norman didn't want to continue with us. He didn't feel he was up to the standard now required.'

For Claction, too, Ian Samwell transferred to bass guitar and a professional lead guitarist working at the camp was brought in for the Drifters' appearances.

When they reached Butlin's John Foster was once again delivered of a shaft of promotional inspiration.

'They wanted us to wear the usual red coats that entertainment staff had become famous for. But we weren't Redcoats, I told them. We were Cliff Richard and the Drifters – something different, even though Roy Hudd, the comedian, was there as a Redcoat!'

Foster won. They were given white shirts – on which was emblazoned a red V, which no one seems able to explain.

The camp management, however, couldn't quite make up their minds where to place this ambitious but pernickety bunch of youngsters.

'They put us in the ballroom,' says John, 'but we didn't quite fit. "We're a rock 'n' roll band," I told them. We played one night and they took us out. So they tried us in a sort of Hawaiian room and again I protested that we were a rock band. Same thing, one night and they took us out.

'Next they put us in the rock 'n' roll room – where we should have been from the start. Anyway, we played there lunchtimes and evenings. All the time Cliff was getting better and better and the reaction was fantastic when he tried out "Move It", which was the side we liked better and always played.

'Norrie rang while we were there to tell us that "Schoolboy Crush" was to be played that night on Radio Luxembourg. There was great excitement and we all crowded into a chalet to hear it. Funny thing, but Luxembourg turned the record over as well and played "Move It" instead of the A-side, "Schoolboy Crush". We were delighted.

'"Move It" started to show some signs of really moving. Other disc jockeys began to play this side now and "Schoolboy Crush" was forgotten.'

Someone else had turned Cliff's record over – a young television whiz-kid named Jack Good, who could scarcely believe that anyone British could sing rock 'n' roll as good as this. 'Get him!' the order went out . . .

When Cliff and the lads returned home after Clacton there was a message waiting from George Ganjou. 'It was sensational,' John Foster says, still with much enthusiasm.

Cliff Richard and the Drifters had been signed for their first tour in the coming October on a bill headed by a bright new duo from the United States, the Kalin Twins.

It was all happening and seemingly at once.

It was goodbye 2 i's, farewell Soho. No more cramped cellars, no more Five Horseshoes. Big time, here we come – at £200 a week for a start . . .

# CHAPTER FIVE

# OH BOY! IT'S CLIFF!

One record hit was enough to bring the Kalin Twins, Hal and Herbie, hurtling across the Atlantic to tour Britain. That was the power of a shiny, spinning disc in 1958, a year in which the industry really didn't know where it was going: wondering if rock 'n' roll was here to stay; wondering if ballads – still popular with such stalwarts as Dean Martin, hitting big with 'Volare', that year's winning song at the San Remo Festival in Italy – would take over once more; wondering if there would be something completely new from Latin America.

Elvis had been drafted into the American Army and was now a number – 53310761 – serving in Germany, leaving behind a stockpile of records to keep his fans happy. But, it was asked, would his absence for two years tend to make people forget him?

America's merchandising merchants did their best to keep him very much alive. During the eventful July of the advent of Cliff Richard in Britain, a million and a half youngsters in the United States bought bracelets, anklets and key chains featuring an autographed picture of Presley, his army number and his blood group.

The new disc names launched to fill any gaps included the smoothie Johnny Mathis and the vivacious Connie Francis. A sixteen-year-old Canadian named Paul Anka sold a million copies in Britain of his teenage love song 'Diana'. Sinatra sang 'Witchcraft', Max Bygraves came up with 'You Need Hands', which he's still singing. Jim Dale, now a Broadway star, was hosting the BBC's pop show 6.5 *Special*, Buddy Holly was big with 'Oh, Boy' and 'Peggy Sue'. And to prove that Discland really was scratching its buzzing head in the great search for something different, the Parlophone label burst forth with their discovery, Sparkie Williams, who recited nursery rhymes and give a reasonable impression of an American TV cop-show. He was a budgie living in a cage at Forest Hall, near Newcastle-upon-Tyne.

Thus this headlong pursuit for something fresh off the disc presses resulted in the pairing of newcomers the Kalin Twins and Cliff Richard and the Drifters on a variety tour of Britain.

At twenty-four, the Kalins were almost old men in this world that was getting younger and faster every day (on 12 August a Comet IV jetliner set up a new record for a transatlantic flight from New York to Britain with a non-stop crossing in 6 hours 28 minutes; six days earlier Australian runner Herb Elliot cut the mile record to 3 minutes 54.5 seconds in Dublin).

But in the Kalin's favour was the fact that they were new and in the charts – and that was what mattered most. Their lone hit song was 'When', a runaway smash. Yet a year earlier Herbie had been a salesman in a clothing store in Washington and brother Hal had been a singing telegram boy for the famous Western Union cable company, standing on Washington doorsteps warbling 'Happy Birthday To You'.

'We made a private record and took it to New York,' Herbie said, 'but nobody wanted to know. Three minor disc companies turned us down, so we took our record home again.

'Then we met songwriter Clint Ballard, who had more faith in us. He took the record back to New York and managed a hearing with a big company.'

The result was a first record that missed hopelessly, followed by 'When' and blast-off!

What they didn't know was that Cliff Richard, who had been clerking at his desk only months earlier, would prove to be an even greater sensation, but when they arrived to top the bill for their first British tour he was just a kid with a first record on the market and as yet looking nothing like a threat.

To vary the possible monotony of the show, top heavy with singers, the promoters had put in golden-disc-winning trumpeter Eddie Calvert, blowing his middle of the road tunes. Also on the bill were the Most Brothers, a twosome who weren't even related, comprising Mickie Most and a fellow named Alex Murray. Before long they parted, Mickie would later become one of the world's best-known record producers in his own right, watching over the disc destinies of top-line British and American artists. As yet, however, the Mosts were as raw as the Kalins and Cliff and the Drifters.

While they waited for the tour wagon to roll, the all-important call came for Cliff to make his bow on television for the first time. The programme was Jack Good's *Oh Boy!* The date was 13 September.

This programme was Independent Television's answer to *6.5 Special*. The brain behind both shows had been Mr Good, an unlikely, studious-looking genius in his mid-twenties, bespectacled and with an Oxford degree in philosophy and English language.

*6.5 Special* had been born in February 1957 and was initially meant as a magazine programme for young viewers. There was a sports section introduced by one-time British boxing champ Freddie Mills, for instance, but the main presenters were DJ Pete Murray and hostess Josephine Douglas. Gradually the show became a pop showcase, especially for the stream of rock 'n' rollers who included such rising stars as Marty Wilde.

Cliff and his Drifters had been invited to audition for 6.5 as 'Move It' came out. Astonishingly they failed – perhaps because Mr Good had already fled the coop across channels to ITV with the ABC company. He readily welcomed Cliff Richard into his rival camp instead and immediately became a tremendous influence on him and his career.

The one thing Jack Good didn't want was a carbon copy Elvis. What he did to Cliff could well have been reported to any Society for the Prevention of Cruelty to Rock 'n' Rollers.

First he took his guitar away, leaving him feeling almost naked. Then he ordered 'off with his sideburns!' He left him the curl of the lip and the shocking pink jackets and glowing, matching socks.

This was the advent of Smoulder Eyes, as Cliff was dubbed in the *Daily Mirror*. And it worked . . .

Jack, who today lives in the United States between show business commitments in both Britain and the United States, told us, 'You have to remember that Cliff was one of the few people I discovered for television who, in fact, I heard on record first rather than saw first.

'I saw Adam Faith singing with the Worried Men first and saw Jim Dale at an audition. P. J. Proby and Cliff, I think, were the only two I heard first on record.

'I was thrilled with both of them, but I was even more thrilled by Cliff because in those days it was unheard of that a rock 'n' roll record coming out of Britain should sound as genuine as "Move

33

It" and be performed with such confidence and assurance. He *sounded* like a rock 'n' roll singer. Better than anything we had.'

Jack spun the disc for the already established Marty Wilde, who had also crossed channels. Marty, too, couldn't believe that this was a British-made effort. From that moment on Cliff Richard was a must for the *Oh Boy!* show, but not without a stack of fears on Jack Good's part.

'I was very worried about the audition,' he says, 'because I thought he would probably have a terrible squint, or an uncontrollable twitch or two heads or three fingers or something, but anyway he was all there and he was quite normal and, in fact, quite a good-looking young man.

'So I was delighted, but he wasn't a strong personality in his performance. He was terribly shy and inexperienced, as most of them were.'

Jack knocked some of the rough edges off his new find with a week of gruelling rehearsals – not only for Cliff but all the cast. These were held at the Four Provinces of Ireland Club in Canonbury Lane, near Highbury in North London. A tattered run-through schedule still in John Foster's possession gives the details.

Rehearsals began on Sunday 7 September 1958, and the schedule points out coldly that each time shown 'is the time that the artist is expected to be in the rehearsal room, set up and ready to go'. Cliff and the Drifters had to be in full throttle on the dot at nine-thirty on that Sunday morning.

This meant an early start from Hertfordshire to reach the venue, cart the gear in, put it into position and full electronic working order with instruments tuned, and somehow manage to look daisy fresh when Jack Good raised his finger to let the rock 'n' roll rip.

From nine-thirty there was an hour and a half of rehearsing 'Move It' and another song called 'Don't Bug Me Baby' before the Vernon Girls and Dallas Boys were called upon to do their bit at eleven.

There was an hour's lunch break and at four o'clock a tea break of twenty minutes (on another day they managed half an hour).

Monday was a free day, then off the artists went to Canonbury Lane again on the mornings of Tuesday, Thursday and Friday for more rehearsals.

Live transmission of the programme was scheduled for six p.m. on Saturday 13 September, going out to millions of viewers from the variety stage of the Hackney Empire in East London. It was another never-got-a-minute day for the artists, who had to be present and correct by eight-thirty in the morning for 'preliminary sound balance'.

From ten till one o'clock there was a 'vision only' rehearsal. At two o'clock there was a 'sound and vision' rehearsal. By the time six p.m. came around and the expectant viewing public were drawing up their chairs to make themselves comfortable for the rockin'est show on the box, there were those taking part who had had a real bellyful of singing or playing the same songs they had been rehearsing through the week. But that's the way the programme worked and there was a certain excitement about it which gathered in a steadily growing viewership, eventually estimated at five million.

Suffering on that debut programme along with Cliff and his band were Marty Wilde, balladeer Ronnie Carroll and the John Barry Seven. John would later become one of the big screen's foremost composers, making his mark with music for the James Bond films. These were early days for a lot of people.

For Jack Good, a meticulous man who has left his imprint on pop television, the show was all-important. He told us, 'The show came first and the artists definitely came second in *Oh Boy!*

'What you must remember is that compared with Tommy Steele and Marty Wilde, who had already been going round the theatres topping the bill, Cliff was raw and though he threw himself into his songs with conviction he did not project a personality. In fact, he was probably more in a transitional stage than a lot of other young men.

'Not only was he very young [seventeen], he hadn't finished growing. People say he hasn't changed over the years. Well, he may not have changed since about 1961 or '62, but in 1958 he was about four inches shorter than he is now. He was a good two inches shorter than me and I'm about five foot ten. So he was about five foot eight. I think he must be a good six foot now [he is around five foot eleven].

'One noticed how dark he was. He looked as if he had come from a romantic place with a strange-sounding name. His black hair was almost blue-black and I suppose this was accentuated by the grease and the Elvis Presley haircut and the famous sideburns that I ordered off.

'He was a different Cliff Richard and a very shy one and very immature in a way, so one really could pick a personality out of a hat and try to stick it on him.

'Not like Wee Willie Harris, for instance. You had to turn him into a comic. I mean, you had to do something and give him a red jacket and grow his hair long and make it orange, because if you didn't get away with the comedy angle you weren't going to get away with Wee Willie Harris at all.

'What we did with Cliff was give him a persona that he could use in front of a television camera and on stage until such time as he developed his own personality, which he subsequently and so successfully did.

'We had to develop a character and a look that would come across in a couple of minutes. He had to register that he was different from (a) Elvis Presley and (b) all the other seven people who were featured on the show, and memorable in his own right. So, of course, we built the personality that was usable on *Oh Boy!*.

'It was no good creating the Boy Next Door when you had numbers like "Blue Suede Shoes" and "Move It" to do. We had to create a personality that would come across singing these tough songs.

'Now we had a slightly built, romantic-looking young man with fine features,' Jack Good recalls. 'There was nothing coarse about the face – the eyes big and dark, the nose small but well shaped. He looked younger than his almost eighteen years. So compared with Elvis – who looked at least twenty-three and as if he had knocked around a bit and was a good deal more extrovert and vulgar in his performance – what we had here was a teenager.

'We could make him mysterious – the Quiet Smoulderer – the boy possessed of smouldering fires of sensuality of which he was as yet barely aware. That sort of stuff.

'This is what we could make work on our show – that's all that mattered to us. We obviously didn't discuss that sort of thing with him; it would have driven him crazy!

'We gave specific advice. The angle of the head . . . tilt the head down. The eyes . . . look up towards the lens because it'll give a better effect. Shoulder forward, not square on to the microphone . . . grab the arm of *this* line because it will give more impact . . .'

When a rock 'n' roller was performing without a guitar, a good dramatic stance could be achieved by grabbing one arm around the elbow with the other!

Jack Good made it all work superbly. Perhaps too well – within a short time Cliff would be taking the same sort of stick that had come the way of Freed, Haley and Presley.

Meantime, however, while Jack Good had managed to solve his initial problem of what to do with the lad, the Drifters had problems of their own as the tour with the Kalin Twins drew uncomfortably nearer. They were still without a regular lead guitarist now that Ian Samwell was playing bass.

There was only one way out of the difficulty, John Foster decided, boarding the 715a bus once more to visit the place that seemed to have all the answers – the good old 2 i's in darkest Soho.

'I dearly wanted a fellow named Tony Sheridan,' he says. 'He used to knock about in the 2 i's – everything seemed to happen there.

'When I went up to meet him there, they told me he'd be in soon, so I waited about and waited, growing very annoyed when he didn't show up. I'm a busy man, I kept saying. What am I doing, hanging about here? While I waited, a guy wearing glasses walked in, carrying a guitar case. I watched him unpack it and I heard him play. He could fit the bill all right, I thought.

'So later I went up to him and asked him if he had ever heard of Cliff Richard.'

He had. He had heard 'Move It' on the radio and liked it, he reported.

'Well,' John went on, playing the big time, 'I'm his manager. Would you like to go on tour with Cliff? My name's John Foster.'

'I'm Hank B. Marvin,' the bespectacled fellow said in a Geordie accent that didn't exactly tie up with such a distinctly American-flavoured name.

After John had outlined the rough details of the tour, Hank B. Marvin nodded his head. Yes, he would like to go on tour with Cliff Richard on one condition – 'that's if my mate can come along. He's Bruce Welch.'

Hank and Bruce, like so many others, had trekked from New-castle to Soho in search of stardom and in July, only some weeks earlier, had taken a tilt at Discland as members of a group calling themselves the Five Chesternuts.

A private backer had heard this teenage quintet performing in an espresso parlour in Hampstead and splashed out £40 to make a production record of them which was good enough to lease to EMI.

Leader of the group was a sixteen-year-old schoolboy named Peter Chester, who penned both the songs on the disc: 'Teenage Love' and 'Jean Dorothy', inspired by a thirteen-year-old girl-friend.

What the backer and EMI didn't know until the release date

was set early in July 1958 was that Peter was the son of the celebrated comedian Charlie Chester.

They went on TV with their disc in *6.5 Special* and, what's more, proud Dad introduced it. The two sides were no better and no worse than some of the American teenage offerings that had hit the top of the best sellers. But the Chesternuts failed to set the world ablaze and here were Hank Marvin and Bruce Welch, ready and waiting to become Drifters instead.

'Up till then they had been living on baked beans in a flat at Finsbury Park.' John Foster smiled.

Within months of their joining Cliff Richard after John's on-the-spot invitation at the 2 i's they would become two dominant members of the Drifters, later to emerge as the Shadows and as international stars, standing on their own without Cliff singing in front of them. It would be an association that would last through the years . . .

What of Tony Sheridan, the guitarist Foster had gone in search of? He went off to Hamburg, where in 1961 he recorded a rock arrangement of the traditional song 'My Bonnie' with a British group labelled the Beat Boys. It was the record that would lead to the discovery of the Beat Boys under their rightful name – the Beatles. Tony Sheridan never did share their fame . . .

Cliff reached his eighteenth birthday during the tour with the Kalin Twins, and also reached high in the charts with 'Move It'. It zoomed to second place, overtaking the Kalins' number 'When', which had been a topper but which now slipped as Cliff became Britain's newest rock 'n' roll sensation. All of which made it an embarrassing tour for both Cliff and the Kalins.

The contract had said that Cliff and the Drifters would open the second half of the show, immediately preceding Hal and Herbie, who would close it with a big finale.

But as 'Move It' got its big move on, the twins were shouted down each night with cries of 'We want Cliff!' from the audience.

Says John Foster, 'There's no doubt that Cliff was *the* star of the show. He was mobbed every night. At one stage the Kalin Twins asked us if Cliff would close the show, as they had no chance now that our record was higher than theirs. No one could follow him, they said. But we stuck to the contract.

'We were now seeing what fan worship meant. Cliff couldn't move without girls clamouring and chasing after him. One night, at Hanley, we had to pull a real nasty trick. Cliff said he was starving and wanted to go across to the café near the stage door to get a bite.

'The stage door was besieged by girls, about fifty or more. So we put on an act. Cliff pretended to be ill and I told the girls he was pretty grim and coughing something awful and I had to get him to a doctor. They parted like the Red Sea.'

He made a remarkable recovery when he had eaten, even though it was only baked beans. 'The fans were a forgiving bunch,' John recalls.

Cliff spent the evening of his eighteenth birthday rocking 'n' rolling on stage at the De Montfort Hall in Leicester. It was a touching, unforgettable scene. Fans littered the stage with flowers in his honour and lifted their seats to stand like a massed choir to sing 'Happy Birthday' to him.

For Cliff these were not only crucial, formative days, but also long, wearing days that would soon threaten to take their toll. Things were beginning to happen swiftly to him and around him in that all-important autumn of 1958.

Around the start of the tour with the Kalins he found that he had acquired a new manager.

He was the singer and music publisher Franklyn Boyd, the man who had first interested Norrie Paramor in 'Schoolboy Crush', only to see it crushed by Ian Samwell's bus-top hit 'Move It'. Not that this could have worried Mr Boyd unduly. The publishers of the songs on both sides of a disc shared an equal royalty on sales of the record.

Agent George Ganjou told us: 'I appointed Franklyn Boyd.'

The deposed John Foster, who took the new appointment philosophically, says that he thought Boyd had been brought in by Paramor. There is no doubt that it would have been a move approved by Norrie.

John Foster reflects, 'I was beginning to learn the business, but I had begun to realize my limitations as well. I was naive and so was Cliff. We never had a contract between us and we took each other totally on trust. It was a big mistake, I suppose.

'However, I'd gone as far as I could as Cliff's manager. He was in great demand and now in the big league. So when I stepped down, I became his personal road manager at eighteen pounds a week.

'To be nearer things, Cliff and I had taken a flat together over Sainsbury's in Marylebone High Street in town, sharing the expenses fifty-fifty.

'Of course we entertained girls there. We were normal, healthy young men, so why not? We took a drink at times as well.

'There was one night when we both felt a bit down. I can't remember why, but we were going on tour the next day. We had several bottles of stuff in the flat and we poured the lot in together and made a punch. It packed a punch all right. We drank ourselves paralytic and didn't feel very well in the morning.'

Some weekends John's mother, Carol, would pay a visit to the flat – 'to give it a bit of a tidy up,' she says.

For years she treasured a Yardley pink heather compact which Cliff gave her. 'Thanks for everything. Love . . .' the inscription reads.

'He was like another son,' she recalls, looking around the lounge at her home in Hertford Heath. 'Many a time he slept here in this room.'

She treasured as well a signed photograph of the young rock 'n' roller on which he wrote 'lots of love and beans'.

'He loved baked beans in those days,' she explained.

CHAPTER SIX

# THE WILD ONE

For Cliff Richard 1958 was undoubtedly the most astonishing year of his life. From being an obscure clerk at the beginning of August he was within weeks a rapidly rising celebrity rushing headlong towards a sensational December.

All in quick time he had become a recording star, a television personality with five million or more pairs of eyes on him during his now regular *Oh Boy!* appearances and a film actor in the making, George Ganjou having booked him into an unpretentious movie called *Serious Charge*.

In the midst of it all, following the tour with the Kalin Twins, the Drifters were having more teething troubles. Ian Samwell was replaced on bass by Jet Harris, an impressive guitar man with blond hair who would emerge as a personality in his own right.

He had come to notice during the tour, where he appeared in support of the Most Brothers.

At the time it was said – and has been repeated since – that Samwell, having been a guitarist for only a short spell, had decided to stand down because he had not yet reached the professional standard required. What's more, having penned a walloping great hit in 'Move It', he would like to devote more of his time to songwriting.

He had been approached by a publishing company to work for them but didn't want to leave the group.

'It was a mixed-up situation,' he recalls, 'and I wasn't all that happy about it. I would have liked to have continued with the Drifters and, given a little time, I think I could have been good enough to carry on as bass guitar. I felt sad, but there was nothing I could do about it. It was a *fait accompli* – they wanted Jet Harris in and me out.'

Not that he was left completely in the cold. After 'Move It' he wrote Cliff's follow-up hit, 'High Class Baby', which reached number seven in 1958. Another success was 'Dynamite', a 1959 chart entry.

Later he penned 'Feeling Fine', the first solo record by the Drifters when they became the Shadows. He also acted as their temporary manager for a period.

'I have tremendous admiration for Cliff,' he says, 'and we are still friends today.'

Following Samwell's dropping came the resignation of the only remaining founder member of the Drifters, drummer Terry Smart.

Says Cliff, 'It was his own decision. Terry felt that he was not able to keep up the standard and that the way we were developing was beyond his capacity. "I think you should get someone else," he said. It's always been like that – all very friendly. Nothing like the story of the fifth Beatle.'*

Drummer Tony Meehan replaced Terry Smart, but this upheaval amongst the Drifters was, in comparison, only a minor event.

As the season of goodwill to all men approached, not everyone was entering into the spirit just yet. There were rumblings that parents were now showing some considerable concern about Cliff's act on *Oh Boy!*. His movements on screen were being viewed with alarm and deemed by some people to be exceedingly sexual.

A crushing criticism came from the most unexpected quarter. Around two weeks before Christmas, the trade weekly *New Musical Express* astonished its mainly young readership with a sensational attack on Cliff Richard, describing his performance on the small screen as 'the most crude exhibitionism ever seen on British TV.'

His violent hip-swinging, it went on to say, was 'revolting' and 'hardly the kind of performance any parent could wish his children to witness . . .'

The *Daily Sketch* headline on Monday 15 December asked, IS THIS BOY TV STAR TOO SEXY? The story repeated the *NME* blast and ended, 'This is Show Business 1958 . . . Do you want it?'

---

* The fifth Beatle is a reference to Pete Best, who was the Liverpool group's drummer for two years before being sacked suddenly in 1962 shortly before they made their first British record, 'Love Me Do'. In an interview in 1980 he told Patrick Doncaster that he still didn't know why the other Beatles dropped him to make way for Ringo Starr. 'It will always be in the back of my mind,' he said. 'When they became famous I just couldn't ignore the fact that I should have been part of it. I don't try to forget that I was ever a Beatle.'

*NME* tried to temper its outburst against Cliff by apportioning some blame to producer Jack Good.

Jack, then aged twenty-six, took it like a man. 'If there's anything too sexy or offensive about the show, it's my fault,' he said. But he pointed out, 'I can't see anything wrong with the act. I don't intend to do anything about it.'

However, in the *Oh Boy!* programme following the trade paper tirade, the *Daily Sketch* noted that 'the cameras showed little more of Cliff than his head and shoulders . . . In the finale, the cameras revealed a display of knocking knees.

'But all the way through, the teenaged audience squealed with ecstasy over the half-closed eyes, the pouting lips, and the agonized Presley look . . .'

Cliff's reply to all this mud-slinging was careful and considered for a lad not long past his eighteenth birthday. 'I don't set out to be sexy,' he said. 'If people want to find me sexy they will. If they want to laugh then they'll laugh.

'We are a lively, jumping-bean generation who don't have time to sit down and listen to Beethoven. Rock expresses our feelings and gives us a chance to let off steam.

'I am not violent – nobody I know is violent. Rock won't inspire violence in anyone who is not inclined that way already.'

Jack Good, thinking back today to those controversial appearances by Cliff in his *Oh Boy!* show, had this to say to us: 'We were accused of wild bumps and grinds and all that sort of thing, but it was not so.

'What helped to make such an impact were the close-ups and the carefully considered cutting [from camera to camera] on the beat to the line of the music that gave the impression that there was something really wild going on.

'I worked very close to the artist, physically close, to show how close the image would be to the viewer at home. Even the mere flicker of an eyelid counted.'

Jack confessed that he sometimes discussed the feeling to be got across in a song, 'but obliquely', he says, giving as an instance, 'You know, "Here you're waking up in a hospital in a daze. You've just had some sort of injection that makes your head fuzzy", that sort of stuff. Anything to give him something to think about, something to direct his performance towards – without saying "You're a teenage idol" . . .'

Appearing to be sexy, it would seem, was hard work in those days, even if it was largely an act. But nevertheless, here was Cliff

Richard, the nice Boy Next Door from Cheshunt, picking up a new label as the Wild One.

More viewers – people who wouldn't normally watch a television show beamed at kids – switched on to see what all the fuss was about; but there were no protest marches to the ABC studios by furious parents or a storming of 10 Downing Street, where Prime Minister Harold Macmillan was in residence; and there was no instant change in Cliff Richard or his act.

There was, as Christmas neared, something of a silver lining. He was starring at the Finsbury Park Empire, just as John Foster had said he would one day.

'They were really tough days,' John remembers. 'Cliff was getting up at five in the morning to start filming in *Serious Charge* and doing two shows a night at Finsbury Park. It was all too much for him and his voice went on the Saturday night, last night of the engagement.

'He was obviously being worked too hard. When Franklyn Boyd arrived in the dressing-room we were melting butter on a hot spoon to try to ease Cliff's throat. I told Franklyn to find an all-night chemist and get something for the boy.'

Nothing could have worked the miracle that night. Cliff *did* go on stage for the final performance and mimed – not to his own records but to the voice of unseen rocker Wee Willie Harris, who gave a Cliff Richard impression from the wings. No one in the audience knew the difference, not amidst the squeals and screams that tended to drown Cliff's act anyway.

It spelled the end for Franklyn Boyd. After three months as Cliff's manager he was out. Some days before Christmas a letter from Rodger Webb told him that his services were no longer required.

On 20 December 1958 the *Melody Maker* carried the headline: CLIFF RICHARD'S FATHER SACKS HIS MANAGER. In the text Franklyn Boyd explained that he had no contract with Cliff other than a verbal agreement and a letter empowering him to sign contracts.

Mr Boyd lamented, 'I got him the *Oh Boy!* series and his film work.'

Cliff's mother said that the firing of Boyd 'was a family decision'.

She told how Cliff had been up at dawn to film *Serious Charge* while singing twice nightly at Finsbury Park and that on the Sunday following the loss of his voice he had been due to rehearse for another *Oh Boy!* appearance. Instead he was in bed. He had collapsed into it as soon as he reached home after the final curtain and in the morning croaked, 'Mum, I can't stand this life in show business any longer. If it's all going to be like this past week I'd rather go back to my old job at Atlas Lamps.'

His mother later said, 'After that my husband wrote to Mr Boyd saying we didn't need him any more.'

Cliff's father explained, 'We hadn't realized that Boyd was a very busy entertainer and music publisher. This meant he just didn't have time to be with Cliff as much as we would have wished.'

Clearly both parents were worried about their son, who had now become the hottest property in British show business. Cliff, of course, soon conquered his bout of depression, regained his voice and bounced back into the pell-mell life of a rock 'n' roller. But still the Webbs had fears about the kind of life he might be living, fears that resulted in the exit of John Foster within a few weeks.

'There was a letter from Cliff's dad waiting for me in the flat at Marylebone High Street when I returned one day in mid-January 1959,' he says. 'It was to give me two weeks' notice.

'When I saw his father he complained that Cliff wasn't being looked after or eating properly. "Look," I said, "I love your son. I'll cook for him!" We had a big blazing row and Cliff walked out. He was sickened, but there was nothing he could do about it.

'"I'm leaving you," I told Cliff afterwards and packed my bags and went home. We'd come through a lot together, but we were both too young to make decisions in the big business that was happening around us. Meantime, I'd got the sack from the sewage works for taking time off!'

Foster was still only nineteen and legally unable to sign anything. The *Daily Sketch*, announcing his departure, described him as Cliff's personal bodyguard. There was a quote from Cliff saying, 'He's pulled me out of a few jams, especially with fans in the north, but now he is to try to do better for himself. I'll miss him.'

John went on to become Walt Disney's London publicity chief before setting himself up in his own public relations business.

'I have no regrets about those days with Cliff,' he says. 'We are still pals . . .'

Appointed to succeed Franklyn Boyd as personal manager was Tito Burns, a former popular band leader.

Strangely it wasn't until September 1960, nearly two years later, that the Sunday newspaper *The People* worked itself up about the saga of John Foster and Franklyn Boyd. The story was headed, 'To the girls he's a heart-throb. To his two ex-managers CLIFF IS A

HEART-BREAKER!' (The words in capitals were in type an inch and a half high.)

Excerpts from the story are worthy of repetition because here was one more rare occasion of our number one rock idol being knocked not only so long after the events, but for two happenings which, as a minor, were beyond his control.

The article, signed by Peter Bishop, began, 'He is short, plump and curly-haired and has a remarkable knack of appearing to rotate his knees in opposite directions as he bellows out the latest pop tunes.

'Cliff Richard is the name, and he's the current dreamboat of rock-'n'-roll-mad teenage girls.

'But last week two men who helped this bouncing small-town clerk to climb to stardom confessed to me that sometimes Cliff features in their dreams too. And they wake up screaming.

'Why? Because both of them were his managers . . . once.

'Since he dropped them they have seen him soar to the stage where his weekly pay is about £1,200.

'And to think they might have had five or ten per cent of it. It's enough to break any man's heart.

'Take tall, quiet-spoken John Foster, for example . . .'

The article then tells how John discovered Cliff at the Five Horseshoes in Hoddesdon and of his efforts to launch Cliff.

The piece continues, 'For months John tooks days off from his labouring job to hawk his "find" around the West End agents.

'But no one was interested. Everywhere he met shrugged shoulders when he played the boy's tape-recorded voice and was told "rock and roll is on the way out".

'Then one day he walked into Mr George Ganjou's office. And they clicked.

'Ganjou, an agent, signed Cliff Richard on a five-year contract – his cut being ten per cent on all earnings.

'John was naturally delighted. His parents urged him to get a contract from Cliff's parents. But in the glow of success he didn't think it necessary.

'Cliff was my pal and I was confident he would look after me,' said John.

'But it turned out that Cliff, being under twenty-one, had very little say in the matter. A new manager with a greater knowledge of show business was called in, singer and music publisher Franklyn Boyd.

'John Foster – discoverer of the Cliff Richard talent – was

relegated to road manager . . . His duties: book hotels, and play strong-arm-man if the fans got out of hand.

'But he wasn't worried. He thought his turn in the Cliff Richard organization would come when he had learned more about show business.

'He got his first sharp lesson in January 1959. It was a letter from Cliff's dad, Mr Robert [sic] Webb, giving him the boot . . .

'But by that time Franklyn Boyd had got his cards too . . .

'Said Mr Boyd at his tasteful Byfleet, Surrey, home, with a sleek grey Jaguar car in the garage: "I've never been so stunned or hurt in all my life as the day I opened that letter [from Mr Webb].

'"At the time my wife and I were living in town and for six weeks Cliff stayed with us because his home was too far for convenience.

'"I spent days with him during those early recording sessions, guiding him, trying to inject some professionalism into his act."

'Mr Boyd's pretty wife broke in: "We took him out on his first big social engagement. Franklyn spent a lot of his own money on Cliff. We even borrowed an evening suit for the boy to wear at the Tin Pan Alley Ball at the Dorchester."

'Why did Mr Webb sack him?

'"He thought we were working his son too hard," said Mr Boyd. "But we had to work the boy pretty hard to get some polish on his act fast. Anyway, we're still pals."

'After Mr Boyd came manager No. 3, Mr Tito Burns . . .'

*The People* writer then went on to ask Mr Webb why so many changes had been necessary.

'Mr Webb shook his head as he sipped a glass of beer.

'"I was green in this game to begin with and I wanted good advice for my boy," he said.

'"Foster? He didn't know enough about show business.

'"Boyd? He didn't quite suit. He seemed to work my boy a bit hard.

'"But Mr Burns now – we get along fine. He seems just right for my boy.

'"But managers," he reflected again, "you got to keep your eye on 'em."'

However, in the midst of all the managerial hoo-ha of December 1958 Cliff could at least take some heart. The *Daily Mirror* disc page bestowed on him the title of New Boy of the Year.

# CHAPTER SEVEN

# THE GREAT TRANSITION

The pace wouldn't slacken during 1959. It would be another helter-skelter year for Cliff Richard, watched over now by the experienced Tito Burns, a forthright man who said what he thought and usually got what he wanted. There would be some brickbats to take – some of them physical – along with the bouquets, and they wouldn't be long in coming.

There would be the achievement of one of his great ambitions: a number one record selling a million; a performance before royalty, despite the wrath rock 'n' roll was still bringing down on its head in some quarters, and another film to make.

The Cliff Richard story was beginning to shape up like one of those old Hollywood movies in which the underdog becomes the toast of the world all in twenty-four hours. Things began to happen almost at machine-gun pace although, strangely, this year of the Great Transition from rocker to Mums' Delight would not be all that obvious at first and the protests about his being too sexy would be slow to diminish.

For Tito Burns the going wouldn't be easy at the outset. 'In those days there were a lot of knockers in the business,' he said, 'and I was battling my arse off trying to batter them down. When they knew I was looking after Cliff Richard they'd say "that little bit of rubbish, that rock 'n' roller", dismissing him. They couldn't see the talent that was there, that he wasn't just a rock 'n' roller.

'I didn't know in those early days that Franklyn Boyd had been involved with him. Anyway, it didn't seem to be a full-time job for him and he was mainly a music publisher.

'Cliff's father had now become very strong behind the scenes when he approached me. I had a message asking me if I would be interested in managing this new boy. So I had a look at him and was quite enthralled with his image. He looked good and was so great – *is* great, not only *was*,' Tito corrected himself.

'He had made *Serious Charge*, was on television and making records and it looked like he was really going to take off.

'I had two or three meetings with his parents. It had to be that way because Cliff was under-age as far as contractual matters were concerned. I explained to them what I would do and what I was looking for in the end, but I felt that the old man [Mr Webb] was a bit suspicious.

'I wanted Cliff to stand on his own two feet. I didn't want him to die with rock 'n' roll, if ever it was going to die, that is. Who could know?' Tito shrugged his broad shoulders.

'Cliff took direction beautifully and understood what I was trying to do. "I see what you mean," he said. And he would do it.

'I began negotiating things for him on his own, away from the Drifters, as they still were, when Cliff came to me. They were marvellous now in their own right, but I had to bring him to the stage where he wasn't depending on anyone else.'

The transition began slowly, with minor adjustments. 'When he went on *Sunday Night at the London Palladium* – then the top ITV slot – he was preparing to go on without a tie. So I pulled mine off and he went on in that. Ties were important at that time. But he did begin to come away from the Elvis thing and he did agree with this. Never once did he say, "Don't try to change me, I'm a rock 'n' roller". He always understood what I was trying to do. He is the easiest man in the world to work with. What you see – that is Cliff. No façade, no bullshit.'

While 1959 was still an infant, Cliff found himself standing on his own two feet for a different reason. On the evening of Monday 2 February, when he opened his act on his first night at the Lyceum Ballroom off London's Strand, he found himself on the receiving end of an uncooked omelette of eggs and tomatoes hurled his way by a bunch of Teds. There were also some bottles in the barrage of missiles, along with rolled-up balls of newsprint.

Cliff stood firm and tried to continue singing. A gang of louts then stormed the stage and he found himself ready to trade punches with at least one of them until the ballroom manager held him back.

Some time earlier, when the bills first went up announcing him as a forthcoming attraction, this hooligan element had been boasting around that they were preparing a welcome for him. They kept their word.

After the third number the management brought the act to a close.

Cliff came through it all not particularly dismayed. He knew exactly why he had been on the receiving end and said, 'Boys out for the evening with their girls get jealous. It's nothing personal, just jealousy . . .'

Anyone watching a Cliff Richard performance at that time would have to agree. He had only to twitch a knee and a thousand girls would begin to scream. He had only to mouth the word 'you' in a song and young hearts accelerated. He had only to be in range for a hundred girls to try to tear him to peaces.

It was something that irritated boyfriends everywhere.

He would have to endure more eggs and tomatoes or a shower of copper coins at Chiswick, at the Trocadero, Elephant and Castle (already a sad landmark where his amplification gear had failed at an early talent contest), and in Manchester and Nottingham. But nothing would stop the onward march of Cliff Richard – certainly not a handful of Teds.

One song from the film *Serious Charge* proved to be the great turning point in his career: 'Living Doll', which had been sung on to a tape by the much-gifted songwriting Lionel Bart, the washboard player from the 2 i's. (Lionel couldn't put music down on manuscript paper or play the piano – someone else had to do this chore for him.)

In case there is still doubt, let us emphasize that the title of the song was 'Living Doll' and not 'Livin' Doll', as it is referred to so frequently. The word 'Living' with a 'g' is on the original record label and on the sheet music copies. The confusion possibly arises from the fact that, prior to its release, Cliff recorded an entirely different song entitled 'Livin' Lovin' Doll' earlier in 1959. It reached twentieth place in the main chart of the day in the *New Musical Express*, and it upset Mr Bart considerably.

He saw this overlapping of titles as an attempt by the powers that be at Columbia to move in first and therefore take some of the shine off his effort, which by contract Cliff *had* to record to tie in with the film's release.

Bart need not have had any fears. 'Living Doll' was the runaway victor, romping to number one and doing extraordinary things for Mr Richard.

*Serious Charge* was the story of a clergyman (Anthony Quayle) working amongst a bunch of yobs. Cliff, as Curly Thompson, more or less played himself as an embryo pop singer, although

Curly was something of a delinquent. There was also a background of homosexuality. But all that mattered really, in retrospect, was the one song.

In his book *Pop from the Beginning*, published in 1969, author Nik Cohn is emphatic about it.

'"Living Doll",' he writes, 'was by far the most influential single of the whole decade. It was cute and sweet and bouncy. It was tuneful and ingenuous. It was the British equivalent to highschool – and it was desperate. In months it took over completely. No rage, no farce, no ugliness left . . .'

It was certainly sugary and catchy, with a lilt far removed from the rip-it-up type of rock 'n' roll. And it certainly knocked some of the fire and smoulder out of Cliff Richard, who despised the song from the beginning, thought it was 'chronic' and says that he sang and recorded it 'under duress'!

Certainly, as well, it chipped away at what was left of his Elvis image. You couldn't sing 'Living Doll' with a snarl or a curl of the lip or be mean and moody about it. It was too nice.

'"Living Doll" changed the whole course of my career,' he has said over the years. 'I parted company with the greasy-haired rock 'n' roll scene and began attracting the mums. And that's how it stayed.'

It was also, he said, one of the key factors in his life, ranking with his becoming a Christian.

On subsequent tours he was astonished to find grandmothers in the front stalls. 'Aged sixty-five at least, some of them!'

Before 'Living Doll', he felt that he had been acceptable only to the teens. Now in came the family, dads as well.

'They came along to see what the apparition was all about,' he thought. But they stayed and were converted. He was still a rocker at heart, but there would be no going back. 'Living Doll' paved the way for more up-market ballads – hits such as the standard 'It's All In The Game', works with a more sophisticated lyric.

This was a number that simply oozed 'establishment'. The tune had been written in 1912 by an ex-vice president of the United States who had also been ambassador to Britain, General Charles G. Dawes.

He penned it as a waltz. It was simply called 'Melody' and was played mostly by military bands, although Kreisler did have a go at it.

Some years later lyricist Carl Sigman gave it some words and changed the title to 'It's All In The Game', which resulted in waxings by jazz king Louis Armstrong and Nat King Cole. In 1958 American singer Tommy Edwards had another go at it and this version carved a niche in the British charts at the same time as Cliff's 'Move It'.

General Dawes, an eminent banker as well, died in 1951, never knowing that eventually he would have his melody warbled by a rocker who had been called the Wild One!

Despite his initial loathing for 'Living Doll', he took it very seriously when he went into the studio to record it and demonstrated how much a professional he already was at the age of eighteen.

Says Tito Burns, 'He hated the up-tempo treatment of the song in the film and when he made the record he slowed it down. It was his own idea. Nobody told him to do it.'

Bart, then aged twenty-eight, was on holiday in Spain in early August when 'Living Doll' reached the number one position in the charts, on its way to a million sales and a coveted gold disc. Patrick Doncaster rang him up from the *Daily Mirror* office in London to tell him the good news. It caused him little excitement.

'I was on the beach working on *Oliver!* when you rang,' Bart said flatly, as if he really didn't want to be disturbed.

At that time he, too, had moved away from the simple early rock that had helped to put Tommy Steel on the show business trail and had scored some of the music for Tommy's latest film, *Tommy the Toreador*, which featured the Bart hit 'Little White Bull'. He had also written the lyrics for the Bernard Miles hit show *Lock Up Your Daughters*, for which Broadway was hankering.

Now his mind was fully occupied with *Oliver!*, which would be a resounding hit and all his own work. He went back to the Spanish beach to slave away at it, not dwelling overlong on the fortunes of 'Living Doll'.

Lionel Bart has said in recent years that when he was asked to write the songs for *Serious Charge* he suggested Cliff for the role of singer after having seen him at the 2 i's.

Cliff agrees that this could very well have been the case but has no recollection of having ever seen or met Lionel at the coffee bar.

'I remember how disappointed I was when we played the 2 i's that Lionel wasn't there. I'd hoped that he would be one of the people we might meet.

'My memory of first meeting him was at his flat. I remember that Larry Parnes [then a pop impresario] was present and that when you went to the loo and shut the door it switched on Handel's "Water Music" somewhere!

'I think we talked about the music scene, but there was no discussion about a film part that I can recall.'

What has to be considered is that all these events took place when the principals concerned were young men living and working in a breathless, thriving and thrusting new world where more could happen in a day than in a year for most people. What was indisputable at that time was that Cliff's stock was now rising with each day that passed.

Tito Burns recalls that he was receiving fifteen telephone calls an hour from people who wanted Cliff Richard – impresarios, agents, bookers, promoters, television – people who were now seeing the great potential. 'The demand was fantastic,' he says, 'and it really wasn't necessary to have an agent, although George Ganjou was still acting in this capacity and getting his ten per cent every week for doing practically nothing! It became easier and easier to look after Cliff.'

*Serious Charge*, which has been described as a moderate success, smoothed the way for a more ambitious film for Cliff, *Expresso Bongo*. Laurence Harvey was signed to star and Cliff was again a rock 'n' roller, playing Bongo Herbert to Harvey's manager, Johnny Jackson.

With the shooting of *Expresso Bongo* there came a slight hint of scandal. Or was it merely a groping for publicity?

On 30 September 1959, some weeks before the film was premièred, the headline over Peter Evans's Inside Show Business column in the *Daily Express* said, 'This love scene makes an hotel angry.'

The story read, 'The Dorchester Hotel, the London resting place of many international stars, has taken legal advice over a scene in the new film *Expresso Bongo*, in which Yolande Donlan, playing a famous star, seduces a young rock 'n' roll singer, Cliff Richard – in the hotel's famous penthouse suite.

'Last night rock star Richard said, "It's not a sordid scene. I play a youngster infatuated with an older actress. And she likes me.

'"Then one night I go back to her suite at the Dorchester Hotel and I've had a bit too much to drink, and you know, I'm feeling a bit tired.

'"Then she begins to sort of, well, take my tie off and that. And, it's very delicate really, the camera moves down and you see her take her shoes off. And that's it.

53

'"I wouldn't say it was sordid or torrid."'

One more event that year did much to dispel any adult doubts that might still have lingered on about Cliff Richard and rock 'n' roll: he was invited to appear before the Queen Mother at what was seen as a mini Royal Command Show at the Palace in Manchester.

Show business writers were stunned by his inclusion and wrote about 'the biggest surprise in years'.

Cliff was in august company, with such pillars of variety as Tommy Trinder and Arthur Askey, and there to bring a touch of culture to the proceedings was the celebrated Hallé Orchestra under Sir John Barbirolli. Rock took another step forward and Cliff enthused about the graciousness of the Queen Mother, whom he saw as an example to every woman in the land. Performances before members of the royal family would become commonplace for him before long and one day reach the ultimate with an invitation to a matey lunch with the Queen and Prince Philip at Buckingham Palace, with only a handful of guests all at one table.

As the fifties gave way to the sixties there seemed to be few ambitions left to be realized. Once he had merely dreamed of making a disc that would reach the hit parade. Now everything he recorded seemed to head there automatically. Even his number one ambition, to win a gold disc, had come true – when he was nineteen.

The odds against having a number one record were at that time assessed in the *Daily Mirror* disc columns as being 125 to 1. The reasoning was that of the 2,000 or so discs issued during a year, an average of only sixteen occupied the number one position during the twelve months. As the majority of the top perch residents were established stars, the odds must have been considerably lengthened for a new boy – possibly to something like 250 to 1, it was argued. This shows what Cliff's 'Living Doll' was up against.

There was still an important ambition to fulfil – to tour America. It wasn't long in coming. In January 1960 he flew off to take part in a rock 'n' roll package playing venues in the United States and Canada. With him went his father and Tito Burns, and as the plane winged high above the Atlantic Cliff, scarcely able to believe it, said to Tito, 'We're *actually* going to America!' Understandably. So much had happened since he quit his desk at the Atlas bulb factory, less than eighteen months earlier, that life sometimes seemed to lose reality.

The tour, a barnstorming series of one-nighters spread across five weeks, was a strange and largely disappointing introduction to the nation that had given the world the rock 'n' roll music that had produced Cliff Richard.

Because of the gruelling itinerary, most of the time was spent in the tour bus, where the artists ate and slept. The packed schedule of a different town every night meant journeys of eight to fifteen hours between dates. Few of the venues were theatres and many were in vast stadiums with sometimes only a makeshift stage.

Cliff was billed as an added 'attraction from Britain' and introduced on stage as Britain's top singer in a cast that was headed by Frankie Avalon and included such hit-makers as Freddy Cannon, Bobby Rydell and Clyde McPhatter. Any of these could have topped a bill in Britain but Cliff was given third billing.

He left his guitar at home – nothing negligent – and explained the reason at the time, 'My act is so short I didn't want to play the guitar on it. I just sing here and leave the instrumentals to my group, the Shadows.'

These, of course, were the former Drifters with Hank Marvin and Bruce Welch and company, who had been obliged to change their name to avoid possible confusion with an American outfit recording as the Drifters. Watching over the Shadows on this trip as acting manager was Ian Samwell.

Cliff, who by this time had been appearing on stage at home in a white jacket, black trousers and white leather shoes, wore all white for his American debut. 'I thought I'd go all the way,' he said.

Strangely, he gave the Americans back their own songs, singing 'Forty Days', 'My Babe' and 'Whole Lotta Shakin' Goin' On' – the Jerry Lee Lewis classic and 'a real wild one to wind the act up with' said Cliff – wedging 'Voice In The Wilderness' from *Expresso Bongo* and 'Living Doll' between them.

The tour played to thousands of American youngsters, but Cliff didn't reach the pinnacle of fame that was his at home in this competitive company.

'He did sensational,' said Tito Burns. 'My one regret is that we didn't conquer America when I first took him there, but there were so many artists doing the same thing and Cliff was singing other people's material.'

It was all experience, of course. For the 'Whole Lotta Shakin' Goin' On' finale he would go down on one knee – but first pull a white handkerchief from a pocket to kneel on.

'The stages are so dirty,' he explained, 'that my trouser leg would be black if I didn't. And that mustn't happen because it's the only white suit I've brought and it has to last till 21 February.'

That was when he left the tour to fly home to Britain for a day to receive an award as the country's favourite rock 'n' roller. Then he winged back across the Atlantic to rejoin the whistle-stop bus tour – taking his mother with him because, he said, he was homesick.

'I'll be glad to be back in Britain. I've had four weeks in America and I'm a little bit sick of it.'

For Mrs Webb it was her first flight and she confessed to having 'butterflies'.

Three stage suits had been ordered for the visit to North America, but only one was ready in time, mainly because the tour had been so hastily put together. 'Living Doll' had begun to attract some chart attention in America and reached number 30 there, which resulted in his inclusion in the tour.

It was the number that really 'sent' the American kids, staff correspondent Stan Mays cabled to the London *Daily Mirror* from New York.

Cliff's big regret was that he rarely met these young Americans who had taken him to their hearts because the police, nightly fearing fan hysteria or rioting, hustled the artists out of the stadium via an escape route straight into the waiting bus, engine purring, which then hurtled off into the night. Even so, the American fans he did manage to meet did not impress him much and he found them and Americans in general lacking in manners. 'Fans would ask for an autograph as if they were doing me a great favour.'

On the credit side there was some television exposure here and there, principally in New York when Cliff guested on the *Pat Boone Show*. The clean-cut, all-American Boone allegedly talked like an Englishman in a banal exchange of scripted words.

Example: Boone tells the viewers that Cliff was 'born in India but left when he was a year old. How was that?'

Cliff: 'Frankly, Pat, when you have shot one elephant you have shot them all!'

There was some compensation on that show: Cliff did sing 'Living Doll', which no doubt helped to lift American sales of the record.

During the tour he also had a meeting with Elvis Presley's colourful manager, Colonel Tom Parker, and wondered when he might meet up with his idol.

Parker said that he would like the two to meet sometime but

couldn't arrange anything because when Elvis (still in Germany) was due to leave the American Army Cliff would be back in Britain.

They would never meet. It would be the one great unfulfilled ambition.

Said Cliff, 'I almost made it when I was in Germany during his Army service. The first time I went to see him he was away on manoeuvres. The second time he was in hospital having his tonsils out.'

The nearest he would come to meeting Elvis was in 1962 during a promotional tour of the United States to boost the showing of his film *The Young Ones* (retitled there *Wonderful to be Young*).

'Elvis was filming on the west coast when we hit the south, but there was a phone call from his father inviting us over. We saw Elvis's home and we were treated with that old southern hospitality.'

He found the Presley home 'a bit frightening', he admitted, with its white leather chairs, the bed with gold panels at the head, and Elvis portraits everywhere, including one woven into a carpet.

In those days Cliff carried his worship of Presley to extremes, even to trying to copy his eating habits. At a swish dinner he ordered sauerkraut because Elvis liked it. He called it ghastly stuff and said that his hero was welcome to it. But he did like the peanut butter and banana sandwiches that were a favourite of Presley's and said that this was one recipe he intended to keep.

The adoration would not last for ever. After Elvis died in 1977 and the stories of his sexual exploits and drug addiction began to creep out, Cliff said in a *Daily Mirror* interview: 'It makes me squirm to think this is the guy I idolized for so long.

'He may have been the most successful artist, but as a man he never made it. I don't mean sexually, but just as a human being.

'When I think of what my sister [Donella] and I went through all those years ago with Elvis as our pinnacle, it's sad.

'I didn't want to read that he picked up a girl out of the audience and within a week she was an absolute wreck on drugs. Or about the pills he was taking. Pills to make him thin, pills to make him fat . . .'

But back in 1960, during that first American tour, Cliff's admiration of the man who had been his inspiration continued unswervingly.

On his return from the States, a year of triumph awaited Cliff: his first 'full' royal show, a long summer season at the London

Palladium, his first television series, plus negotiations for further, more ambitious movies. And, of course, more records.

The pattern would be set, in fact, for his show business future during the relatively short term that Tito Burns would be his manager. The forthcoming years would be much the same except for changes of venue or location. Cliff Richard had truly arrived and was here to stay.

Only now was the big disc money beginning to roll in – royalties can take an age to come through – and only now, after his return from the largely disappointing American tour, did the Webb family leave their council house at Cheshunt to move into their first home of their own.

It was a modest little place, even so, and bore no comparison with the big luxury homes that would be a feature of the pop star life style for years to come.

Their new house was a semi-detached in Percy Road at Winchmore Hill – not so very far away in North London – which cost around £7,000. Cliff had a bedroom decorated in primrose yellow where his mother would bring him a cup of tea in the mornings and he would sometimes ask her to pinch him to see if life was real.

To save space he had the attic converted into a room to house his stage clothes. In his bedroom a wardrobe was set aside for shirts. And, according to one report, he was becoming rather blasé about his footwear, wearing a pair of suede boots only two or three times before giving them away when they needed cleaning.

Now he drove a red Thunderbird with white hard-top that at £4,000 cost nearly as much as a lesser home in those days.

Cliff described it as one of his proudest possessions and drove himself to the Palladium and back during the five-month-long season.

When this same-every-day life tended to become monotonous he would sometimes drive aimlessly around quiet streets in the early hours, soul searching, occasionally feeling low in trying to cope with the penalties of fame and wondering if he might be far happier as just plain ol' Harry Webb instead of Cliff Richard. When he arrived home, his mother would always be waiting.

Says Tito Burns, 'Material things never seemed to bother him outside of his big love for cars. I went with him to Lex in Brewer Street in Soho to buy that Thunderbird. He loved that car.'

What did begin to bother Cliff at this stage of his career was the weekly siege of Percy Road. At weekends upwards of a hundred fans would descend on this hitherto quiet suburban haven for a glimpse of their idol and perhaps an autograph. Some just gawped, peeping through cracks in the seven-foot-high fence that had been put up to provide some privacy. Others lolled around on the walls of nearby gardens, which didn't please Cliff's neighbours.

A woman living opposite the Webbs thought this fan activity lowered the tone of the area. 'When I went out to water the hydrangeas,' she said, 'I asked the girls to move away, but they were very rude and one of them said, "Why should I? This isn't bloody Russia!"'

The woman had decided that she would have to set up home somewhere else if this kind of behaviour continued, she said.

Cliff's mother had some sympathy for the neighbours. 'I know this must be annoying for them,' she said, 'but some of these youngsters come all the way from Scotland and places as far off as Leeds. Cliff can't just turn them away.'

Whenever he did appear he would sign autographs and tell the fans as pleasantly as he could to move off from the house.

If the good neighbours of Winchmore Hill had yet to take this rock 'n' roll star to their hearts, they were lagging a long way behind the Establishment. A few weeks after moving into his new home, Cliff was chosen to sing in his first full Royal Variety Performance at the Victoria Palace on 16 May before a smiling Queen in white satin.

The Crazy Gang were in attendance and, with their usual impudence, walked on stage wearing bridesmaids' dresses that were exact copies of the one Princess Anne had worn ten days earlier at the marriage of Princess Margaret to Mr Antony Armstrong-Jones.

It was a mammoth evening featuring more than 200 artists, numbering Nat King Cole, Sammy Davis Jr and Liberace, who closed the show. The cast was thick with comics apart from the Crazy Gang and included Max Bygraves, Benny Hill, Bruce Forsyth, Jimmy Edwards, Harry Worth, Frankie Howerd, Norman Wisdom and Charlie Drake.

Rock 'n' roll, along with pop, was squeezed in early as Item 5 in the first half of the show. Still, it was a start.

In the programme the item was described as 'Focus on Youth', which was one smart way of not having to mention either pop or rock. It consisted of Cliff, Adam Faith and Lonnie Donegan performing their hit songs. Also in attendance were the Vernon

Girls. But the big sensation of the evening was the sparrow-like little one-eyed Sammy Davis Jr.

Cliff was still packing 'em in at the London Palladium to the accompaniment of thousands of girlish squeals twice a night when he said goodbye to his astonishing teen years on 14 October 1960.

'Just think – I'm twenty!' he said incredulously. 'When I was fourteen I used to think how marvellous it would be to be twenty and shave every day. Now I shave every day and I wish I didn't. That's life. Always want what you can't have.'

Asked what he thought he might be doing in a further twenty years' time in 1980 he said, 'Well, I see myself doing a bit of singing, a bit of acting. A sort of Bing Crosby type.'

He wasn't far out.

They had been magical teens for Cliff Richard. He was up there with the greats of show business, playing his part, standing on his own two feet the way Tito Burns had planned it.

He was earning more than the entire British Cabinet put together and the Great Transition from Wild One to The Boy Next Door was almost complete.

Leslie Grade would see the job through.

# CHAPTER EIGHT

# THE IMAGE AND THE MAKERS

Leslie Grade was a sandy-haired, pleasant man with large blue eyes who didn't look much like his two brothers, Lew and Bernie. They were the fabled, all-powerful brothers Winogradsky, whose family had come from Russia to settle in London's working-class East End.

Lew and Leslie anglicized the name to Grade; Bernie called himself Delfont. Between them, in 1960, they controlled or watched over a lot of ground in show business: theatres up and down the country, including the historic London Palladium and television via ATV, where brother Lew was the big wheel with the big cigar. The new thing from the Grade Organization was going to be nice, clean musical films for all the family, masterminded by agent Leslie.

With all this going for them, the Grades were super people to have on your side. Those who weren't with them, or were untalented and unwanted or both, made envious jokes about Lew and Leslie Greed or Low and Lousy Grade. It didn't matter. In the end there would be Lord (Lew) Grade and Lord Delfont and the jokers would be nowhere.

The perceptive Leslie Grade saw the potential in Cliff Richard early on and knew that here was a very hot potato indeed. It was inevitable that he would eventually become his agent, but first there would be some hard bargaining between Grade and manager Tito Burns and a deal with agent George Ganjou.

'Leslie was never Cliff's agent in those days when I was operating as manager,' said Tito, 'but he'd been after me for Cliff and he wanted to "buy" him for a period of weeks, as it were, as a promoter, putting him into theatres in various places, good spots such as Coventry.

'I wanted something as well in return. I wanted the Palladium for Cliff and a series on television. So I asked for twenty-five per cent over the going rate if I were going to let him have Cliff – plus the guarantee of an ATV series and the Palladium.

'Leslie eventually agreed and "bought" him for thirteen weeks, six days a week. I leased him, you might say.

'Then I got him into Leslie's films with a deal for three movies. There was a lot of argument and to-ing and fro-ing. "Look what I've done for the boy!" Leslie said when I asked for a certain figure plus a percentage of the film profits. "I can't give the boy away because you did something for us," I told him. I got the deal as I asked in the end.'

To clear the way for the Grade films Cliff had first to buy himself out of a contract negotiated two years earlier with another British company. The price for his freedom was reported to be in excess of £10,000. Said Tito at the time, 'It was hefty, but we feel that it was worth it. The contract was signed when Cliff was only just becoming known. Now he is free to take up one of the bigger offers that has come his way.'

In retrospect the sum was peanuts. For the first film would be *The Young Ones* – one of the most successful British-made movies ever – which began to evolve on the drawing board in November 1960.

At this stage freelance producer Kenneth Harper, who had joined Leslie to set up the Grade Organizaion's film section, had been observing a new phenomenon – that when Cliff Richard and the Shadows appeared at a cinema in place of the movies, they did more business at the box office than any film did.

'We must make a musical film with those boys in it,' Harper told Grade.

It sounded a good idea and the people concerned started remembering the smash-hit films Hollywood had made years back with young ones such as Mickey Rooney and July Garland, all-time musical winners like *Babes in Arms* and *Babes on Broadway*. They were nice, clean, homely films that really entertained, caused nobody any heat under the collar, had good songs, good dancing and some laughter and maybe a tear or two.

Writers Peter Myers and Ronnie Cass were called in to produce a script for the Grade musical; a young Canadian named Sidney Furie was invited to direct, and choreographer Herb Ross was whisked across the Atlantic from America to put some zest into the dancing. For too long the dancing in British films had always managed to look as if it belonged in a parish hall production.

The story was simplicity itself. A bunch of kids put on their own show (*à la* Rooney and Garland) to stop their youth club being taken over by some spoiling bigwig. That was it. First rehearsals were called for May 1961, at the Elstree Studios in Hertfordshire. But Cliff didn't arrive . . .

The year had started troublesome and by May the Webb family would experience a crisis.

But first, on 4 February 1961, a headline in the long-gone *Daily Herald* read, 'Cliff and his boss part – so amicably'.

The story beneath began, 'Pop idol Cliff Richard has broken away from his manager, Tito Burns – the man who put him at the top.

'He announced it yesterday in a joint back-slapping statement with Mr Burns that emphasized the parting is amicable, by mutual consent – and not caused by any row.

'The end of the two-year partnership was announced by Richard's publicity agents, the Leslie Perrin organization. Richard had agreed on the wording of the statement with Burns's lawyers.

'The statement added Richard's thanks for his work. Burns said he had "enjoyed" their association. Then each wished each other "the best of luck" for the future . . .'

The headline on the *Daily Sketch* story the same morning was nearer the mark: 'Now dad handles disc star'. The text was terse: 'Cliff Richard, £1,000-a-week rock 'n' roller, has broken with his manager, Tito Burns. The hinted reason: a difference over his contract.

'Commented ex-band-leader Tito, who "owns" ten per cent of the singer: "Cliff and I have separated as from today, but that's all I can say."

'Last night a spokesman for both the singer and his ex-manager said, "Cliff's father, Mr Roger [sic] Webb, is now looking after him."

'Twenty-one-year-old Cliff signed with Burns after a wrangle with his first manager, Franklyn Boyd.'

Cliff, of course, still had a great chunk of the year to go to reach twenty-one which, in the circumstances, was important. Legally he was still under-age and considered a minor. But what was more important at this crucial time in his development was that his father was far from well. He had been seriously ill for several weeks at home in Winchmore Hill during Cliff's previous summer season at the London Palladium. To be with him as much as possible at this time, Cliff cancelled a number of other personal appearances and engagements.

Tito Burns didn't mind recalling those days. 'We agreed to separate because of Cliff's father, who fancied himself to be the power behind the throne. It's funny,' he smiled, 'but all kinds of people in England seem to have two businesses – their own and show business! Anyway, Cliff had to be pushed to the front and stand on his own two feet and I just couldn't work with his father. He, like a lot of others, thought he knew it all, but maybe that was because he was a very sick man.'

Sadly, Mr Rodger Webb was dead a little over three months after the announcement that Cliff and Tito had ended their partnership.

He died from heart trouble in a North London hospital on 15 May 1961. He was aged fifty-six and had been in and out of hospital since the previous October. Said Cliff, 'I never did anything without consulting him first. He helped me in everything.'

Because of his father's death he had to call off the first rehearsal at Elstree of *The Young Ones*.

Now Leslie Grade would loom larger than ever in Cliff's career. He got what he wanted. 'In 1961 I sold Cliff to Leslie Grade for £12,500,' George Ganjou revealed to me in 1981.

'So Leslie, who was a great friend of mine, became his agent. I was sorry to part with him because Cliff was just wonderful to me and very grateful for what I did for him.'

Brought in to succeed Tito Burns as personal manager was a shy, reticent but forceful man from Australia named Peter Gormley. His predecessor, Tito Burns, said of the events of those early days of 1961: 'At the time Peter was managing the Shadows and had proved a very knowledgeable person. So when Cliff's father and I could no longer get on together Peter became the automatic choice to take over from me as Cliff's manager.' Like most other people, Tito had nothing but admiration for Gormley.

Peter Gormley, born in a Sydney suburb, was drawn towards journalism in his teens and joined the staff of a country paper as a cub. At eighteen he left to go into films with a company that also turned out a weekly newsreel. Then the Second World War came along to take a slice out of his life and he saw service in the Solomon Islands.

When peace came Gormley went first into film journalism and then into cinema management, being responsible for a group of cinemas that sometimes put on live entertainment, all of which

64

was to lead to a meeting one day with a country and western singer named Frank Ifield.

Their liking for each other was mutual and Gormley now devoted his energies to managing this good-looking green-eyed lad who yodelled and didn't give a cuss for this thing called rock 'n' roll.

The Ifield–Gormley partnership boomed, but an artist can go only so far in Australia. Then he has to spread his wings and take off for Britain or America to find new and more rewarding fame. The ties with Britain, naturally, are strong and were particularly strong for Frank Ifield. He had been born in Coventry in 1938 when his father – who had hailed from Australia – was working in the motor trade. The family returned Down Under when Ifield was eight.

So Britain was the choice for Frank's future – and Gormley's. But the methodical Gormley didn't arrive here in 1959 with his charge and start pounding the streets and knocking on doors looking for the big, elusive break for his boy. Instead he arrived three months ahead of Ifield with tapes, Australian records and press-cutting albums to sell him first, and had a start neatly packaged for him with radio and TV appearances when he did touch down.

By January 1960 Ifield was making his bow on the Columbia label with a song called 'Lucky Devil' – all very pleasant, but not ear-catching enough to start a stampede to the record stores. That would come some eighteen months later with the Ifield yodelling smash hit 'I Remember You'.

The year 1960 would be a turning point year for Peter Gormley rather than for Frank Ifield.

While the Shadows were appearing with Cliff in the Palladium summer show they cut a solo record, a home-grown composition penned by singer-songwriter Jerry Lordan, an ex-London bus conductor. Title: 'Apache'.

Norrie Paramor, who was guiding the disc destinies of Cliff, the Shadows *and* Frank Ifield, thought its potential so high that now was the time for the Shadows to employ a full-time manager. Gormley was the right man, he decided, and approached him. After seeing the group in action and hearing 'Apache', Gormley agreed.

'Apache' (Cliff played a Chinese drum on it) became a block-busting international hit after its release early in July. At this time in 1960, of course, Cliff was still in the capable managerial hands of

Tito Burns. When Tito departed early in 1961 the lifeline was thrown Gormley's way. He was now on the threshold of becoming one of the most successful managers in the history of pop, but it wasn't a lifeline that he hastily grabbed. He weighed the situation carefully and particularly didn't want to tread on the toes of any predecessor.

'Do you know,' Cliff confided in a great tribute to Gormley, 'Peter didn't take a percentage of my earnings for a year after becoming my manager, saying that they came from arrangements made by Tito. Where can you find people like that in a business that is notorious for its rip-offs?'

In 1961 the final image of Cliff Richard was perfected under the guidance of Peter Gormley and Leslie Grade. It was an image that Cliff was naturally assuming as the days of wild rock receded. The real Cliff.

There would be no more managerial upheavals to complicate his professional life; there would be two more Grade movies in much the same nice-guy groove as *The Young Ones*, and records that would continue to hit. No more would anyone see even an itsy-bitsy suggestion of offensiveness in anything that Cliff Richard would do.

The path into the future had been determined. Not even the fantastic explosion that was the Beatles in 1962–3 would ruffle a hair on his head . . .

*The Young Ones* not only packed the cinemas of Britain when it was screened but caused a sensation in the movie world when the money was counted. Cliff, it was announced, was the nation's most popular film star of 1962 – head and shoulders above anyone Hollywood could offer. This was the finding of the *Motion Picture Herald* in its annual survey and poll of the film business in the United Kingdom.

The movie itself came second in the money-spinning league, which was topped by *The Guns of Navarone*, which cost around £2 million to make. *The Young Ones*, with an original budget of £100,000, had eventually cost £230,000.

Headed by Cliff, the list of ten most popular stars showed an astonishing array of talent that just couldn't keep up with the boy from the council house at Cheshunt.

His idol, Elvis, was second, Peter Sellers third. After this the runners-up were: 4, Kenneth More; 5, Hayley Mills; 6, Doris Day; 7, Sophia Loren; 8, John Wayne; 9, Frank Sinatra; 10, Sean Connery.

With his usual modesty Cliff told interviewers that it was 'ridiculous'. It wasn't, of course, and there were the box-office totals to prove it.

He went on, 'For my own ego it's great to be named the top star, but my next film may be a flopperoo. Of course I'm not as big a draw as Elvis. He's made a lot of pictures. It's not just a oncer for him. After I've made more films I'll be in a better position to judge my own worth.

'I dare not compare myself with established stars like Sellers. That would be stupid. Let's face it, I didn't do anything at the box office with my other two pictures, *Serious Charge* and *Expresso Bongo*.

'*The Young Ones* was just meant as a happy little film, or so we thought. It was Sidney Furie who injected the magic.'

He summed up, 'It really is fantastic. I'm terribly proud, but if I was making the choice I wouldn't choose me!

'I know I was being used as a guinea pig to see if a British musical could be a success and I think it happened because it was a simple film with a kind of amateur charm. But the public like something simple.'

Ironically, a vaudeville segment in the film was shot in the old Finsbury Park Empire, which Cliff used to pass in the Green Line bus before he was a star and where he lost his voice. It was, when used as a location for *The Young Ones*, a doomed theatre, killed along with variety by television . . .

The *Motion Picture Herald* poll and survey results came just a week before the second of the three Grade films was due to be premièred in London's West End – *Summer Holiday*, which was screened at the Warner Theatre in Leicester Square on 10 January 1963. It was a première that Cliff missed.

More than 3,000 fans were swarming around when his car arrived in the square. Hundreds pressed in close and twice when he tried to leave the car the sheer weight forced him back.

Worried police advised his chauffeur to try to make his way out of the square through the throng. He managed to edge the car out and drive Cliff to Peter Gormley's flat in St John's Wood, where he watched boxing on television while the première went on without him. 'I am bitterly disappointed,' he said. 'I put off a South African tour so that I could be there.'

One girl fan went to hospital with a leg injury. Others were treated at the cinema's first-aid centre.

Cliff was in the Canary Islands a year later shooting the third

Grade film, *Wonderful Life*, when he received a cable which read, YOU'VE DONE IT AGAIN BOY.

It was to tell him that for the second year in succession he had topped the poll in the *Motion Picture Herald* survey and was the most popular film star in Britain still. This time Peter Sellers was second and Elvis third. The other placings were: 4, Sean Connery; 5, Hayley Mills; 6, Elizabeth Taylor; 7, Marlon Brando; 8, Albert Finney; 9, Dirk Bogarde; 10, Norman Wisdom. *Summer Holiday* had done the trick.

The now completed image of Cliff Richard, top pop star and top film star, was far different from his original stage image. Gone was the chubbiness of the early rock 'n' roller, along with the dreadful drape jacket and pink, light-up socks. He was neat, well groomed and now ranked amongst the nation's ten best-dressed men.

A few years earlier he had been shocked one evening as he sat watching television to hear Minnie Caldwell – a character in *Coronation Street* – saying, 'I love that *chubby* Cliff Richard.' He decided to do something about it. As Tito Burns says, Cliff's a believer in not abusing his body. Not that he's a health food nut, but he will eat the right kind of food – except for curry!

'He was tending to be a little plump when he was with me, but no one gave him a diet sheet. He sorted it out himself. He also had the usual teenage problem of acne. He found out what to do about it himself and got some treatment.'

Some of this early skin trouble was caused by using the wrong stage make-up and not taking it off afterwards in the approved fashion with cold cream.

During the mid-sixties he could be observed arriving at the Palladium, where he was resident in *Aladdin*, carrying a string bag holding a mysterious package. What dark secret lurked there? Just a whack of cheese, it transpired, mostly Cheddar.

Cheese, he revealed, was his staple diet. By nibbling at it instead of wolfing curry he had reduced his weight to ten stone from his former twelve stone seven pounds.

'I have one real meal a week,' he confessed to Patrick Doncaster's column in the *Mirror*, 'and I had it last night. A tin of stewed steak.'

He also admitted to indulging in his mother's home cooking on his one day off on Sundays. 'I'll eat anything then, but I know exactly what the result will be. I'll put on four pounds.'

The spartan cheese diet shed it again, almost as quickly, he reckoned.

This then was the prototype of the Cliff Richard, superstar, we know today – the Cliff who has endured in a business as hard as steel and strewn with pitfalls.

The final image was not the work of one influence. No one could point a finger at any one person and say that's the man who made him what he is today. Cliff Richard evolved because of a bunch of people who were close to him or simply crossed his path.

In chronological order they were his father Rodger; John Foster; Ian Samwell; George Ganjou; Norrie Paramor; Franklyn Boyd; Jack Good; Lionel Bart; Tito Burns; Leslie Grade; and Peter Gormley.

Cliff admired his father very much, but has always said that they were really never close until his father's last illness. He had been strict and something of a disciplinarian.

'There's no doubt he was a great influence,' Cliff told me. 'He was also very much a balancing factor. He liked to know exactly what was going on and whether or not it was good for me. Whatever he did was for me and when he felt that I had too much to do he put his foot down.

'Yes, he taught me guitar – he'd played a banjo in a jazz band when we were in India, but not professionally. The original guitar he bought me on the never-never when I started out professionally was stolen on the first tour when we played the Colston Hall in Bristol – before he'd even finished paying for it!

'He was a great Jerry Lee Lewis fan and loved "Whole Lotta Shakin' Going' On".'

This was the rock classic with which Cliff closed his act on that first American tour in 1960. Cliff said at the time, 'My father is really enjoying himself. Like me, he too has never been to America. He fusses over me.

'During the show he sits in the stalls and listens to how the mike is reacting to the other singers' voices. Then he tells me how far away from it I should sing.'

The record of his son's which he most liked, Cliff told us, was 'A Girl Like You', which reached fourth place in the charts the year that he died.

'It would have been lovely if Dad had stayed alive to see all that has happened,' Cliff says a little sadly . . .

He will always be thankful that John Foster strolled into the Five Horseshoes at Hoddesdon that memorable evening in 1957.

'He was the first to have any faith in me,' Cliff says now. 'He gave me confidence – as well as a giggle and laugh on the old 715a bus to London!'

And he will always be grateful that his first agent, George

Ganjou, took the private recording to Norrie Paramor and wonders – almost with a shudder – what might have happened if he hadn't. 'Because no one else was taking much notice of us. George knew nothing about rock 'n' roll, but he saw the potential that was there,' Cliff says.

He remembers ex-Drifter Ian Samwell not only for writing 'Move It', the song that began it all, but for a master stroke in having suggested that the letter 's' be dropped from Richards when Harry Webb was looking for a new name. 'Brilliant!'

Samwell, who now has his own music publishing company and also produces records, says he still collects royalties from 'Move It'. He works in Britain and the United States and commutes across the Atlantic. When I talked to him, he said, 'Cliff's recorded about fourteen songs of mine over the years.'

Norrie Paramor died in September 1979. Five years earlier he had ended the long association with Cliff when he went to work for the BBC in Birmingham. He felt that he should make way for a younger man to preside over Cliff's recording career, he said.

Remembering him today, Cliff says, 'What can I say? He was a kind of father figure. He gave me fifteen years of consecutive hit records. I never had a miss – until the first record I made without him. It was called 'Brand New Song'. A sort of epitaph in a way. It's nice to think – with no disrespect to his successor – that the first record without Norrie didn't make it. It was the end of an era.'

Norrie once paid this tribute to Cliff: 'He's always so unassuming. Above all he has humility – the humility to listen and take advice even though he has firmness of opinion. In his position he could easily throw his weight about and make demands, but he never does.'

Cliff has long forgiven Jack Good for taking away his guitar and curtailing his Elvis sideburns and he never forgets that Jack turned over that first record in favour of 'Move It', the B-side. Jack's *Oh Boy!* programme pushed him to fame, and some notoriety, in those all-important early days.

'I used to look glum, sad, brooding – whatever word you like,' Cliff said. 'That was the way I was told to play it in close-up on telly. But,' he added, 'that wasn't me. After a few years I tried to set a happier mood.'

Jack Good agrees, of course, that the personality he developed was only a temporary one for television and that Cliff would grow out of it.

Answering my question, Jack says, 'What were my thoughts

about his future prospects at that time? I didn't think about that at all. We lived from day to day and it all seemed rather a joke. I wasn't prepared or cut out for this sort of career and in a sense neither was he, because rock 'n' roll had only just happened.

'Cliff and I just grabbed on to it. I said publicly that I thought he was going to be a huge star.'

Tito Burns left his mark on Cliff Richard as well. 'I have him to thank for my early film entry,' Cliff says. 'Again, when our association came to an end, it was an amicable parting. I can't pay tribute enough to all these guys. You know what a rip-off business this is. I have been fortunate, but of course there have been little bits of sadness – and some smiles.'

Tito himself, today an impresario who represents in certain countries such names as Victor Borge, Sacha Distel and Tony Bennett, says, 'I look back on my association with Cliff with great satisfaction and the big thrill for me these days whenever I'm in California is turning on the radio and hearing a Cliff Richard record. He has an incredible love of music. That's his whole world and his whole life.

'Only once did we ever come near to possibly breaking up while he was with me.'

It happened towards the end of 1959 when they were preparing for Cliff's first American tour early in the coming year. Cliff was recording twelve songs that could be released during his absence when Tito noticed that something was lacking.

'He had only two more songs to do and there was not a song yet from his new movie, *Expresso Bongo*,' he tells us. 'So I suggested one.

'"I don't like it," Cliff said.

'"You have to learn politics," I told him. "You have to back up your own movie." But he still didn't like it. "It's obvious," I said, "that you've reached the stage where you don't need me any more. Okay, you can carry on on your own." I walked out, but he ran after me.

'"You have to take my advice," I told him. "Oh, all right!" he said and everything was well again.

'The song was "Voice In The Wilderness". The record reached number two in the charts.'

This was one of batch of songs from *Expresso Bongo* written by Norrie Paramor and Bunny Lewis, a former Decca executive who had guided the early career of the powerful-voiced hit singer David Whitfield.

Cliff's EP from the film also hit the singles chart.

His memories of Leslie Grade illustrate how thorough he was, giving his attention to the slightest detail, however busy he happened to be. 'He was a workaholic,' Cliff says. 'We got on very well together and he was always very thoughtful. His main aim was that I should be happy when I was working for him. If I found myself in a show where someone was using any blue material, I would tell him that I was concerned because of the number of kids in the audience and he would remove whoever it was.'

Leslie Grade died in October 1979, only weeks after the death of Norrie Paramor.

One other member of the entourage for whom Cliff had much respect was Leslie Perrin, without doubt the best-known and best-loved public relations man in show business.

He represented Cliff and the Shadows for many years. Also in his fold for a long time were such diverse luminaries as Frank Sinatra and the Rolling Stones.

His publicity campaign to back up the launching of the Shadows' first big hit, 'Apache', is still recalled affectionately by Cliff. 'Les sent all the record critics and columnists a story with an arrow stuck through it!' It was a slick way of drawing attention to a group that was trying to make it on their own without Cliff and the critics certainly paid attention.

But Les's task was not only to put his clients' names in the papers. His more important duty was to act as their spokesman – frequently in some difficult situation. On all his press releases he gave his home telephone number for night calls and there were many long nights when the phone never ceased to ring, often with calls from many parts of the world.

As Cliff said, paying tribute to him, 'We needed a buffer and Les was a buffer, taking the weight whenever necessary.'

He died in 1978 at the age of fifty-seven. No one over the years has taken his place. Cliff's immediate publicity has largely been handled by the press office of his only British record company, EMI Records, and there can be few quibbles with their loyal efforts. Cliff has never been *au fait* with much of British music journalism, apart from such senior and experienced writers as David Wigg of the *Daily Express*, and a relatively small number of others. Generally, those allowed to pen more in-depth features have written good copy, and not sensationalized what has essentially been ordinary, but he feels the same cannot be said about some tabloid newspapers, and this was especially true during the Cliff and Sue Barker saga. Equally annoying are the guarded allusions to unprovable sexual desires, often the province of fantasy journalism and published because it is felt they sell newspapers. But there have been solid, well-researched articles in tabloid newspapers: one instance can be found in the *Daily Star* of Friday 12 October 1990, when the former feature writer and the then news editor, Derek Johnson and Alasdair Buchan, published a tasteful, well-informed article on Cliff's life and music.

Arguably, Cliff needed a strong public relations service more in the 1980s than at any other time. The music scene has greatly changed; it still retains a strong teenage strain – witness the success of a magazine such as *Smash Hits* – but the teen print world is nowhere near as effective or important as it once was. Successful teen magazines in the late 1980s and 1990s mix their input much more and are no longer so pop-star orientated, an editorial strategy well illustrated, with sales to prove it, in *Smash Hits'* sister paper, *Big*.

Although Cliff cannot be considered a prime feature subject for a magazine aimed mainly at girls between the ages of eight and seventeen, he will still occasionally make pop paper columns, but the essential directive that he should be there no longer operates. For the most part Cliff is covered in the entertainment sections of daily and weekend papers, allied chiefly to the women's magazine market; he has been much featured in the British *Woman's Own*, and he has appeared in the fastest-growing general journal of the past ten years, *Hello!*. Even with Cliff's track record in music and other areas, it simply isn't the case that people come running if it is announced that he will give interviews, which rarely take place except in the context of a new single or album, video or tour, an award or television or radio special. There is always an element of 'What's new?' from long-standing editors. By and large, though, journalists will say 'yes' to an interview invitation.

Sometimes something special will be planned. It may be a general press conference, perhaps a rather lavish launch of a new album in most congenial surroundings, attended by several hundred writers. Here, Cliff may give a speech, and take questions from the floor. Often he will close the occasion by meeting a few journalists. I recall how EMI organized a special lunch for journalists from provincial newspapers. They met for drinks, and then sat around the large table in EMI's swish executive boardroom for an excellent meal, with Cliff at the head of the table. Later, journalists had their own fifteen- to thirty-minute audience.

Augmenting arranged interviews is the inevitable round of telephone chats, mostly with papers in far-flung corners of the world. Running parallel with this are extensive interviews for the ever-growing number of radio stations. Sometimes, while on tour, Cliff will visit a local station, but he prefers to do promotional exercises before the tour begins rather than when he is under the stress of performing. He likes to relax and ensure he is ready for his concerts.

In addition to radio, there is television. Even here he doesn't accept all invitations, perhaps only those that may be most effective for a particular single or album. He has also to consider the demands on his time that may be made by the television station, apart from the relatively brief interview.

While the EMI marketing and promotional machine has been extremely important over the years, the real power base lies in offices in the Esher area of Surrey. (Originally Cliff's affairs and office were based in Harley House, off Upper Harley Street and Marylebone Road in north-west London.) Here, the best-known names in current Cliff activity such as David Bryce and, more of a visible presence for media people, the genial and gentlemanly Bill Latham, are to be found. Most writers will probably talk to Bill Latham, who has the ability to make them feel at home and who will gently enquire what angle they may have in mind. Cliff is spared the day-to-day running of his business, his mind eased by the professional people in the Esher office, but is still central to major decisions.

Much of this may lie behind the promotion of any artist, although some artists can prove inflexible and lack understanding. Cliff has never been obdurate, nor has he exercised the vanity and arrogance of some major stars who will only be interviewed for a narrow band of journals, radio and television programmes. He has talked with the least significant, in promotional and marketing terms. For that, sadly, he has gained little credit. He has never engaged an independent public relations office to say a continual 'no' or to give highly edited versions of events.

However, what of the 'image' concept if, in Cliff's case, it is not in the hands of those who spend their days and time trying to formulate marketing ploys? Bill and Cliff deny that there is any deliberate 'image' building for Cliff. Undoubtedly, there have been times when extra push has seemed necessary but equally, it has often been when they realised they had something special, as at the end of the 1970s with the classic 'We Don't Talk Anymore' or with 'Saviour's Day'. But it hasn't entailed a revamping of the way in which Cliff should be seen. Nor has it engendered a host of fictitious stories to capture the headlines. When Cliff has been in print and when the news has been significant, it has almost always focused on a worthy charity or religious happening.

Bill has said, with a wry smile, 'There are no meetings about his hair, what he will wear. He is aware of current fashions and he takes note, but it's always down to his personal preferences. Obviously, more than most people, he is aware he is in the public eye, but he has his own self-image. But then I think "image" is not the right word, it can mean something contrived, and that isn't Cliff. I think he has inner strengths and outward projection.

'Cliff has never felt he has had to adopt a degree of aloofness to maintain the mystique that some have felt in the industry. He has been accessible to a degree.'

Cliff has also made it clear that he felt 'no need for all the publicity machinery that goes with George Michael or Michael Jackson. I'm always "me", this moment, and any moment. Even in my early days I don't remember someone sitting down with me and saying this and that would aid me, although, of course, there was the time when Jack Good suggested a few things, but that was very early in my career. I just remember I used to bring clothes, a shirt, jacket, trousers and shoes, that interested me and seemed right. I've always been interested in fashion. But I've always thought most other stars have been into "image", and I know some of them have had managements very concerned with how they shall be projected. And see what has happened to most of them – their careers have ultimately nose-dived.

'I know I have cultivated certain things. I've always kept care of myself, and yes, remained slim as the years have passed. I try and think of what I should do. I listen to what is around me. And why shouldn't I still be as contemporary as the next person? I don't know about all this talk of me being the oldest teenager for I don't think that way. I'm getting older, I know that. I am not, though, trying to reflect something I am not.

'I simply want to keep my career and that will not be so if I lose my fitness and spend my life in nightclubs.'

As he put it in his book *Single-Minded*: 'Sure, in ordinary life I'm not different from anyone else, and certainly no better.' He goes on: 'But on stage it's a different world, and I'll pull every trick in the book to look different, sound different, be different, in order to express that piece of fantasy which I believe is exactly what the audience wants and pays for. They ask to be wafted away into another realm, and how can that even begin to happen if on stage I'm the spitting image of the bloke next door?' And he added, 'Being separate doesn't mean being aloof.'

Later in the same absorbing chapter, 'Now and Then', among many trenchant comments on the attitude of record companies to their so-called artist rosters, Cliff says with despair, 'Now the priority criterion is who looks right for the day. And when the day's out, why worry? There's always plenty to choose from for tomorrow.'

Cliff and his management team may not sit down and plan his image for tomorrow, next week, next year, but they take care to use only quality product in photographs, posters, advertisements, record sleeves and any printed material over which they can exercise influence. The Cliff output has become synonymous with high standards, although not all may like the finished product. And, yes, despair has been expressed about his 'goody-goody', and 'squeaky clean' image, even by some fans. It all sounds so banal.

In the end, of course, it all boils down to the right songs and Cliff's vocal ability: find the wrong numbers or if Cliff is suffering from throat problems, it all dissolves – at least as long as Cliff doesn't see himself as a mere purveyor of 'my greatest hits', which doesn't seem likely.

# CHAPTER NINE

# NEAR AND DEAR

There was no escape for the Webb family. The big breakthrough made by Harry while still in his teens would touch them all in some way. They could never be ordinary people again, able to live a normal life going quietly about their day-to-day business while the eldest child was moving towards his peak as a pop and movie star in the swinging sixties.

Fingers would point at them, at both the parents and the three sisters, and voices would whisper, 'That's Cliff Richard's mum!' 'That's one of his sisters!' Fans would beg favours of them. An autograph of Cliff's; a lock of his dark, romantic hair.

The family home, when Cliff's father died in May 1961, was still the house at Winchmore Hill, where the siege would never abate. Some nights a handful of girls keeping a round-the-clock vigil outside would be invited in for a cup of tea brewed in the wee small hours by a patient Mrs Webb, sitting up awaiting Cliff's return from an engagement.

Jacqueline and Joan, the two youngest daughters, were still schoolgirls, but the eldest, Donella, was moving towards womanhood.

Cliff was now the man about the house whenever he was able to be there, but still had several months to go until he attained his majority on reaching twenty-one, then the legal age. Until that time someone else would have to sign all documents on his behalf (it had been his father up to his death). And according to the law he was not yet old enough to enter a pools coupon, which was hardly a burden when his yearly earnings were now estimated to be in the big pools win bracket, anyway.

Within twelve weeks of the loss of her father, Donella was married at Waltham Abbey parish church in Essex. She was eighteen and Cliff gave her away.

It was 5 August 1961, a Saturday, and frantic scenes made

acres of picture space in the Sunday newspapers. The fans turned up to scream and mob Cliff rather than Donella, who fainted when they forced their way through a cordon of police to reach big brother and knocked her veil askew.

Cliff did a man-size job, gathering up his sister and carrying her into the church, although hardly getting her there on time. The service was delayed for fifteen minutes.

Donna, as the family called her, looking radiant in white, had her veil neatly arranged once more before Cliff escorted her up the aisle while the bridegroom, a young man named Paul Stevens, waited anxiously.

After the ceremony there was the same frenzied activity as the fans surged forward, many of them with cameras, when the newlyweds tried to leave the church to escape into the wedding cars.

This time Cliff stayed inside until the rest of the wedding party had managed to drive away. When he did make his exit he was surrounded by six brawny bodyguards.

In November 1963 the remaining Webbs – Cliff, his mother and two younger sisters – folded their tent at Winchmore Hill and moved off into Upper Nazeing, just across the Hertfordshire border in Essex, into a spacious, sprawling £30,000 mansion with elegant chimneys.

It was called Rookswood, had six bedrooms, four reception rooms, four bathrooms, a billiards room, a five-car garage, stables, greenhouses and tennis court, and stood in eleven acres. Cars crunched along a 300-yard drive to reach the entrance, which opened on to a large hall panelled with oak that had once looked out on history at Hampton Court. Cliff's bedroom looked as large as or even larger than, the famous cellar at the 2 i's.

'This house is essentially a family home and that's the way Cliff wants to keep it,' said manager Peter Gormley.

An aunt and two teenaged cousins also moved in to live with the diminished Webb family, now without Donella as well as a father.

But the fans found the place. They arrived on foot and in cars and the police had to clear them from the driveway and grounds, where they churned up the turf. Only after the gates had been strengthened, and Cliff departed for his long sojourn to film *Wonderful Life* in the Canaries, did the siege begin to ease.

Sisters Jacqueline, then sixteen, and Joan, thirteen, felt the loneliness of Rookswood at the beginning, set as it was in a comparative wilderness. For them the transition to such splendour was wondrous, after the modest semi-detached at Winchmore Hill and the council house at Cheshunt, where the rent had been 30 shillings a week (£1.50) and the residents looked into each other's gardens.

Only Joan was still at school – Cheshunt Secondary Modern, where Cliff had been a pupil – while Jackie, as she was known, had already started work, pounding away at a typewriter. What made them different was that they travelled each morning in a chauffeured car to their respective destinations. And each morning the postman brought them mail, mostly from girl fans of their famous brother wanting to become their pen pals – anything to reach a little closer to their idol.

At school Joan was taking a daily dose of ragging. The Beatles had now arrived to challenge Cliff as lord and master of the British pop scene and a lot of youngsters were transferring their affections and letting Miss Webb know.

The Webb girls began to take an interest in another fast-rising name in the group business, the Dave Clark Five, who in January 1964 achieved national acclaim by unseating the seemingly immovable Beatles from the top of the charts with Dave's smash hit 'Glad All Over'. They became such admirers of Dave and the Five that they became their fan club organizers and were even pictured at their task. It's a free country, they might have said . . .

Some two and a half years later the calm of Rookswood made way for some new excitement in the Webb family saga. On Monday 20 June 1966 the *Daily Mirror* broke the news at the top of page three with bold black headlines: CLIFF RICHARD'S MUM WEDS HIS EX-DRIVER.

The text ran, 'Pop star Cliff Richard's mother, Mrs Dorothy Webb, forty-five, has married his 24-year-old former chauffeur, Derek Bodkin.

'Last night Dorothy and Derek were on a touring honeymoon in Cliff's white E-type Jaguar.

'Their wedding was such a well-kept secret that not even Cliff was told until AFTER the register-office ceremony on Saturday.

'Mrs Webb telephoned Cliff, twenty-five, from a call-box at Epping, Essex, and broke the news.

'Then she and Derek drove back to Cliff's £31,000 [sic] Tudor-style mansion at Upper Nazeing, Essex, for an impromptu champagne reception.

'It was strictly a family affair,' the story went on to say, 'with daughters Jackie and Joan present along with Derek's parents, who had also been present at the wedding ceremony.'

At some stage Cliff arrived and took photographs of the newly-weds on the lawn. After waving them goodbye on the first stage of their honeymoon he was reported as saying, 'I'm not worried by the difference in their ages. Derek is an old friend.

'Mum has told me that the reason she kept it all secret was that she didn't want it to be a showbiz wedding with lots of people there.

'She wanted to be married quietly and this was the only way she could do it.

'She wanted to be just plain Mrs Webb getting married, not Cliff Richard's mum.'

Cliff had been missing from the family home because he was filming *Finders Keepers* at Pinewood studios in Buckinghamshire, with Robert Morley and new leading lady, Viviane Ventura. The journey from Rookswood to Pinewood at daybreak would have meant an hour and a half drive, Cliff explained later. Bill Latham – who had been a master at his old school and one of the people whose advice he had sought about Christianity – lived with his mother, Mamie, in North London, midway along the route to Pinewood. To save Cliff time he suggested that Cliff should stay with them during the six-week filming, to make the hard movie life that much more bearable.

Cliff accepted the offer and it was the beginning of an enduring friendship.

On that Monday in June 1966, when the news of Mrs Webb's secret marriage came out, Cliff held a press conference at Pinewood between filming at which he announced that he was going to buy a house as a wedding present for his mother and new stepfather, who was younger than himself. He referred to him as Derek and smiled, 'I can hardly call him Dad!'

He added that on the wedding day he had gone out and bought some wine for a celebration with them and that they would continue their honeymoon at his villa in Portugal.

Discussing plans for the future, he said that the house he would buy for his mother and her new husband would be in Essex and not far from Rookswood.

'My sisters and I naturally want our mother and Derek to build a happy life.'

The plans also included a new home for his two sisters and a third for the aunt and cousins who were living with them. He envisaged a smaller home or flat for himself.

'We all met Derek,' he went on, 'when he applied for the job of chauffeur with us years ago, though he has not worked for us since my father died. We all regard him as a friend.'

The first contact with Derek had been when Cliff frequently booked vehicles from the car-hire firm for which Bodkin worked. Later he became Cliff's personal driver for a period.

Within three weeks of the marriage Cliff had sold Rookswood for £43,000. The buyer was a director of the London Rubber Company. At the same time it was announced that Cliff had bought a detached house at Broxbourne, only a few miles from Nazeing but in Hertfordshire, for his mother and Derek, plus two other houses in Broxbourne for sister Jackie and the aunt who had been living at Rookswood.

Six months after the wedding, Bodkin went on record to say that Cliff did not know about the marriage until after the ceremony but that he did know 'we were going to get married'.

He also said that he didn't treat Cliff 'like a son'. And he now had his own car-hire business.

Some years later Cliff stressed that the marriage had not upset him. 'It was the nicest thing that could have happened, both to her and to me. My father's death was a great loss to her and although she married someone very much younger, he has been a stabilizing factor.'

However, the union did not last, leaving Cliff once more with the close relationship he had shared with his mother between his father's death and her remarriage. She continues to enjoy healthy and good living and some of the best pictures in his career photo library show the two of them together. She obviously feels for Cliff when he is confronted with a negative press, and is offended by suggestions that he might be gay. She attends many important and more social gatherings, and is sometimes seen with Cliff on outings: during the early months of 1992 he took the family to the Jack Good musical *Good Rockin' Tonite*.

But it would seem that age and distance from his father's death in 1961 have increased Cliff's desire to see their relationship in a better light, and on a number of occasions during more personal press interviews he has brought it up. He has said that when his father became ill, 'we finally understood each other better', for otherwise 'my memory would have been of a man bordering on the tyrannical. In fact he was just very firm and I now recognize that I actually needed the discipline he imposed on my life.' In other contexts, he has taken his father's stress on discipline and applied this to his thinking on how he might bring up children, if he were a parent. Cliff despairs about the lack of discipline in current family relationships: 'Children who are not disciplined grow up to have no respect for other people's property, or bodies.'

All his sisters married and, not surprisingly, Cliff's mother would love to see her son find someone special. Speaking to Judith Simon of the *Daily Express*, Cliff said, 'When I was fourteen, and beginning to get interested in girls, I had a mental picture of my marital future. I figured I'd get married at twenty-seven, which seemed a nice, mature age, and have two sons and two daughters. As it turned out I'm still a bachelor and the main children in my life are my ten nephews and nieces.' And indeed one of them married on 14 January 1992. This was Clare, aged twenty-one. Cliff lent her a Rolls-Royce for her big day with Matthew Payne. The manager of the local leisure centre was reported saying that Cliff got on well with everyone at the reception.

Fame, though, does not spare anyone pain and he was particularly upset when his sister Jackie's baby son was born with his internal organs joined together. His survival rate was given as fifty-fifty with an operation immediately pencilled in before he was a year old. Thankfully, in spite of early difficulties and set-backs, progress has been made, although Phillip still warrants major medical care and attention.

There is, too, his wider 'family'. He has often said that Peter Gormley, who has managed his affairs since 1961 (although he now oversees, for the day-to-day running has passed to a team management), became a 'father' figure, as did his big-standing musical arranger, the late Norrie Paramor. Office staff have often stayed and this longevity is unique in a musical world where managers and agents come and go. Over the years there has been his long-standing friendship with Bill Latham and, until she died, Bill's mother Mamie, which has been worth so much.

Peter is very much someone who keeps in the background. Any collector over the years of Cliff interviews will know there has been precious little comment. He says simply, 'Why have me chattering? It's Cliff who matters, surely?'

Over the years he travelled the world. He arranged the tours, decided where Cliff went and kept a close watch on contractual and recording matters. Now that he is in his seventies, he has handed over the day-to-day affairs.

David Bryce handles Cliff's recording and touring affairs and is expert in handling the lighting for Cliff shows. Like Peter, he is an outstanding and much respected person with an honesty not much in evidence in the cut-throat world of the 'biz'. He is a brother of the late 1950s British singer, Dickie Valentine. Bill Latham takes charge of Cliff's Christian and charity interests, personal and general public relations and liaising with the media, and Malcolm Smith handles the business and contractual matters.

Cliff is no playboy and is rarely seen at parties and London clubs. He does not usually find his friends in the ephemeral world of pop, except a few, one being the popular disc jockey and writer, Mike Read. Those friends he has from the music business have known him for a long time, and include, not unexpectedly, the Shadows, especially the best-known trio of Hank Marvin, Bruce Welch and Brian Bennett. Obviously they aren't as close as they were when they played and toured together, but there is still much affection between them, even if as Bruce put it, 'We only seem to meet these days for anniversaries and awards.' It's now over thirty years since an early financial arrangement eased and cemented a friendship. 'The very first tour we did, Cliff just split the money with the group – five ways. I think we got twelve quid each. Then in 1959, when he was big, we got twenty-five quid a week. But for twenty-five quid a week in those days, I had a flat in the West End. I was married and I still had money left at the end of the week.

'We travelled everywhere together and that is how the song-writing developed. Coaches, cars, trains – we just used to get our guitars out all the time . . . that's how all the music came, just from that sort of atmosphere.

'I remember the first time I met Cliff. He looked at us and thought we were yobs. Mind you, he was right.'

Hank recalls how Cliff brought back from the States a Fender guitar which gave the group a very American sound. Critics remember how Hank's use of the treble arm, allied with the Shadows' twanging, made them special.

Cliff says of them, 'They were the motivators of myriad instrumentalists. Hank was the only guy who could play Buddy Holly's solos note for note. That made you stardust.

'Hank was the king. In Italy they said that without the Shadows there would have been no pop music. After we started there were Italians up and down the country wearing pink jackets and doing the goose step in the background!'

Acknowledgements have come from such famous rock people as Pete Townshend, Jeff Beck and Eric Clapton, all still playing, especially Clapton.

Last but not least – except the fans – of Cliff's friends are those he has made among fellow Christians, such people as David Winter, Nigel Goodwin and Cindy Kent. Winter still smiles broadly when he recalls how he gave Cliff around five years in Popsville, although on normal reckoning such a time-scale might seem generous in the fast-moving days of the early-to-middle-sixties pop scene. He says, 'He's good at a lot of things. I really think he could have become a professional football player [Cliff played at right back], there's nothing casual about Cliff when it comes to serious things. He's always been prepared to do things. His activity rate is staggering. And through everything he's always suffered from a dodgy throat and a back which used to play up a great deal. My word for everything is "astonishing".' Winter once edited *Crusade*, a lively Christian monthly, then became a producer with BBC Radio for fifteen years. He ended up as Head of Religious Broadcasting in 1987. He is now priest-in-charge of Ducklington, in Oxfordshire, and Bishop's Officer for Evangelism in the Oxford Diocese.

Nigel Goodwin is another of Cliff's confidants, and often arranges occasions at which stars from many artistic areas gather to eat and hear why Cliff is a Christian. Goodwin was one of those responsible, with Cliff, for founding the highly successful and influential (Christian) Arts Centre Group. Cliff was best man at his wedding with Gillian and is godfather to the Goodwin offspring. Some say Nigel is Cliff's principal spiritual adviser. He says, 'To me Cliff is a great ambassador for the good side of the music business. In private he has problems like we all have. For him, it's harder to share them. With someone who is well known there is always the problem of someone saying something in the wrong place and then it's there in the newspapers, even when it's trivial.'

Cindy Kent's relationship with Cliff goes back to his early church attendance in North London, and her work with the Settlers. They played many concerts with Cliff and appeared on many of his early television shows, both religious and general.

Cliff also numbers among his friends the world-renowned evangelists Billy Graham and Luis Palau, while in the more structured areas of mainstream Christianity, his work has been much appreciated by the new Archbishop of Canterbury, Dr George Carey, who expressed how magnificent has been Cliff's witness.

Cliff says, 'I guess it's a family affair. There's been a long-term commitment of people which is fantastic. They worry about me. There's this marvellous solidarity behind me.'

And lastly the fans. Oddly enough, there is no longer an official Cliff Richard fan club. There was once: a girl called Jan Vane ran it from her house and somehow managed to keep a reputed 40,000 fans happy with news of their man. She had known Cliff for some time, even before his first taste of stardom with 'Move It' in 1958. She says she doesn't think much about those early days unless someone broaches the subject. Jan still follows Cliff's activities but as a friend rather than a fan. She pops up at important occasions and celebrations and still phones him. 'They were fantastic days, the early ones. Everyone was so taken with the success. We just enjoyed every moment without really thinking too much. I was just part of the family. I would go shopping with Cliff. I remember once they threw me in the swimming pool for laughs. Fortunately Johnny Foster realized I couldn't swim and he pulled me out.

'We never had much money. I can remember sometimes forking out the taxi bill! They were great times. An official fan club was necessary because all sorts of people were trying to jump on the Cliff name bandwagon and fans were powerless.'

There were several later attempts to set up a fan club, but the operation ran out of control. Cliff and his management stepped in to sort things out, ensuring that no one was financially deprived.

Since the late sixties there has been the International Cliff Richard Movement (ICRM) which is run from Holland, where Cliff has always enjoyed considerable popularity. Anton Husmann and Harry De Louw chase Cliff closely in age, and their *DI* magazine is published bi-monthly, containing lots of information about Cliff's movements. Other meeting houses and fan groupings pay allegiance to the Dutch shrine, and many of them, including the Cliff Richard fan clubs of London and Surrey, Avon and Somerset, and Yorkshire, produce their own, often very bulky and informative, magazines. Cliff United is run from southeast London base by Christine Whitehead. Her magazine of the same name can run to sixty-four pages, and had just launched when the first edition of *Cliff* was published in 1981. Oddly enough, Cliff United was outlawed by ICRM in its early days, the organization issuing a stern warning in its *Dynamite International* magazine of April/May 1982, number 81, in which they said that Cliff United claim not to be a fan club but act as if they are. 'The

ICRM certainly does not support this "club".' But times change in politics and religion – and also in the world of Cliff fans!

However, one thriving body stays outside of the world mentioned thus far: Grapevine, which grew from the Colchester Meeting House in 1978. This was basically a dozen or so fans meeting together to share their common interest. As with many splinter groups, they felt dissatisfied with existing groups and wrote to Cliff explaining their intentions, to which he raised no objection. Over the years their excellent magazine grew from the usual typed affair to a printed, glossy number using colour. The office base is Diana Duffet's dining-room.

The fan groupings have continued to lend Cliff enormous support for his many activities and, though not all are interested in the Christian side of his life, they raise enormous sums for charities, mainly for his favourite, Tear Fund, and his own charity fund. Sometimes major gifts have been made to other worthy causes, such as the National Spinal Injuries Centre at Stoke Mandeville, or to the handicapped children of Oakleigh School, north London, who received a new minibus. This gift was received on their behalf by Cliff personally, and had been instigated by Janet Johnson.

Many of those who run the clubs have followed Cliff since their own teen days. One is Jennifer Chatten, who runs the Cliff Richard Fan Club of Yorkshire. As her club magazine constantly shows, she is adept at having letters about Cliff published in local newspapers when she senses the most tenuous link between him and a current news subject. She even found herself with celebrity status when on 31 January 1986 the *Harrogate Advertiser* ran a full-page story on her support for Britain's top male artist. Her love for Cliff began when, as a thirteen-year-old, she caught sight of him performing on *Oh Boy!* in 1958. 'When I saw him I instinctively knew that he was different. Obviously, I didn't envisage it going on for so long.' Later in the same year she found herself in his presence. During a break when Cliff and the Shadows were rehearsing, one of the theatre staff mentioned to him that a young girl was desperate for his autograph. 'I was so awestruck. I didn't say anything to him at the time. The first time you meet him is something you never forget.'

She told the newspaper that running an active fan club is an exhausting affair, especially since they spend so much time involved in charitable activities.

One of her greatest achievements has been in activating a

campaign to bring Cliff to the Harrogate Centre. The town never featured on his itinerary, or at least had not for twenty-six years, so when he came in 1986 it was in part due to Jennifer's constant letters in which she pointed out the splendours of the town's conference headquarters. Her devotion was shown even more when she queued outside the centre's booking office for twenty-two hours to ensure she got her tickets: 'I wanted to be there when he came back.'

Like many fans, she has stayed with Cliff simply because his lifestyle has been sensible and responsible, and the kind of image she would present to her own daughters. 'I know he gets the mickey taken out of him because of his religious beliefs, but he has the same moral outlook that we were brought up with and the majority of people respect him.' She says, 'I have to cringe when they [pop stars] flaunt their drug-taking and everything else. Cliff has never let us down.'

Cliff himself says, 'My fans are pretty vocal at concerts. They wait respectfully for me at the stage door for autographs. No hair-pulling, chair-smashing mobs. The fever has been cured. I find these destructive crowds most unhealthy. It smacks of anarchy, and that philosophy is so childish.' But it wasn't so when he first began his career when there was a definite air of hysteria.

In the 1950s several music papers found his act objectionable and a thoroughly bad influence, but a few years later in the mid-sixties those, and others, saw Cliff as British, Pat Boone-ish, endowed with good looks, a constant toothpaste smile and a casual, immaculate appearance. Writing in 1963, Colin Frame claimed, 'The adulation, crazy, vociferous, hysterical, followed him – still follows him – like a pack of baying hounds.

'And he knows how to handle it – the thousand eyes adoring him, the thousand hands held out to him, the thousand voices calling his name.

'He knows when to please, when to tease, when to disappear.' Frame called it 'orgiastic self-release' for the girls. The fans' behaviour was sometimes extreme: one girl sent Cliff a piece of chewing gum, asked him to chew it and then return to sender. Another, showing a certain creativity, had herself posted to him as a parcel. Inevitably some have gate-crashed theatres and television dressing-rooms, or shinned up a drainpipe and appeared at the window.

Fans are not always contented: Janet Johnson, a most loyal Cliff follower and organizer of the active London group, caught the flak from fans, fan club organizations and the Cliff office when she burst into national newspaper tabloids saying she was completely fed up with the way Cliff and his management treated fans.

The best-selling *Sun* newspaper, never one to allow its readers a peaceful breakfast, screamed in agony: CLIFF RICHARD SPURNED ME, SAYS NO. 1 FAN JANET and sub-headlined: CLUB BOSS QUITS IN RAGE OVER TICKETS. Janet was quoted as saying, 'It has taken me thirty years to open my eyes and realize that neither Cliff nor his staff care anything about the fans.'

It appeared that she was 'given the worst seats in the house' for his 1988 tour, but a spokesperson for Cliff denied that the star didn't care, while stressing that the office could not give priority to particular individuals or clubs.

While many deplored that this issue should reach the pages of the major press, it cannot be denied that the central core of the Johnson case is one that frequently arises, with anger expressed in letters carried by the fan club journals and most recently in 1992 issues of *Grapevine*. Short of a stage stretching a mile or two, it is difficult to see how each and every fan can claim a front seat.

That grievance aside, Cliff fans are usually even-tempered, the most loyal, and arguably the best bunch in artist fan club land. And his followers are worldwide, with most countries boasting some kind of Cliff information service and a place for fans to meet, catch up with the news, hear records and watch videos of the man who means more than anyone else.

# CHAPTER TEN

# LOVE AND MARRIAGE

By the time you reach this page Cliff Richard may well have surprised us all and married. 'I would like to be married sometime,' he told me. 'I hope so. But falling in love is not something you can plan. It's something that happens.'

He has made similar pronouncements over the years, almost since his entry into the big time in 1958. Of course he would like children, particularly a son, he has said. But, as he points out frequently, the problem of whether or not he will marry or why he isn't married is one that seems to concern other people more than himself. In *Which One's Cliff?*, written in collaboration with Bill Latham, he says that he is content as a bachelor, although marriage and children around the house are desirable.

'I don't have any great urge to be married. No, I'm not a mass of sexual hang-ups. Yes, I have had girlfriends in the past and, who knows, I may have another in the future and end up married. In the mean time, I'm not pursuing anyone and feel very fulfilled, thank you very much! Perhaps I'll give the next interviewer who starts the well-worn romance routine a copy of this book – it will save a lot of time and a lot of tedium.'

At a subsequent interview, I asked Cliff if these sentiments still applied. They did, he said, and repeated that he would still like to be married sometime.

Since he became a star he has always tried to keep his private life private, although this has not always been easy. But in 1968 he did have this to say: 'People were always trying to find out who I was going with, but really I have been in love only three times.

'Once was when I was planning to marry Jackie Irving. We met when she was dancing in my show at the Palladium – but then she went and married Adam Faith. So that was that.'

He went on to say, 'I'm going to get married when I'm ready – and not before. I may not get married at all.'

The Jackie Irving romance blossomed in the early sixties when Cliff was the number one pop and film star and Britain's most eligible show business bachelor.

In July 1963 he said, 'There is one girl I'm very friendly with – dancer Jackie Irving – but she and I know that marriage is out of the question.'

Yet he had thought seriously about marrying her and let it be known some three years later when he said, 'The Shadows had all married and I'd been going around with Jackie Irving for three years and we'd got along very well.

'I did think about marriage then, but I decided I couldn't love her or we'd have been married earlier.'

He was twenty-three when he considered marriage to her and still had some time to go before he reached twenty-five, the age he had designated several times as probably the right one at which to wed.

When he did reach twenty-five he was reminded of this and admitted that 'there have been three or four false alarms which I don't regret. If I meet the right girl then I'll marry straight away . . .

'How can you say that you'll marry at such and such a time? Who can plan for the right girl to turn up?

'Too many of those I do meet are either sarcastic or over-keen. They put me off – it's my job to do the chasing. I much prefer a reserved girl who doesn't do all the talking to the type who charges up and never stops. And I want a girl who is interested in me as a person rather than the pop singer she has read about.'

He did update the marrying age to twenty-seven and later to thirty-two as the bachelor years moved on. After all, he recalled, his father had been in his thirties when he wed Mrs Webb.

Cliff was a few months short of his twenty-third birthday in 1963, when he was dating Jackie, when he said, 'The girl I marry will be a girl I'm in love with, and that's not likely to happen for some time yet. I don't plan to marry for another four or five years yet. When I do, it will be for keeps.

'My wife, whoever she is, will have to put her foot down with me. She'll have to speak her mind and not be afraid to say what she thinks. I can't stand insincerity. There's nothing like a bit of straight talking.'

The romance with Jackie Irving has been the only one that he has talked about at any length and where the name of the girl has been mentioned. It seems to have foundered while Cliff was in the Canary Islands shooting *Wonderful Life* early in 1964. Miss Irving, who was then a dancer in the Lionel Blair troupe, lamented, 'I don't see Cliff any more. I haven't heard from him since he went away filming. Not a letter or a postcard, nothing.'

She, for her part, denied that there had been any romance or that there was any secret engagement. They were, in the time-honoured show business quote, just good friends. They had worked together in Cliff's shows in Blackpool and in South Africa.

'When we were in South Africa we often went out, but with a crowd of people from the show,' she said.

'While we were in Blackpool [in the summer of 1963] we went out together quite a lot.'

In fact, she added, 'Cliff and I only seem to have gone out together while we were working together.'

After the Blackpool summer show closed they met only at parties. Said Miss Irving, 'I realize it wouldn't do Cliff's career any good at all if he married. It would only annoy his fans.

'We went out together because Cliff didn't want to be with other fellows all the time. It was just a boy and girl friendship. He doesn't know many girls and he doesn't have a lot of time to go out with them and get to know them.'

Cliff has admitted that he has been 'rather shy' about contact with the opposite sex. 'It takes me a long time to pluck up courage to talk to a girl. If a girl makes the first move, I'm off!'

Some twelve years after the Jackie Irving episode he was more positive about the romance when he recalled in 1975, 'I was madly in love, but I had doubts at the last moment.

'Jackie is the only girl I have ever contemplated marrying. Now I'm glad I'm not married.

'I'm glad I'm not in love with a woman who is going to make me want to come home all the time. My whole lifestyle would have to change.

'What I'm doing now is so valuable for myself as a man, and for the things I believe in, that they come first.'

The dimming of his image with his vast following of female fans used to be an important factor to be considered whenever romance was hinted.

One night, during his early appearances at the Finsbury Empire, a girl could be seen sitting on his lap in a crowded car as he was driven away from the theatre through a swarm of fans. The reaction was alarming. Several fans flung their autograph books and pictures of him into the gutter in their obvious anger and jealousy.

In those days he often wondered what difference it would make to his career if he did marry. It was a difficult question for anyone to answer, but one adviser thought that maybe some ten per cent of his followers would cease to be counted among his faithful. It was perhaps a conservative estimate. The real answer would never be known.

What was true was that a lot of them really believed they were in love with him and cherished a dream that somehow one day they would become the chosen one who would walk proudly down the aisle on Cliff's arm as his bride.

In 1962 the show business departments of the Fleet Street nationals worked themselves into a frenzy when some watchful tip-off merchant reported that the banns had been called at a church in north-west London for the forthcoming marriage of one Harry Rodger Webb to a Miss Valerie Stratford, who lived in Willesden.

The big day had been set for 10 February. Cars had been arranged to call for the bride and the guests on that date and a present list had been circulated. It all sounded like the real thing. The only person who appeared to know nothing about the great day was the intended bridegroom, Harry Webb, now trading as Cliff Richard.

Reporters descended on him and some of them took a lot of convincing that he was not planning to wed in secret.

'The story was printed in some papers,' Cliff said, 'and I didn't understand it until I realized that the girl who had made all the arrangements without asking me was a girl who had been following me around so much.

'She had been writing to me and waiting for me outside my office, my home and theatres for a long time. Although I was amazed at her devotion, our friendship never exceeded the "good evening" stage.'

The girl had to admit that the whole thing was a hoax, explaining that three girlfriends had dared her to do it. 'It was just a practical joke,' she said. Her worship of Cliff could be gauged by the fact that she possessed 3,500 pictures of him.

He said at the time, 'I'm not annoyed. Teenagers often do things without thinking. She has apologized to me and I'll forget all about it.'

Valerie still continued to be a fan – and thousands of other girls nursing the same impossible dream of becoming Mrs Richard breathed a sigh and went on hoping that one day their turn might come.

It is easy to understand how a girl fan could be wafted away into a fantasy of believing that she was *the* one who would spend the rest of her life with her idol.

This is the type of letter that in those days nightly awaited Cliff in the dressing-room when he arrived at a theatre:

'Dearest, darling Cliff, I know you are basically a shy person, but there's no need to be shy with me. I am deeply in love with you and I know that you feel the same way about me, because you keep singing the songs I like best of all. If you want me to make the arrangements for a quiet wedding, just sing "Living Doll" tonight when I'm in the audience and I'll go straight ahead with all the plans.'

It scared him enough to go through his act that particular night without singing the already scheduled 'Living Doll' – probably to the disappointment of all the audience.

This was not an isolated incident and was a simple method that could be employed by a fan to reach to an idol; to form some secret means of communication that only the two of them would understand. Thus the performance of a requested song could mean only one thing – that the star had understood and was answering in the magic code that only they shared. It was a method not confined to Cliff Richard fans, and it could spell trouble . . .

The severed romance with Jackie Irving early in 1964 had barely cooled before Cliff's name was being linked with another.

This time the girl was actress Susan Hampshire, his co-star in *Wonderful Life*. They had spent three months in the Canary Islands – the shooting had been delayed by unkind weather – and show business gossips wondered how it was possible for them to be together for that length of time without forming some kind of intimate relationship.

Miss Hampshire was livid when she returned to England. 'Of course I'm in love with Cliff,' she said, very much tongue in cheek, 'just like the bulk of the female population of Great Britain. But we are definitely not having a romance.'

She wished that people would understand that the movie life is not exactly a bowl of cherries, even on location on an island. 'It's sheer hard work from dawn to dusk,' she explained. 'Most nights I was in bed and asleep by nine o'clock.'

Although she was his leading lady, she went on, it was Cliff's picture and the life was considerably harder for him. Also, she said, 'He's such a positive person and he knows exactly what he wants – particularly in his choice of girls. He believes in one marriage and one girl in life.'

Cliff's first ever girlfriend, he has said, was one he met in India. A little lady named Joan. It came to nothing. They sat next to each other at school. He was seven.

There is little doubt, however, that he experienced the pangs of young love when he was in his teens at Cheshunt. One of the earliest mentions of a girlfriend after making his break into show business was of a damsel named Janet, though it is not certain that this was her correct name. It was reported in an early fan publication that he fell in love with her but was 'in despair' when he discovered that she already had a boyfriend.

In a 1963 interview in a now-defunct magazine he said, 'Just before I had my first big break in show business I was courting a girl steadily. We'd been going out for about a year and I guess she was the most serious girl I ever had.

'My career took an upward leap when I signed a record contract and her mother saw a few snags about our association, with me entering show business on a full-time basis.

'Anyway, she called us both together one afternoon. We talked about the situation, which wasn't helped because my recent stage appearances had prevented me from seeing her for three weeks. The result was that we went our separate ways.'

He said in the same interview that he 'wouldn't marry a girl in show business'.

As his fame grew he had only to be seen in the company of a girl – however innocent the reason – to raise questions about romance. In October 1960 he accompanied American singing star Connie Francis to a midnight supper at the White Elephant, a renowned show business rendezvous in Mayfair, chaperoned by manager Tito Burns. It was fun. 'But it wasn't really a date,' Cliff had to explain, adding that he didn't have much time for dates, working six nights a week at the London Palladium, as he was then, rarely leaving the theatre before midnight. His free Sundays he spent with his parents and sisters and managed to watch some television or gather round the table for a family Scrabble tournament.

He appeared to be extremely cautious in those days.

When he was conducting *Sunday Pictorial* columnist Jack Bentley on an inspection of the new family home at Winchmore Hill the same year, they stopped off at Cliff's bedroom, where three walls were 'painted in a lemon colour and the fourth papered in an animal design'.

Cliff revealed that he was going to put on one wall 'a pin-up picture of Carol Lynley, who starred in the film *Blue Jeans* . . . I think she's terrific.'

Wrote Bentley, 'Cliff caught the look in my eye.

'"Oh, no!" he said. "I have no serious romantic ideas about any girl."'

Again in 1960, still showing caution, he had this to say: 'If I had to choose between marriage and my career, I'm afraid I would put my career first. You see, so many people depend on me.' He had just reached his twentieth birthday.

Pairing or attempting to marry Cliff off has been fair game through the years. Even in 1974 he was denying that any romance existed, this time with the delightful Miss Olivia Newton-John, whom he had known for many years. So much so that 'people think I discovered her,' he said. 'But I didn't. My agent did. We are great friends, but I haven't asked her to marry me.'

As his involvement with Christianity became more apparent the evergreen question about marriage needed more studied replies.

'I happen to be a Christian,' he said in 1967, 'and I wouldn't live with someone to whom I wasn't married. If you throw marriage out, what do you put in its place? The whole point of marriage is that it keeps people stable. Marriage is binding and living with someone isn't.'

On another occasion he said, 'If you're a Christian like I am you need a real spiritual affinity with someone.'

He once defined wedlock: 'Marriage is the public commitment of two people who are free to marry, who want a life together, who cannot live without each other and who want to cement their relationship.'

He will know when the right girl or woman comes along.

With the stretching of the years towards his thirties and beyond, a new question about the reasons for his continued bachelordom began to arise. Was he gay?

He dealt with it briefly in *Which One's Cliff?* when he said that, 'I'm not a mass of sexual hang-ups.' He has indulged himself in a few more words with several interviewers, however, who noted that he showed some signs of irritation and anger when the subject was mentioned.

To *Daily Mirror* columnist Don Short he said in 1969 (one of the earliest references to the question), 'Of course I've heard stories that I must be a homosexual because I've never married. That's terrible, but there's nothing I can do about it.

'People must do and think and say whatever they want to. As long as I know the truth, that is all that matters.

'If it is not God's wish for me to marry, then it is something I must accept. He may feel that my work can be achieved more purposefully by remaining single.

'One day I hope to marry and have children . . . I believe that the girl I marry will be a Christian. It is essential that two people who are going to be together for the rest of their lives should think the same way.'

Asked if he were gay by a London *Evening News* writer in 1976, he replied, 'It's untrue, but I have given up even talking about it because I think nothing I say will change anything. People are very unfair with their criticisms and their judgements. I know I catch the brunt of it, but I don't give two hoots.

'I've got a lot of living to do and I'm not going to spend my life either proving that I do believe something or that I'm not something else.

'I'm not going to get married just to prove it. I'm damned if I am. Of course I've heard the rumours, but I know what I am and my friends know what I am.

'What the mass public thinks doesn't bother me as long as they buy my records.'

In a reference to extramarital sex he disclosed, 'I don't sleep with women at all now – not since my Christian conversion.'

In 1977 he told *Evening Standard* interviewer Charles Catchpole, 'Let people think what they like. I've had girlfriends. But people seem to think that if a bloke doesn't sleep around he must be gay. I've never ruled out marriage. I'd love to marry one day, but I just haven't met the right girl yet. Marriage is a very special thing to me. I'm certainly not going to do it just to make other people feel satisfied.'

He used similar words to *Daily Mirror* writer Alasdair Buchan in the following year, repeating that the accusation didn't worry him any more. Marriage, he felt, would be the easiest thing in the world, 'but I would find myself in a position where I get married to clear people's minds about me and I don't intend to do that'.

He also commented, 'Nothing, I suppose, will take the place of normal sexual relations. But I never feel I've got to get up and rape someone. Maybe I've been given the personality to cope with the fact that I won't get married.'

Cliff's former manager Tito Burns summed up with these words: 'When anyone asks me if he is gay, I say nonsense. He had some little romances during those early days when he was with me, but nothing that amounted to anything. He just wasn't interested in going into a deep romance.

'As I've said, he has a great respect for his body and didn't seem interested in sex, but no – never anything approaching gay. No way. I always felt he was waiting until the right girl came along. He was very close to his mother and he treated women the way he would treat his mother – with great respect . . .'

Undoubtedly Cliff's career and his devotion to it was a major obstacle in the path of marriage for many years.

The show business life of constant travel and upheaval, of new places and new faces, would never have contributed to a stable home life. Even when he felt he did not have to worry any more about losing part of his vast army of fans if he wed, his lifestyle still had not changed. And he had seen many marriages of show business people around him founder along the way.

When asked at a press conference if he was thinking of marrying, Cliff replied, 'No, but when I am you will probably know about it before I do!'

It could happen that way . . . on a 29 February perhaps! But, as the 1990s progress, it would be a major surprise. Fans have their own ideas, particularly if they're very young. According to Mrs P. Bewick of Hull, penning a letter to a British tabloid newspaper, her eight-year-old daughter remarked, 'Oh, yes, he looks really young, doesn't he? That's because he isn't married.' Yet the 1980s had their matrimonial possibilities, although in one or two instances it seemed that the media was working overtime to maximize what little potential there might be in an effort to find a story. In Cliff's life, the presence of a girl within arm's length is enough for the word 'friend' to be replaced by something a little more speculative. Such was the case of Sheila Walsh, a talented, classically trained singer whose own faith had led her into the world of Christian music, its attendant gatherings and recordings. Bill Latham managed her for a time, and Sheila made a brief excursion into the wicked land of pop when she was signed to DJM Records. She was launched with a fanfare, and Cliff lent considerable practical support to her first recordings, though she only found minor success. One press source, captioning a picture of the two, neatly said: 'Presenting the new girl in Cliff Richard's life. She's Scots lass Sheila Walsh, who persuaded the bachelor boy to produce a record for her three months ago.

'Now Cliff, whose duet with Phil Everly, "She Means Nothing To Me", is high in the charts, plans to sing with Sheila on his next record.

'A friend says: "Sheila's thrilled to be in partnership with Cliff. But any relationship is strictly on the record."'

It was a caption that said everything. Sheila was seemingly not 'a friend' but the 'new girl'; Cliff was the 'bachelor', she was 'thrilled' to be 'partnering' and, well, 'any relationship' is not closed, merely at present 'on the record'. They could have added that Sheila had personality, was a trained Bible school student, and, yes, those were starters in proving the two could make a great partnership! However, it was a story that never came to anything, although the two met at frequent intervals, and obviously enjoyed these meetings. The public were to catch sight of Cliff and Sheila at religious gatherings in Britain, Europe and the United States. They even pre-planned a dance step or two at some Christian gatherings. And Sheila would always introduce Cliff with great gusto, both at concerts and on her BBC TV *Rock Gospel* shows. However, any question of romance was a non-starter and, besides, Sheila had interests elsewhere – with a record A&R man called Norman Miller who would eventually manage and marry her. These days, she lives in America and is influential in the more modern wing of the American evangelical world, with close connections with the evangelist, TV personality and erstwhile politician, Pat Robertson. She continues recording and is occasionally spotted in Britain.

There was also the time when Cliff was spotted escorting the separated wife of Status Quo stalwart, Rick Parfitt; with her Christian faith it seemed a more than interesting development, which appeared to interest fans more than any ongoing developments with Sheila Walsh. Marietta was described by Cliff as a 'good friend', but although the two had meals together, there was no romance.

The 1980s began – as also the 1990s – with some spice. Bursting into print in February 1982 came Carol Costa, who told the world that she had had a passionate affair with twenty-year-old Cliff. She described his love-making skills as 'terrific' and said it had made her feel 'a complete woman'. As to why this enviable state of affairs should end, Carol, once married to one-time Shadows' guitarist Jet Harris, said the news of their relationship would have killed Cliff's father, who was very unwell. Cliff, responding from Bangkok, where he was on tour, said she had 'her reasons for publicizing what was very personal. She has the freedom to do that. But I also have my freedom and I don't wish to publicize anything that personal.' The singer put the record straight in terms of his own accepted morality by stressing that since his conversion to Christianity his attitudes had changed. Carol Costa, forty-eight, brought the story back into prominence during the early autumn of 1990, as the *News of the World* reported that she claimed she had aborted Cliff's baby. She said the two had made love twice before Cliff broke off their relationship.

Fans, of course, have often had a special relationship with Cliff, ranging from the famous story already told of the girl who had church banns called, to the more up-to-date and equally astonishing saga of family dedication found in Raye and Collette Williams. Raye is quoted as saying, 'We don't look upon Cliff as a star. He's very much part of our lives as if he were one of the family.' The family has every video, disc and book produced on Cliff. It seems Collette, standing 4 foot 9 inches, once carried a 6 foot by 3 foot figure of Cliff by train. She says, 'Cliff is the best sort of man, he'd never let you down.'

For one woman, at least, the 1980s promised the real Mr Richard: Sue Barker. She had two immediate plus points: first, she had become a Christian through the powerful Christians In Sport network, pushed effectively by Gerald Williams; secondly, she was a well-known tennis player who, perhaps, always promised more, especially at Wimbledon, than she realized. Tennis became Cliff's great passion during this decade, so much so that he has named tennis as a worthy substitute for a rock career, should a second life be granted. At the outset the press remained ignorant of the relationship. It was only when Cliff attended church with Sue and Gerald Williams that phone calls were made and the press alerted. Journalists went through a list of possible sources in their search for information, and finally tracked down a Liverpool vicar, Alan Godson, who had considerable association with Christians In Sport. Godson has always denied the quotes attributed to him. But that he said anything gave the story credence, and it was soon everywhere.

In the furore created by the press, the leading Christian youth journal of the time, *Buzz*, took the higher line by saying: 'We would like to think that other Christian publications would also give Sue time to breathe – at least in the near future,' and pointed out: 'After all, her survival as a Christian is far more important than a scoop news exclusive or a few extra copies added to the circulation.' Their sub-headings expressed the attitude: 'mis-quoted' and 'no more publicity'.

The Cliff–Sue saga excited the press, and for those given to write headlines and sub-headings the tennis 'match' was a veritable godsend. To take a little walk through headlines means meeting such smash hits as LOVE-ALL! CLIFF'S IN A CLINCHER, CLIFF COURTS HIS No. 1 SUE, CLIFF AND SUE TAKE A WALK UP THE AISLE, CLIFF AND SUE'S CENTRE COURTSHIP and TENSION AS SUE LOSES.

This Cliff–Sue story was based in fact as well as fantasy. When they were together the chemistry was noticeable and few would dispute that there was passion. Those who witnessed Sue's sur-prisingly flurried and indifferent display at Hurlingham club in a pre-Wimbledon tune-up in 1982 will recall the anguish on Cliff's face, and indeed that of his mother. Sue was comforted in her sadness by Cliff. She told the press that her relationship with Cliff was not affecting her tennis.

The fan magazine *Dynamite International* wrote: 'At this time of the year, with new flowers popping up here and there and even the sun making an occasional showing, many people take to holding hands, cuddling and kissing and even falling in love.' They found that among those currently engaged in this time-honoured pastime were 'Cliff Richard and Sue Barker'. Obviously aware of how difficult it must be for true fans to stomach this, it added 'theirs is one of the most curious cases of love we have witnessed'. They wondered how deep was this love. Cliff's man-ager, Peter Gormley, said, 'I have no idea', which was comforting to those who entertained thoughts of eternal bliss with Cliff. Sue's tennis coach, the late Arthur Roberts, was also less than fulsome: 'I don't talk to her about it.' Certainly, the magazine concluded, the two were hardly out of each other's arms, off court. And when Sue was on court, there was 'the stealing of kisses between sets', meaning kisses blown rather than that the two had something going on behind the barley water and umpire's stand, as Sue changed court sides. The final word in the piece gave hope: 'Our opinion is that this is one of the greatest examples of platonic love around and that the chances of hearing wedding bells are distinctly remote.' The sighs of relief must have been enormous.

Yet Cliff said continually that the two were just good friends, even if some of their gestures strained the usual definition of such an expression. Perhaps it was a case of kidding the press along when Cliff, hugging Sue, told reporters, 'We're the new Charles and Di. There had to be someone to take over once they got married.' He would talk of early days long after the first meetings. He was more definite on whether the two would have a love trial, either bedding down together or sharing a home. 'It would conflict with our Christian beliefs,' he said. 'I just believe it'd be better for me not to dabble in sex outside marriage. Also, I don't need it. But by practising restraint, I'm more likely to have a good relationship if it does turn up.' On another occasion, Cliff said he 'might' be in love with Sue, but most certainly they were 'terrific' friends.

However, with their careers causing gaps in the relationship, he would talk of such moments being 'a testing time for our romance'. On one occasion work prevented him from dining with Sue and her parents, and it was said that he sent a salmon supper by taxi. Her mother, Betty, told the press, prior to meeting Cliff, 'Obviously he's just the sort of chap that any mother would like to see her daughter with. Because Cliff has never married there have been some very nasty rumours about him, but I can tell you they are not true.' She thought it sounded like a similar saga which had affected her daughter in the tennis world. 'Sue suffered the same innuendo when there was all that fuss about lesbianism on the tennis circuit.'

To those who pressurized him, Cliff would say what was patently obvious to those with eyes to see, that 'my bachelorhood seems a much greater problem to others than it is to me'. *The People* gave their verdict on the affair when, from the hindsight of 1990, writer William Wollf wrote: 'Cliff and Sue Barker: at one time they seemed a real love match. She improved his tennis but taught him that he'd never make a husband.'

Whatever the case, the relationship ended amidst rumours, during late October and early November 1984, that there would be a reunion. By coincidence, both found themselves in Australia early in November: Cliff was touring with his show while Sue was competing in the Australian open. It was in Sydney that she chose to talk to the press and said, 'If people are waiting for us to get married, they are going to have to wait an awfully long time.' She recalled when, after a Brighton tennis tournament in 1981, Cliff had phoned and asked her out for dinner. 'It grew from that

– we cared a lot for each other and it did become serious but we never reached the point that we were going to get married.' Bravely, she said, 'But if we don't get married, it means that Cliff and I can still be great mates. And that's super.'

They seemed to be words fighting tears, especially when placed against personal reflections on an earlier occasion when she said, 'It's not Cliff I am not sure about, it is myself. I want to slow down and not rush into anything. It is silly to say we are just good friends. Anyone can see it is much more than that. He understands me. He can psych me up before a match. He can cope with my highs and lows before and after a game. He lets me rattle on and just listens.' Yet even then she admitted, 'Tennis and the need to win is still in my blood.'

It is a pity for Cliff if the romance was lost to work. Sue's life has turned in another direction since then: the big tennis days have gone. By December 1984 the press was reporting that she had formed a new friendship, with Stephen Shaw, at twenty-one seven years her junior. A family friend was reported as saying, 'Steve was absolutely terrified that when Sue put the record straight on Cliff, people would find out about them. They are definitely fond of each other.' In 1988 Sue married a London policeman but she and Cliff have become occasional partners on the celebrity tennis circuit.

For the time being, Cliff and romance is a dormant theme. He speaks of feeling positive about singleness. He talks of his home with its tennis courts and swimming pool, of being surrounded by those who love him, and continuing career success, and there is the deep underlying satisfaction of Christian faith. He still says, 'Marriage is not entirely out of the window,' but that it does not stand high on his list of priorities – although he loves female company, always will, and women continue to swoon over his slim, trim looks. And unless a secret signal was wrapped up in an outburst that hit the British press in February 1992, he will definitely not be marrying Madonna. 'We are all sexual animals, but to me there is more sex in Olivia Newton-John than any video I've seen of Madonna's.' Being reported off the transcript of a BBC Radio 2 series on his life, he added, 'I don't like Madonna because she does all the things that to me are the most obvious hypes ever. She is a poor man's Marilyn Monroe.'

In London's *Evening Standard*, Nicholas Hellen commented, 'He has the reputation as one of the cleanest-living performers in show business,' but in the late 1950s, 'the combination of Cliff's looks and Jack Good's perception of what those looks should be like on television made Cliff in the early days of *Oh Boy!* probably the sexiest animal on television'.

Ah, well.

# CHAPTER ELEVEN

# A FEW SLIPPED DISCS

EMI Records had a pleasant problem in 1977. They had decided to release an album of Cliff Richard hit singles encompassing his complete record-making career.

Usually such compilation albums have anything from twelve to twenty tracks. The eventual figure is arrived at after long discussions on what are fondly called the prevailing winds of the market place at the given time of record release. The agreed total may, though, not entirely reflect what is claimed on an album cover. Few artists have had twelve, let alone sixteen or twenty hit records. Yet the companies have deemed that a sixteen-track album is most acceptable to the public and indulge in 'padding', including a few non-hit but generally popular tracks of the particular artist. Joe Public rarely notices he is the subject of a minor sharp practice. As the record companies well know, Joe Public likes to think he has a large number of songs by a popular artist at a fraction of the price he would pay if he bought each song on a single record.

Cliff, though, is different from anyone else bar Elvis. Prior to 1977 he had achieved sixty-eight chart hits!

The Head of Marketing at EMI, John Cabanagh, ruefully told me it meant one big headache.

'Well, it was obvious Cliff had too many hits for one LP. Half the number could span his career but even then we had to decide which tracks should be included and, I suppose, more important in terms of the buying public, which would be excluded.'

In the end EMI issued a *40 Golden Greats* collection. It was given a major TV promotional push and a special trade launch at the Carlton Tower Hotel, London. Its release followed extensive market research.

'We really wanted to know what the public wanted and which numbers they knew and remembered.'

The market researchers questioned male and female groups from two age groups: sixteen to twenty-four and twenty-five to forty. The sample groups all thought the project was a good one but in true British fashion, exercising both caution and a reticence towards committing themselves, they were less sure whether they would buy the record. Some of them felt a single record would be enough.

Among the final conclusions came statements that for females aged twenty-five and over the appeal of Cliff lay in his early material. Interest in the middle period was low and even non-existent. Cliff's golden era was identified with the Shadows.

The group samples said his music changed from approximately 1964 onwards, as did his image and also his interests. The gradual diminution of the Shadows' associating with Cliff was one of the reasons for a drop in popularity but this decline was also blamed on his becoming religious, adopting 'preachy' attitudes and a 'safer' style.

Other reasons for the so-called low-key middle period in Cliff's recording career included his becoming a solo singer without a group and that the music scene of the middle and late sixties moved and changed so fast, leaving him unfashionable.

There was a positive reaction towards his singles of the mid-seventies. It seemed that those hit songs – 'You Keep Me Hangin' On', 'Miss You Nights', 'Devil Woman', 'I Can't Ask for Anything More Than You Babe', 'Hey Mr Dream Maker', 'My Kinda Life' – had indeed revived and rejuvenated his appeal and made him acceptable to the young.

EMI had another problem, and that was image. 'To the committed, Cliff may not appear to have altered,' said Cabanagh. 'But when EMI's planners looked at pictures of Cliff over the years, it was clear that the hair, the glasses and the clothes were not the same. It was very important to get the right Cliff there on the front cover, the one to whom people respond.

'It took a year of planning – you have to plan when you're spending a great deal of money and also when the project involves a major artist like Cliff.

'EMI put the album into the top spot and that was no mean feat. Outwardly the whole exercise looked easy but when you look at the possible complications then it's not by any means that simple.'

A music critic might not agree with the kind of divisions the public suggested were applicable to Cliff's career although it should be said that a division was made for them when they actually listened to extracts of the proposed running order for a double-record album.

The sample heard records from the periods 1958–61, 1962–3, 1964–7, 1968–77. The length of the last division illustrates Cliff's lack of releases and success compared with previous years.

The first division naturally includes the first hit, 'Move It'. This remains a classic. David Winter, author of the early Cliff biography *New Singer, New Song*, writes an appreciation better than any other attempted: 'It is pure primitive rock 'n' roll. It builds up in the traditional way: a few sharp chords from the lead guitar, then the whole thing is transferred to its rhythmic foundation, an insistent, vibrating bottom E on the electric bass, which, apart from half a dozen Bs in the central section, is plugged relentlessly all through. Upon this foundation the drums and rhythm guitar build the fast, pulsing tempo of rock 'n' roll, the lead guitar links the vocal sections, and the voice, inescapably young, tops the whole thing with its emotional appeal.'

The voice hovers around middle C for most of the time but, as Winter also noted, the whole technique is the introduction of sudden trills or runs above and below the note, where it drops a full fifth and does so rather surprisingly. It was an excellent record and an amazing start for an unproven seventeen-year-old. 'Move It' still possesses an impact which allows a contemporary DJ to segue* it into any current recorded hit without embarrassment.

Looking back on it today, Cliff says, 'It was great at the time. We were over the moon. I've a different version for the American tour and when I compare now with then I know I've progressed.'

Several attempts have been made at re-creating the hit feel via another artist, but without success. One of the best-known attempts came from Alvin Stardust in 1975. At the time Cliff said, 'Yeah, it's all right. I love the backing but I don't like his treatment of the lyric. It lost something. I did a version of the song live in Japan two years ago.

'It was really heavy and funky. I prefer that live version even to the original. I sing it better.'

It was the first recording of 'Move It' which made the music critics sit up. Many of those who now write books and are DJs

* Segue is the process in which a DJ will play two records consecutively without his vocal interruption. Generally, he picks up the mood and musical note and feel of the first with the second.

106

were young at the time, like Cliff. 'Move It' has stayed with them. When it first came out it helped Cliff to gain critical acceptance during a period when, for most people, the only good music came from America.

One of rock's most respected chroniclers, Charlie Gillet, wrote in his classic book *Sound of the City* of the times after 'Rock Around The Clock': 'The most accomplished and successful British singer was Cliff Richard, with a style and image originally modelled on Presley but subsequently located somewhere between Rick Nelson and Paul Anka. Compared to the other British rock and roll singers, Richard had good vocal control, access to writers who provided competent and suitable material and an unusually capable and disciplined rhythm group.'

Another well-known rock chronicler, Nik Cohn, admired the early Cliff for the way he dominated British pop for years but Cliff did not achieve this through raw and rugged rock 'n' roll. Reflecting on 'Move It' and its follow-up Cliff says, 'There was an immediate need for a follow-up. We had no background. We didn't write our own material, "Move It" was written by Ian Samwell and he'd written this other song, "High Class Baby", but when we went into the studio the magic didn't happen, and I thought, "Oh no, it's gonna be the end of a great career," and I went home and cried.'

Of course it wasn't the end but his music changed during this early period, rather than in 1964 as the market research sample group appeared to believe.

Within a year Cliff had passed from the rock-for-the-kids class into singing ballad-style material. This gained him an audience which spanned the generations but lost him the kids who wanted a music and a star adults could not relate to. The record which heralded the new era was 'Living Doll'.

There were, of course, fans who loved any record Cliff made – whatever the style. Typical of these is Cliff Marshall of the Cliff fan club in Southend. 'In 1958 I was fifteen years of age and like most fifteen-year-olds in those days an ardent rock 'n' roller and mad about Elvis. Here in Britain we had nothing to compare with the then king of rock ... but in August "Move It" was released and immediately I had to sit up and take note of the best rock record I had ever heard.'

Marshall heard more of Cliff's material and after four singles and two albums he decided he would rather hear Cliff than his childhood idol.

Cliff's early album material maintained his touch with rock 'n' roll. His second LP saw him singing 'Blue Suede Shoes' (which Elvis sang) and 'Twenty Flight Rock' (Eddie Cochran) and to fans like Cliff Marshall it was Cliff who won hands down. The singles differed. They became more polite, even wholesome.

Writer Peter Jones saw that Cliff had introduced something new. 'Before Cliff all pop singers sounded what they were, solidly working-class – but Cliff introduced something new, a bland ramble, completely classless.'

He sees 'Living Doll' as the most influential British pop single of the sixties.

'He's been followed through his long career by a positive horde of imitators, copyists and plain apes.

'That's why he's a great one. He's lasted the pace, pleased millions, offended only a few – and he's still producing hits. Not as from a mass-production line, but in a variety of styles, moods and atmospheres.'

Nik Cohn is less reverential. He talks of Cliff as akin to a magic slate, 'a pad on which almost everyone could scrawl their fantasies and rub them out and try again. He was the nice boy that girls could be proud to date, the perfect son that mothers could be proud to raise, the good nut that schoolboys could be proud to have as a friend.'

Cliff merely responds to such comments with a cryptic, 'I'm hysterical about it . . . if someone thinks I'm goody-goody I think, well, whey whey, I'm winning out – at least I'm achieving an end.'

In the early sixties Cliff hit the charts with records like 'I Love You', 'Theme for a Dream', 'Gee Whizz It's You', 'Please Don't Tease' and 'A Girl Like You'.

'One thing I remember about it was the way my dad loved it. My dad died not long after and he missed all the success that was to follow on from the films like *The Young Ones* and *Summer Holiday*, but whenever I think of "A Girl Like You" I always remember how he said that was the best record I ever made up until that point.'

'A Girl Like You' charted in June 1961. Six months later another major happening in Cliff's disc career occurred. It centred around the single 'The Young Ones'.

The headline in the music paper *Record Mirror* for 13 January 1962 ran, 'CLIFF BEATS ELVIS.'

'British singer Cliff Richard is now the holder of the record for advance sales with his new disc "The Young Ones".

'He beats the previous record holder, Elvis Presley.

'Official figures released by EMI state that the advance orders by day of release reached an all-time peak of 524,000 copies.'

As a film *The Young Ones* was equally a stupendous box-office success. What thrilled Cliff was that he and the Shadows had the chance to write songs for the film. The Shadows wrote several numbers.

The only sour note from *The Young Ones* took place across the Atlantic. In the United States Connie Francis recorded Cliff's UK number three chart smash from the film, 'When The Girl In Your Arms'. Cliff's management felt release of the song should have been held up until the film had been screened in the States. The resulting row saw Cliff leaving ABC Paramount and signing with Big Tree. Needless to say, Connie had a big hit with the song and Cliff badly needed a major US success.

Films and hits went together and with *Summer Holiday* Cliff emerged as a songwriter. He wrote 'Big News' with Mike Conlin and his co-writer on the massive hit 'Bachelor Boy' was Bruce Welch.

'It was always an ambition of mine to write and I thought I would keep on just as long as the tunes would keep coming,' said Cliff.

The hits kept coming. In 1963 there were four hits, and in 1964 the total was a staggering six. The following year it was down to four and that set the pattern for every year until 1970. It meant Cliff was rarely out of the charts. He was never missing from the public ear.

Cliff comments, 'All through my career I have always had pretty much the last word on what I record, although I don't lay down the law.

'Peter Gormley still tells me if he thinks that I am wrong and if he is forceful enough about it, then I usually succumb. When I worked with Bruce as producer he also had a big say. If everyone is against what I feel, then I give in willingly.'

The prolific hit period from 1963 onwards saw chart-toppers like 'The Next Time', 'Bachelor Boy', 'Summer Holiday', 'The Minute You're Gone' and 'Congratulations'. Somehow Cliff could sing in the familiar way and manner when the rest of the pop scene was raging with the Beatles of *Sergeant Pepper*, the Stones, the Who, the Animals, flower power, acid rock, West Coast sounds, blues, the birth of Pink Floyd and Led Zeppelin. Though they all made the news, he continued with the hits.

He says in reflection, 'I know a lot of people hated me for doing

the Eurovision-type numbers, particularly "Congratulations".
They thought it was a terrible compromise, but the fact is that
there were 400 million viewers when I performed that song and
you just can't argue with those viewing figures.

'I've never considered recording something because I think the
style or the trend is paramount. For me the song itself counts.
Actually I don't know if you know how I'd heard "Love Me Do"
from the Beatles in the early sixties. Now that was a good song. I
really liked it. I never dreamed that the Beatles would be a hit,
particularly with a name like that. I thought "insects"! Anyway, I
took "Love Me Do" to South Africa with me. I took it to all the
studios and every time they said, "Can we play a record for you?"
I said, "Yes, please", and I'd hand over "Love Me Do". And I'm
sure it didn't help their career in general but I always think that I
had a part in it in South Africa!'

Cliff's Christian commitment may have hastened his split from
the Shadows, but whatever the market research group may say, it
didn't really change the kind of song he sang. Norrie Paramor
remained his producer until 1973. His song lyrics did start to
change from 1969: 'Throw Down A Line' was more socially conscious, though quite polite when compared with other rock scene
material coming from people such as MC5, Jefferson Airplane and
the Doors.

However, the research sample group was right in suggesting
Cliff's momentum was running down, but in terms of actual chart
and sales achievement Cliff still ran strongly. It was not until
midsummer 1971 that one of his songs failed to reach the top
thirty.

The dubious honour for this belongs to 'Flying Machine'. In
relation to other songs it hardly deserved the fate!

There was still life left in the old but ever-young man. 'Living in
Harmony' reached number 12 in 1972 and thanks to a return visit
to Eurovision circles there was a number four placing for 'Power
To All Our Friends'. But just before this, real calamity had
occurred when 'Brand New Song' failed to chart.

Norrie commented in 1978, 'We'd had a lot of fun and a lot of
success, but I felt Cliff had reached the stage where he should
work with a younger producer. I knew that it was time for me to
move on, although I was sorry to see the end of our partnership.

'I remember the day when I decided to put Cliff in a studio with
an orchestra instead of with the Shadows. I can still remember his
face when he walked in and there were about forty-five musicians

sitting around waiting for him to arrive! However, he enjoyed the experience.

'The first song we did was "I'm Looking Out Of The Window" – and after that he liked the idea of using strings on his recordings. We also started doing the same thing with the Shadows' records.'

The period from 1973 until early 1976 was not happy from the point of view of hits, high chart placings and sales. For a time Dave Mackay produced and the partnership came up with the very much underrated album, *The 31st of February Street*. That album actually laid the foundation for Cliff's return to major contemporary prominence via 'Devil Woman' in February 1976.

There was another slipped disc in 1975 when 'It's Only Me You've Left Behind' missed out on the charts. The 'Honky Tonk Angel' fiasco followed and certain sections of the press, general and music, had a field day. There were those who said they could not believe Cliff would one day record a song about loose-living girls. And now he had. Naturally, they were not saddened. Obviously, from their oceans of copy, they were happy but, alas, they did not say so.

Quite what happened remains in doubt and there are a number of conflicting accounts and statements. However it seems Cliff was not conversant with what the term 'honky tonk' could mean. The major upshot of the affair was a definite cooling towards the record. It was another slipped disc in the UK, while in the world at large it did rather well.

Fortunately the dark days appeared more or less over with the charting of the spine-chilling 'Miss You Nights' in February 1976 and the album *I'm Nearly Famous* in May of the same year.

Said Cliff, 'It was really up for grabs who produced me around this period. Peter said that the first person to come up with the right songs could produce me.'

The producing angel of mercy and release was nearby. It was Bruce Welch of the Shadows.

'Cliff wasn't averse to a change of musical style, what was important was the fact that he should love all the songs,' said Bruce.

'When we first went into the studios it wasn't with the idea of making an album at all. On the first session we put down three songs and they were all successive hits – "Miss You Nights", "Devil Woman" and "Can't Ask For Anything More". We were looking for a single but ended up making an album.

'I think the great thing which came from our sessions when we were making *I'm Nearly Famous* onwards was that Cliff became much more interested in his career.

'For a long time he had just been going into a recording studio and putting down the vocals to a pre-recorded track and then going home again. He realized recording techniques had changed and started sitting in throughout the entire recording sessions.

'After all, Cliff had been making records for more than sixteen years. My object was to make him see that he had started as a recording star, and take him back to those roots.'

Cliff was so excited with 'Miss You Nights' that he postponed his planned trip to Russia. Rock star Elton John was reported to be quite crazy about the record. He released the single in the States on his own Rocket label.

The album's self-deprecating title was another positive plus. EMI records man Brian Southall thought *I'm Nearly Famous* was memorable and EMI staff seemed just as revitalized and excited as Cliff was.

Cliff waxed eloquent and talked miles of tape on his *I'm Nearly Famous* spectacular. 'It's the best thing I've done for years. It may be the only hit album I'll have had in years.

'And I was excited. It was like a new thing. I would meet students and they would actually talk about music to me, whereas before it was like a joke. "Oh," people said, "didn't know he did that sort of stuff." All kinds of people were knocked out by this album.'

Even the International Cliff Richard Movement caught this sense of 'didn't know he did' for in the July 1976 issue of *Dynamite* they began their review of the album and of the first track with, 'If you walked into a party while "I Can't Ask For Anything More Than You" was on the turntable, you'd just laugh if someone said it was Cliff. The funky, super-cool, high-pitched vocals belong to our Cliff. This, and most of the other songs too, really stretch Cliff's vocal range.'

'Devil Woman' followed. It was a monster hit, giving Cliff another market, the disco world. The media buzzed with Cliff. He appeared on all the major TV and radio pop promotional outlets. A new day was dawning.

Brian Southall of EMI wrote, 'While Cliff Richard was achieving even more fame and fortune with his truly memorable *I'm Nearly Famous* album and his string of hit singles, it mustn't be forgotten that EMI were also rewarded handsomely for their efforts during the last year.

'In addition to the satisfaction of re-establishing Cliff as a major force in British rock music, David Munns, marketing manager of the Group Pop Repertoire Division, and his team, deservedly won the *New Musical Express* award for the best marketing campaign in 1976.

'We had great music supported by a great marketing campaign – virtually an unbeatable combination, and now we are gearing ourselves into that position again.

'Cliff has done his bit . . .'

You could hear the grunts of support for miles from the huge record company's headquarters in London's Manchester Square.

The music press loved it. So did the public. Yet the euphoria of this period was slightly misplaced for the old times of hit after hit were not forthcoming. Dark days still remained. There was another lurch and it was worse than the previous one.

The following year saw release of the album *Every Face Tells A Story*. 'My Kinda Life', a Cliff and Bruce song from the *Every Face Tells A Story* album, reached number 15 in the singles chart. The follow-up was a touching ballad, 'When Two Worlds Drift Apart'. It reached a mere 46. Then came real disaster of a magnitude which Cliff had never previously known. It was a cruel finale to the hopes and joys which had been raised since the late winter of 1975.

Cliff wanted to release a religious song as his next single. It came from his album *Small Corners*, issued in November 1977, and was an excellent gospel record. 'Yes He Lives!' was the title. It had the authentic beaty pop feel. It was ignored. It didn't chart. Cliff was hurt, more so because he badly wanted the world to hear the record's message.

He says, 'I tried to do an album that is in exactly the same bag as *I'm Nearly Famous* and *Every Face Tells A Story*. I tried to find some really good songs. The fact that they happen to have depth of meaning is, I think, a plus factor.'

He knew there were problems. 'All I have to do is get past the DJs, because I believe the DJs say to themselves, "Oh, well, gospel format, not for my breakfast show," but they haven't heard "Why Should the Devil Have All The Good Music?", 'Hey Watcha Say" or "I Wish We'd All Been Ready", or any of the songs, and they're just great songs. I'm so overboard about them . . .'

However, the DJs quaked and the producers pretended not to know.

113

In his London office Cliff told me, 'I think you could say all my religious records have been failures – when issued as singles.'

He smiled momentarily and then laughed. 'Life is short and there is no point in forcing things. But the response to, say, "Yes He Lives" was really disappointing. I mean, look at "Brand New Song", "When Two Worlds Drift Apart" and "Throw Down A Line". I felt like screaming about their being ignored. After all, God sent Jesus, the most important fact in the world. I want to tell people of that.'

He does; but in the form of hit pop singles the message was not for telling, until his Christmas hits of the late 1980s.

*Green Light* was issued in October 1978. It produced, if nothing else, headlines like 'Green Light For Success'. It was the third album produced by Bruce. It hurled Cliff once more back into the general musical fray. Well, so the reviewers said. The public remained unmoved. The singles disaster area continued. There were slipped discs all over the place.

'Can't Take The Hurt Anymore' didn't chart. 'Green Light' spent three weeks in the then extended industry chart of the Top 75 and went no further than 57.

Yet again, however, there was light at the end of the tunnel. A whole series of media happenings took away the sting of the singles failure. Cliff and the Shadows reunited for a season at London's Palladium, which was an instant sell-out. An album followed. EMI issued the *40 Golden Greats* with a superb marketing campaign. No one waited for Cliff's twenty-first anniversary in the music business. His twentieth year in 1978 released an avalanche of tributes from the music press.

Cliff and the Shadows were honoured by Europe's most influential music trade paper, *Music Week*, at their yearly dinner at the Dorchester. The media queued for interviews and Cliff told the history of his years. In 1979, it was the case of:

'I was back. "We Don't Talk Anymore" was a five million seller. I was number one in Britain for the first time in eleven years. Marvellous.' So says Cliff and there were beaming smiles everywhere. The media ran a solid barrage of articles proclaiming, 'Cliff does it again'. Bruce produced the single. In every way it was how quality pop should be, with the right touch of commerciality.

Cliff was the perfect white rock 'n' roll singer. He had excellent pitch and purity of tone. He showed consummate skill in handling words and tune.

*Melody Maker* editor of the time, Richard Williams, spent half a page extolling the record's virtues and from the more hardened punk, new-wave quarters there was grudging approval.

Williams pointed out the superb nature of the backing track, with the on-the-beat drums and the haunting synthesizer, and felt the delightful, sparse production was one of the best pieces of work in the history of pop.

Cliff told Richard Skinner, a well known DJ, that although the song had become a disco hit, as well as a pop smash, it wasn't intended for that market in the first place.

He says, 'It appears on my album *Rock 'n' Roll Juvenile* but that wasn't intentional. I'd started recording the album, which I wanted to go in a specific direction, and when they said to me, "We need a single now," Terry and I said, "Don't rush us, we're not ready. We don't have one ready for you." Then Bruce found an Alan Tarney song. I listened to it and got goose pimples, which is a good sign. Bruce had them as well, so we both went into the studios and recorded it in about forty-eight hours.'

It was inspired spontaneity – but, then, this process has brought into being many great records.

As Cliff says from his vast experience of records and recording, 'You can't really plan a number one. I'll be singing "We Don't Talk Anymore" for ages, maybe not in the same style but the song is good. It's going to be here for a long time.

'I'm not sure though that it's my best record. I think that "Devil Woman" is going to remain my favourite.'

So the stopgap single brought Cliff his biggest sales success ever. He sang the song at Greenbelt, the now massive Christian music festival which covers a wide range of subjects and idioms. It seemed right that Cliff the Christian should celebrate the best thing in the singles market for eleven years in such a gathering. The 17,000 audience agreed.

'I consider myself a current Christian singer who sings songs like "We Don't Talk Anymore" but I also have in my repertoire a few more overtly Christian songs. The religious world, for want of a better phrase, has some really fantastic singers and musicians who are denied worldwide fame because the world is not as free as we are musically. They still think that rock 'n' roll is something and gospel is something else . . . It's the Christian world which needs to come out and say, "Look, we're rock 'n' roll singers and we want to sing about God in our own way."'

Naturally, *Rock 'n' Roll Juvenile* was a success. Alan Tarney was the bass player and he produced the next Cliff album, *I'm No Hero*. It too has been a major seller and from it have come the massive-selling singles 'Dreamin'' and 'A Little In Love'. Those two tracks plus 'Suddenly' (with Olivia Newton-John) from the *Xanadu* film soundtrack gave Cliff three records at one time in the *Billboard* Hot 100, and paved the way for his 1981 US success story.

'As for the title, I tried to find another anti-title. I liked *I'm No Hero* because it was tongue in cheek and I thought there aren't many heroes in the world, and I'm certainly not one of them. And I thought it's just a nice title so I had an idea for a boxing motif and there I stand with my knock knees with boxing gear on – Lonsdale shorts and stuff. I tried to make the sleeve describe what the album's like, just a fun album . . .'

Cliff covered a lot of ground between 1958 and 1981. He disliked being placed in any particular musical bag. In the beginning he was the lad who was attracted by the rawness and energy of rock 'n' roll. He was a kid without real rebellion for he loved his family and rock 'n' roll wasn't his way of rebelling. Initially, his music and stage shows caused some sections of the press to urge parents not to let their offspring see him, though his appeal was soon wide and the music accordingly became mostly softer.

'I can't say that I actually planned it that way. You can't plan, as such. I suppose one could analyse it by looking back at my career but it was a challenge for me – to make sense to all ages. The only way you can do it is to go the whole gamut of rock 'n' roll.

'I think I'm ordinary really. The only thing I do know is that out of my throat comes this noise that people like.'

Cliff these days sings 'When I Survey The Wondrous Cross' side by side with other music without it seeming the 'gospel spot'; and there is always the comforting thought that he's seen off most musics and fashions.

'I don't know that I've seen them off. I've joined in with them. I've been having an affair with rock 'n' roll for a long time. I've liked rock 'n' roll in all its aspects and to me it's a musical culture and not just a tempo. For me as a vocalist rock 'n' roll is so wide. I can keep on as long as my voice lasts out,' said Cliff at the outset of the 1980s. And the voice continues to last – and how! For if the story thus far has been an almost constant succession of top ten hits, the 1980s decade would see another twenty-five chart listed titles, with only four of these failing to make the top forty, and a mere seven not appearing in the upper thirty. No other artist can touch such a singles success story and Cliff's albums are inevitably top five.

As he moved into the 1990s, he had sold a total of 45 million singles worldwide, more than any other act except the Beatles. His top ten hits span a period of over thirty years. He has had a much longer span of number one hits than any other act, 31 years and 153 days between the first, 'Living Doll', and 'Saviour's Day'. He has achieved more top ten hits than any other act, with over thirty top ten albums and second only to Elvis Presley for top ten albums.

But all this is racing ahead of the travelogue through the hit record story. As briefly mentioned, the album *I'm No Hero* produced the big hit tracks 'Dreamin'' and 'A Little In Love' but the 1980s had begun with 'Carrie', a slow, beautiful, emotive ballad culled from *Rock 'n' Roll Juvenile*. Interestingly, in Australia 'Carrie' had two issues, with differing B-sides, one with 'Moving On' and the other with 'Walking In The Light'. 'Hot Shot' had provided a weak follow-up to 'We Don't Talk Anymore'.

This was a high period for Cliff, full of delightful tracks that begged for single release, for after 'A Little In Love', which, surprisingly, went no higher than 15, it was time for 'Wired For Sound', the title track of his top five album of late 1981, and, tailor-made for Christmas, 'Daddy's Home'. The latter, in its original form by Shep and the Limelights, was one of the titles on Cliff's own jukebox, splendidly displayed at that time in his Weybridge home. It had been a hit in America in May 1961, and reached number two, the same position as Cliff's record at the end of 1981. Sadly Jim 'Shep' Sheppard was found dead in his car on the Long Island Expressway on 24 January 1970 – he had been robbed and beaten to death.

There was considerable media promotion for the next single, 'The Only Way Out'. This was popular with many, but lacks the overall marketing appeal usually necessary for a single to make the top five. In Cliff terms this means that a wide cross-section of the public want to purchase the record, rather than just immediate fan club members. The same might have been said about the next release, 'Where Do We Go From Here?', but inexplicably it did no better than 60. This is puzzling as it was a well-received number during concerts, but its inability to move upwards suggests that even the fans deserted this title.

Fortunately, Christmas was on its way after the autumnal failure of the latter title, and Cliff corrected an unexpected downward lurch with an excellent Christmas single, 'Little Town', which reached 11 and deserved at least top five. It seemed far better than some others in a higher position.

But rosier times were ahead, particularly with the appearance of his delightful single with Phil Everly entitled 'She Means Nothing To Me'. This was released on Capitol and not EMI. It was written by John David, bassist with the Dave Edmunds Band. The idea of Phil and Cliff recording had come from their get-together at London's Hammersmith Odeon, when Cliff celebrated his musical career for a BBC special. 'Top musicians Mark Knopfler and Terry Williams of Dire Straits and keyboards man Pete Wingfield were enlisted for the recording. The song was recorded for Phil's next album. The two also recorded 'I'll Mend Your Broken Heart'. The association with Phil recalled the marvellous times of the Everly Brothers.

With his next single Cliff took us back to the great Buddy Holly, whose version of 'True Love Ways' had charted in 1960. Cliff did rather better than Holly, charting number eight to Holly's 25. On this Cliff was joined by the London Philharmonic Orchestra, the recording coming from the album made live at the Royal Albert Hall, *Dressed For The Occasion*. The flip 'Galadriel (Spirit Of Starlight)' was also taken from the release.

Cliff duetted once more when he agreed to aid Sheila Walsh's career and laid down 'Drifting'. It was Sheila's release, part of a new contract with DJM. Interestingly, it appears in the *Guinness Book of British Hit Singles* as a joint issue and Sheila and Cliff described as a 'UK, female/male vocal duo'! It was hardly a success, a two-week chart placing, and a highest position of 64.

In the autumn of 1983 Cliff released 'Never Say Die (Give A Little Bit More)' which was followed by a Christmas period top ten hit, 'Please Don't Fall in Love'. Both singles came in the period when his *Silver* album was released, and coincided with the Silver Anniversary tour. Both 'Please Don't Fall In Love' and 'Too Close To Heaven' were written by Mike Batt, famous for his Wombles music, some solo success and a number of concept albums. He wrote the glorious 'Bright Eyes' chart-topper for Art Garfunkel. Fans were quick to spot the mistake on the single's front cover, that both, rather than the A-side, had been culled from the *Silver* album.

Arguably, Cliff might prefer to write off his 1984 record data: it was a most unsatisfactory year. There were three singles – four given the recasting of 'Oceans Deep' – and one release failed even to make the top 75, a deafening silence from the loyal fans. The year began with a 27 placing for 'Baby You're Dynamite', which came coupled with a particular favourite from his stage show, 'Oceans Deep'. Fans insisted that the flip side was the strongest, and so the record was flipped. It had a 12 inch release but the decision proved disastrous, though made with good intentions and promptings from fans. In the new label credits form, it had a one-week run and went no further than 72, and merely proved an unnecessary blot on Cliff's singles listing. Even that was better than the total blow-out of 'Two To The Power', coupled with 'Rock and Roll'. The latter was a duet with Janet Jackson, although the nearest the two came together was in the splicing of tapes. It remains another of those release mysteries even if Janet Jackson had yet really to fire on all cylinders.

Bad times would not go away. 'Shooting From The Heart', released in October 1984, and 'Heart User', issued in January 1985, reached 51 and 46 respectively, leading into another of those periods when people began to speculate on whether Cliff was at long last slowing down. Both tracks came from the *Rock Connection* recordings at Strawberry Studios South in July 1984. Hard as it may seem, those sessions and the ones in June yielded material that did Cliff little service, although many remained nonplussed at the rejection of the pacey 'Heart User'. Also, Cliff recorded with Elton John on the track 'Slow Rivers' at the SOL studios, but when this was eventually released a considerable time afterwards in late 1986 the expected big hit never materialized. The song reached a top place of 44 although it lingered for two months in the national top 75. In another of the *Guinness British Hit Singles* quirks, Cliff is named with Elton as a British male duo, as though there was a career in the offing. Under 'Cliff Richard' and 'subsequent work with others' there is no clue that he might have recorded with the mighty Elt.

Not enough tracks were put down for an album during the summer of 1984, and eventually a remixed version of the Phil Everly duet plus other tracks, six in all, from the *Rock 'n' Silver* collection were served up as the *Rock Connection*. In album form this period brought no more joy than the singles, with the album reaching a very low position for Cliff, a miserly 43.

For a brief moment life returned to something approaching normal when 'She's So Beautiful' from the *Time* musical headed towards the big time in the autumn of 1985, but even that surprisingly fizzled out at 17. It was quickly followed by 'It's In Every

One Of Us', which hit the market on 21 November. This was intended by EMI to score heavily at Christmas, and it had a religious–spiritual flavour. The song was written in 1973 by David Pomeranz and found on his own self-titled album issued by Arista in 1976.

The February 1986 *Cliff United* magazine said it was a great album track but not single material, yet, as the journal added, it, was better than many hit songs of the period. This Cliff single went no further than 45. And if the pits hadn't exactly been reached on the chart front, it certainly seemed so with the next single, which also came from *Time*, namely 'Born To Rock And Roll'. Some thought it might run to the very top, whereas it never even made the top 75. It was provisionally scheduled for release on 3 March but was held back, eventually coming out in May. Some investigation seemed needed among the regular fan buyers: had they all emigrated, become penniless, or even bankrupted by excessive watching of *Time*? Even the *Cliff United* reviewer thought it would go far, and said it was a 'great song, and will put Cliff back into the charts'. How little he knew. Of course, it must be stated, as Peter Gormley has said, that even if the hits had temporarily dried up, Cliff had hardly been out of the limelight, and without success somewhere. This was particularly evidenced with his long-running engagement in the musical *Time*.

However the release of the record with a TV satire group, the Young Ones, with Rik Mayall, Nigel Planer, Ade Edmondson, and Chris Ryan, fortunately intruded upon Cliff's miserable run of poorly placed or failed chart singles.

In order to raise money for a series of projects, and several charities, they had established Comic Relief and decided to record a new version of the hit song they had loved when they were younger, namely Cliff's 'Living Doll'. An approach was made to the original hit man himself – would he make a fresh version along with the 'fun' people? Cliff says, 'I liked the idea. I didn't see very much of the television series and some of what I did see was ridiculous. I didn't mind the Cliff Richard jokes. It was quite flattering to be filtered into the scripts.' Thankfully, he agreed. 'We went into the studio, had a lot of laughs and worked really hard for a couple of days.' Producer Stuart Colman was congratulated by the Yorkshire Cliff Richard Fan Club, since he was a former Harrogate School pupil. Colman thanked the club and remarked, 'Cliff's so good to work with, he is such a great artist.' And suddenly as a by-product to the money made, Cliff Richard had a number one hit. He became one of only two artists (the other was Gerry Marsden of Gerry and the Pacemakers, and The Crowd with 'You'll Never Walk Alone') to reach number one with two different versions of the same song. Cliff says, 'It's really great to think that a record that has already been at number one can be number one again!' For one letter writer in the *Daily Mail*, John Docherty of Old Trafford, Manchester, it was important to say: 'It underlines that many of today's hits will never be remembered in twenty-seven weeks' time, let alone a year. Bridging the gap of twenty-seven years is remarkable. But the best part is that Cliff is still strong in purpose and in heart.' But Cliff did not see it as any more than reviving an old hit for the purpose of making money for charity, and certainly not as an older man consorting with younger artists to make a record.

However, it brightened up the lives of all true Cliff fans who had cried long into the night at this mid-decade lurch that was reminiscent of difficult times in the 1970s. Sessions for the charity single were recorded under the auspices of WEA. Hank Marvin was one of the guitarists for the session and, with Bruce Welch, Jet Harris and Tony Meehan, had adorned the original session at the end of April 1959 at Abbey Road, as they recorded music for the film *Serious Charge*.

Only in two years has the solo Cliff failed to chart a new record, the first being in 1975 and the second 1986. However, 1986 did produce a couple of duets. One, with Elton John, has already been mentioned; it took two years from its time of recording to hit the schedules. Far more successful and preceding the Cliff–Elton release, was 'All I Ask Of You', which brought him together on record with Sarah Brightman, which reached number three in a sixteen week, top 75 chart run. It had been recorded in August at Abbey Road, with Andrew Lloyd Webber producing. But if 1986 seemed bare of the solo Cliff, at least he was busy in the studios, laying down material for *Always Guaranteed*, an album that would once more restore his chart fortunes.

But it was a long wait for devoted fans. 'It's In Every One Of Us' had entered the UK chart listings in December 1985 and departed after two weeks in 1986. There were no solo hits until June 1987.

Of course, when 'My Pretty One' hit the shops, and was followed by 'Some People' in late August, it suddenly seemed good again. The former title reached number six and the latter halved that, and might have made the top spot but was prevented by such epic records as 'Never Gonna Give You Up' by Rick Astley and 'Pump Up The Volume' by M/arrs. 'Remember Me' became the third single to be lifted off the top five *Always Guaranteed* set but while it may be one of my top Cliff singles, this view was only partially held by the record public who bought enough copies to see it reach a ridiculously low 35. As was usual with the marketing of the time, 'Remember Me', like the previous two singles, came out in a variety of forms with spaced date releases to maintain a selling momentum. Each had four stages of release: the basic 7 inch, followed by 12 inch, CD and then a special 12 inch. And 'Remember Me' had a hitherto unreleased track as its extra flip side on the 12 inch, namely 'Brave New World'. The initial B-side, which was designed to lend impetus for the coming Yuletide, was 'Another Christmas Day'. The CD added the recent top three single 'Some People'.

*Always Guaranteed* also received particular attention, being presented, doubtless, with the Christmas market in mind, as a special boxed edition including a signed print, coloured postcards, album, a 7 inch specially recorded Christmas single, and a handgraved, hand-written message from the man, plus a poster. In the British Granada and Central Television areas there was a £200,000 TV ad campaign, with advertising also in other regions of Britain. EMI's TV advertisement had Cliff telling everyone how he was away on tour but would soon be home. He was seen sitting in front of a fire, holding a copy of his album. Cliff was full of praise for the production and writing work of Alan Tarney. Tarney said, 'It's always incredible working with Cliff. The enthusiasm, the show-biz sense, the professionalism, the voice all make for something that is fabulous.' Without seeming arrogant or pushing his own undoubted high standards and ability, Tarney remarked, 'I think at this time Cliff needed a pop producer. I produced his big album *Wired For Sound* in 1981, and so I was really thrilled to get involved with this one, and he needed something great.' One other plus at this time was the record photography of Paul Cox. He captured a delightful sense of reflection and assurance in his studies of Cliff. Over the years a number of photographers have been employed to take Cliff for either sleeve pictures or promotional material, but Cox certainly lays claim to be one of the best, alongside, if not ahead of, Brian Arris.

But was there the possibility of a fourth single from *Always Guaranteed*? As often happens, EMI and Cliff suggested that the fans might have the answer, although some might have remembered the disaster of 'Ocean Deep'. Notwithstanding that this had topped the annual *Dynamite International* magazine poll for the top Cliff recording of all time in 1987, it had hardly sold in May 1984. 'Two Hearts' was billed as his ninety-ninth solo release until someone did some reckoning and decided it was number ninety-eight, thus winning the fans' vote. On 1 February, it appeared in 7 inch and 12 inch form, the latter also including 'Yesterday, Today, Forever' and 'Wild Geese'. Since the track obviously had Valentine's Day appeal, there was a special 12 inch gatefold sleeve in the form of a Valentine card. But, yet again, the fans failed to deliver the goods, for the record only got to 34 and, horror of horrors, only just survived Valentine's Day itself, lasting a pitiful three weeks. Once again there was a minor crisis, with two releases in a row not performing as they should. Even the bi-monthly *DI* magazine said it was 'a little disappointing'. It sure was. The single would also feature on a PMI Cliff Richard Video EP that bore the last album title and carried the released single video promotions for 'My Pretty One', 'Some People', 'Remember Me' and 'Two Hearts'. Cliff introduced the eighteen-minute video and remarked that it was the first time that four singles had come off one of his albums. Somehow it didn't seem right that in this thirtieth year of recording his singles were not zooming into the top twenty, let alone the top ten. 'Some People' topped the *DI* readers' choice of top songs in his career in their 1988 poll, pushing 'Ocean Deep' into second place. 'My Pretty One' was four, 'Two Hearts' ten and 'Remember Me' twelve, a rather more healthy position for two of those hits than that found in the actual record sales chart!

Still, it is now becoming obvious that just when he is down, Cliff comes back to the surface, for now would begin, from the Christmas period, 1988, a hat-trick of top three singles with 'Mistletoe And Wine' reaching number one, 'The Best Of Me', two, and 'I Just Don't Have The Heart', produced and written by Stock, Aitken and Waterman, stripping away the years and having him sound more relevant even than Jason Donovan.

'Mistletoe And Wine' was issued on 21 November, in a picture bag, and in the simple 7 inch form had 'Marmaduke' on the B-side. But, of course, there was much more to come. In 12 inch format the buyer could own a poster bag and calendar and have 'Little Town' as an extra track, while the CD had a Christmas card and 'La Gonave'. Apart from 'Living Doll' with the Young Ones, this was his first solo number one since 'We Don't Talk Anymore' in the summer of 1979.

The single topped the UK chart for Christmas and, to everyone's joy, Cliff gained the coveted UK album chart top spot the same week for the double-record set *Private Collection*, which was to sell a cool 1,500,000 copies. It was the third time Cliff had achieved this: he had done so in 1962 with the album title track and single of *The Young Ones*, and the following year *Summer Holiday* topped both listings. *Private Collection* achieved a sales figure of 620,000 in just forty-two days.

'Mistletoe And Wine' has the schmaltz Cliff, some found it too sugary, but it became the highest selling single of 1988 with sales in excess of a million, and for Cliff the sales were the highest since 'Living Doll' in 1959. Some people were reminded that a long time back, in 1962, he had had advance sales of 524,000 for 'The Young Ones', and here he was, twenty-nine or twenty-six years later, with a million-plus selling single and album. And the single was his fifty-fifth top ten hit, if duets are included, equalling the record set by Elvis and soon passed . . .

Once this headed towards its success all attention was turned toward the hundredth Cliff solo single. It was rumoured that he would throw caution to the winds and join the techno-dance beat of the moment. It was known that he would be recording with the whiz pop-dance team Stock, Aitken and Waterman, a trio who were having phenomenal success, albeit hardly applauded either, by the industry or the critics. Early in 1989 Cliff said that he was meeting with Alan Tarney to see if he could write something tailored to the occasion. Cliff said, 'It would be fantastic if the hundredth single was a number one. Everyone wants the hundred single to be really special – and a very strong commercial song.' It was at this point that the 'dance' element came into play, for he added, 'I've been thinking of doing a dance-orientated single for some time now. I'm always looking for new challenges. They make incredible dance records these days but my one criticism is that dance records do not often go hand in hand with great songs. If we could succeed in marrying the two together I think we would have something very special. It will be a contemporary record. Of that you can be sure.'

In the end, it was the strong traditional ballad 'The Best Of Me' that won the day but, sadly, the record jumped into the singles chart in Britain at number two and went no higher. In a way, it was all the more romantic, even if Cliff himself had wanted the top spot on this special and unrepeatable occasion, for his first hit, 'Move It', reached no further than number two in 1958. He was prevented from reaching the number one spot by the new single from Jason Donovan, one of the many highly successful acts from the Scott, Aitken and Waterman stable. Some thought the trio should have waited a week, and allowed Cliff to have a free run, especially since they were in the running for the hundredth single, and his next record, solo release 101, was theirs. Perhaps business is business.

Fans had a considerable wait for this hundredth solo single, with May set for the release date, six months on from the November release of his Christmas number one. However, it was into June before it all happened.

Alan Jones, in the pop weekly *Record Mirror* (which, alas, no longer exists, having been incorporated in part within the pages of the industry trade journal, *Music Week*), remarked how Cliff was Britain's representative in the Eurovision Song Contest in 1968 when Jason was born! It was a pity that the Donovan record, was a reworking of an oldie, the Brian Hyland hit of 1962, 'Sealed With A Kiss'.

It was late summer when Cliff stole the headlines, as he debuted at 10 with the Stock, Aitken and Waterman number, 'I Just Don't Have The Heart'. It was the first time he had had three consecutive records entering the top ten. It was also another extra-special landmark since it was his hundredth chart hit, comprising ninety-four solo hits and six with other artists. By the following week the record had become his third top three in a row and it became his best run since 1962–3, when seven top threes followed upon each other.

It was another golden period, untouched and unequalled by someone with such longevity at the top, and almost ranking with the likes of Madonna. There would now come a list of extremely high quality singles – the haunting 'Lean On You', the vibrant 'Stronger Than That', a sparkling revival for 'Silhouettes', the powerful ballad 'From A Distance', and as 1990 waited to go away, there he was again, for the third Christmas, at the top of the charts thanks to 'Saviour's Day', which was infinitely better than 'Mistletoe And Wine'. All of these deserved at least to reach the top five, but 'Lean On You' peaked at 17, 'Stronger Than That' at 14, 'Silhouettes' at 10, and 'From A Distance', 11. (The flow of his own name singles was interrupted by the release of a duet with Van Morrison entitled 'Whenever God Shines His Light', which was mooted in 1989 as a possible Christmas number one single but only reached number 20 in the chart. It was recorded for Morrison's album *Avalon Sunset*.)

'From A Distance' was the single to celebrate his fiftieth birthday. (*DI* magazine asked its readers, 'Have you ever seen Louis Armstrong or Frank Sinatra do when fifty what Cliff is still able to do?') It was a good title for this half-century since it led to all kinds of writers reflecting on Cliff 'from a distance' as they culled facts and figures from a long past, and fans from around the world could send their greetings 'from a distance'. In Cliff record landmarks, he was twenty when his 'Nine Times Out Of Ten' was faring well, at thirty it was, 'I Ain't Got Time Anymore', and a decade on, at forty, there was the superb 'Dreamin''.

'From A Distance' had been featured in the finale to his Wembley Stadium concert of 1989, and had long been anticipated as a future single release. In only one of pop's occasional chart chases in which two artists chart with the same title, Cliff did rather better than Bette Midler, the American artist; later, her version was reissued and charted much higher.

'Saviour's Day' by Chris Eaton was released on 26 November 1990. It had already been sung by Cliff in a week-long engagement in the autumn at the Savvas Club in Usk, Gwent, and was featured during this autumn tour. Chris had formerly been responsible for 'Where Do We Go From Here?', the music of 'Little Town', and the popular song, 'Joanna'. At Cliff's birthday concert at the NEC, Birmingham, the Midland-based singer-songwriter joined Cliff on stage to sing the song. Cliff announced that he was definitely aiming to take the Christmas number one spot. He had recorded the single's video on 25 September near Lulworth Cove. Filming had begun at eight in the morning, and some 400 people were gathered for later film shots.

There were also exceptional sales of his albums during this time. *Stronger*, released in October 1989, had spawned four hit tracks, the already mentioned 'Stronger Than That', 'Lean On You', 'I Just Don't Have The Heart' and 'The Best Of Me'. Many thought another album track, 'Joanna', would have made a fine single but it only appeared as the flip to 'Stronger Than That'.

November 1990 saw the album *From A Distance – The Event*, a record of Cliff's historic concerts at the massive Wembley Stadium when, over two days, 150,000 people saw a show that must rate as one of the finest to grace a stadium that can be booked only for the mega-stars of the day.

It was hardly surprising that 1991 did not have the fizz of the past three years. In recording terms the main event lay in his putting down material for a Christmas album. Otherwise it seemed a time of relaxation. There was a rumour that 'Miss You Nights' or 'We Don't Talk Anymore' might be reissued in the UK, the latter remixed, but it did not happen. However, it was issued in Germany and eventually appeared as a track on the 12 inch record of the lacklustre main side, 'This New Year'. Cliff, in denying the rumour, said there was too much new material clamouring for issue, but fans might be forgiven for wondering just what.

Still, a new single came in September, entitled 'More To Life'. It was specially written by Simon May (writer of major British TV themes for *EastEnders* and *Howards Way*) and Cliff's friend, DJ and writer, Mike Read. 'More To Life' was the theme song of a new BBC drama series, *Trainer*. Somehow it never really clicked, although initially there were chart possibilities and Cliff appeared on *Top Of The Pops*. The song entered at 23 but then dropped a place, even though sales had increased from the previous week. Unfortunately the British media tend to view any drop in position as the end of the road. The track is also found on the album of the series, which was released by EMI in October 1991.

As Christmas approached the inevitable speculation arose that a promised new Cliff single might hit the top spot. The track chosen off the Christmas album, *Together With Cliff*, was 'We Should Be Together'. It had the 'come home' call for Christmas appeal in its opening moments but soon became no more than a good record, lacking the overall class and appeal that defeats competitors. At one time it hovered and had a late dash to number ten when EMI released it in another format, but never seriously challenged Queen's 'Bohemian Rhapsody' reissue, which sprang from the tragic death of their lead singer, Freddie Mercury. However, it provided Cliff with his fifty-seventh solo top ten hit. A video accompanied both single and album, and in promoting the visual, EMI – via its PMI release label – stressed how *From A Distance – The Event* was number two in PMI's all-time-best-selling video list.

The album comprised Cliff's past Christmas numbers and a selection of traditional Christmas fare such as 'White Christmas' and 'Have Yourself A Merry Little Christmas' (he had sung this on a TV show in 1968 joined by Bruce Forsyth and Anita Harris). Perhaps his manager, David Bryce, had something to do with the

127

choice of 'Christmas Alphabet', since it was previously a number one in 1955 for Dickie Valentine. Many thought this might have been Cliff's Christmas release, and perhaps it ought to have been rush-released once it was realized that 'We Should Be Together' was not heading into the big hit territory. Even 'White Christmas' would have been an inspired choice, since it is one of the most familiar and often-played Christmas songs, and has not been a top ten hit since 1977. The talented Chris Eaton was responsible for a new version of 'O Come, All Ye Faithful', which might have been a single contender. Bruce Welch penned 'I Love You', which is only found on the video, and not the album. It was issued on the CD single of 'This New Life' at the end of 1991. For some season 'Scarlet Ribbons' found a place, and some may have recalled the 1957 version by Harry Belafonte. Paul Field, a contemporary writer much involved in the Christian world, contributed 'Christmas Never Comes', with its inbuilt cynicism about the world and its often tragic events balanced well against a rather sugary rendering of 'Silent Night'. The latter also had a spoken passage by Cliff which grated on my ears but elsewhere received the stamp of approval. It was another Chris Eaton song, 'This New Year', that would eventually give Cliff his first single release of 1992. It had an optimistic air but did not really suggest itself as a major hit, although it had a 'growing' quality about it. It was marketed with a limited edition 7 inch with an engraved photograph on one side, and the limited edition 12 inch came with a giant poster of Cliff and a 1992 calendar. The 12 inch and CD included a remix of 'We Don't Talk Anymore', with the added date 1991. This was released on 30 December which was not the best of choices. The New Year quickly disappears from people's minds, and the record was a rather ponderous affair. After entering the chart at 30, it was at 52 within a fortnight, and lost. Should this follow past patterns then it means another possibly lacklustre chart affair before a sudden resurgence of sheer Cliff power. It would seem right that this should accompany his major UK tour, which began in early October.

# CHAPTER TWELVE

# INTERNATIONAL CLIFF

The stage suit was carefully handled, neatly folded and hung on a battered coat-hanger in the dressing-room wardrobe. He changed into sweater and slacks.

'Wow! You know, I've been eating corned beef like mad recently because it said 240 calories on the outside of the tin and I thought it was non-fattening until I discovered just how fattening 240 calories can be. I think I'll have a quick omelette for lunch.'

Still, as he had said a few moments previously, he had lost three pounds thanks to an instant diet. Pop reporter Ian Dove from *Record Mirror* was less concerned with Cliff's midriff than with how the 22-year-old looked so fresh. After all, Cliff had only been back from the United States for a day or so and since then he had had long consultations with Peter Gormley and had rehearsed, with his usual zeal and professionalism, his coming stage presentation at London's Palladium. It was October 1962.

'Coming home is as good as a rest. We've been working hard in America. I've done about seven cities in two weeks, and that means starting at breakfast and meeting the press, doing radio and television shows from nine a.m. until nine p.m.

'I believe our American visit is paying dividends – which is unlike what happened when I first went over, when I was right down at the bottom of the bill.

'I am satisfied with my home country. There's nothing in America that I want. It would just be a feather in my cap, a kind of challenge.'

His expression of satisfaction with dear old Britain was doubtless felt but it was also a good public relations comment. Cliff's home-based fans were not too keen at the thought of their artist being taken over by others – across either the Channel or the Atlantic. They wanted Cliff for themselves.

With some successful pop groups and artists, fans have little cause to worry. Cliff though, like the Beatles, was different. Almost from the start he was international property. America was just one of the markets clamouring for his records and his presence. One album and six singles preceded his first top-of-the-bill foray overseas. Scandinavia was first on the schedule sheet. The tour took place in October 1960 and was not without immediate problems. Tony Meehan had to have an appendix operation. Laurie Joseph took his place.

There was one week in the early sixties when Cliff topped the charts of six overseas countries. 'Lucky Lips', released in May 1963, gave him the number one spot in Israel, South Africa, Sweden, Holland, Norway and Hong Kong. The magazines called him, with slight generosity, 'The World's Most Wanted Man – in the pop world, that is', and asserted that he was 'the greatest INTERNATIONAL British singer – and certainly as big in the world ratings as any American – including Elvis!'

Cliff fans purred assent.

These days the tall and imposing Peter Jones is British Editor for *Billboard*, the trade paper of the giant US music industry. In 1963 he was a pop paper reporter. He remembers Cliff in South Africa, and looking back after all this he still radiates enthusiasm and incredulity that a mere twenty-year-old should achieve such world prominence so soon.

'I remember Cliff in South Africa. He caused more mob-gathering, more riot-raising, more honest to goodness noises of appreciation than most political revolutions. He took the place by storm. He could have stayed for a lifetime.

'And what's more, he did more good for British pop music than anyone can imagine. He waved a flag. He took over a whole country.

'Do you ever read anything derogatory about Cliff? Have you ever heard of him being off-handed? Or big-time? Or indulging in the favourite show business pastime of running down competitors? Or even throwing a tantrum? Of course a lot is due to the excellent and understanding management.

'I remember Cliff appearing in the office just after his first-ever record had hit the shops. I remember him coping with a mass press conference at the time. In between these two meetings, one so informal, the other so charged with formality, he had nothing but success. Worldwide success.

'From £20 per week to more like £2,000 – and the brown-eyed, dark-haired bachelor boy hadn't changed at all. I once said, "I don't know if you like oysters, Cliff, but the world's your personal oyster."'

It was this image which guided various persons to suggest Cliff might give a very special concert in the East African country of Kenya on 11 February 1963. It was held in Nairobi and was in aid of Kenya's under-privileged children. It received the imprimatur of Kenyan lead Tom Mboya.

Cliff, at the time, was extremely popular in this African country. Months later the Kenyan *Sunday Post* said Cliff had topped its Kenya Top Of The Pops poll. Largely instrumental in furthering Cliff in Kenya was the British Forces Broadcasting Service, normally known simply as BFBS. A DJ of the time (later with BBC Radio 2, Radio Hallam and Yorkshire Radio), Keith Skues, says Cliff achieved his East African success because nothing was too much trouble for him.

'He didn't have too much time while in Kenya but he gave BFBS his special attention and of course we were heard throughout the country. I remember four Nairobi teenagers – Gillian Duncan, Valerie Flatt, Karen Bell and Valerie Maskell – being absolutely knocked out by him. They interviewed him for one of our shows and I did my stuff with him earlier in the day at the concert.

'We received many complimentary phone calls about its success and in response to numerous requests it was repeated the following Sunday afternoon.'

Skues, still maintaining a DJ's rapidity of speech, says Cliff was one of many stars who came out with the hope of finding African success. Cliff, he feels, was different from most others.

'He looked good. He was polished. He had a varied offering. He had a genuine air about him. He had professionalism, everything had to be right. And then he had time for everybody. That matters when you're overseas. I mean, here he was, a major world star, he could have had an arrogant air but he didn't. People liked him. There was time for everybody, whatever the work load.

'I remember how, a few years later, I was walking down London's Savile Row, the street which had Cliff's management offices. He was on the other side of the road from me and he saw me. He let out a yell, "Cardboard Shoes!" I've met up with him subsequently. He makes friends. It's an invaluable asset, really is.'

In those early days Cliff recorded many of his songs in foreign languages. Nowadays he remembers this with some amusement. Between words he chuckles.

'I used to record my hits in German, French, Italian, Spanish –

even some Japanese crept in. I couldn't speak the languages. I sometimes wonder what they made of them! But then they bought the records. Amazing, really.'

He laughs at the memory but he knows it helped. It gained him respect. People felt that he had gone out of his way to communicate on their level. He wasn't just a show business foreigner out for every penny he could get.

'I did it all by phonetics – where you learn to imitate the sounds of the lyrics. French and Spanish were the easiest ones to come to grips with.'

Not surprisingly, German, with its many throat-clearing gutturals, provided him with most difficulty. No matter, struggle or no struggle, Cliff's attempts at foreign languages were the best commercial plus for him at the time. They gained him air play. They pitted him against the locals. He wasn't an ordinary damn foreigner. They served him well.

'I reckon it's fairly easy to make hit records once you have the formula but it's the individual who has to make something of himself. Since quite early in my career I have had a definitely long-term attitude.

'It's a problem, though, keeping all the countries happy. They all want you and from early times I was popular all over the place.

'It's easy to lose territories. For a time you can sell records but in the end you have to go and let yourself be seen and heard. I lost the German market. I stopped going there, not for any particular reason, but it was difficult to fit things in.

'I stopped going to Germany for nine years. I've regretted that. It just seemed that every time I wanted to go something else would happen.

'So in 1977, maybe '78, I said to EMI that I wanted Germany to happen for me. I suppose it was a good time, with some strong records coming out. Well, it has happened and I'm knocked out. I'm back in the *Award* listings and at the age of forty-one in the top three with the young stars of today.

'I'm glad those early days gave me this world base. It wasn't easy. It was hard work. You know, the routine of flight, airport, car, hotel, rehearsal, concert, hotel, car, airport and off to somewhere else. Still, we had some great times, we really did.

'Japan is another place I've a little neglected. But what do you do when so many things happen? Places like Hong Kong, South Africa, Holland and Australia have always remained loyal.'

He could have added some less likely places – Korea, the

Eastern bloc countries and, amazingly, the USSR, which has played host to a mere handful of Western pop artists.

Year in and year out Cliff has sung for his supper somewhere other than the UK and with his Christian interests increasing from 1966 onwards some territories have fought for either a secular or religious tour. In 1964 he toured Europe along with the Shadows, including a week at the Paris Olympia. In 1965 there were visits to Spain, Switzerland and France. The next year he toured behind the Iron Curtain and in 1968 Turkey, Hawaii, Israel, Australia, Japan and Spain saw Britain's top pop star.

Before the sixties had come to an end Cliff had visited Germany, Japan, Norway, Israel, Romania, Czechoslovakia, South Africa, Scandinavia and Holland once more. That he should go anywhere at all was amazing, considering that the last half of the sixties saw him involved not merely in hit records but a plenitude of TV and radio shows, films, plays, gospel lectures, media presentation, general cabaret including various seasons at London's Talk of the Town and the London Palladium, and the time-consuming activity of the Eurovision Song Contest.

The USSR was the event of the seventies, though there was a sudden splurge of interest from the United States just past the halfway mark which for a time looked as if it might be Cliff's long sought-after breakthrough.

Some 91,000 Soviets heard Cliff via twelve concerts in Leningrad and eight in Moscow, with several matinées in both cities. At Leningrad the stage and orchestra pit were level and therefore accessible to the audience. Such was the hysteria on the opening night that the orchestra pit was dropped by some feet for subsequent performances.

'It went fantastically well, amazing reception. I think it certainly proved rock 'n' roll is an international language. It was a marvellous opportunity,' says Cliff.

Peter Gormley was stunned by the reception given Cliff. 'It was just fantastic – Cliff was absolutely knocked out. It was even more amazing considering his records were not even on sale in the USSR at that time.'

The £8 tickets fetched £40. It was a case of 'comrade' Cliff rocking the Reds, though one song was removed from the tour programme. It was 'Love Train'.

The major objection to this seemingly harmless bland homage to universal togetherness came because the lyric mentions the state of Israel, with which the USSR at that time had no diplomatic relations. It might be argued that Israel is speedily dispatched, as are most other named places in this song which was popularized for the Western hit parades by the black Philadelphia group, the O'Jays. This and other arguments were put to no avail. 'Love Train' did not run in Cliff's Russian shows.

Cliff's visit had been requested by the Russians. They had seen him perform in Copenhagen and they liked his style. He was considered the most acceptable of Western artists.

'It's only because I don't smash up hotel rooms,' is how Cliff sees it, though he didn't look too serious when saying this.

So there he was on the late August evenings of 1976 on the stage as the first invited Western pop artist in the USSR. He wore his white suit, which looked a dream as he still sported a Barbadian suntan handily acquired some weeks previously. He moved in his usual fashion.

One Russian girl told a British pressman, 'It's the way he moves that's so exciting.' It was like yesteryear, only then the audience was British and it was 1958, with Cliff eighteen, not thirty-six.

Payment was mostly in roubles. Hard currency was limited but everyone agreed the tour was not for money. It was an experience and it opened the possibility of record sales. For the general Western music business, the Cliff visit suggested promising sales days ahead.

While the USSR, for its very uniqueness, stands out as the international event for Cliff and perhaps the British music business as a whole during the seventies, Cliff himself seems more affected by the short tour he made the same year in Asia.

At first it took him back home to the sprawling and heavily populated land of India. There he soon knew that many young Indians who are familiar with Western pop culture fervently claim him as part theirs. He was born on their soil. Public appearances were made in Kalamandir Stadium, New Delhi, on 7 and 8 December 1976. The show bore the advertised title 'A New Message, A New Song'.

For much of the time he was involved in Tear Fund activity, outside the musical sphere, but what he saw in Bangladesh had an indirect effect on his career. Appropriately enough, the chapter in his religious autobiography which deals with this visit is titled 'I'll Never Be The Same Again'.

He says he felt at one moment that it seemed almost a cheat that he should return to Britain and resume his career as Cliff Richard – the International Pop Star.

'It was all so easy. I would go ahead and do my twenty concerts for Tear Fund and raise £25,000 and I'd enjoy every minute of it. Compared to what others were contributing it seemed so puny.

'I see now that that was illogical but it took one of the girls to help me realize it. "Without you and other Christians at home," she said, "we wouldn't be here! We need each other." That was real consolation at the time and the words stuck.'

Cliff says he learned the simple fact that in real cold terms he had nothing to contribute in Bangladesh. Yes, he could sweep floors. So can others. True, he could hump materials around but then it's a task most can do. Few, though, can command the kind of audience and respect which he has in show business.

For former EMI Head of Marketing John Cabanagh, worldwide Cliff is a precious possession.

'He's one of the few whom you can speak of anywhere in the world and they know the name. No discussion. No questions. They know Cliff.

'We have what we call local companies virtually everywhere and if we do not have a specific office someone represents us.

'The marvellous thing about Cliff from a selling point of view is the number of markets which can be tapped. He has fans right across the musical board.

'He's been with us at EMI since he began and the same is true worldwide save for a few years in America. He had some success just after the mid-seventies with Rocket – Elton John's company – but when he signed a new deal with us it was an international deal.

'He's always relevant. There's a constant cry from overseas for a Cliff visit. His records are always being released and foreign licensees can choose their own way of issuing material.

'Internationally he's big. Actually these days he sells more units in Germany than the UK. I'm not saying he's a bigger artist there, merely in sales terms.

'Japan and France are big. His best-selling single in France has been a record which was never issued in that form in the UK – "Early In The Morning".

'The States have always been tricky. It takes an eternity to come big there. But Cliff can sell in millions. He had three records in the early 1981 US *Billboard* Hot 100 charts.

'Then again, he's someone who can capture the feel of other homegrown culture. I mean, when you hear "The Minute You've Gone" you realize he could be an acceptable country singer. He doesn't sing another idiom badly. He has a Latin feel which the continentals like. Let's face it, Cliff's appeal is astronomical. It's amazing really and a lot of people use that adjective but who else makes sense to Japanese, Koreans, Germans, Italians, Australians? What diversity!'

With Cliff it's not so much a question of where he has been, rather where he has not. Where would he go next?

'China would be interesting,' he says.

So it would, if international Cliff could find the time.

The 1980s saw him travel through familiar European venues and countries, as he did during October and early November of 1982 with Germany, France, Finland, Belgium and Denmark in the 'call-in' diary listing.

His concerts were little different from that performed in Los Angeles during the spring of 1982. He would begin with 'Green Light', and make his way through 'Dreamin'', 'The Only Way Out', 'Better Than I Know Myself' and 'Broken Doll', while in part two there would be his rock 'n' roll package of classics from the 1950s, including 'Tutti Frutti', 'Great Balls Of Fire', 'Lucille', 'Long Tall Sally', 'Rip It Up' and 'Blue Suede Shoes'. However, his encore saw changes, depending on the venues and reaction. While at Hanover's Kuppelsaa, he would end with 'The Young Ones', 'Do You Wanna Dance' and 'Move It', at other points he sang 'Living Doll' and 'Gee Whiz It's You'.

Early in 1983, in Singapore at the Goodwood Park Hotel, he was greeted by fans from the host country and Hong Kong, with plenteous supplies of Cliff's favourite flowers – orchids. Eight thousand attended his two concerts at the National Theatre. On the second night there was an unexpected delay when drummer Graham Jarvis penetrated the outer skin of one of his drums during Cliff's singing of 'Dreamin'', and a replacement was needed.

Cliff's sartorial sense was noted when he reached Bangkok from Singapore – sports trousers in grey to match a blue T-shirt, with fetching grey sports shoes. During his concert he even wore a T-shirt presented to him by the British Embassy and, thanks to its staff, many in the audience waved the Union Jack in a variety of sizes.

When his Singapore Airlines flight arrived in Hong Kong he might have felt a touch of déjà vu since those who greeted him had met him in Singapore and Bangkok and returned by an earlier flight. He was soon acclimatized and followed the pattern of many British tourists by going shopping, and purchasing a Sony

Walkman. On meeting his dedicated Hong Kong fan club he spoke of plans for his Silver Jubilee, and in reply his hosts gave him a silver plate that bore the inscription 'Cliff Richard 25 Years In Music'. He signed a number of posters and stickers with his silver-ink-equipped pen. During his concert he tried a little of the local language, and since it was near the Chinese New Year he said, 'Kung hai fai choi', which means 'good fortune'. And yes, he did say thank you in Chinese, 'Doi tse'.

His next port of call was Manila, where he performed only part of an expected programme, and spent Valentine's night at the Folk Arts Theatre. (At least Sue Barker, back in Britain, would know where he was.) He made a few changes from his most recent programme, and even dropped his previous opening number, 'Green Light', as well as certain more rowdy rock 'n' roll numbers. Not unexpectedly, since it had just been issued as a single in Manila, he sang the fast-moving 'Where Do We Go From Here?'. In reality, that was Australia, where his tour had sold out in ninety minutes. It was at this point that his goodwill showed, for even if he was tired after his recent haul through the Far East, and with this major tour in the offing, he was still saying he would perform at a special benefit concert in Adelaide to help victims of a bushfire. It was a vital day off 'gone missing' but Cliff felt it was something that must be done.

All this was a prelude to the enormous barrage of media interest back home, as Cliff went through his twenty-fifth anniversary celebrations from August onwards. It was a time of reflection for some, including the artist, and in Britain a major Silver Tour. Some believed it might be his last year, the right moment to bow out, not because the looks, stamina and ability were fading, but on a pleasant anniversary note. It was certainly felt by some fans abroad who wondered if his visit during 1983 might be the last they saw of him.

But then, to anyone who knew him even only moderately well, the thought of retiring was no more in his mind than it was in Mrs Thatcher's, nor would he stop jetting round the world, which he had done so many times that some countries could be seen as his extended back garden.

During 1984 he took part in the 24th Montreux Golden Rose Festival and joined Duran Duran, Joan Jett and Gloria Gaynor. His performance was watched through twenty-three countries, with some Americans viewing through their biggest cable station, Showtime.

South Africa received him for a series of concerts that opened in 1985; his visit was not without controversy, and there were reports that he was on an artists' blacklist for playing in a racially disturbed country. Cliff then, and before, defended his right to play in South Africa in spite of international bans. His decision was questioned by some of his fans, not least his close Christian friend, Garth Hewitt, who roundly attacked Cliff's position. Some South African Christians felt betrayed by Cliff's insistence on coming, although not all saw it that way, as they attended his concert at the Christian Community Centre in Pretoria. Said Hewitt, 'Christians felt betrayed, and I felt black Christians in particular were saying "don't go", but then we all make mistakes. I had been in South Africa previously with Cliff, and we had tried to woo people to the concept of multi-racialism but I think we were naïve, there were greater things at stake than a localized situation. I felt some of our white friends were not giving us the whole picture.'

In conversation, and in his book *Single-minded*, Cliff has defended his visits to South Africa and stressed they have been specifically for Christian purposes. In his mind, his contacts have helped bridge misunderstanding, and he feels that to some degree they have righted the manner in which much of the condemnation was expressed by anti-apartheid groups. 'It has hurt and disappointed me – not because I feel the the condemnation was unjust, but because it has been delivered so often without love and without compassion for all segments of the community.' He objected vehemently to a cruel satirical song that was carried on the British television show *Spitting Image* that had the refrain: 'but I've never met a nice South African'. In *Single-minded* you can almost hear his anger as he writes, 'Well, I have – many of them, of all races – and I feel really offended when the world tars every one of them with the same apartheid brush.' He talks of his bond with Christian South Africans sweeping away geographical and race problems. In the end, Cliff agreed he would not play South Africa until the political situation was resolved.

But he also encountered protests in Britain: on 27 June 1985, the Bishop of Sheffield, the Rt Rev. David Lunn, led a delegation from the city's anti-apartheid movement who met Cliff – he was appearing on stage at a Billy Graham Mission England meeting – and asked him to renounce the South African links that had led to his blacklisting. He said if it would help them, 'I would guarantee not to do a commercial concert there,' although he had done so for ten years. He also said, 'I go for one reason and that is to do gospel concerts and raise money for black problems.'

However, his position became clearer when on 6 October it was announced that his name had been removed from the United Nations Anti-Apartheid Black List. Cliff said that he had given a twofold assurance to the UN body, 'that I shall not perform in South Africa until the apartheid policy is abolished, and secondly, that any future religious visits there will not follow racial or segregationist procedures'. Cliff added that this stance had always been his policy even though, as it has already been pointed out, some black Christians felt he should not come, even for Christian gatherings.

By late summer of 1985 Cliff was making a few brief forays into Europe and beyond before commencing a tour beginning on 4 October at Essen, Germany, and ending in Munich on the 29th, but in the interim taking in other dates in Germany and elsewhere. Towards the end of August he had visited Oslo for a Red Cross Charity Show, and then taken part in a large youth conference in Warsaw, Poland. The latter was in his capacity as Vice-President of Tear Fund.

But even Cliff, with all his apparent health, suffers from illness. Apart from back trouble he, as with many other vocalists, is subject to throat difficulties, and this led to cancellations, in early October, of European tour dates. He had previously cancelled five of his British gospel concerts, although he manfully struggled through a special concert in Colorado with Sheila Walsh at the beginning of August.

The advent of *Time* and Cliff's starring role meant that his globe trotting suffered a severe setback during 1986. *Time* was premièred on 9 April. Cliff expressed regret that many of his activities would have to take second place to the musical, and visiting friends in so many countries would be one area that would suffer, although he had been careful to ensure that recorded material would be available including, before the show and during it, some of his songs from the musical. Such is the work involved in arranging international tours of any size, that plans were being mooted while he was strutting the boards at London's Dominion Theatre.

While his British fans were pleased and even elated by his performance in *Time*, his long run in the musical obviously caused tensions. Anton Husmann Jr wrote in his editorial for the excellent *Dynamite International* magazine for October/November 1986, 'though Cliff is still doing the *Time* musical there are signs of planned tours in the coming years. Many fans are waiting impatiently for those concerts.' In the magazine's state of tension they even misplaced the year in their credits, writing 1987 and not 1986. Certainly Europe and Japan seemed frontrunners as soon as Cliff could forgo *Time* and once more hit the road, but later Australia joined Japan as a possible venue.

On 13 April 1987, Cliff's world audience breathed a sigh of relief for it was then that the American David Cassidy took over Cliff's role as Chris Wilder in the *Time* musical. There was some rest for Cliff, and then a series of gospel concerts in Britain during a fortnight of June. The European tour would commence in September. And when the date list was announced there were more than a few drawn-in breaths and audible sighs, for it seemed as if he was determined to recover lost ground. Apart from the odd day, he was scheduled to tour from 1 October until a lengthy return to Britain when he would play from 7 to 12 December at Birmingham's 12,000-seat National Exhibition Centre. In all, there were forty-five dates outside the UK, and of these twenty-one were in Germany, well and truly impressing upon everyone his enormous popularity in that country. There was also a handful of dates behind the still-existing Iron Curtain. It was pretty good going for a 47-year-old (which is what he would be by the time he completed those dates).

His European tour was preceded by three dates at Wimbledon Theatre late in September. And at the other end of the spectrum, bookings were announced for Australia in February 1988.

His tour went out under the name of the new album, *Always Guaranteed*, and in programme it was a mix of his gospel tour earlier in the year, songs from the new release and some oldies. Certainly gospel and secular came together with the opening number – 'I'm Alive'.

At the outset of the Australian tour his throat kept him confined to his room. During a sound check at the stadium in Canberra he found he had no voice, and concerts scheduled for 12 and 13 March were hurriedly rescheduled for a fortnight later. Torrential rain threatened another concert in Rockhampton, Queensland, but here the large audience received an unexpected treat for, rather than postpone the event, the rain making it very dangerous for the musicians and their electric gear, he decided he would sing to backing tapes, and did so for two hours. Another surprise during the tour occurred in Perth when Hank Marvin from the Shadows, who lives in Australia, joined Cliff on stage, not repeated the following evening. It inspired a version of 'Living Doll'. Also for Australian ears was 'All The Time You Need', a new song by Chris Eaton that Cliff said he was trying out on his world tour to see if it should be recorded. Apart from his throat and the rain problems, Cliff may well recall that the temperature in Perth was thirty-seven degrees centigrade.

He scheduled eleven concerts for New Zealand, his first visit in three years. The final night of this tour was 14 February, and for Valentine's Day he received from the active Cliff Richard Movement fan club of New Zealand a huge red heart comprising ninety fresh carnation heads, which eight members spent three hours assembling. Apparently, it was one of 'the' presents of his career. Naturally, flowers were augmented with special hand-made chocolates but it's doubtful if more than one or two found their way into Cliff's mouth.

During April he recorded material for a show that celebrated Israel's fortieth year of independence. He arrived for his first visit in sixteen years. He toured the old city of Jerusalem and taped the English version of an Israeli song, 'Jerusalem Of Gold'. He appeared as part of a live show at the Malcha Stadium and sang 'Happy Birthday To You' to a delighted audience instead of 'Congratulations', a gesture that seemingly made a very positive impression. Soon he was off on a European mini spring tour that began in Oslo on 8 May and finished at the Osteehaller on 21 May. At his German concerts he wore a black suit, black tie with diamanté across it, and white shoes with black and diamanté. He changed into a red pin-stripe suit and red shirt for the second half. In Oslo he assured journalists that plastic surgery had not been performed on his face, and remarked, 'though you keep expecting me to look like Michael Jackson', and added in conclusion that he enjoyed singing much more than in the old days, mainly because he had made sufficient money and he could sing for enjoyment.

In Stuttgart he featured 'All The Time You Need', among familiars from the old days. He told the audience, 'I have had a really wonderful career, singing rock and roll songs for thirty years.' Cliff's often expressed antipathy towards some areas of the British and German press came to the fore once more when he said, 'The newspapers in Britain, as well as in Germany, write many things about me . . . And sometimes I read what they write

141

about me, and I don't understand how they can tell such lies. It's not always the case. I am thankful. I know I cannot correct everything.' His finale was 'Share A Dream', 'We Don't Talk Anymore' and 'Wired For Sound'.

During his Hamburg concert someone presented him with a big gingerbread heart with 'Lucky Lips' (*'Rote Lippen Soll Man Küssen'*) written across it. It was noted that he dined at the Shalimar and ate onions and spinach baked with Indian cheese, and later he signed a visitors' book that contains a number of known musicians' names. His visit to Kiel was the first in twenty-four years and the most enthusiastic response led him into saying, 'I really don't know why I haven't come to Kiel for twenty-four years.' The German press praised him effusively, and were particularly taken by his youthfulness. They called him 'the eternal pop boy' and remarked that his career began at the time Madonna was born. 'It seems to be a reward for living a God-fearing life.' His own youthfulness obviously does have transference power, with one German, forty-four years old, saying, 'Already after the first half of the show I felt twenty years younger.' Of his German hosts and audiences, Cliff would repeatedly say, *'Ihr seid sehr nett,'* 'You're very kind'.

He was back in Australia on Wednesday 28 December to take a well-earned holiday and see, by coincidence – well, not really – the Hopman Cup and several other major tennis tournaments. Cliff took part in the Pro-Am doubles tournament at the Burswood Superdrome. Partnering the German superstar Steffi Graf, he ran out winner. Later at the Hopman Cup New Year's Ball on the last day of December, he sang a dozen or so songs in a 45-minute set. His golden jacket was auctioned for charity. In June 1989 he found himself another top notch partner in Ilie Nastase, the colourful Romanian player. Again, Cliff, the tennis man, won.

Cliff's gospel work took him to Budapest on 7 April 1989, when he helped further the mission work of Luis Palau. Few events with a religious flavour have featured an artist singing 'Heartbreak Hotel' and 'Living Doll', among a programme that also included an interview about his faith with Bill Latham, and songs 'Lord, I Love You' and 'I Will Follow You'. Cliff's contribution concluded with 'When I Survey The Wondrous Cross'.

Nineteen eighty-nine ended with Cliff once more undertaking a mixture of dates and promotional work in various parts of the world. One of the highlights came when he topped the bill at the

Diamond Awards Festival in Belgium before 17,000 people. He was back in New Zealand on the last day of January 1990 for a month-long tour of eighteen concerts. He began with 'The Best Of Me' and moved into 'Green Light', followed by 'Dreamin''. He closed many songs later with 'Share A Dream' and 'From A Distance'. He had several changes of clothing, including an appearance as a ship's officer for 'Sea Cruise'. He also danced a little. Another apparent first was his wearing a little Walkman-appearance earplug that could give pure sound from the stage. The show ran for 150 minutes.

In the spring and early summer of 1990, a major tour took him through Scandinavia and much of Europe beginning on 1 May at the Ice Hall, Helsinki, and closing at the Zenith, Paris. The tour went under the title of his album, *Stronger*. Here again, 'The Best Of Me' was featured with the band joining in on this song, his hundredth solo single. In Finland, ICRM member Pirjo Paavola thought Cliff's dance steps left Michael Jackson well behind in the movement stakes. The secretary of the CRFC in Austria, Christina Schauer, wrote in *Dynamite International* that when she met Cliff she was suffering from a voice ailment, so much so that when 'I started to speak, he heard what was left of my voice and said "Stay away from me."' But apparently she was allowed to take some photographs.

British Cliff expert Eileen Edwards was among those who saw Cliff in concert in Brussels during May. When the British tour bus reached Dover they found themselves parked next to a coach taking Phil Collins fans to see him perform in Lyons. Cliff fans noted theirs was a double-decker, whereas the other was a small vehicle. For Eileen, the major question was 'Could Cliff ever follow The Event extravaganza at Wembley stadium in June 1989?' That evening he wore a mauve shirt, purple trousers, black jacket and shining black shoes. He began by singing 'The Best Of Me' unaccompanied and the band joined in after the first verse. In her lengthy report for the always excellent *Cliff United* magazine, she noted Cliff's reminding the audience how he had cold feet as the two June nights of 1989 had approached, but fortunately 72,000 had attended both evenings to fill the stadium. On this occasion he sang 'Anyone Who Had A Heart', a massive hit for Cilla Black and Dionne Warwick in the 1960s. It seems a pity that this song has not been recorded and released by Cliff. As in New Zealand and Australia, he closed with 'From A Distance', and left the stage after curtain calls to the band playing 'We Don't Talk

Anymore'. But what did Eileen finally say in relation to the question she raised? Was this a damp squib after The Event? She commented on the Stronger tour concert, 'Be sure to see it,' and as she concluded her long review for *Cliff United*, she exclaimed, 'Oh, what a wonderful weekend.' Other fans would describe the concert as 'magic'.

And there he was again in the winter of 1991, escaping once more to the sun, with dates in New Zealand and Australia commencing in Auckland on 14 October and finishing in Sydney at the end of November. The tour was another complete sell-out. He opened on his birthday and, for being in New Zealand for the first time on his special day, he was the happy recipient of a splendid birthday cake that had been made and decorated by the New Zealand fan-club president, Katrina Richards. Another member, Sue MacKinven, presented him with a special teddy bear that had around its neck a cheque with the money designated for Tear Fund. The active club made another presentation later in the tour for the South Island Bone Marrow Trust. But while fans in Australia and New Zealand saw their hero yet again, it was not such a happy scenario for fans in Japan, as their Cliff visit was cancelled.

In 1992 he made public appearances in Europe. If that seems an off-beat note on which to finish another Cliff travelogue, so be it. Amidst the gloss and razzmatazz of concerts, airport welcomes, personal reunions and presents, there was an ever-running tide of media engagements; not perhaps greatly enjoyed by Cliff, but as Bill Latham once said, 'What he does, he does professionally. If he says he will do something, then he will do it.'

And that is one of the overriding reasons for the continuing success of Cliff, at home and abroad. At a time when amateurism has been elevated foolishly into some kind of 'art', or at least worthy of high salary and media exposure, he stands as one of *the* professionals. To Cliff, the second best is no starter: around the world people can testify to his supreme skills. And in a roundabout way, he is Britain's most eloquent ambassador, not just to music people, but to citizens of many lands and identities. He communicates to them all, rarely embarrassed, mostly celebrative.

# CHAPTER THIRTEEN

# RELIGION – ODE TO BILLY

The gulf between Church and people in Britain had been widening for more than a generation. Church attendances were declining. The drift from the Church was touching all sections of the community.

Clergymen wrote increasingly of their amazement at the indifference to religion expressed by the young and their ignorance of the Christian faith.

Others were complaining of a sharp decline in the observance of moral standards, and they instanced a growth in crimes against the person, in juvenile delinquency and in sexual laxity.

Some, of course, blamed the impact of two great wars for the disintegration of religious life in Britain. Others said that the aloofness of the working classes from church life was hardly the consequence of two wars, however terrible they had been in terms of loss of human life. They traced the problem's beginning back to the industrial revolution.

So the arguments raged in the British Christian community in the early fifties and in fuller form they found their way into a book by C. T. Cook, *London Hears Billy Graham* (1954).

Billy was a young American of unimpeachable record. He was known for his strict morality. Why, he even said, he didn't kiss his wife Ruth until they were engaged. Billy was a solid evangelical. He knew where he stood. It was with the Bible. He believed he taught what the Bible said. When he preached his long sermons he would continually say 'the Bible says', for it was his authority.

He was an orator, not exactly of the old school, more akin to, though not quite like, a super-salesman. He was charming. He was eloquent. The cynical said he was just like some of the

145

old-time preachers who made converts and took their money. These critics said Billy sold Jesus as a product and took himself a mighty salary from the free-will offerings which flowed from those who had made their decision for Jesus.

Most of the Christian leaders and writers of the fifties spoke differently. They saw that he was a man of God with a definite calling for this age. They saw him as a man of dedicated spirit, with a passionate desire to make people face up to the reality of Jesus's claims and the consequences for their lives, their families and the country at large.

They welcomed him when he arrived in Britain and conducted a massive campaign of revivalist meetings. These gatherings were simple in outline. There was a huge choir which led the singing of noisy and boisterous hymns. There was a soloist named George Beverly Shea, a man equipped with a rich baritone voice which could silence the cynic, at least as long as George sang. There were people who came on stage and spoke of how their Christian faith meant everything to them. And there was Billy, good-looking, suave, cultured, with a resonant voice and radiating conviction. He didn't roast the listeners over the fires of hell like preachers of old, but he posed life and death questions.

It was in the spring and early summer of 1954 that Billy conducted his first Christian campaign in Britain. Rock 'n' roll was just beginning to breathe. Bill Haley was emerging and Elvis would soon come on the scene. Harry Webb was thirteen at the time. He didn't hear Billy this time around. He was more concerned with playing football and being an ideal son for his hardworking parents.

'There was a Bible about the house. I don't remember my father talking to me about faith. I was conscious of Christian things but that was all.

'I had been baptized and brought up as an Anglican. I had been taught my religion in school but I remember when I was fourteen refusing to go to confirmation classes.

'I had rejected religion, or rather I had rejected what most people take for religion but which to me seemed no more than lip service to the Christian code.

'I was, I suppose, looking back, a kind of dormant Christian. It's funny really – I say now that many kids do not give Christianity a chance. They say it's a stupid, staid thing. But I don't know if I gave things a chance when I was younger!'

He didn't dream that one day a pop writer called Jan Iles would

*Top:* The Elvis twitch of the leg. It was all part of the early Cliff Richard act. *Above left:* The agonized
sley mood . . . while the Shadows kick a leg. *Above right:* In the beginning . . . Harry Webb has become
Cliff Richard. Shy, a little plump, hair greased in Elvis fashion. He is seventeen.

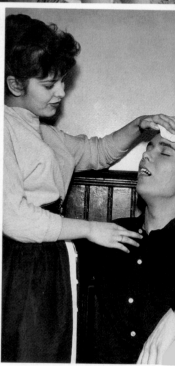

*Top:* Time out in Blackpool. Cliff's mother wears the sun hat. Skiffle king Lonnie Donegan stands between them. *Above left:* Togetherness on tour . . . Cliff and the Shadows book in at a German hotel in 1964. *Above right:* Post-performance aid administered by no other than Cliff's eldest sister, Donna.

*op:* South African pop organist Cherry Wainer appeared frequently with Cliff in the early days. His first effort as a songwriter was for her 'Happy Like a Bell' written in 1960. *Above left:* You meet the nicest ople in showbusiness. The armful is singing star Millicent Martin. *Above right:* Well, you can't go round smiling twenty-four hours a day!

*Top:* Cliff! Meet Cliff! Shaking hands with a puppet of himself created for the *Thunderbirds* TV series. There were puppet Shadows as well. *Above left:* Studio rehearsal. The Shadows pay attention. *Above right:* The strawberry blonde is the late Jayne Mansfield, pictured with Cliff during her British tour shor before her death in a car accident.

*Top left:* Rockin' on to the seventies – and remaining spectacularly successful. *Top right:* And still he oves what he does! *Above left:* Cliff's courtly romance with Sue Barker never got as far as marriage.
*Above right:* It's all down to Timing!

*Top:* Cliff with radical new hairstyle as Chris in *Time*, 1986. *Above:* With Freddie Mercury at the *Time* party.

*Top left:* John McEnroe, eat your heart out. *Top right:* The party of a lifetime. 1989's Event. *Above:* 'With a shirt like mine, you could make it to the big time, Jason!'

The varied stage personas of Cliff: as wild rocker, glitzy superstar and slick Teddy Boy

in a flight of racy journalism write, 'From Living Doll to Living Legend? Rebel to Christian? Raunchy, Risqué Baby-Faced Rock 'n' Roller to Mature Balladeer.'

Or, of course, that one June day in 1966 he would stand next to American Billy Graham as he conducted a further series of revival meetings, this time at Earls Court. Or that he, the one-time Harry Webb, would bewail the ungodliness in British society.

Cliff did at least grow up aware of religion. It was through several members of his family and his group, the Shadows, that his dormant interest in Christian things wakened, so much so that at one point he considered joining the heretical Christian body who call themselves Jehovah's Witnesses. (They, of course, would deny any charge of hereticism and would call into question the beliefs of orthodox Christendom.)

Cliff's sister Jackie is a Jehovah's Witness. Donna almost became one. Cliff's mother was baptized into the movement. Within the Shadows interest in the movement came from Liquorice (Brian) Locking and then from Hank Marvin.

Hank says, 'I'd always been a fairly directionless person and didn't need a path but, like everyone else, sometimes I sit down and I wonder what I'm doing here. I always felt that life went on no matter what but that there had to be an answer to it all.

'Jehovah's gave me that answer . . . Jehovah's believe there are things that are totally wrong – they don't have the confusion most other Churches have.'

Cliff says, 'What attracted me to the Jehovah's Witnesses was Liquorice Locking leaving to join the movement. It made me think.

'And then there was the time when with the Shadows I was touring in Australia. Dad had died and I had this desire to make contact with him. I thought I would go to a spiritual séance.'

Liquorice thought he was making a mistake and said so clearly, and it was the way he explained his reason which made Cliff take notice.

He asked whether Cliff had ever bothered to find out what the Bible said about this. Cliff had not. He was then shown a number of Bible passages, some of which suggested dire consequences for those consulting mediums.

Not surprisingly, this discussion about spiritualism veered into general religious questions of belief. Informal Bible studies became frequent amongst the touring Shadows and Cliff. They were joined by some of Liquorice's friends. It was 1961.

Cliff was now an established international star. Outwardly he had everything which any kid who dreamed of fame and riches could imagine. Yet something was wrong. The *Daily Express* caught the scent of personal upheaval beneath the outwardly smiling pin-up pop star.

On 14 December 1964 they headlined: 'Cliff Richard Thinks About God'.

The *Express* staff reporter described Cliff standing near the gate of his £30,000 home in Nazeing, Essex and reported his saying, 'I am thinking about God. This is a very personal thing. It was Liquorice Locking who set me thinking. I am not considering joining the Jehovah's Witnesses. Do you know what that means? It means being baptized in the faith. No, at the moment, I'm just thinking a lot about God. That's all. It's very important to me.'

And with that Cliff drove off in his American car, ready for a day's filming on *Wonderful Life*.

'I became dissatisfied with things generally, and if you're upset in life, then it affects everything you do,' says Cliff. 'It was beginning to get me down. My whole career was affected.

'I spent two years with the Witnesses, listening to them. After a while I felt like I was a Jehovah's Witness but for some reason I held back from baptism.'

It was now that another group came on the scene. It began by accident. Towards the end of 1964 Cliff visited his old English teacher, Mrs Jay Norris. Cliff couldn't resist speaking about the Jehovah's Witnesses. Mrs Norris seemed unimpressed, though worried. She was a Roman Catholic whose ideas of God, Jesus and the Holy Spirit differed from the Witnesses'. She suggested Cliff should meet a bright young religious instruction teacher from her school. Cliff agreed and a meeting was arranged at his house.

Jay came, together with the religion teacher, Bill Latham, and a friend of his on the school staff, Graham Disbrey. Cliff was not convinced by their arguments but was impressed with them as people.

David Winter, in *New Singer, New Song*, recalls what Cliff said about his feelings that evening. 'They were the first real Christians I had met, talking about the real thing, appealing only to the Bible, but interested in me as a person, not a scalp.'

Jay invited Cliff to a party where he met Bill once more. The upshot was an invitation given by Bill and a nod of assent from Cliff. The world pop star said he would come and look at the Christian activities which took much of Bill's time.

What followed next almost lies in the bizarre and its very eccentricity speaks volumes for the genuineness of Cliff's later orthodox Christian commitment.

There are those who constantly, even now, suggest that Cliff's Christian interest is merely a promotional gimmick. If so they must ask themselves why it was that a pop millionaire with millions of fans across the globe should begin a so-called promotional con by spending days, even weeks, with a bunch of teenagers, learning from them and their leaders of Christian things.

Cliff recalls that his former mates were struck dumb with cold and awkwardness. It wasn't what they expected of a superstar. And the younger element – the people who bought his records and imagined from afar that he had all life's answers – what did they make of him drinking coffee from cardboard cups and sitting in a circle of intent Bible students?

Days and weeks stretched into months. Cliff had many questions needing answers. He had spent two years exploring the Jehovah's Witness faith within his own close circle of friends and it was most unlikely that he would commit himself without another thorough investigation. In any case, his busy, crowded career continued with its many engagements.

This time, though, there was a definite response. He had been appointed an assistant leader of his local church's branch of the Crusaders and when he could he would spend hours there with his new-found mates – schoolboys who had ceased wondering at the astounding fact that a pop and film star was around the place without expecting trumpets and fanfares.

Life was changing fast for Britain's long-lasting pop star. He took less and less interest in show business activities. He was noticed for his absence. He spent his time at Crusader meetings and sharing in their various social activities. David Winter says he even sang at St Paul's (his church) a version of 'Blowing In The Wind' and the older members hadn't a clue they were hearing someone who could fill stadiums as far away as the Far East, Australasia and the Americas. He recalls in his book how Cliff toured the local hospital wards at Christmas and one lady kindly remarked that he ought to take up singing full time.

In the sixties David Winter was a schoolteacher and a prominent member of St Paul's church long before he became a priest. He has always maintained a great personal friendship with Cliff.

'It was quite staggering really. Can you think of another star who was up to this kind of thing or anything remotely resembling it?

'Remember this was an artist who had done it all. Here he was, so casual, at the church with, if you like, ordinary folk; they didn't have to pay! He was so utterly genuine. It was quite remarkable. Don't mistake Cliff, he's a very determined person. He makes up his own mind.'

Cliff decided he would become a Christian. He felt he could say Jesus was his personal saviour. However, the scene was not yet right for the appearance of American evangelist, Dr Billy Graham. Cliff had heard the evangelist when he attended a Graham meeting incognito with his youth group. Like many Londoners at the time, they wanted to know just what made this famous evangelist tick.

Somehow this activity was missed by the press. They certainly did not miss out on the eventual public meeting between Billy and Cliff at Earls Court on the evening of 16 June 1966.

On that evening the 25-year-old pop star who was dressed casually and soberly in his brown corduroy jacket told 25,000 people, 'I have never had the opportunity to speak to an audience as big as this before but it is a great privilege to be able to tell so many people that I am a Christian.

'I can only say to people who are not Christians that until you have taken the step of asking Christ into your life, your life is not really worthwhile. It works – it works for me!'

After he had finished his testimony, which told of his new life and his commitment, Cliff sang the familiar gospel song of personal witness 'It Is No Secret' which has the added punchline of 'what God can do'.

Outside Earls Court countless thousands of fans had gathered but they had been unable to gain admission, for there were 'house full' signs everywhere. Cliff told them how he found Christian faith utterly relevant.

Though Cliff's past Christian explorations and expeditions had escaped much attention, the following morning's daily press and ensuing interest from weekly and monthly journals made up for it.

But not everyone had been caught napping. Maureen Cleave in London's *Evening Standard* had remarked in December 1965 how Cliff's friends were mostly teachers and were interested in religion. Cliff had told her of his own Christian base.

'It's a kind of way of life, it's a moral way of life. I've always tried to be a bit moral, a bit Christian and not ashamed of it.'

He spoke of reading the Bible nightly and of taking his Crusader group to Whipsnade, for trips in his Cadillac and for a week the previous April, sailing on the Norfolk Broads.

'It's a new way of life for me. I came into show business when I was seventeen and when you come in you lose your childhood immediately. I find all this specially fun because I never did youthful things.

'At the moment I feel dissatisfied. I don't get the same kick out of my life as I used to. I always said that if I didn't feel completely happy I would retire. I feel I could do more with my life.

'I would have to go to college for two years because I only got English Language in GCE but then I would be equipped to teach English and Religious Education.'

The night after the Earls Court meeting much of the press picked up on the observations Cliff had made to Maureen Cleave. They wondered aloud whether Cliff the pop star had run his course. They saw the end. They shouted of possible retirement. Cliff fans frothed at the mouth. It was dreadful news for them. They wrote pleading letters. They bombarded the music press with anguish.

The fans had cause to ponder and wonder and shed some tears. In the *Daily Express* of 20 September 1966 writer David Wigg said, 'It is now generally known that Cliff Richard wants to retire from show business and teach religion in a school. These days he regularly telephones his office to say which days he must have off for either religious studies or religious work of some kind.'

Cliff said, 'I have always believed in God and always prayed, but that doesn't make me a Christian. Being a Christian, to me, has been a step I didn't realize I had to take.

'I've enjoyed every second of show business but now I've found something else I would like to get into.'

He told journalist Rhona Churchill, 'I was thrilled to be invited to sing and give my testimony at Earls Court, thrilled by the size of the audience, but scared to death. You see I couldn't rehearse my testimony. If I had it might have sounded like an act. So I went forward knowing what I wanted to say but not how I would say it.

'I steadied myself by gripping the lectern. Then when I tried to move my arms I found I couldn't. I had pins and needles.

'At church one day someone said to me that if I wanted to be a real Christian, I must go to church, testify to my faith and set aside a fixed time every day for Bible reading and prayer, as they did.'

151

Rhona Churchill concluded her feature by saying, 'But his faith is real. It is no publicity stunt. He merely feels it's his duty to testify to it when asked to do so.'

Later, a few years on, Cliff had put behind him thoughts of giving up show business and becoming an RI teacher. 'I'd like to be a successful evangelist. I would love it. But I don't think I could make it, I am not a leader.

'Show business is the only thing I can do properly. It is certainly the only thing I've succeeded at. It's good for me – I can sing a bit, and act a bit, and in show business all I have to do is what I'm told.

'I make the most of my career to do Christian things. I'm not just a pop singer. I'm a Christian pop singer. I don't like the permissive society. I am not shocked by it, but as an individual I am allowed to show my distaste.

'Before I became a Christian who knows what I was heading towards, greed, sexual lust, who knows . . .'

*Reveille* magazine writer Jane Reid says she found Cliff at that time the epitome of the man mothers would like their daughters to marry. 'Handsome, gentlemanly, well groomed. To many young people Cliff is a bit of a square . . . Despite his religious fervour, Cliff must be one of Britain's most eligible bachelors.'

Cliff's association with Billy Graham led him into making the film *Two a Penny* for the Billy Graham Organization. It was not without immediate controversy.

'I didn't want paying. I saw it as an evangelistic effort. Union regulations compelled me to accept a fee, which I have returned to Dr Graham.

The fee was £40 per week for ten weeks. Billy was proud of Cliff. He talked of Paul McCartney and Cliff. Paul disturbed the evangelist by proclaiming he had taken LSD and that he had seen God through taking the hallucinatory drug.

Billy said, 'Cliff has found what I think Paul is looking for. My heart goes out to him. He has reached the top of his profession and now he is searching for the true purpose in life.'

Cliff's announced conversion led to numerous offers of Christian witness and work. For a brief period he appeared on television, arguing for his faith. In ABC TV's *Looking for Faith* series Cliff engaged in a dialogue with Paul Jones, former lead singer of Manfred Mann.

Jones said Cliff was letting himself be exploited by the Church. The programme itself had an opening sequence which stressed

Paul's point. Jones had been in the film *Privilege* where he had acted a pop star cynically manipulated by the Church. An excerpt from this film began the programme and this was cut into a shot of real-life Cliff singing a hymn at a Billy Graham meeting.

Intellectually it was an unfair situation. Paul Jones had been to university. Robert Kee, the interviewer, had a similar background and was regarded at the time as one of television's most knowledgeable and perceptive interviewers. And there was Cliff, bright and verbally cogent but with no training in the finer points of semantics and debate. As it was, he came through. His genuine witness won him respect, even if in the battle of words he did not win the final comment.

Cliff was a guest on a number of similar programmes. Some might have argued it was often placing him in invidious situations, particularly when he talked at universities and colleges where there was always someone who could outwit him in words. Yet he survived and there are those who maintain that whatever the situation Cliff's basic sincerity would always win through and make a lasting impression on many.

Magazine interviews were easier for Cliff to handle. There was a situation where he could plainly say how he felt without intellectual riposte coming his way. Indeed the Christian message was heard in all kinds of quarters where previously it might have been regarded at best as quaint but possessing no relevance to the teenage girl whose greatest concern was with cosmetics and clothing.

His diary soon read quite unlike that of any other pop star. There were the expected items like routining, recording, photographs, the occasional press interview, radio and television and basics from time to time, the doctor, dentist and hairdresser. Then there were evening meetings – showing that Cliff was making forays into churches, schools and youth gatherings. Somehow he managed to pursue a pop career and witness at the same time.

Soon came invitations to speak at a variety of meetings and adult conferences, his involvement with Tear Fund, and gospel tours where the proceeds went towards the named charity.

He recorded several albums and cassettes during the seventies where he sang or put across the Christian message. He took part in a Japanese religious crusade and earned from Mary Whitehouse the comment, 'In my view he is precisely the type of young Christian one wants to see.'

It was the kind of remark which, while approved by some, did little to enhance Cliff's standing in the rock world, where it's never been too fashionable to express Christian sentiments. Much more in keeping is the profession of faith in some obscure cult.

By and large Cliff has escaped criticism but there have been a few problems. Sometimes he has deliberately courted the angry riposte.

He had hard words for those he termed 'Gay Lib banshees' who disturbed religious meetings in London and Lancaster University.

'They came in camping about and screaming and there were almost fights. The public hated them. I really prayed hard and said, "Please, God, don't let this turn into a fiasco."

'I wrote to them and suggested we had a meeting on neutral ground and no publicity. I said they could bring twelve of their thinkers and I would bring six of mine. I approached some friends and a couple of Christian workers but never had a reply to the letter.

'Everybody knows homosexuals exist, but I don't think an honest homosexual wants to be known as gay for a start. The homosexuals I've met – and I haven't met hundreds of them – are different from the Gay Lib people who come crashing in dressed as nuns or something.

'Don't think those people who take pills or who smoke marijuana are being tough. That's not toughness. It's weakness.

'Pop stars should show a greater responsibility for what they say and do.'

Such comments brought verbal comebacks but Cliff seemed perfectly happy to deal with whatever came. Less easy to deal with was the carping from some extreme quarters of Christian evangelicalism.

The Christian monthly *Crusade* in its time carried some very bitter letters about the pop, gyrating Cliff.

For some Christians pop is anathema. It is the kingdom of the devil. They see its system perverting the minds of youth and encouraging immoral behaviour, leading to eventual destruction of the spirit. They see rock music as ungodly. They regard dancing as one step towards worship of the flesh.

These days Cliff is far better able than he was at the outset to deal with carving knives from within the camp. He takes it all with a shrug of his shoulders but admits it gives him no pleasure and at times causes him some distress. This is made worse in that generally his attackers are people who have never met him face to face and are not even prepared to declare their identities.

'You can only do what you feel is right and what they say doesn't add up to me,' Cliff says. 'I don't know what God has in mind for me in the future but at present I am sure I am doing His will where I am. I can only say, "Here is me, this is what I am", but really in the end what matters is how people respond to Jesus.

'Through being in the pop world I believe I've brought the Christian message to masses of people who otherwise would have heard nothing. And, of course, on a very practical level I've been in part responsible for founding and ensuring the success of the Arts Centre Group where Christians in the media can talk and pray together, compare notes and gain strength.

'I am constantly thrilled by the Christian faith, and what we offer. Christian faith doesn't depend on your emotions. It's a stable, solid factor. It gives us ground to feel confident and positive, whatever happens.

'What we have is a reality, there are roots in the Christian faith. You can't live up there on some high plane, you have to come down to reality and survive in the world as we know it. I'm worried by some young people who think everything must be high all the time and they get so down when they find you can't shout hallelujah all the time. You have to work for a living and so on.

'I'm not trying to be high and mighty but I mean it. I know what I believe. If some people feel I've sold out or whatever, then OK, they've sounded off but I'm confident.

'Some of the criticism comes because there are Christians who are genuinely frightened of all this media stuff. But I've used my career to further Christian things and books have been one of the recent means.'

Of course, meeting the criticisms of rock fans on the pop level is another thing, but since the album *I'm Nearly Famous* there has been a much more healthy regard for his music. He has become more contemporary and the sing-along days have to a great extent been pushed into the background.

Cliff frequently says he's a singer and that his whole object is providing entertainment. This attitude has resulted in the uncanny ability with which he has successfully courted up to five generations of fans. People come and they assume they will receive a wholesome show. It's not a sentiment which would necessarily be shared by the rock-orientated young. They expect some spice and a few verbal fireworks. They want the music and the presentation to give them a solid smack in the guts. And some expect their hero to take a definite political or social stance.

The Christian attitude to stage presentation does no more than expect the artist to be sincere and not misuse or exploit the audience for dubious ends; but as far as politics is concerned, a definite concern for society and the individual is an intrinsic part of the Christian faith. It may well be that if Cliff wishes to make a late major impact upon rock-orientated kids he must dig for radical roots in the Bible. Certainly, the evangelical Christian world is very conscious these days of social and political matters. It is true of an evangelist as persuasive and powerful as Billy Graham.

As it stands at the moment, Cliff will never capture rock adoration and commitment as John Lennon did. Cliff has never dug as deeply into the ways in which people respond both to themselves and the world at large. He may never trot out stirring sentences on major social issues but in the end that is his choice.

It seems churlish for some people to write off Cliff Richard as anaemic. Such criticisms are the product of condescending, spiteful minds. Cliff may not wax eloquent on racism or nuclear misuse but the time he gives to charity, the money which he donates to causes, is considerable. No other star of his stature devotes so much time to non-musical activities, and it is not totally his fault that he attracts some well-wishers who find scant sympathy among today's young people.

He has probably addressed more young people than any other Christian speaker of the past decade. Certainly his work is highly valued by Maurice Rowlandson, who leads the continuing ministry of the Billy Graham Organization in Britain.

'I've known Cliff now for a long time. He's matured a great deal over the years. There is no one like him. For many youngsters he is good news. My two said to me one day that since I knew Cliff, why couldn't I get him to the house one day? He kindly agreed. There was a whole crowd of youngsters. He came and he stayed an hour and a half and he had them totally spellbound. The answers he gave to the many questions asked were fabulous.

'His whole contribution has been fantastic. He's always been ready to do what we've asked. He's always kept close contact with Dr Graham and although they come from different generations they have a rapprochement. And there's been all this work he's done for Tear Fund. I said jokingly once to Billy, "You needn't come back, we've Cliff."'

It's an assessment shared by people like David Winter, who also observes quite rightly, 'Cliff is a professional in everything he does. He's never casual when it comes to work. Gospel concerts have never been an extra to his so-called secular activities. He spends days with a band, rehearsing those gospel programmes.'

Of course Cliff could easily stroll on stage with a guitar, serve up some three-chord magic, sing a few songs and, with a word of witness, depart. In fact, he spends hours perfecting those concerts. The only real difference between gospel and secular, according to many fans, is the informality of the former. He chats and talks rather than presents.

Billy Strachan is the principal of Capernwray Hall and is responsible with Cliff for one of the cassettes in the Scripture Union *Start the Day* series. Both were at Eurofest and Spree 73.

He is one of Cliff's admirers and says, 'People criticize the rock 'n' roll side of Cliff, but what have they got to offer in its place? You see, the people who say "We prefer the old hymns" little realize that when the hymns were written, they were in the music which was popular.

'So all Cliff is doing in the media is to satisfy what people want today. If you can't appreciate the new generation, don't enter it. You'll never satisfy everybody.

'Many Christians are critical of him but they don't know anything about him. Their criticism is from a distance, they don't know what he is achieving for Christianity because he never tells anybody, so they are wrong. They condemn a man without giving him a hearing, and just because he does not do exactly what they expect of him, to have their approval of him as a Christian or spiritual person, they don't give it.

'Then Cliff Richard, like any Christian, has to learn to leave it between himself and the Lord and not between himself and the churches, and I think he is doing that.

'I have observed in him a strength of character and Christian growth that is lacking in many people.

'Watching his various appearances on television, I find he never has to bring up his faith, they always bring it up, and he is very open and honest in his response to the commentators.'

Ron Palmer of the now defunct magazine *New Christian Music* said that Cliff is someone who sees his career as part of God's ordained plan for his life.

'It is clear that Cliff has a very healthy understanding of the

157

Bible, which he has been able to translate into a well-balanced view of life.

'He, in turn, has been an encouragement to others in similar situations to express their faith and to develop it within the crucible of their own professions.'

Cliff himself is reticent about accepting the praise heaped on his shoulders. 'What I really want is to be seen to actually be this Christian that I claim I am – not so that people will say "What a sincere bloke Cliff Richard is", but simply so that Jesus will be noticed. What other people think of me is becoming less and less important; what they think of Jesus because of me is critical.'

This is how he ends his book *Which One's Cliff?* On stage one evening for a gospel concert he said, 'No Christians own Jesus. He belongs to absolutely everyone – anybody who is willing to say, "Jesus, I know you're there. I would like you to come into my life."

'I didn't know how he was going to come into my life. I asked him to do it because I believed he could somehow. And he did. So it hurts, it upsets me sometimes when I meet people who know a great deal about Jesus, they know a great deal about the Church and yet somehow they just hold back. They hold back, because they will not step forward and say HELP – the magical word . . .'

He told us, 'My career comes second to Jesus. Nothing would really disappear if it all ended tomorrow. I don't think it *could* collapse, mind you, *that* quickly!

'No, it all depends on how you view life. I can survive without stardom. I like it but I have other things to do if it disappeared.

'I feel God is with me. If He said tomorrow that I should go and do something else, then I would, whatever the pain. I've no ultimate fears. I don't fear for my career.'

The cynic will give a wry smile. Others will shout hallelujah! Whatever the case all this makes him a pretty unusual star.

Oddly enough, when EMI Records researched for their *40 Golden Greats* Cliff Richard album they found that all groups spontaneously mentioned his Christian beliefs, and it was an aspect of which most people disapproved. Some males resented his 'preaching' attitude. It was felt that post-conversion he had a much 'safer' style in his singing.

In the meantime Cliff marches on and Billy is proud. Writing to me, after my request for an entry in the book *Survivor*, the great evangelist was hardly brief (although the printed comment was much reduced) in his effusive praise and thanks for Cliff's efforts.

In Europe, Cliff continues to support any Graham campaign (the last time was in 1989) and if he always hungered after real American music success, then Dr Graham may well reflect how his ministry would have assumed a much broader profile back home if he had a gigantic star on board.

Dr Graham was not the only major name who agreed to write a tribute to Cliff in *Survivor*. Among numerous others, there was Robert Runcie, former Archbishop of Canterbury and his successor Dr George Carey – evidence that Cliff remains well and truly within the Christian camp. While some pop stars with Christian convictions run scared from public pronouncements, accepting hysterical public relations advice that such associations might disturb their image and tone down their record career, Cliff has completed another decade of major Christian witness. It was startling that this stance did not find him a place in an otherwise excellent treatise on music and religion, *Hungry for Heaven* by Steve Turner (Virgin Books, 1989). For who else has made such an impact? And even a cursory glance at Cliff's stage repertoire and album tracking through the progression of the 1980s shows how closely the two worlds have merged. At one time he kept the secular and gospel tours very distinct but now the major arena shows see him talking about his faith, and the shows include overtly religious numbers and others where the allusion can be taken in a religious framework. To be sure, the gospel concert is what it is, and is naturally devoted to a public statement of his faith in Jesus, but the lines have blurred. In an interview, unless kept on tight rein, Cliff is always happy to talk about the faith that governs his life and ultimate happiness.

Yet, it is still amazing to find that there are Christians who doubt his ministry, and who constantly ask if Cliff is genuine. Some express disquiet with a logic that defies any reasonable explanation. Perhaps a book such as *Pop Goes The Gospel* by John Blanchard (Evangelical Press), which proved a bestseller in more rigid religious circles, might be blamed for its overall insistence that in Discland the devil reigns, and therefore it should be avoided.

Cliff, perhaps more than anyone, is quite aware that pop territory can be an unbridled expression of decadence, but then so can much elsewhere in the modern world, even down to the squalor and misery of many poor and neglected peoples and communities for whose wellbeing some Christians show not the slightest interest.

Some believe, cynically, this whole Cliff religious orientation is no more than a devious marketing exercise, and, above all, a means of extending his record sales. Does anyone seriously think a few album sales is commensurate with attending a variety of religious functions, or taking himself off to a school for an evening of question and answer? Bill Latham says, 'Cliff has become more confident in his faith. He doesn't hold his faith in some kind of know-all manner, rather it's being sure that God *is*. That God loves. No doubts here. It's reflected in his communication. It's allowed him to be more relaxed. And in a quiet way, he's become more involved.'

Latham has been the tower of strength behind Cliff's involvement in Christian matters ever since Cliff chose not to become a Jehovah's Witness like some of the Shadows and most of his immediate family. (His mother and sisters are still Jehovah's Witnesses.) Latham's involvement and commitment has often been underwritten, and he has remained, and accepted, the position of a background figure. Again, it has been Bill Latham, and to some degree a former director of Tear Fund, George Hoffman, who brought Cliff into an appreciation of the work of that charity to which Cliff has been a generous giver, as also he has helped to provide it with an excellent public image. It has been Latham who has transposed into book and booklet form many of Cliff's thoughts on religion. Prominent in the publishing field of the 1980s decade has been *You, Me and Jesus*, and *Which One's Cliff?*

*You, Me and Jesus* was published by the children's section of Hodder and Stoughton, since originally it seemed a good idea that Cliff might endorse a series of Bible stories. In the end, springing from Bill's questioning and greater sense of what could be achieved, it became a book of readings with Cliff adding explanation. They had in mind a teaching element that would push the book's intent beyond instant reading, although ensuring an element of humour. *Which One's Cliff?*, issued in several forms, and eventually replaced by *Single-minded*, took almost a year in preparation, with Cliff talking into a tape-recorder.

When the book was reprinted a small piece was added inviting those who might want to know more of the faith that Cliff accepted to write to the given address. Bill Latham says hundreds of letters were received; the sentiments and self-expression varied, and some respondents were at the end of their tether. They know that a number of these enquirers have become Christians. Obviously, Cliff has not been able to answer more than a few, leaving the work to those who understood his mind and that of young people, but the person who replies always says he or she is not Cliff, merely a good Christian friend. People are often directed to someone in their own locality who can help them. Cliff magazines, especially *Cliff United*, where Christine Whitehead, the editor, is a strong Christian, have often told of, and printed letters from, people who say Cliff's Christian writings and overall public witness have led them into accepting the Christian belief. Many converts have resulted from the Bill and Cliff chat shows that have taken place in many different circumstances, from business lunches to youth clubs. In this context Cliff usually sings some songs, with just his guitar playing as backing, and then joins in a discussion with Bill. Admittedly, Cliff is aware that Bill is hardly likely to throw a wobbly or toss in the unexpected question, but for all that their conversations usually have a lively, informal freshness. In any case, Cliff is now well able to hold his own against anyone, but for the most part this has been an extraordinary double-hander, one of the few communication teams in the field of Christian evangelism that talks and meets people far outside conventional religious terrain. More obviously, Cliff has carried the gospel into the expected arena, namely his own world of showbiz, in the dinners he gives, mostly under the auspices of the Arts Centre Group.

The 1980s, no less than the previous decade, saw Cliff participate in many gospel tours, with proceeds channelled into charitable areas. These events come under the direction of Bill Latham, and may be either short or extensive. Most years include one, and along with the worldwide tours, there are one-off events, not all large-scale. To take a few examples: Cliff was at the second Banquet in 1983. This pop-styled religious meeting, held at Wembley arena, brought together many of the more youth-orientated speakers and singers. Cliff appeared on Sunday 30 May, when with Sheila Walsh he sang 'Drifting', her single which he co-produced. His association with Sheila led to both being on the Radio 1 *Newsbeat* programme during the same month. Oddly, the presenter described the Scottish singer as a comparative newcomer in the UK but well established in the gospel circles of the United States. Cliff mentioned that Sheila had supported him on his last gospel tour and that for both of them the word that summed up everything was Rockspell, 'because it conjures up everything we want to say. We don't know how to do anything else except rock and roll, it is all I have ever known and loved all my musical life, and to combine your message, which is a Christian one, with the music that you make turns it into Rockspell, but it is no different from any other kind of music. It is just that we are far more positive about our approach to life, and therefore our messages are more positive.'

During 1983 he also performed in a Youth for Christ tour in Europe, taking with him, as he has on other occasions, Garth Hewitt, a talented singer-songwriter, who opened the proceedings. Cliff started his set with 'Why Should The Devil Have All The Good Music?', 'Where Do We Go From Here? preceded some humorous chat, largely centred around foreign language pronunciation for this particular evening in Brussels. He then sang the first gospel song that he had ever written, 'Of A God', a ballad, prefacing it by reminiscing how he used to wonder if his new-found faith would last but how, in those early days in the 1960s, he found enormous support from Christian friends. The song 'Lord, I Love You' came next and Cliff expressed how he felt he had received so much from God. The flow of gospel material was interrupted by his announcement that in the UK his record 'True Love Ways' had reached number eight in the charts, and so he sang it. He went on to explain that he would not be present if it were not for his faith that Jesus is alive today. A medley followed: 'Yes, He Lives', 'Up In Canada', 'Be In Heart', 'Whispering My Love', 'I Wish We'd All Been Ready' and 'The Rock That Does Not Roll'. He would also sing 'How Great Thou Art', with the audience joining in on the refrain. He posed the question 'Would you be ready to face him?' (Christ) answering, 'I know I could face him, if he came in ten minutes from now!' There would be an encore of 'When I Survey The Wondrous Cross', a hymn that he has sung many times, and with such depth.

The same year saw Cliff at Greenbelt. It was good that while he celebrated the silver jubilee of his career, he also underlined importance of his faith to all aspects of his life. He was interviewed for *Strait* by Stewart Henderson, the journal associated with this August Bank Holiday event. This event became the major festival of that holiday, although the media were obsessed with the Reading Rock Festival, held annually on that weekend, but without equivalent numbers.

Arguably, this interview is one of his best to be found in print, and it appeared in *Strait*, issue 7, ranking along with two consecutive interviews in *Hot Press*, the Irish rock paper, volume 14, issues 3 and 4. In answer to questions, the 42-year-old Cliff spoke of his total commitment, both to music and faith. In answer to a question from Henderson, he talked of areas of general music that he found uncomfortable, the trends he had found most disturbing and specifically anti-Christian during his career span.

He said he thought of the whole flower power era as nothing more than a subtle breaking down of true spiritual values. 'There was a fake spirituality which moved into the whole humanistic area . . . what we should have been saying was that all we needed was God's love to show us how to truly love one another.' He did not issue a blanket condemnation since he admitted there had been a degree of good intention, reserving his strongest approbriums for certain aspects of the punk movement. 'There were these guys of eighteen or nineteen screaming about things in such a childish way . . . let's do our own thing and kick the next guy. Doing just what pleases you.' When Henderson enquired if he thought any bands reached some semblance of maturity and had something creative on offer, Cliff named Squeeze and Police.

Was Cliff a charismatic? After all, he spent time in circles that encouraged this mode of religious expression. He answered no, yet felt he liked being amongst it, and admitted that he got more from a charismatic service than more staid congregations. When Henderson wondered how he maintained some form of spiritual discipline, Cliff talked of 'my Bible reading every single night' but admitted 'there is a danger when some nights I find it hard to take in because I get so tired'.

As people know from his perceptive poetry, Henderson pulls no punches, and in his interview with Cliff, he produced an unexpected question: 'How would you answer those critics who say that some of your stage shows, especially those with gyrating disco dancers, female, are not just entertainment but acceptable carnality, that you're paying lip service to the titillating spirit of the age?' It nonplussed Cliff momentarily, and his first words were, 'I can't really answer.' He thought first and foremost that Christians hadn't really sorted things out when it came to apparently sexual expressions. He mentioned how Sue Barker had been pictured in *Woman* magazine covered head to toe in a body stocking, and this had upset some Christians. But he liked to feel that his dancers were not playing on their sexuality, and he spoke approvingly of an American review that talked of the asexuality of his show. The dance element was raised again when Cliff talked of not minding being on the then very popular Kenny Everett TV show. The Everett show had the rather raunchy dance

163

group Hot Gossip, and Cliff said, 'I would not have Hot Gossip, definitely not [on a show of his], because what they are out to do is to sexually titillate. The thing I have to admit is they are not hacks, they are brilliant dancers, certainly misguided.' He even saw Everett as misguided but 'he's so hysterically funny when he's not being blue'. For Cliff, it was worth asking 'How do we affect people for good unless we're there, being salt in a very grubby area?'

The *Hot Press* interviews, while they concentrated on Cliff's religious views, also sought his opinion on feminist approaches to his music, and feminism as a subject in itself. There was, apparently, loud laughter from Cliff when it was suggested that the reason why he was not married lay with his inability to commit himself because he was either too immature or too much in love with himself. In this interview, one of countless excellent features by Joe Jackson, Cliff was asked for a response to the remarks made by the editor of the *NME* that most of his readers would see Cliff as a wimp, or a form of soul-brother to the Christian Mary Whitehouse. Cliff said, 'Back in the sixties they wanted to believe that Mary Whitehouse was idiotic, whereas in point of fact she was prophetic.' He dismissed the description of himself as a wimp, and defended himself as someone who had beliefs. Cliff told Jackson that he could be as tough and forthcoming in his views as anyone else and still be a Christian. In the 1990 *Hot Press* interviews Cliff said he was 100 per cent led by Jesus. He also spoke of his respect for Margaret Thatcher, then the British Prime Minister, and did so again in an interview for *21st Century Christian*. His political views and allegiances have stunned many Christians of more overt social stances, although others, such as Cindy Kent, herself an admirer of Mrs Thatcher, have applauded his courage in being so outspoken in his appreciation. Speaking of his frustration with the problems in Northern Ireland, he both deplored inhumane killing and the complexity of the overall situation. He ended the first printed interview by stressing the concepts of world peace, love and Christian ideals, and asked, 'They can't be wrong, can they?'

In 1985 Cliff attended the celebration service for David Watson that was held a little over a year after his death from cancer at the age of fifty-one. As Christine Whitehead reported in *Cliff United*, it was surely what the speaker-evangelist would have wanted. 'We reflected, laughed, sang, we were entertained, and we worshipped, in the presence of the Lord Jesus – we remembered and we rejoiced!' One of Cliff's musical associates, Dave Cook, played a song he had written, entitled 'Better Than I Know Myself'. Cliff was heard humming along in the front row. When he took the spotlight, he talked of his appreciation for David and sang 'The Rock That Doesn't Roll'. He talked of how one member of his band, John Perry, had become a Christian and sang John's lovely ballad, 'Be In My Heart', followed up with 'Where Are You?'

In the early part of 1989 Cliff was in New Zealand and, among other events aimed at raising money for Tear Fund, did two chat shows. He sang nine songs, accompanying himself on an amplified acoustic guitar. Bill Latham was joined in the question-and-answer session by the New Zealand Youth for Christ director, Ian Grant. The wide-ranging session covered Cliff's Christian beliefs and his fifteen-year involvement with Tear Fund, of which he had been British vice-president since 1982. There was also a series of questions, previously submitted to him, including whether he had had plastic surgery (answer: no), ever been given a speeding ticket (answer: once) and whether rock is permeated by satanic spirits (answer: neutral).

In the concluding remarks Bill said it must be obvious to all who had attended that Cliff spoke with a tremendous enthusiasm about his faith, and he asked him to say why this was so. Cliff talked of how he had come to faith twenty-three years before, and that in Jesus he had found absolute truth, that he was amazed, and pleasurably so, that Jesus still affected the lives of tens of thousands of people in a deep and personal way, 'even a rock 'n' roller like me'.

One of his shorter appearances was at the Royal Albert Hall, London, on 3 January 1992, when he lent his support to the two evenings organized by Dave Pope's Saltmine Trust which, beneath the title Fan the Flame, centred on the potential for mission in Europe. For these evenings, Cliff sported Cuban-heeled boots, a multi-coloured shirt and a stone-coloured suit. After singing 'Saviour's Day', he spoke of his unease at the suffering of so many during the transformation of Eastern Europe, and of the lack of Bibles and books in Christian countries that had suffered under Communist rule. He said he thought few people in the West realized how fortunate they were with all their possessions. After singing 'Love And A Helping Hand', he talked a little with Dave Pope, mentioning the variety he had in his life, which included tennis and *Top Of The Pops*. Someone wheeled a phone on stage and, being told the call was for him, Cliff found himself engaged in a conversation with Paul, the pastor of the church Cliff visits when he takes a break in Portugal. We learnt that the congregation had grown from sixty to about 150. As it happened, the whole Portugal phone-line was a charade for suddenly Paul and his wife, Madeleine, came on stage to the bemusement of Cliff. His quick wit enabled him to respond 'This is a bit like *This Is Your Life*, and this is why you'll never find me on it!' Cliff's last song was 'Flesh And Blood'.

Of course, Cliff's Christian witness has been far beyond circumscribed events: it can happen, for instance, even at one of the now so well-established pro-celebrity tennis tournaments. On 17 December 1989 the Salvation Army took the court, after a rather languid, below-form appearance from Cliff, who had perhaps not been able to put in his usually serious practice sessions beforehand, due to his thirtieth anniversary tour and a number one single. The tennis players joined the audience and band in singing the traditional, loved Christmas-time hymns, 'O Come, All Ye Faithful', and 'Hark! the Herald Angels Sing'. Jimmy Tarbuck, who had been one of the tennis players, briefly joined for 'Move It' before, more sensibly, it was back to seasonal song with 'Another Christmas Day'. Mike Read joined Cliff for 'Silent Night' and proved a most capable singer. A solo, 'Little Town' from Cliff, followed before there were thanks to everyone. And last not least – it had to happen – Cliff sang the number one single, 'Mistletoe And Wine'.

Apart from the now more obvious Christian sentiments finding their way into the stage shows, and sometimes general charts, Cliff has made a number of religious albums, gathered together by Word UK, under licence from EMI. In 1986 came the release of *Hymns and Inspirational Songs*, on which Cliff sang familiar and mostly traditional hymns reverently, with no attempt to modernise them. He says of 'What A Friend We Have In Jesus', 'It's the song I identified with when I first started looking towards Christianity. This fantastic hymn states very simply the basic truth of the relationship we have in Jesus.' In addition to the familiar songs found in most Christian hymn and song books, the album contained numbers such as 'Higher Ground', 'Day by Day', and several spirituals, often given a bluesy feel, including 'Just A Closer Walk With Thee' and 'Take My Hand, Precious Lord'. He saw 'Just A Closer Walk With Thee' as the perfect expression of the personal relationship one can have in Jesus.

This chapter can never hope to cover more than a tiny portion of the Cliff 'Christian' involvement but hopefully it will put to rest (some hopes!) the nonsense that Cliff Richard is no more than a Christian fraudster.

As he says, when speaking about 'Take My Hand, Precious Lord', 'Today, I no longer feel as though I'm singing about a "second hand" experience. Now, quite genuinely, I can give it "heart and soul".'

## CHAPTER FOURTEEN

# THE NEW COLUMBUS

Some of the natives were anything but friendly when Cliff Richard arrived in the United States late in February 1981 to try once more to conquer the New World – his last frontier.

His first attempt in 1960 had been, as we have seen, something of a hurried, slapdash rock 'n' roll tour featuring a bunch of recording stars among whom Cliff was a mere fledgling. He was included because 'Living Doll' was beginning to bite in America.

Since then he has made several promotional visits to the States, but not until 1981 did he return to the challenge and set forth to tour again with the hope of winning what was for him virtually uncharted territory.

It was a different story this time. There was nothing hasty about the preparation. The much-experienced Peter Gormley, in his usual wisdom, had gone ahead to smooth the path. This time it would be Cliff's own show plus a few supporting acts. There would be six highly competent musicians behind him and a trio of professional back-up voices.

Three successful Cliff Richard recordings which had found their way into the charts had ensured that a lot of North Americans knew the name and no doubt would like to see Cliff in the flesh. ('Devil Woman' alone had sold 1,300,000 copies in America – without even reaching number one. Its highest placing was fifth.)

It would be a lengthy visit of seven weeks with thirty-five concerts scheduled in a coast-to-coast venture taking in Canada.

The party flew out from England on 27 February after long days of rehearsal at Shepperton Studios and made landfall in Los Angeles where, before the tour wagon could even begin to roll, some West Coast natives went into the attack.

A lorry loaded with £40,000-worth of Cliff's equipment – guitars, keyboards, sound gear – was spirited away by thieves from outside his hotel in Hollywood. The haul included three of his favourite guitars.

It was a hit below the belt that shook every one on the touring party. The opening date in Seattle was only three days away. What was the point in trying to carry on?

Said Cliff, 'The temptation was to say "to hell with it". But then an inner voice – that of God – told me, "Cliff, you have to do it. You have a responsibility."'

That the thieves showed something of a sense of humour was little comfort. They left behind a note that said – in typical Californian fashion – 'Have a nice day!'

Cliff and company recovered and hustled around, buying or hiring new equipment. By the time they reached the east coast early in April, with several successful concerts now behind them, they were in good cheer.

'Everything's going well,' David Bryce, Cliff's Man Friday and lighting expert, told me when they arrived in New York. 'But nothing has been seen of the truck,' he added, 'and chances are that we'll never see it again.'

Saved was Cliff's stage wardrobe – much of it leather – and there was no repetition of the 1960 foray when he landed in the States with only the one white stage suit.

After the initial shock of the robbery, the party had set off undaunted for Seattle on the first leg of the tour.

The theatre was only something like half full for this opening shot in the campaign to conquer America. Nevertheless, 1,200 young people had handed over their money to see this new Columbus of rock 'n' roll looking much younger than his forty years.

They screamed and squealed like the fans of yesteryear and Cliff was both grateful and somewhat amazed by the size of the audience. He had genuinely not expected that many to buy tickets.

Modest, as always, he told me when he reached New York, 'I wouldn't have been surprised if nobody had turned up. I'm not known here. It has been like starting again, going back to square one and all those years ago.'

At this stage of the tour he had given three concerts in the States and worked his way from west to east across Canada.

The excursion was showing definite signs of success.

'The reaction has been fantastic,' he told me, 'and the reception better than we ever dreamed of. The audiences have been alive and vibrant. I'm staggered.'

He particularly recalled the one-nighter in the Chester Fritz Auditorium at Grand Forks, North Dakota. 'The reception was so deafening that the band were sticking their fingers in their ears!'

One of the songs that had audiences screaming for more was 'Move It'. Strangely, it had been omitted during the abortive attempt to capture North America on the 1960 tour. Wrote a Canadian critic, reviewing one of the 1981 concerts, 'A version of his very first record, "Move It", almost sounded like it could have been written this year . . .' And it was noted in Canada, where Cliff is certainly better known than he is in the United States, that audiences ranged 'from teeny-bopper to grandmother'.

There were those present as well who knew what they wanted of Cliff. 'One fellow kept calling out "sing 'Lucky Lips'!" Right, I said to myself, if he calls it out once more we'll have to do it. He did. There was no music and the band had to busk it.' Proving that the customer is always right. He pays his money and is entitled to make his choice, it seems. The object of the tour was not, however, to return home with sackloads of dollars.

Cliff felt from the start that financially it would be a failure and anyway, he said, he didn't need money. What he needed most was to be recognized as a true star of rock 'n' roll in America – its birthplace. 'It's something I want badly,' he said. It was an ambition that he had achieved almost everywhere else in the world.

The party travelled from venue to venue in a luxury bus or, where distance demanded, by chartered aircraft.

'The bus was very comfortable,' David Bryce reported. 'We had video aboard and could watch concerts or movies.'

Headlines in the Canadian newspapers reflected the ecstatic reception given to Cliff wherever the tour bus halted. Some typical examples: 'Reception proves Richard still rock's most durable icon.' 'Cliff wows 'em.' 'Pop's perfect prince.'

But still there was the odd snag, such as industrial trouble reaching out to reduce the shine a little, as the *Vancouver Sun*'s music critic, Fiona McQuarrie, wrote: 'Cliff Richard's latest album may be called *I'm No Hero*, but you would have a hard time convincing the devotees who came to see him Thursday night. It was Richard's first ever Vancouver appearance, in a career that's covered almost twenty-three years, and although the show concentrated on his more recent material, it was slick enough and clean enough to satisfy fans of every age.

'The show was switched from the strikebound Queen Elizabeth Theatre to the Italian Cultural Centre; the big losers, besides the audience members at the back who had to crane their necks to see anything, were Richard and his band. Ten musicians were crammed into an area the size of your standard high school gym stage. One could imagine only too well how stunning the skilful lighting and effects would have been in a proper theatre.

'Richard, who at forty doesn't look a day over twenty, is a spirited singer who infuses finely crafted pop songs with feeling and life. At times, his dramatic poses and karate movements become hammy, but generally Richard puts his songs across sincerely.

'Where he really shone, though, was in his departure from the pop fare. He went back into the mists of time for a driving version of his first hit, 1958's "Move It", and he obviously enjoyed performing two gospel rock numbers. "Why Should The Devil Have All The Good Music" (by gospel rock pioneer Larry Norman) and "The Rock That Doesn't Roll".

'Richard is a professional who knows how to pace a show and how to present a song, but if all his material was performed with the joyous energy that he puts into his gospel rock numbers, he would be truly outstanding.'

In the *Winnipeg Free Press*, critic Glen Gore-Smith certainly backed up Cliff's description of his reception as fantastic. 'You could almost call it Richard-mania,' the writer reported.

'The Centennial Concert Hall stage wasn't stormed by swarms of screaming, barely nubile bodies, but Richard's fans skirted the outer edges of Beatle-era madness.

'Just about everything Richard did touched off a ringing hallful of applause, hoarse shouts, stomping feet, and the kind of screeches and screams that rock 'n' roll fans supposedly deposited in a time vault along with video tapes of the Ed Sullivan Show.

'Fans didn't want the British superstar to quit the stage, even after four standing, leaping ovations had exhausted his current repertoire.

'Cliff Richard was legend in the UK before the Beatles started playing the Cavern, and he's managed to ride out the Fab Four, folk rock, art rock, heavy metal, punk and new wave.

'Richard stands virtually alone as a first-generation rocker who hasn't become a relic, and last night, he showed why he is pop music's most durable icon . . .

'Richard's stage savvy was evident in special effects, like rolling colored fog banks spilling off the stage, sci-fi and Vegas touches with a glitterball, and in his unerring control of body language . . .

'Cliff Richard has lived on the edge of North American superstardom, for two decades. Judging by the reception here last night, it would appear that he is close to conquering his final frontier.'

Then there was the critic who could only accuse him of being too good!

'Watching Richard in concert,' he wrote, 'is more like an ITV Celebrity Concert than a typical pop show. Every turn is calculated for effect. Every phrase his six-piece band and his trio of back-up vocalists add has been measured and remeasured, until the final tracking is perfect . . .'

Observed Cliff, 'If that is the worst thing anybody can find to say about us this is going to be a great tour!'

Like his Canadian concerts, his New York appearance at the Savoy, a former Broadway theatre that has been turned into a 1,000-seater club something like London's Talk of the Town, was a sell-out.

Not only the box-office take impressed him. He was the first star to perform there following the completion of its transformation.

'It was a great honour opening it,' he told me.

There is no doubt that Cliff was pleasantly surprised at the warmth he generated during this most recent tilt at America.

Even the natives of Los Angeles eventually demonstrated how friendly they could really be. When the box office opened for bookings for the last concert of the tour there on 18 April the queue stretched round the block.

The new Columbus had arrived at last, or so it seemed, considering the apparent enthusiasm from major American cities on both west and east coasts.

And even the British fans had decided this was his time to take the world's biggest and most influential record market by storm, for some forty of them travelled around 5,000 miles to see him perform in Denver, and then at the Los Angeles evening. The visit had been arranged through the London *Daily Mirror* pop club. Not long after 8.00 p.m. on 14 April 1981 he took the stage at the Rainbow Music Hall and began with 'Son Of Thunder', followed by 'Monday Thru Friday', and then 'Dreamin'', 'When Two Worlds Drift Apart' and the 1979 album title song, 'Green Light'. He reached back to very early times particularly in a walk popularized by the Shadows and now given expression by the combination of Cliff and guitarist, Martin Jenner. He sang his version of 'Heartbreak Hotel' and recalled when he was first starting out and Elvis was his hero. And, of course, when he had toured the States in the early 1960s he and the Shadows had visited Elvis's Graceland home in Memphis but, alas, the King was out of town, filming in Los Angeles.

It was in Denver that he told listeners to television channel 2 that he found the current attempt to storm the US a more pleasurable experience than former occasions. He commented, 'It's really nice to be able to come over, have the security of a career already in the rest of the world and just come over and say, "Do you like me? If not I'll go home and work somewhere else."'

He talked about his visits to the States in 1960 and 1962, a long time back, and how he had died a death but in 1981 he was in the States with five recent hit singles behind him, although in America even that was no guarantee of coast-to-coast fame. Wise words – but he had the Los Angeles triumph to come, and certainly he took the audience at the Civic Auditorium in Santa Monica by storm. Before some 3,000 people he appeared resplendent in red satin jacket and black trousers and shirt, and, while the programme was the same, the fans saw him perform against a different backcloth, especially in the greater drama of its lighting. Perhaps some of the enthusiasm was misleading, for Los Angeles is known for its expatriate community and many were there for his show, including Susan George and an old mate from early Shadows' time, John Farrar.

He returned to the States in 1982, with the focus this time centred on two Los Angeles concerts held on 15 and 16 March with almost all tickets disappearing before the official ticket sale date. These events were attended by numerous American celebrities including Jim Stafford, Phil Everly, Kim Carnes, Rick Springfield and Cliff's friend from the contemporary Christian scene, Larry Norman. By now he was into his eighth US hit, 'Daddy's Home', a song featured on this occasion. It also found its way into his guest appearance on the television show *Solid Gold*. He also sang a rock version of 'Dreamin''. Also, Cliff had a short comedy routine with a puppet called Madam.

Dixie Gonzales, a former president of the Cliff Richard Movement in the USA saw this visit as proof that Cliff had part-way conquered America, and certainly he was willing to claim with some exuberance that 'the city of Los Angeles has surrendered her heart to him already!' But with no disrespect to America's most ardent Cliff fan and worker, it had not been quite such a triumph. Perhaps it might have been if Cliff had decided to stay in the States and risk punishing himself with an extensive tour, but this was not in his reckoning. He had many other pressing engagements around the world which he would have had to cancel.

On 1 August 1985 Cliff made another of his rare appearances in the USA to support Sheila Walsh. The two performed at Praise In The Rockies – a Christian artists' music seminar – on the Thursday evening of this week-long event, which drew many of America's leading Jesus Music artists. Sheila opened her set by singing 'Light Across The World' with Cliff on back-ups, as he was for 'Under The Gun'. After being properly introduced, he duetted with Sheila on 'Jesus, Call Your Lamb'. Unfortunately he was still suffering from the viral laryngitis that had caused havoc with his planned programme in England. With some humour, Cliff told the amused audience, 'My voice does sound stranger and stranger as I speak, but if necessary, I shall *recite* it.' However, he did sing 'Lord, I Love', accompanying himself on acoustic guitar. And not even his vocal problems prevented him from giving a rousing version of 'Why Should The Devil Have All The Good Music' before lending more back-ups as Sheila performed 'Triumph In The Air', and the two duetted on 'We're All One', the lovely Bryn Haworth rhythmic number.

Conversations with various US critics and industry figures over the years suggest that he should have based himself in America if he was to achieve his long-held ambition. Of course, it is easier said than done, and the expense would have been high, even horrendous. Cliff rested his hopes on more hit records and an increasing penetration of the market, accompanied not only by successful singles but best-selling albums. That he deserved this few would question, even if they are hardly fans. In 1988 *Billboard* writer Steve Gett told me that he considered six months' constant US public appearances and concerts the barest mandatory stay for an artist interested in succeeding in America.

However, America would not go away, even if it was only a gospel tour, which seemed possible in 1987 or the following year. But early in the autumn of 1987 Bill Latham hit hard on reality in saying that Cliff was not well known in America. He stressed the enormous cost of transporting the entourage across the waters, admitted that Cliff needed more US hits, and that the early momentum seen towards the end of the previous decade and into the 1980s had all but disappeared. It seemed hardly likely that hard-bitten US promoters would bother with someone who was not riding high in the current scene. Polydor had issued 'All I Ask Of You'.

Still, Cliff didn't entirely forsake North America: on 28 and 29 January 1991 he spent two days in Toronto, Canada, promoting the *From A Distance* album. For someone with few recent hits he did well in the media stakes, appearing on numerous radio and TV chat shows. During his CTV visit he was reported to say that he had no qualms about coming back and touring Canada but he was aware of the high costs. He was well primed in the non-starting element in Canada of his recent UK happenings. The *Stronger* album never appeared either in the US or Canada, although the title track charted to 16 in the US disco listing. He told the Canadians that he had contacted his record company to ask why he was not being given a vital push and 'I got this message back saying that the record company in America was not really excited about my material. So I thought to myself, "Well, I can't fight the competition as well as my own record company."' As he put it succinctly, 'I have to fight and find my way to another label, because I don't think I'm going to get any help from EMI America.' Cliff rarely issues critical statements in public, but on this occasion something snapped. He was very much to the point in saying a little later, 'The work of the company is to present the album and get the album in the charts. I actually had an album called *I'm No Hero*, from which I had *three* top thirty singles, and the album didn't break the hundred.' He thought that if this has happened to Elton John no one would have believed it, yet 'it happened to me'. He changed his record company, albeit sadly since his association with EMI had been worldwide, and had begun in those far-off days of 1958. But even that change produced little, except one top ten on Rocket, the excellent 'We Don't Talk Anymore'.

Since the record world is so unpredictable it's always possible that even a 52-year-old can make an impact in the States, but it seems unlikely. Cliff may find another single success with a classic number but as his run of hits showed, it is no guarantee in such a large record market that success would be anything more than momentary. Yet it seems sad that Britain's giant of a pop artist should be denied the recognition that has come the way of Sting, Bowie or Jagger. Erudite music critics might find reasons why they have succeeded rather than Cliff. They may point to those and other major British acts possessing a particular quirk or style, a difference, an appeal to something other than a bubble-gum buying market. There is truth in such observations but in the end such views presume that Cliff must be seen as a singles artist, rather than someone who delivers depth albums, and who, given the chance, could be as weighty as any. Indeed, numerous conversations with Cliff over the years always seem to include some reference to his despair that some music critics never really listen to what he does on an album. Arguably, Cliff has sometimes not 'sold' his albums because he has spent much of his show time recalling the hits fans want to hear rather than saying to them, 'Well, yes, fine, but this is me now, and the past has its place but not now when I'm promoting my new album.' And he has given the impression that he is a singles artist, albeit with a performance none can better in British chart music history.

In the end the only satisfactory reason for Cliff's apparent lack of major success in America – meaning, for example, top ten albums fetching a few million sales apiece – lies in the already stated view that if he wanted US fame then he should have taken off to the States, and delivered a total commitment. Some artists have done this and found to their cost that the home base has disappeared by the time they have returned, sometimes with no US response; others have not had a negative response. It seems a question and a problem that will occupy Cliff in old age when he has time to ponder the missing elements in what otherwise has been a fabulous career, and which has taken most of the world's applause in a way few other artists have achieved.

Still, it would be pleasant to find all this disproved if one day he takes his deserved crown of number one in Britain and America simultaneously, on single and album format! For in the end, even taking into account all the reasons that may be put forward for establishing why he has not been the new (music) Columbus, there is no conclusive answer. He may be a giant in British music history but in the US he means little. That, sadly is it.

# CHAPTER FIFTEEN

# TWENTY-FIVE AGAIN

The year 1983 will be remembered by Renee and Renato, Phil Collins, Men At Work, Michael Jackson, David Bowie and Bonnie Tyler, for they were among the artists who topped the chart, and others, such as Bucks Fizz, Ultravox, Fun Boy Three and Duran Duran, will also have their fond memories. Golden-oldie programmes keep some of these names alive, while, of course, several are still prominent. For Cliff and his fans, however, all pales into insignificance compared with a single event: 1983 was the year of Cliff's silver jubilee, his amazing twenty-fifth year in the music business.

Cliff was still creating music in 1983 – not for him the role of a desperate 'look back' soul vainly trying to relive the past. By now he was heavily into tennis, thanks to Sue Barker, and having at least six hours' thrash a week on court. Admittedly, it seemed then that it was what he termed 'pat-a-cake stuff', but this was hardly so by the end of the 1980s. By then he had become a useful player and was devoting energy into finding youthful talent. He was still finding Christian faith an adventure, and telling people that their concept of God was too small. But contact lenses were still uncomfortable – and Cliff has often walked on stage without, risking a fall into the orchestra pit.

Nineteen eighty-three saw a carry-over from the previous year of his charming reworking of the Christmas favourite, 'O Little Town Of Bethlehem', the moving 'True Love Ways', the more pacey 'Never Say Die (Give A Little Bit More)' and for the Christmas market, 'Please Don't Fall In Love'. There were two hit albums, namely *Dressed For the Occasion*, and, of course, the record that would be expected for such an important anniversary, and with the right title, *Silver*.

It was certainly not a year for waiting around until the anniversary date. Cliff was in South-East Asia twice, for there, as elsewhere, people wanted to congratulate him. He went to Australia and was presented by the Australian fan club with a silver watch, the face of which bore the inscription 'Cliff Richard – Silver Jubilee – 1958 to 1983'. He produced material for Sheila Walsh at Rick Parfitt's studio in Surrey, and there was also much gospel activity, with support for Youth For Christ in Gothenborg, Sweden. He took John Perry with him, and said goodbye with 'How Great Thou Art' before an encore with 'When I Survey The Wondrous Cross'.

But how did Cliff see himself in 1983? Sue Barker was very much in his mind, and so, too, was the press treatment he had received. He admitted, 'I shared things with the press that I shouldn't have shared. In future, I'm not gonna say much.' It wasn't so much the speculation but the misreporting of which he despaired. 'Why don't they just tell the truth? With the press, the guy asks a question, and one gives an answer, and yet one reads it, and it's different.'

He also wanted to make the anniversary year something special, and although he was thrilled to renew friendships in areas already mentioned, he said, 'It's in England I'll be celebrating most, so I'm gonna do a monstrous tour that will start up in Scotland and bring us right down into the North, the Midlands, then I'll do a month in London.' He instanced the high drama content of a show that starred David Bowie and Kate Bush. Speaking of his own performances, he added, 'I've brought a little bit of drama into my set but I still do basically a concert with a little drama thrown in. I'd like to do a show where I go in and record a hit album as the musical. And I don't see why that shouldn't happen.'

It is still a mystery why Cliff has for the most part neglected the thematic album. Arguably, on this level, his best album is the underrated *The 31st Of February Street*. (Bill Latham would choose *Stronger Than That* as his favourite.) This 1974 album rode free from the collection of rock-pop-religious material that pervades most of the other sets, although many of these are some of the best in pop terms, especially in the 1970s *I'm Nearly Famous*. It would be true to say that, overall, Cliff has kept on improving without, as some of us see it, really producing the great one that could stop the music world, and even bring him a top five US album seller.

His silver year did not pass without a little controversy. During May, the Consumers' Association in Holland protested at a concert he gave on 26 April in the Sportpaleis Ahoy in Rotterdam. This was one of his Rockspell events, but some people thought it was going to be a major pop concert, and were unaware of its promotion by Sportpaleis and Youth for Christ. Both were sued and on 20 May, Mr Niek van Exel, managing director of Youth for Christ, said money would be refunded to those who complained that 'reborn' Cliff had only sung religious songs.

The great moments of the anniversary year came in late summer, spread into the early winter months, not to be pushed out of the way until Christmas. In celebrating twenty-five years the International Cliff Richard Movement headlined *Dynamite International*: 'CLIFF RICHARD – 25 YEARS ON AND STILL MOVING IT.' Said its writer, Sue Russell, 'He's never thrown TV sets out of the window, smeared walls with jam, got involved with drugs – or done any of the things usually associated with pop stars.' She talked of the flak he had taken in his career: 'his clean-living-boy-next-door image just didn't go with the legendary decadence expected of rock 'n' rollers'. Cliff was quoted as saying, 'My career can break and it won't break me.'

He would tell the late great disc jockey Roger Scott on Capital Radio that there was a little bit of luck behind his twenty-five-year career. 'You can have some talent trapped away in some town somewhere who might never get to meet the right doorway that will swing open and allow that talent to blossom out.' He added that even the best sound in the world won't last for ever: 'it will last a couple of years'. What, then, had been particularly important in keeping him at the top for so long?

'I have had the really good fortune in finding really great songs . . . You get something like "Never Say Die", you can remove the track, you can probably do it in a different way, and it would still be a good song.' He instanced his own musical upbringing, an era when people were given basic studio time and were expected to lay down so many tracks. He remembered how he grew up in a period when people wrote songs to last three minutes. 'If they couldn't do it in three minutes, they didn't do it.' (Nowadays it is not unusual for a singer or band to take a month to lay down one track. He recalled writers Terry Britten, Alan Tarney and John Farrar and he reminisced about the great rock 'n' rollers. Then the conversation veered into discussion of the material Cliff had drawn from past times for his rock 'n' roll section of the *Silver* album. 'There are certain records that come out that hit you between the eyes. Elvis's "Heartbreak Hotel" was the one that I remember the most, but there were also the songs of Ricky Nelson, Jerry Lee Lewis, Buddy Holly and Gene Vincent.' Of the latter's records, Cliff said, 'I can remember running down with the record, and it must have been at least half a mile to my mate's house, because he had a better record player, and playing it, and playing it, and playing it, and holding the arm up, you know the old stack-up stuff, and letting it play, over and over again. I mean, it was magic.'

*Silver* was an album with a surprising hard rocker, namely 'Love Stealer', again proving that Cliff can cope with most kinds of music, or at least sound convincing in many styles, without these interpretations having to be considered against vintage creations in the respective genres. Mickie Most, the British record producer and owner of RAK Records, one of the finest pop instigators, once said of Cliff, 'He's a good singer, with a good record voice, the "mic" likes him – and with that you either have it or you don't, and he does.' To Most, Cliff has even a 'black music' edge to his voice, 'but he's always been someone who has never got silly, and imagined he could do more than he is able. He could ride with what I call urban black music of the type of Alexander O'Neal, and Michael McDonald. But he's also been different, there is something instantly distinctive about his vocal sound. He's constantly sounded fresh. Anyone who has survived for so long is unique. Before the 1980s he had seen off a whole host of musics, even the powerful Liverpool sound. And going back a little before, what happened to the Wildes, or Adam Faith? And then there was glam rock junk, and the punks, and the technical people. He's won more musical Derbys than Lester Piggott.'

While the celebrations were progressing, nearer and nearer came his forty-third birthday. 'I love being forty-three,' he said, even before the day had arrived – the Scott interview was on 7 September.

Zzzzzzzzz – yes, it's been said so often, but standing there on stage at the Victoria Apollo, London, he certainly didn't seem that age. And if his generation was about basic recording professionalism, then it was carried into the show, for there he was on stage at 7.30 p.m. promptly, wearing black trousers, silver shirt and white jacket. Immediately, he concentrated on the twenty-fifth anniversary album, *Silver*. He started with 'Making History', followed by 'The Young Ones' after which Cliff remarked that now he was forty-three it seemed to have a lyric far from his age. He talked of recent travels around the world that had fulfilled his hopes for how he might spend this special year. Among the next selection of songs came 'Donna', recorded, he revealed, again (it was on his first album) because he adored the song, though he had a sore throat for this new version. He rocked with 'Love Stealer', and many remarked both there and in various magazines that even Iron Maiden might be tempted to lay down this track. There was a 2,000-strong help-out for 'Summer Holiday' but how could he celebrate the twenty-five years and come up with everyone's favourite song? The fans screamed titles long into the show, some hearing their favourites, others not.

A clothing change – a striped T-shirt – heralded the look Cliff had chosen for the second half. Songs included 'Be Bop A Lu La', 'Never Say Die', 'Galadriel', 'Devil Woman' and 'Ocean Deep', with the latter having a most stunning visual, in which Cliff looked as if he were drowning, occasioning screams of anguish from the crowd. Well, it *was* improbable that he would sing in a vast tank of water, but it looked so *real*. It was one of David Bryce's great moments with the light teams: a shiny dazzling silver ball adorned his version of 'Devil Woman', the song that has led to many narrow-minded religious people accusing Cliff of taking devil worship and occult observance into his thinking – a ridiculous suggestion, but critics often assume rather than listen.

In the *Silver* tour programme Cliff wondered, 'Where did it all go?' It seemed less ominous than asking where the twenty-five years had gone. He particularly praised his British fans: 'I've always thought that if you enjoy what I'm doing artistically then I can face even failure in other parts of the world. This is home – it always will be. I feel good here with you!'

He was at the Apollo in London for a staggering twenty-seven nights following his other dates in Southampton, St Austell, Cornwall, Bristol, Nottingham, Liverpool, Coventry and Ipswich. He also played Blazers for six nights from 8 to 13 October. The Apollo event was a huge success but so was the entire year. And apart from the concerts and the two albums released (*Dressed For the Occasion, Silver*, and in limited edition with the latter, *Rock 'n' Roll Silver*), there were other noteworthy happenings. Cliff appeared at the Greenbelt Festival at the end of August, ensuring that his great anniversary year was seen as more than just a celebration of an outstanding musical career. He was on stage at 11 p.m. on the Bank Holiday Saturday for a rock 'n' roll set. However, his Christian commitment was evident and, as Marian Donovan wrote in *Cliff United* for November 1983, 'people left singing "Our Lord Reigns", praising Jesus and not Cliff'. Earlier in

181

the year Cliff had supported the Luis Palau mission that was held at the Queen's Park Rangers ground in London, and a Billy Graham campaign in the UK.

It was also a major time for the Shadows as on 8 September, Music Therapy hosted an event to celebrate their own silver anniversary. They had toured from 30 July through until 2 September. A few weeks later Cliff, taking full advantage of his silver anniversary year, occupied more column spaces and news stories as Hodder & Stoughton published his *You, Me and Jesus*, the title springing from one of his gospel songs, and providing clearly and cogently his interpretation of certain biblical passages. It was illustrated throughout by John Farman, with the addition of sixteen pages of colour photographs of Cliff visiting the Third World for Tear Fund, as well as some concert footage.

The media busied itself around the time of album and tour release, and fans ensured radio stations liberally dosed their playlists with his records. Indeed, some fan clubs gave their members strict orders not to let the event pass!

All the fan clubs were busy but the Yorkshire Fan Club went to town and gave him five special presents, first, an engraved silver gallery tray, then a silver jubilee cake, made by Sheila Bennett, and third, silver-framed pages from the *Daily Mirror* and *Daily Mail*, including material by Patrick Doncaster who claimed he was the first national journalist to sense Cliff's oncoming greatness. The latter two items were given to Cliff at his Manchester concert on 30 April. A huge birthday card was assembled for him by Jeanette Nicholson and, lastly, a Silver Jubilee Book of Tributes which came with a satin and sequin cover, designed and made skilfully and tastefully by Susan Heath. The Yorkshire Fan Club President, Jennifer Chatten, said she had spotted the silver tray at Inglis and Sons of Stonegate, York, and knew it was the ideal present as Cliff would be able to use it, rather than keeping it as an ornament. She says, 'It was a patterned design, and there was an oval of plain silver in the centre which was ideal for the engraving. The card had a gorgeous picture of two puppies, one a Labrador.'

Several clubs gave anniversary discos and played Cliff tracks into the early hours of the morning. Others watched videos. Some, of course, were fortunate to obtain tickets for one or more of the shows.

The Cliff Richard Fan Club of South London and Surrey organized their first convention, which I attended, on Saturday

25 October at All Saints Church Hall, Shirley, with Eileen Edwards reporting that 'members signed a card for Cliff's birthday, and we also sent him a silver jubilee rose to celebrate his twenty-fifth year in show business.' Eileen and her helpers obtained many items from some of their honorary members for auction. One bidder paid £7 for a pair of black trousers once worn by Cliff himself. Other items included key-rings, notebooks, signed photographs, and an initialled handkerchief from Cilla Black. Proceeds went to the Croydon Darby and Joan club.

The Cliff Richard Fan Club of North London invited me to a dinner and dance at the Empire Rooms in Tottenham Court Road, London, organized by Janet Johnson, which provided a disco and sit-down buffet. During 1983 the club raised money for much-needed equipment for sick children.

The fan club of Avon and Somerset held a grand charity disco on 24 September that had a ploughman's supper plus lots of Cliff music – and if Surrey had Cliff's trousers, then Avon and Somerset had his shirt! Radio West supplied a good friend in Trevor Fry, 'good friend' meaning someone with a particular propensity to play the man's records! Fry presented a Cliff Jubilee show. Enterprisingly, the club informed the Cliff office and, to their joy, he recorded a message for the show. The club's journal, *Sci-Fi* carried various tributes to him, his music and professionalism, and the words of his songs. Other people recalled their earliest meeting with Cliff, with club member Margaret Watson recalling how, in 1958, with five other girls, she was rehearsing for a school concert at the Colston Hall. Their rehearsal happened to be taking place on the same day as Cliff was due to give a concert. Seeing him coming down the stairs and looking rather lost, they told him the direction he should take, and he was promptly ambushed by a group of cunning but friendly schoolgirls. Cliff signed his autograph on six sheets of music, and Margaret has retained hers until this day.

It was quite a year: shows, singles, albums, special radio and television presentations, and *The Video Connection*. This brought together many of Cliff's hits, including 'Wired for Sound', 'Devil Woman', 'Carrie', 'Dreamin'' and 'We Don't Talk Anymore'. From all accounts, it seems that fans particularly liked previously unseen holiday shots from Portugal. Cliff devised the idea that he should be seen being assailed by and ducking thrown plates. The video lasted fifty-five minutes.

It was a great year and no one had any doubts that there would be many more to come. Cliff commented, 'I didn't think it would last this long or be so good.' But he had said the same thing many times before. Speaking to William Marshall in the *Daily Mirror*, September 1983, Cliff said, 'If my voice is still OK in twenty-five years' time, I'll still be singing. What songs I don't know.' A streak of realism and humour followed, for he said, 'But there will be a different way of performing for a seventy-year-old man. I'll have to gain a certain amount of dignity with age.' Marshall described Cliff as 'lean and tanned as though he had just been released from a time warp where miraculously the physical and mental fizz of his early days had been pickled and preserved'.

I was present when Marshall met Cliff. It was at the Roof Top Gardens in Kensington, and the event one of the many celebrative occasions in his silver jubilee year. I remember noticing that Cliff was wearing jeans and a cotton armless T-shirt and, a little surprisingly considering his usual sartorial style, scuffed trainers. Disciplined living, a careful diet, the right exercise, no drugs, no cigarettes, and frequent early nights, had contributed to his glowing health. Cliff once mused about the physical state of Mick Jagger of the Rolling Stones, when Mick said he was now running to keep fit. 'Has he left it too late? I ask myself. What has happened to all those early years? He wants to be fit for his tours. Well, you know, I've thought of that for years! I've gone to bed at a reasonable hour so that my voice would be good the next night. I rarely sing duff on stage because I care about it.'

Marshall did find one or two things to suggest Cliff was forty-two, fast approaching forty-three, smallish but present. 'Only the slightly crêpey wrinkled neck and a few crow's feet around the eyes were a giveaway.'

'I still look like a fourteen-year-old trying to look forty,' he told *Sunday*, the weekend colour magazine of the *News of the World*. He explained it was his face. 'I think I do look forty, but there are certain face shapes that have a younger look about them.'

Some fans did not like his look of this time. There was his chin stubble, an attempt to add some age. Obviously Cliff pre-dated current stars like George Michael, who have adopted the policy of not shaving regularly.

Cliff didn't see it that way, although he didn't keep his stubble. He was more interested in stressing his continual enthusiasm. 'A lot of people get bored with their careers or they think they've done it all. I've never felt that. I've never taken it for granted, it's not a noose around my neck or a millstone – it's a great pleasure for me to be in the rock 'n' roll scene. I love it.'

He would say the same thing in 1992.

# CHAPTER SIXTEEN

# TIME

The words 'There has never been anything in the theatre like *Time*,' might well give hope to any interested party that a favourable review is in the process of unfolding – misleading in the context of John Peters' piece in the *Sunday Times*, 13 April 1986. The banner headline read: A SPECTACULAR LOAD OF BILGE.

Perhaps, even to this day, the critic should feel relieved that Cliff fans may not be readers of this organ, since there have been no reports of Peters' untimely demise. Cliff fans, and thousands of them every week, were besotted both with the musical's theme and with a rock singer called Chris, played by Cliff, a role that caused Mr Peters to comment, 'I don't think Cliff Richard could act his way into a deserted railway station.' Both fans and newspaper columnist were united in thinking that the sets by John Napier were breathtakingly audacious, but diverged when Peters noted that their 'swaggering opulence is matched by the spiritual poverty of the show'.

*Time* was Cliff's return to theatre. At long last he had found a production that took him away from the endless cycle of album and single, promotion and tour. There was no doubt that his first foray into the land of stage since *A Midsummer Night's Dream* with the Riversmead School Dramatic Society, or perhaps in professional terms, since *The Potting Shed* at Sadlers Wells, in London in May 1971, was for him a career high. He believed that *Time* was a gem, and this was how the fans also saw it.

*Time* was the creation of Dave Clark, a rock 'n' roll hero from the 1960s, along with music from Jeff Daniels and book and lyrics by David Soames. The story was of a trial set in space: since man was venturing to the stars, and had already walked on the moon, the Time Lord, Melchizidek had decided earth people must be brought to trial to ascertain if they would be an asset or threat to universal peace.

Clark's production came apparently brimming with the best. In John Napier, he had someone well accustomed to accepting design and creation awards, and who had recently stunned many with his sets for *Starlight Express*. He engaged Larry Fuller as choreographer and director, a major name in the all-powerful US theatre and musical world, whose credits ranged from the London production of *Funny Girl*, starring Barbra Streisand, to international productions of *Evita* and *Sweeney Todd*. Clark promised at the outset that there would also be top sound engineers, top musicians, a star-studded cast and a plethora of stunning special effects. Prior to its world première, a concept album would be released by EMI, and there would be a series of singles by name artists. And there would be Cliff who, in the role of Chris, would be beamed into space to be confronted by the Time Lords and defend earth. He described himself as the new Flash Gordon, and said he had never heard so many potential hits in one show. He would sing the first single, the rather enchanting song, 'She's So Beautiful'. (A video of the single was produced by Ken Russell.) *Time*, at last, brought back a musical to the once-famous stage of the Dominion theatre, in London's Tottenham Court Road.

Clark was, of course, more than someone with a genial smile, warm welcomes and lots of money – or, at least, access to it. If he was written down as a 1960s pop star and no more, somewhere along the line an otherwise admirable PR machine had let him down. When his pop days ended, he went to the Central School of Speech and Drama, as he wanted to be an actor, and was signed to take several major film roles. But, he says, 'The movie industry was going through a bad spell at that time and in the end none of them ever got made.' It didn't occur to him that he might have cast himself in *Time*: 'I decided I would make a better director or producer.'

In his plush office in London's Mayfair, Clark told me that he had always fancied attracting Cliff back onto the stage. 'I didn't bully Cliff into taking a major role. I wanted to use a rock star for the part and Cliff was my first choice.' Cliff was sold after hearing some songs, and acquainting himself with the script. But Clark had to wait two years, for Cliff's diary was full until then. Clark could have made no greater compliment than to say, as he did, that he would wait until Cliff was free, even though the project would have to be put on ice. He was convinced that he was bringing something new and exciting. Apart from his dramatic training, he had already learned much through involvement in other media such as television and video and had also produced for Channel 4 *The Weekend Starts Here With Ready Steady Go!* He was also aware of the impact of engaging Laurence Olivier, whom he would personally direct, to play Akash. Clark put out a *Time* concept album in advance of the theatre production, which included performances by Olivier and Cliff, plus Stevie Wonder, Freddie Mercury, Julian Lennon, Dionne Warwick, Ashford and Simpson, Leo Sayer and Murray Head. It was the first album to have a holographic cover.

But even if Cliff was looking for something new to add to his illustrious career, Clark understood that he needed to be persuaded: 'I remember he said, "A year out of my life?"' It needed a subtle orchestration by Clark to persuade him that the Cliff world could stop for a year. After all, there would be records spinning from the show and nothing to stop Cliff arranging an intensive recording schedule before his show commitment, so that EMI would have plenty to release if, say, the show music did not entail major record chart action for him. Cliff suddenly agreed: 'I'd love to do the musical. I'd be delighted!' Clark adds, 'The thing I found about Cliff is that when he says yes, he is then full-hearted and enthusiastic, and he never got bored. He is someone who gives 101 per cent. And he had this amazing energy, even at his age. Some actors, I find, pace themselves through the shows, and are not always at their best, but I couldn't say that about Cliff. Maybe it's something about being a musician as well for musicians do not hold back, it's in their nature to give.' And, as Dave would find out, Cliff did not miss a single performance – wasn't even put off by the accident on the way to the theatre when he wrote off his VW Golf on the M4, or when overwhelmed by his grief over the death of Mamie Latham. The only 'miss' night came when the stage computer system failed to perform; the show was cancelled, and Cliff rushed off to visit Mamie.

On my visit to his office, Clark recalled the rehearsal period. 'Remember, he was up against people from the National, so he had to be really good. His dedication and work output gained their respect, for, after all, being who he was, his every move was being watched, and he had to convince people he wasn't just a pop star playing a pop star. I remember he was off the book before anyone else. People said he was a professional. I think his attitude in rehearsal and later showed clearly one of his underlying beliefs: anything is possible. And if you fall flat on your face, then you do so, but you may find you're brilliant.'

For Clark, his work with Cliff brought back old memories. 'I knew Cliff from around 1963 and, oddly enough, his sister Jackie ran my – or the Dave Clark Five – fan club, although I didn't know the connection at the time. I remember getting this telegram from Cliff, congratulating us as we began our first tour. Then I got invited to the home and I met his sisters. So in a way there was a twenty-five-year relationship beginning its growth. During the run of *Time*, I learnt how good a voice he possesses – great on record and it transmits to the stage. I fancy though he is really a rock 'n' roller at heart. But he always believes the song itself is important. He is the ultimate professional. And to think once I saw him at Finsbury Park in London in his pink jacket, quiff and bright socks – and then to see him on stage for my musical. That man is one of the greats.'

Cliff began rehearsals in January 1986 for his long run in *Time*. The show was at first warmly welcomed by fans but less so as the months rolled by. Those who couldn't get to London and those who had seen *Time* increasingly yearned for the good old tour schedules, while overseas fans muttered long into their nightly prayers, 'How long, Lord, how long?'

But how did Cliff feel? 'I had to make up my mind without really knowing how it all might happen. Once I got into the actual production it was different from my early impressions but also much better. I was told about the set, for instance, but I couldn't imagine it, and when I did see it, to me it was the impossible taking place – twenty-three tons of machinery on the move and it's silent.'

He talked of shows he had seen, and felt, 'The only show you could compare it with was *Starlight Express*. I've seen *42nd Street*, *Guys and Dolls*, and loved them. Oh, I should say I've seen *Starlight* many times. But *Time* is the most sensational thing in my experience. I mean, I like shows for different reasons, and comparisons are hard but *Time* was definitely something.'

But what about the year or more out of his life? 'I committed myself. And I loved it.' Not that Cliff made no criticisms: he was a little unhappy about the initial, rather than cast, concept album. 'I'm not saying that it would have been any more successful if I had sung all my own songs, I just think the public would have related to it.' (On the concept album, several artists had been gathered together to sing material that would eventually be

189

performed by the show's stars.) Cliff added, 'I would find it nice if EMI said, "Let's have an album of Cliff doing *Time*," ' but this was not to be. And in any case the musical did not produce major hit songs, apart from 'She's So Beautiful', for as I mentioned in Chapter 11, other numbers found little public favour, even one of the show's great pop numbers, 'Born To Rock 'n' Roll', generating little radio play. 'No one would play it,' Cliff commented to us. It was a source of bitterness to him, and also to Dave Clark.

*Time* had its première on the evening of 9 April. The crowds came with the critics. Before they were even through the theatre doors they were warned that the lighting and special effects could cause problems to those suffering from medical ailments. Quite why would soon be evident from the opening moments of sheer noise and light confusion, as earth seemed to leave, and a new existence was brought into being. For fans of Britain's longest-standing rock 'n' roller, the moment they wanted could not come soon enough – and there he was in a black leather waistcoat and T-shirt, adorned with badges that mostly said 'Ban the Bomb'. Immediately, it was an all-energy Cliff, which caused a few gasps, and even worries over whether he could last the frightening pace he set. He shouted his message, 'Make this world beautiful, while we've still got time.'

Apart from Cliff, the sound effects and the amazing stage props, many were stunned by the 14-foot-high fibre glass head, revealed from within a giant globe, hovering, so it seemed, in mid-air. On this was projected the face of Lord Olivier, in his role of Akash, the Ultimate Word in Truth, who spoke on the themes of existence, of good and evil.

The musical's message lay in exhorting Earth to change its ways, to learn more of love and understanding. The *Sunday Times* critic, John Peters, said, 'The whole thing is like a demented cosmic church service, except at the end you can't shake hands with the vicar.' He was not persuaded by the torrent of worthy slogans that emanated from it. Not that he was alone in his verdict: one of theatreland's most revered and long-standing critics, Milton Shulman, thought you had to be under twenty-five for even the possibility of enjoyment; ideally the age range should be eight to fourteen. Sheridan Morley thought it was one of the worst musicals of the century, and was totally bemused as to why Olivier should associate himself with it. At least the *Observer*'s critic, Michael Radcliffe, thought it was the greatest light show in town. Cliff was hardly enamoured with some of these comments, and neither was Dave Clark. Cliff has told us that he has always remained puzzled as to why the show did not receive both praise and awards. He saw it as symptomatic of cultural élitism, for Clark, not a recognized impresario, had gate-crashed theatreland.

The fans, including some Radio 1 jocks, begged to differ, and did so passionately. Dave Clark's persistence against the voices that said he should not try to break into the closely knit West End theatre fraternity was much praised. The *Cliff United* magazine reviewer Eileen Edwards pronounced it all most satisfying, and exclaimed 'even my husband insisted on seeing *Time* again'. As for the 'boy', she neatly caught the feelings of fans by saying, 'Cliff once again managed to pursue his career to a greater height. His debut appearance on a West End stage has proved successful and will continue to be so for as long as there are people who demand to see entertainment that is "out of this world".'

Crowds came, many admittedly were Cliff fans, and some saw the musical many times. The Cliff magazines printed numerous tributes from fans, including Judith Winder, who said, 'How glad we were we had not let the critics put us off. What a magical show – we enjoyed every minute of it. As usual, Cliff was wonderful.' Denise Taylor wrote, 'It was fantastic and impossible to explain to anyone not in the "know", although we've bored our friends trying. On our way out of the theatre, still shell-shocked, all I could think about was when we could book to see it again.' Sandra Taylor felt 'I think a lot of people will be surprised how good he is,' and Gwenda Carpenter of Worcester Park, Surrey, thought Cliff was the ideal person for the lead role – and so the praise continued.

During Cliff's residency around 650,000 people saw the show with an 85 per cent capacity. By the time it completed its run, *Time* had been seen by over a million people and grossed in excess of £15 million. Cliff left the show on 11 April 1987 with one-time pop and television teen idol David Cassidy replacing him. John Travolta had been rumoured as Cliff's successor, and even Freddie Mercury had been mentioned, which seemed most unlikely, even if it would have given *Time* a further major audience explosion, Cassidy had an odd connection with Cliff, for writer and producer Alan Tarney had penned and produced his minor hit 'The Last Kiss' in 1985, a song with different lyrics which bore the title 'Young Love' on Cliff's *Wired For Sound* album.

HRH The Duchess of Kent attended the Royal Gala Performance on 9 April 1986, along with a number of other prominent people. During the presentation of the stars to the Duchess, she asked the three chorus girls where they hid their microphones. The answer was prompt – the lifting up of their bustles!

Cliff's own birthday on 14 October produced an audience of fans who could hardly wait for the show's completion. Banners, posters, flowers, presents, birthday cards, and persistent chants of 'Cliff, Cliff, Cliff' were his, with the *DI* magazine reporting to its readers that there were at least twenty choruses of 'Happy Birthday'. There were calls for a special birthday song. After feigning surprise that people should remember his 'special' day, Cliff said he would become Cliff Richard, the pop star, and so he sang 'Living Doll'. He had already celebrated on the previous evening with *Time's* cast and crew at a party at the La Barca restaurant in Waterloo. It was also an occasion to celebrate the first six months of the show.

Two days later, Cliff played his first Thursday matinée for months, replacing his understudy John Christie, since it was arranged that Lord Olivier would attend. To ensure there would be a good house, Dave Clark offered free seats to the members of any Cliff fan club who could produce their membership card.

April 11 1987 was a truly emotional and overwhelming occasion. Here was the ending of a major chapter in Cliff's life. For fans, it was their last chance to see him in the musical's title role and, doubtless, they could sit in the theatre in the knowledge that their star was being liberated back into the more safe pastures of his usual round of record activity.

On this final appearance, Cliff needed a police escort to take him through around 400 fans who had assembled outside the theatre. South Croydon fan Hank Pieper, who had seen the musical sixty-four times, arranged an extravaganza with a band playing 'Congratulations', and festooning the immediate area with hundreds of white balloons bearing the words 'Thanks, Cliff'.

'Congratulations' was the tune the *Time* band played inside the theatre, once the evening's show ended. Dave Clark came on stage and hugged the star, and then made a brief speech that also extended into saying a big thank you to all the people who were making the show so popular. Others were saying goodbye too, including Bernard Lloyd, Jodie Wilson and some of the dancers. There was a telegram of congratulations for the show on its first birthday from Olivier. But it was to Cliff that most attention was given.

Dave Clark told him 'Cliff, this is your night, my friend. I know your mum's family, I know they are very proud of you. We have known each other since the sixties. I won't say when in the sixties! Seriously, it has been an experience and pleasure to work with you, Cliff. It is an amazing feat in our business to find a star who has never missed a single performance, who has given 100 per cent every night. Cliff always arrives at the theatre two hours before a performance. He is always on stage five minutes before the curtain goes up, and, for that alone, you are a credit to our profession. Cliff, thank you for your loyalty and devotion to *Time* and to everyone including our multi-talented cast.' He also thanked Peter Gormley and David Bryce, Cliff's managers. Cliff was presented with a picture of the Dominion Theatre, lit up with the word *'Time'*.

In his response, Cliff thanked everyone who had made it possible for him to make his contribution to the show. He refuted the early suggestion of some that he would be bored after a matter of weeks, and said he had not had a dull moment. But, as is often his way in these later years of his career, he did not shy away from venting his feelings on matters about which he felt deeply troubled. The press was told, fair and square, that they had been mostly blind to the merits of this show. He said, 'If there are any press in here, I want you to hear this now. You should write now [said with great emphasis] that this is the greatest thing that has ever hit theatre.' His last sentiment found much favour from the audience, even if it was hardly likely to find support from many other quarters.

It was now that the really unexpected occurred, for even the experienced Cliff was silenced when a Scottish piper came on stage and played 'Auld Lang Syne'. It led to Cliff enacting, impromptu, a fast and furious dance, with the audience clapping along with him. There was time for a few more thank yous and a final 'Thank you and good night'. As the cast departed they sang, from the show, 'It's In Every One Of Us', another song that should have been much higher in the charts than its lowly 45 position, for, schmalzy and sentimental as it might be, it had a definite commercial edge. Christine Whitehead of *Cliff United* reported tears from cast and audience alike, especially during the singing of 'It's In Every One Of Us', when Cliff stopped singing and kissed each of the girl backing singers in turn. The dancers had come on stage by the aisles and not from the side of the stage. Finally, all that bore witness to the emotional ending was the sad sight of flowers crushed on the floor by fans who had dashed out to the front and then rushed away tearfully into the spring air. Perhaps many remembered the odd moment when, during a pause in the last lines of 'It's In Every One Of Us', someone had shouted out, 'Cliff, you're the only artist who can do this.'

And so it seemed that this was the end of Cliff's connection with *Time*, but Cliff could not stay away . . . and, travelling incognito, managed to slip into the theatre at least five times – although, as he told Gloria Hunniford on *Sunday Sunday* on 20 September 1987, 'David Cassidy is in it now . . . not as good as me!' He told her that he went because he found it so enjoyable and still thought it one of the best shows in town.

However, he returned in more tangible fashion on 14 April 1988 when he made a guest appearance in a special presentation to raise funds for fighting Aids. It was like old times as hundreds of girls came with bouquets of flowers or a single rose. Hearts must have almost stopped when Cassidy's successor David Ian hit the stage, but after one verse of the song the bluff was called and Cliff was back on stage. He was joined by Freddie Mercury. Cliff stayed only to sing 'Born to Rock 'n' Roll' and then was seemingly gone for the remainder of the first half. Those with quick ears picked up a new line in the script when David Ian, in response to being asked why he had been summoned to represent Earth said, to great audience amusement, 'Why me? Why not Cliff Richard or Freddie Mercury?' That seemed it, until Cliff and Freddie came on stage to take over from him to sing 'In My Defence'.

The second half proceeded normally until the point was reached when the return to earth is signalled, and it was here, in a plethora of flashing lights, that fans realized Cliff had once more stepped into David Ian's shoes as he sang 'It's In Every One Of Us'. Once more, old times returned for *Time* as girls rushed to the front. But they were lost in several speeches from the stage that stressed the agonies of Aids. Dave Clark told of how he suffered when his young sister died from cancer in her early twenties. There were speeches about and from people connected with the Aids movement, Frontliners. People were assured that the money paid out on that evening would be spent helping Aids sufferers. After the speeches, Cliff and Freddie came back on stage and again sang 'It's In Every One Of Us'.

This was definitely the last Cliff appearance in *Time*. But the *Time* story was not over: it moved to the High Court. Dave Clark's The Right Time Production Company won £400,000 damages against Rank Theatres Limited, claiming that the organization had failed to run an efficient box office and was therefore responsible for the musical's premature closure and loss of income. Clark was also awarded a further £200,000. He had sued for £15 million.

*Time* will remain a treasured memory for both Cliff and fans.

# CHAPTER SEVENTEEN

# THIRTY YEARS

August 1988 saw Cliff begin to celebrate his thirty years in the music business. As I have already noted, he did so by playing the Greenbelt Festival, launching a new book, entitled *Single-minded*, a new single, a new album, and a thirtieth anniversary tour that began in October. This chapter concentrates on the acclaim he received from the music world, which was concentrated in the second half of his thirtieth year celebrations.

'Mary and I very much enjoyed the events,' said the then Secretary of State for Education and Youth, Kenneth Baker. 'It was good of Cliff Richard to say what he did. But there really is no need to apologize for any discourtesy; people in politics – as in show business – must expect all kinds of receptions, which will vary from the ecstatic to the less than reverential.'

It was The Brits 1989, the year made famous for stage chaos, and the unusual compèring of Samantha Fox and Mick Fleetwood. It came to the final award of the evening. The Fleetwood Mac member announced the Lifetime Achievement presentation. Peter Jamieson the then chairman of the British Phonographic Industry, who sponsor the event, was left to fill in the details and explained how the BPI is the voice that unites British record companies, for such causes as the School for Recording Art, that it helps fund numerous projects, that 130 members, large and small, had voted for Brits nominees, but that one honour is not voted for and is given by universal acclaim. He was rejoined by Mick Fleetwood who said that year's winner was someone who had inspired him for many years – Cliff Richard.

Cliff rose from his seat, walked forward and, as he took to the stage, presumably with no relevance as to what might follow, the strains of 'We Don't Talk Anymore' were played. By the end, some might have wished that Cliff had not made a speech, beyond thanking the recipients.

It all started pleasantly and uncontroversially. Cliff said, 'Thank you very much' and that he had had a wonderful thirty years, had enjoyed the record industry, and was thrilled that in recent years much had been given back, noting such charitable ventures as Band Aid, Live Aid and Sports Aid. Perhaps he got slightly carried away, as words tumbled out fast and furious. He talked of the many audiences, the diversity of music and musicians, the sheer scale of the industry, and went on, 'I am grateful for being a part, just a little tiny part of this great industry. Tonight is a night for cheering success. Everybody on this stage has been success-ful. Therefore I am compelled to say at the end of my little thank you speech, and I am grateful for this award, I feel compelled to say that we are supported in our industry by many people from outside it, and we have people sitting here tonight who are not part of the music industry. Therefore when I hear Kenneth Baker booed, I have to say, I am really sorry about that, but thank you for coming, and I hope that you will come back next year. The rest of us have got to grow up.'

Perhaps for the first time ever in his long career Cliff heard himself being jeered and partially slow-handclapped by some of the audience, which subdued a moment when everyone should have been on their feet cheering and clapping back to his seat Britain's longest-standing star.

After the ceremony, Cliff, with his mother, David Bryce and Bill Latham, went to London's Grosvenor House to celebrate. Cer-tainly, he was a popular figure. Few thought there would be considerable furore the next day, when some newspapers went to town over his remarks. Amidst the rabble, it seemed, Cliff emer-ged as the knight in shining armour. Even the *Sun* applauded his comments. They called him a 'true gentleman' among 'the small minded, self-opinionated morons who make up the majority of today's music scene'. They thought he had courage to stand up for 'decency and politeness', and 'apologize to Kenneth Baker for the disgraceful reception he received from the riff-raff'. The *Sun* concluded by asking, 'What did Cliff get from these ill-mannered yobs, when he left the stage? More boos and abuse.' And it had a final verbal cracker: YOU'VE LASTED 30 YEARS. THAT LOT WON'T LAST 30 MINUTES!

The BPI award was not the only honour accorded to Cliff in 1989. He and the Shadows received the Silver Clef, an award given annually by the Nordoff-Robbins Therapy Centre as a reci-procal gesture to the music industry for its help in aiding severely handicapped children. On 8 February, Nordoff-Robbins gave a special lunch to honour them for their part in show business. In spite of the formality of the occasion, it was pretty light-hearted. The diners consumed *terrine de sole* accompanied by *sauce verte*, followed by *suprême de volaille aux concombres*, accompanied by *pommes noisettes* and *légumes de la saison*, and a dessert of *piano de chocolat aux fruits de la saison*. The latter consisted of a triangular sponge covered at the sides by white chocolate, and several different fruits and topped with a chocolate treble clef. To the side of the plate lay some cream topped by a chocolate guitar in two different shades of chocolate.

Once the staff of the Mayfair Inter-Continental in Stratton Street, London, had cleared the tables and served coffee, the award ceremony got under way with an initial reading of messages from two music people who could not be present, namely Marty Wilde and George Martin. Oddly enough, Marty was appearing at Cliff's Pavilion in Southend. Dave Dee, now of major record company fame, and formerly of Dave Dee, Dozy, Beaky, Mick and Tich, read their words and, once completed, handed over the event's programme to the man some say looks a trifle like Cliff anyway – the one-time Radio 1, and now Capital Gold, DJ, Mike Read.

Mike produced much laughter when he said, 'I know you all work for, or with Cliff, and therefore don't go to his concerts,' and followed this a few moments later with a travelogue through the histories of Cliff and the Shadows.

He was followed by L. G. Wood, who had been General Manager of EMI when Cliff signed with the British company. He recalled how a celebratory dinner was planned for Cliff's twenty-first at the Dorchester, the 'posh' hotel in London's Park Lane. Cliff was refused admission because he wasn't wearing a tie! He borrowed one and, once inside, those who had exercised the rules came rushing over to ask for his autograph. Mr Wood, who has since died, praised the Cliff management and asked Cliff and the Shadows (Bruce, Hank and Brian) to join him and Dave Dee on stage for the presentation.

Cliff again said how marvellous the past thirty years had been. He mentioned that only a few days previously he had received an award from *TV Times*, and here he was once more thanking many people for their contribution to his career. He applauded music therapy for giving the industry the chance to contribute something to the lives of the less fortunate. As for the future, and the

1990s, Cliff said, 'Len very kindly mentioned that we will be going on through the nineties and I guess, if we can stand up, we will. For me, every year that I live, let alone have records in the charts, is absolute abundance.'

The major European industry trade paper *Music Week* has its own awards ceremony and if the BPI ceremony had not given Cliff his due reward for 'current' action better than anyone else, then this journal sensibly gave him the top single award for 1988, with 'Mistletoe And Wine'. Of course, there was the album category for *Private Collection* but while it would easily outsell the winner, none the less it was placed second to *Kylie* from Kylie Minogue. In the marketing category, *Private Collection* from EMI was placed second to the London Records' marketing of the album *Bananarama*. *Private Collection* helped EMI into third place in the category for top albums – obviously the company could well do with a few more Cliffs!

For fans, the thirty-year celebrations continued with EMI issuing a special video, *Live and Guaranteed 1988*, the first 'live' video since the 1984 *Rock In Australia* concert. This new video had been filmed during part of his world tour, and centred on performances in April 1988. It gathered together many of Cliff's all-time classics and some more recent hits. It also had backstage interviews with both the band and Cliff, with Cliff talking about his life, his beliefs and his work as a rock 'n' roll star. It ran for sixty minutes and cost only £9.99.

Fans had another Cliff goodie in store with the release of the sparkling new album, *Stronger*, in October 1989, but long before the day of release – and by then into year thirty-one – there was a preview of some tracks on 3 April, although the main purpose was to ask fans to name the track they would like to see released as his hundredth single.

It was an extraordinary event with some 2,000 people attending. It began at 2 p.m. when Mike Read walked on stage to introduce Cliff. Cliff said a few words, enquired about the distances people had come, and then sang 'Move It'. Mike Read reminded him of past fan choice of material, including '1960' and 'Nine Times Out Of Ten', for some so far back that they could not have been born.

Then the main point of the preceedings began in earnest with 'Stronger Than That'. Cliff mimed to the record, danced and was photographed. The second contender was 'Joanna', a ballad in sharp comparison with the strong beat of 'Stronger Than That'.

Next came 'The Best Of Me', 'I Just Don't Have The Heart', 'Forever You Will Be', and the catchy 'Lean On You'. At the completion of each, there was a short reprise, Mike and Cliff leaving the stage. Then began the voting, with fans asked to put a mark in one of the six boxes. Some thought that although some of the other songs were better for a hundredth title 'The Best Of Me' was most apt – and, anyway, it was a good track.

After Cliff and Mike returned on stage, Cliff sang 'Living Doll', and recalled the story behind the song of how he had been in Sheffield when Norrie Paramor contacted him and said he had to sing the song for the film *Serious Charge*. Along with the Shadows (the Drifters) he disliked the rock version. Bruce had suggested a slower version in country and western style. Initially, Cliff was also against that idea, but was glad there had been a change of mind. Later he told the audience about a fan of his called Julie, who had followed him all around the country in her wheelchair. Sadly, she had died, and for her, he sang the number she loved so much, 'Bachelor Boy'.

Mike Read gave details of a forthcoming gospel tour that would have a new look and be on a smaller scale than previous ones. Cliff sang 'Love And A Helping Hand'. He mentioned that the one-off concert planned for Wembley Stadium had now become a two-day event. The audience heard that the hundredth single in CD form would have re-recorded versions of two old classics, 'Move It' and 'High Class Baby'.

A surprise presentation to Cliff was unveiled: Mike Read had brought on stage what seemed to be nothing more than a large, oblong frame. When it was turned round, there, for all to see, was a platinum disc for the sales of *Private Collection*, now said to be around 1,500,000 copies.

And so the almost Eurovision nature of the event drew to its climax. The result came, naturally, in reverse order and read: 'Forever You Will Be Mine', 'Lean On Me', 'Joanna', 'I Just Don't Have The Heart', 'The Best Of Me', leaving, surprisingly, 'Stronger Than That'. Cliff was amazed, having thought people would have gone for a ballad. But that was it – the hundredth single was to be 'Stronger Than That'. In the end, however, fans discovered that their second choice would be the actual number 100, and 'Stronger Than That' was not released until February 1990, when it did not even make the top ten.

Before the month was out, Cliff had performed at two nightclub venues he had long favoured. First there was Caesar's Palace in

Luton on 20 April, where he announced that he had decided to reverse his fans' decision for the title of his historic hundredth solo release, and then came a residency at the Savas Cabaret Club. At the latter Cliff remarked how people assumed that his big hits were in the late 1950s and the ensuing decade. He told everyone that it was not so, for in 1979 came his biggest selling single of the time, 'We Don't Talk Anymore'. The audience was thanked at the end of helping him through thirty great years. There was time for 'Mistletoe And Wine', and 'Congratulations' for a couple in the audience who were getting engaged that evening, and then came a further reference to the occasion on 3 April when fans had voted for 'Stronger Than That'. He said he was going to make his own choice, and this would be 'The Best Of Me'. He was at Blazers, Windsor (another venue much favoured by Cliff) on 13 May.

Soon would come the hundredth single and those two fabulous evenings at Wembley Stadium (see chapter 18). A gospel tour would take place in July and the thirtieth year of celebrations would be over. While life would be back to normal, with a new autumn album and British tour, it could hardly be seen as anything but busy, and it seemed wise to ensure that the momentum would not slacken – not least for Cliff, who would otherwise be in danger of suffering anticlimax after so many glorious moments during the celebrations for his thirtieth anniversary. Interestingly, Cliff says that he managed to maintain his essential eight hours' sleep each day, even if he got to bed late after a performance and meal. He had also found time for tennis.

One of his last public events in the thirtieth year was at the Harrow Leisure Centre in North London. Ruth Martin, writing in *Cliff United*, saw this as the antithesis of The Event. In the latter he was, for her, a small dot in the distance, whereas on this occasion, in contrast, he was so near. The evening itself had a familiar pattern of songs, and a Bill and Cliff 'chat' time, with the inevitable moments of banter, and none more so than when Bill asked Cliff if he might perform, at the age of eighty, ' "The Young Ones" from a wheelchair'. Cliff's reply was instant, 'If you'll push me on, yes.'

However, if his career longevity had given cause for celebration, there was still his fiftieth birthday, which would fall on 14 October 1990. But before that momentous occasion would come the culmination of this remarkable year at Wembley Stadium: The Event . . .

# CHAPTER EIGHTEEN

# THE EVENT

Cliff has played innumerable concerts all over the world and, since 1958, almost without exception, year in, year out. Playing live is his great joy: there is a radiance about him when he is on stage. For the most part these concerts have been in venues providing between three and four thousand seats, the exceptions being Wembley Arena and Birmingham's National Exhibition Centre. As the 1980s wore on, it seemed Cliff was becoming increasingly obsessed with the idea that he should join the élite of the world music fraternity and book himself into the massive 72,000-seating Wembley Stadium, London, for what would easily be the live playing highlights of his distinguished career.

But doubts crept in that he would not be able to fill the stadium, although it hardly seemed a matter of debate for fans or even, surely, a pop promoter. (Far more people want to see Cliff than can normally be accommodated, and his concerts always sell out within hours. As the sales of *Private Collection* have shown, Cliff has a colossal following that never moves fast enough against the well-organized fan clubs who rush anxiously for tickets.)

Once lengthy considerations and consultations with all parties involved were out of the way, the announcement was made. It caught the attention of the major press. The world's news wires shook with the announcement. It would obviously not be just another booking. Cliff was determined it would be, as its title suggested, *The* Event for music fans. No expense would be spared to ensure that The Event lived up to its title.

It would begin in the late afternoon with an *Oh Boy!* section to revive memories of the once highly thought of and popular television show and would feature bands who were with Cliff during the early years of his career. A second section would star one of Cliff's currently favoured bands, Aswad, with whom he had recorded. In part three, Cliff would team up once more with the

Shadows, who would also have their own solo spot. It would close with Cliff and his band for a set to last ninety minutes. There would also be some surprise guests. The promoter, Mel Bush, told journalists and other media people that he would be spending nearly half a million pounds on the stage alone, which would be specially designed and erected for the two days. Added to this, there would be a sophisticated sound system. Cliff told the gathering, 'It will be one of the world's most sophisticated sound systems, and I'll do everything in my power to ensure everyone goes home thinking they've just seen one of the best rock shows ever at Wembley Stadium.'

Wembley Stadium officers were keen to point out that the stadium had been recently voted the world's top venue by the prestigious American trade magazine *Performance*, and that in the previous year 860,000 rock music fans thrilled to its atmosphere. Sales and events director Roger Edwards said, 'Cliff Richard has long been a credit to the British music scene, and all of us at Wembley are delighted to join in this celebration of his tremendous success. His unique appeal transcends all age groups.' The doors would open at 4.00 p.m. with the show beginning at 6.00 p.m. Tickets were priced at £17.

There was an immediate rush – so much so that some feared they might not get tickets – and the positive early response quickly quieted early fears that this major undertaking would not succeed. Meantime, as the tickets sold so the grand scale of The Event began to unfold, and a soaringly high budget was spent.

It was only after The Event that its financial enormity was known: Cliff had spent nearly £2.5 million and it was announced that every penny of this sum had gone into making the show a true tribute to his thirtieth year in pop. Cliff had even forgone his own £500,000 slice of the profits.

The money division was as follows: £400,000 in wages and expenses for the roadies and technicians who had worked for over two weeks; £100,000 for paying Aswad and the Shadows as the major support bands; a similar sum on stage costumes; £300,000 on marketing and advertising; £50,000 on a champagne party to follow the concerts; £350,000 on a stunning light show; £500,000 on computerized equipment and giant video screens; and £650,000 to hire the stadium, facilities and staff over two days. Said Cliff, 'It cost a fortune but it was worth it.'

Such was the success of The Event that it was hard to find anyone who might proffer a negative response. I certainly enjoyed the whole proceeding hugely, from beginning to end, with the weather allowing it to assume the splendour and free-and-easiness of the best American West Coast festival. However, on the first day, many experienced travel problems as 16 June was the day of a strike by London Transport workers.

North Londoners know only too well the enormous traffic tailbacks and snarl-ups that can occur even on the most ordinary day, but that evening many felt they had never travelled in worse conditions. Wembley Stadium was denied the benefits of the Underground railway network, which meant that only 45,000 had arrived when the show began.

Cliff seemed to appear an hour early, if the tickets were to be believed. But there he was – no double! First came the lingering look back to when the artists now appearing were young, youthful and expectant. There were Hal and Herbie Kalin of the Kalin Twins, for example, who had toured with Cliff on his first British tour, hardly major names, but who had had one hit which lives and lives – the chirpy, up-tempo number 'When', whose lyrics rely mostly on the title word. It was a hit a little before 'Move It' entered the charts in 1958. When Cliff's record first entered the top twenty on the chart for the week ending 4 October, 'When' was at number two, having topped the chart every week from 30 August through September.

Along with the Kalin Twins came The Dallas Boys and the Vernon Girls, among them Kim Wilde's mother. The Kalins sang their British hit single, and then Cliff joined them for 'The Glory Of Love'. More of the past came with both the Searchers and Gerry and the Pacemakers, constituting the 'Mersey Set'. The Searchers began their hit trail in 1963, which was the same year that Gerry and the Pacemakers had had their first hit, also a number one, namely 'How Do You Do It?' Naturally, Gerry and his band sang their anthem 'You'll Never Walk Alone'. For those with long memories it was gold and nothing but gold as Cathy McGowan and then Jimmy Henney talked with Cliff, who hardly seemed old enough to have met some of these guests, in his cerise, black and white outfit. For older music people it was an impressive flashback to the past but some younger ones felt it rather excessive. Catherine von Ruhland, still in her twenties and an avid fan and collector of Cliff material, said, 'It was good but it got a bit wearying. I much prefer seeing Cliff as he is, as contemporary as the next. He performed some of The Event in his next tour and I took my sister, and I had to tell her as the old stuff was poured out that it would not be like this all evening. Cliff is great and I think he doesn't have to keep living off the past. Some people still think he was *Summer Holiday* and no more, and they stop there. When Cliff puts on these oldie bits it only reinforces the ignorant viewpoint.'

Aswad and reggae time followed. Aswad had been enjoying success since 1984 when 'Chasing for the Breeze' had given them a chart entry, not a high one, but enough to make people aware of them and their musical crossover potential. They had two top twenty hits, 'Don't Turn Around' and 'Give A Little Love', and a handful of other less high chart placings. In July 1989 they had a shortish chart run with 'On And On', and 'Next To You' also charted top thirty before 'Smile' in November 1990 seemingly called a halt to their once flourishing career.

Cliff fans recognized their man's costume change, as he shared with them the singing of 'Share A Dream', for it was the waistcoat with streamers he had worn for the video *Together*.

It was time for a pause. The crowd had grown by the time for the reunion of Cliff and the Shadows. Cliff strode out in blue shorts for a run-through of the early hits where he and the Shadows had combined so effectively: 'The Young Ones', 'In The Country', 'Bachelor Boy', 'Willie And The Hand Jive', 'Living Doll', 'Please Don't Tease', 'Dynamite' and 'It'll Be Me'. He then disappeared for some well-earned rest and relaxation, leaving the Shads to their own devices and memories of the times when they too hit the record charts with unceasing regularity. When people talk about the 1960s they often forget the Shadows' magnificent chart run. The facts are simple, that between 'Apache' in 1959 – a number one – and 1964, there were fifteen consecutive top twenty records, and by 1980 some twenty-eight top thirty hits, only 'The Dreams I Dream' at 42 spoiling the tidiness. In the 1960s, the Shadows had twenty-four top thirty hits – putting most artists well to shame.

They sounded marvellous: their guitar sounds bounced off the sides of the stadium, creating exciting ripples of sound. It was one of the highlights of an excellent day.

Tension rose as they reached the end of their set – you could sense that people were willing the minutes away, so that Cliff would once more appear, as he did after another break, coming on stage entirely in white, except for a jacket embellished with rhinestones. He could well have played a brief though rich set – after all, he had thrown himself around with the energy of a teenager not long before. But this was a complete show with stunning lighting that was all the more effective for being in the open air rather than confined to a theatre. It lasted ninety minutes with no break. Many thought the visual side even eclipsed *Time*.

Cliff started with 'Wired for Sound', his top five record from 1981. Then it was more of those early 1980s specials – 'Dreamin'', 'Daddy's Home' – before he split those songs and the splendid 1987 number 'Some People', with a flashback to Christmas 1964 and 'I Could Easily Fall In Love'. Then it was 'We Don't Talk Anymore' and 'Two Hearts', followed by the public reunion of Jet Harris and Tony Meehan, and a slide into a longer, rock version of 'Move It'. Harris said later, 'I had second thoughts when I saw the great crowd. When we got out there it was incredible. After that everything else seemed unreal.' Rock 'n' roll took over with 'Shake, Rattle And Roll' before something comparatively new to many of the audience, Cliff's moving rendition of 'Joanna', and then, from the same source, 'Stronger Than That'. 'Silhouettes' and 'Good Golly Miss Molly' came next, followed by the lovely 1976 song, 'Miss You Nights', with particularly arresting lighting and visual effects. And there had to be a communal outbreak of vocal support during 'Summer Holiday'. Then came his new single set for August release. From the all-hit team of Stock, Aitken and Waterman, the pacey, familiar sound of the trio adorning 'I Just Don't Have The Heart', it firmly put Cliff into the mainstream pop sound. Then it was into 'The Best Of Me', with many in the crowd flashing their free mini torches. Quite a few of the audience joined in on this number, his hundredth single, which was followed by 'God Put A Fighter In Me' and 'Thief In The Night'.

The finale was reserved for 'From A Distance'. The many support artists came back on stage, and provided a tremendous farewell into the night. Said Eileen Edwards, 'Madonna, Michael Jackson and Pink Floyd were only warm-up acts at Wembley Stadium compared with the staggering production Cliff had in store for us.'

The 250,000-watt sound system and 1,600 lamps were just two of the worthwhile costs, and, as for the stage set, Cliff himself said it was 'the largest Punch and Judy box ever'. And when promoter Mel Bush was applying to the *Guinness Book of Records* with the claim that it should be judged as the biggest stage production in the world, he might have humorously added Cliff's remark.

Did Cliff shed a tear as it drew to its close? Those with binoculars said he did. No one doubted why. It was a peak moment for anyone. Few could touch the occasion, and certainly no one of his own musical ilk. A nasty thought struck a few people around me, as they saw him standing there taking innumerable bows and savouring the volume of the applause: he might suddenly announce that this was it, the end, and he was to go out after just over thirty years at the top. There were a few uncertain 'nos'. But the moment passed, and the dreaded announcement never came. Promoter Mel would say, 'He's one of the best rock performers I've ever seen,' but no one could think of another artist who would have performed so long on any one occasion and in so many guises. And the weather was marvellous; the heat of the day lasted late into the evening. It was memorable, it was an event – no, it was *The Event*.

# CHAPTER NINETEEN

# CELEBRATING FIFTY

Fortunately a fiftieth birthday is something special, above and beyond the claims of all previous decades. Some get lost but, in Cliff's case, the media was hardly likely to pass up the opportunity of expressing how time has flown, that it is quite amazing to see Cliff still performing at fifty, that from a distance he looks forty, even younger, and to ask, can he continue and for how long, and – the old chestnut – is he ever going to head for the altar with a pretty woman beside him?

In personal and career terms, the sudden advent of a fiftieth birthday close upon the festivities of thirty years in the business could well have given a sudden jolt to a machine that had eased its way on with only minor technical problems such as the odd sore throat, sinus nuisance, occasional reminders of an ever-present back trouble, a habit of waking four or five times at night, and a slight loss of hearing in one ear. His continuing career might suddenly be questioned, for if fifty after forty may seem aged, what then of sixty following fifty?

For years Cliff has loved a classic programme from Tony Hancock (one of Britain's finest comedians, especially on radio, who took his own life), *The Blood Donor*, in which Hancock waits for what he thinks constitutes taking of blood. He suddenly says to a fat lady, 'If they gave Cliff Richard a pint of yours, that'd slow him down a bit.' Once Cliff said, 'That I'm immortalized by someone like Hancock, it's a fantastic feeling,' but perhaps now he might give a wry smile. These days, had Hancock lived, he would be in his mid-seventies, and on reflection might have felt the line was not strong enough. Certainly, Cliff believes he has cast off the Peter Pan label. When asked to comment upon it in 1990, he replied, 'Yes, the Rip Van Winkle of rock. I think I've worn out the Peter Pan of pop one. I was hoping that Michael Jackson would take that one over [Jackson is only in his early thirties, his career beginning before his teens]. The media want to have bags to put you in. I'm the Christian rock and roll singer. I'm the one who's ageless. They always used the same terminology about different artists. I find it quite flattering. I'm glad, first of all, that they recognize my faith and, of course, it's very flattering to be called ageless. I promise you, it's not true.'

What else could seem noteworthy in Cliff's life against the constant razzmatazz of the year between August 1989 and August 1990?

The thirtieth year celebrations were incredibly successful: they had coincided with an 'up' in Cliff's career cycle, a cycle that has never had any real lows, even when odd records have simply not sold, for there have always been compensations, either through an album, video, stage show (meaning *Time*), overseas concerts and so on. And, in any case, the standard of material in this twelve months, and slightly beyond into *Stronger*, had been extremely high.

As 1990 got under way, Cliff was issuing more single hits off the 1989 *Stronger* album, and at times in the previous eighteen months both single and album sales often ran parallel. It is a pity that, these days, unlike the 1960s, an album cannot chart in an overall sales listing. *From A Distance – The Event* had been a marvellous seller, following close on the heels of the phenomenal *Private Collection*, and if *Stronger* never approached the sales levels of those two, it still sold notably well. The release in August 1989 of 'I Just Don't Have The Heart', the single with the Stock, Aitken and Waterman trademark that proved Cliff could produce the 'in' pop sound just as well, or even better, than those under half his age, had been followed by one of my favourite Cliff singles, 'Lean On You', which did not make the top ten. The onset of 1990 saw release for which the single fans had cried out, namely 'Stronger Than That' with the popular ballad 'Joanna' accompanying. The excellent 'Silhouette' was followed by the birthday month release of the powerful song 'From A Distance' that would preface the run-up to the number one, 'Saviour's Day'. It was another great track run and into this would come Cliff's fiftieth birthday.

While in Britain 'Stronger Than That' was released in February, Cliff was away for ten weeks to tour New Zealand and Australia. In May he began a major European schedule that took him from Helsinki on 1 May through to the Zenith, in Paris, France, on 7

June. To some fans' disappointment, no gospel tour appeared in the diary, with none expected until at least March 1991.

Cliff dates for the UK under the *From A Distance* banner centred around three venues, Birmingham, Aberdeen and London, with the bulk of the event taking place in the Midlands NEC venue and Wembley Arena. It was decided that the evening of 7 November, at the Birmingham NEC, would have a birthday flavour and proceeds from the evening would be divided equally between the British Deaf Association and PHAB.

In February, Cliff had joined the Simon Mayo breakfast show on BBC Radio 1, via satellite from Wellington, New Zealand. He talked of taking a three-week holiday after his New Zealand and Australia tour, before the European dates. He also talked of performing in London's West End: 'I've always wanted to do a concert where I was settled in one theatre for a period of time, so I'll be there for a minimum of three months, possibly six months.' He named the *Time* venue, the Dominion, Tottenham Court Road, as the location. He told Simon Mayo, 'I'll do a concert-style performance specially built for London. I hope it will be exciting and different because being in one theatre for a length of time means I can go overboard with the effects and things as you don't have to pull them down every night.' The official disclaimer came on 9 April 1990.

On 30 June, Cliff was at Knebworth for a large scale music event that was beamed to ninety-five countries, potentially reaching a possible 90 per cent of the global population. The day was a mixture of rain and sun, and was rarely without an uncomfortable wind. Cliff wore a bright pink suit and, with the Shadows, recaptured familiar songs from his early days, adding a few rock 'n' roll numbers, plus 'We Don't Talk Anymore'. With the Shads around, it must have been for fun rather than a mistake that led Bruce into playing 'I Could Easily Fall In Love' while Cliff and the others were singing 'Bachelor Boy'.

On 19 July Cliff appeared at the Queen Mother's Ninetieth Birthday Gala at the London Palladium, where he was the only pop singer invited. It was screened at the beginning of August by the BBC and he sang 'The Young Ones' and 'The Best Of Me'. A holiday followed, before rehearsals with a smaller band than usual with only Peter May and Paul Moesl remaining from the previous one.

Lacking a world disaster to wipe out some or all of the planet, 14 October 1990 finally dawned. Only a hermit might not have known it was Cliff's fiftieth birthday. London's Capital Radio decided the whole weekend of the 14th should be his, playing Cliff music non-stop. Radio 1, often accused of ignoring Cliff's records until chart placing forces them into recognition, made him the most played singer of the day. Cliff could have given interviews to the entire UK network of stations, and beyond but Mercury Radio, Capital and Radio 1 were chosen.

Fans kept a vigil outside his house, while, at times, there was almost a minute-by-minute delivery of flowers, presents, cakes and packages. There were hundreds of telegrams among the thousands of cards and letters and the mountain of birthday greetings came from all over the world.

Speaking on the day, Cliff said, 'I have had some wonderful presents. Peter Gormley, my manager, bought me a pair of marble seats for the garden; someone else gave me an owl's nest – which I had never heard of – you put it as high as possible in a tree, and with a little bit of luck I might have owls living in the garden. My bedroom looks like a bedsit. I have been given a wonderful settee.'

The least unexpected question was how he felt, now that he was fifty. Like many, he simply said, 'I don't feel any more'. And then, with his characteristic deft turn of humour, he remarked, 'A friend said to me that I seem to be getting as much attention for my fiftieth as the Queen Mother got for her ninetieth birthday. It's not quite true, but it seems I am moving with the right set of people.'

He spent the day with his close family and special friends, admiring some of his presents and taking time every now and then to open some letters and telegrams. Fans had a great day as well. The many Cliff groups around the country raised money and some gave a little extra to charity. Cliff United fans normally give their birthday gift to charity, but this one was an exception. Christine Whitehead asked Cliff what he might like, and the fan club gave him some pillars for his intended pergola – an ever-present visual reminder of the club.

In Kingston-on-Thames, so many people wanted to attend a fiftieth-birthday disco that many could not gain admission. At midnight fans sang 'Congratulations' and 'Happy Birthday' with glasses raised to Cliff. There was a large birthday cake for eventual consumption.

The International Cliff Richard Movement's magazine *DI* had its managing editor, Anton Husmann, exclaiming: 'Cliff Richard is 50 years young,' and recalling that he has run the fan club for thirty years, Husmann admitted, 'Indeed, I am only three years younger than he is. But for sure I could not do the same things.' His wish for Cliff was that his physical condition and health will permit a career for many years to come. The front page, apart from the Husmann editorial, was filled with good wishes from individuals and clubs around the world, from Cliff record expert William Hooper to 'Jaquey and all your Kent fans' and 'You were No. 1 in the Philippines in February, but you're always No. 1 with US(A). Happy Birthday, Cliff! Los Angeles News Meeting House.'

Fan clubs, meeting houses and individual Cliff fans gave the ICRM a birthday gift of £2,500, presenting Cliff with a cheque. Cliff said, 'I'm bowled over, to say the least! All I can say is that your money will be put to good use – and a lot of people will benefit! Thanks once again – Love ya! See you around, Cliff.'

The front of *Dynamite International*, from the Cliff Richard London and Surrey Fan Club simply printed:

> What we have to say is very simple,
> For your age you're very nimble.
> You're looking great now you are fifty,
> Those dance routines are very nifty.
> Your shows are great and full of fun,
> You'll always be our number one.
> We wish you joy, we wish you peace,
> Let those great hit records never cease.
> HAPPY BIRTHDAY, CLIFF.

Not great poetry, perhaps, but the message is direct and effective. Extracts from two magazines, *Woman* (they devoted six pages to Cliff in their issue of 8 October) and *Woman's Realm* (the latter being taken from *Survivor*) gave the fan club members an absorbing guide through Cliff's career. *Chat* magazine readers voted Cliff their ideal date, beating off Mel Gibson, Robert Redford and Tom Cruise. The Yorkshire fan club went to town in its magazine dated 14 October. Their front page message was brief: 'From A Distance you look pretty good for a 50 yr old, Cliff. (Close to you look even better!) Have a great time.' Apart from members sending monetary gifts to Cliff's Charitable Trust Fund and a £100 personal gift, the club bought an oval wooden plaque engraved with a picture of York Minster. Above it were the words 'Happy

50th Birthday, Cliff' and underneath, 'Yorkshire Fan Club'. For his thirtieth anniversary they had given him white rose bushes and standard roses.

The fiftieth birthday event at Birmingham's NEC was quite a show, a veritable 'must' for fans. It was certainly special, not the least for the extra emotion generated by 10,000 people. Those attending were given mini torches to switch on during the show, recalling The Event at Wembley in 1989 and thousands of birthday balloons dropped from the ceiling. Cliff told the audience, 'I'm not usually lost for words, but I'm speechless.' Tears were evident. He added, 'I am beginning to feel like the Queen Mum. Our birthdys seem to go on for ever.'

Backstage, Cliff threw a champagne party and naturally blew out the candles on a magnificent cake decorated with an iced statuette of himself in the middle. Mike Read, Kim Wilde and John Reid, Elton John's manager, were among those present and John Reid presented Cliff with a special present from the one-time Reginald Dwight: a £15,000 diamond brooch and fifty-two bottles of vintage wine.

Momentarily tarnishing the wonderful nature of the happenings was a newspaper story in which it was said that some fans were supposedly angry that Cliff had used some backing tapes for more than half his three-hour performance. Naturally, the supposition was that he must be too old to sing and dance simultaneously. Since even teen stars use backing tapes – without a three-hour show of non-stop music and movement – it seemed nothing less than nonsense. And it was a trend at the time to use backing tapes. A fuss over nothing, perhaps, but the criticisms were voiced. Not all appreciated the extra show-biz razzmataaa: some found the loudness distracting, others the new band set-up, and one person was even reported as saying that he had left the show before it ended (he should have applied to the *Guinness Book of Records*). Many thought Cliff's new hair style was terrific and his outfits most eye-catching.

The fiftieth birthday had passed. Within months, following upon the plethora of British dates, he was number one again with 'Saviour's Day'. His age just didn't matter.

'As far as I'm concerned the best is yet to come. Occasionally I have to remind myself that I started five years before the Beatles. When I was eighteen, there were no fifty-year-old rock stars, and at the age of eighteen, I would have thought it impossible. But I can still perform it.'

CHAPTER TWENTY

# AND SO IT GOES ON

Early in 1992 Cliff rediscovered the 1950s.

Along with his mates, Joe Brown, Marty Wilde and Bruce Welch, he took himself out for the evening. Along with Gloria Hunniford, Tony Blackburn, Jess Conrad, Lonnie Donegan and numerous others, they went to see *Good Rockin' Tonite*, the rock 'n' roll musical from the man who had popularized the new pop of the 1950s, Jack Good – soon, it seemed, readying himself for life in a monastery in New Mexico, Texas. And when Joe Brown borrowed a guitar from one of the stage musicians, Ronnie Caryl, it was time for an unexpected 'jam' session. Good was paid a considerable compliment by Cliff: 'He changed the face of rock and roll in this country and he was so special to work with.' Later in the evening, Cliff bopped his way through a special party for Good, spending noticeable time with Gloria Hunniford, the prominent British television personality, presenter and interviewer. The *Daily Mirror* headlined: GLORIA AND CLIFF CHEEK TO CREAK.

Good, with Jess Conrad, Wee Willie Harris and others, took part in a 14 February edition of the BBC *Kilroy* show, a talk-discussion presentation, but while Bruce Welch was in the audience there was no sign of Cliff.

February was a month of extremes. During Willy Russell's comedy *One For The Road* at Exeter's Northcott Theatre, forty Cliff records, donated by EMI, were smashed. The British *Daily Mail* on 26 February advanced Cliff's age to fifty-two, and linked the past with the present, when Cliff recalled bus days with the film *Summer Holiday* as he launched his Tennis Trail scheme at the All England Club, Wimbledon. Sue Barker was among those attending, and indeed received fulsome credit from Cliff as the one who had really fired his enthusiasm for the game. Now, he announced, he would hit the road with some of Britain's leading coaches in an effort to foster and find neglected talent.

214

He also found 1992 a time for commemorating himself in wax, fortunately not ten feet under, but instead providing visual guidance for a lifesize replica by sculptor Willow Legge; this was unveiled in July at Rock Circus in Piccadilly, although work on the statue had begun in February.

Another interesting moment in the same year was an appearance on the BBC TV show, *Wogan*, where he sang with the major group Wet Wet Wet, prompting speculation that they might combine for a major chart assault. There was also the wedding of his 21-year-old niece to Matthew Payne, with Cliff lending his Rolls-Royce for the couple's big day.

Less pleasing was the now-usual backlash over distribution of tickets for the 1992 concerts, with fans saying ticket agencies were being given priority over fan club members. It led to Val Sanderson of the York Meeting House writing to Cliff's office. She was told in response that agencies are the lifeblood of ticket sales, and that it was the policy of the office to give fan clubs advance information of Cliff tour dates so that they could gear themselves for the expected rush. Matters were not helped for the 1992 season when, according to Cliff's office, 'the Sheffield venue management took it upon themselves to issue a press release about the Sheffield dates a week before the official press announcement. This, as we told them, blew our whole publicity campaign and our displeasure was made evident.'

Nineteen ninety-two has also seen Cliff take a well-earned holiday, skiing in Europe, and he has been in the recording studio for his new album which should coincide with the autumn tour if completed in time. In view of lacklustre singles from last October onwards, it's fingers crossed for a real record revival, as can often happen when a few records have slipped. Mike Read linked a six-part BBC Radio 2 series on Cliff. This spring he appeared on the Bruce Forsyth show, with Pat Cash and during September there was considerable rehearsal time for the Access To All Areas tour. Instant ticket take led to extra dates, with Cliff commenting at the time, 'The tickets may go on sale a year in advance, but the fans are getting autumn '92 tickets at autumn '91 prices! I'll be putting on a spectacular show.'

In the meantime, the Cliff show goes on, and Christine Whitehead of Cliff United continues to receive between 500 and 2,000 letters a week!

The year should end with another Cliff music and stage explosion. The Cliff story cannot be tidily concluded. A postscript is in the same position as an introduction. This an ongoing saga, and there is no sign of this story ending.

As Mickie Most told me at his RAK studios, 'Artists have a hit or two, they get into yachts, girls, Hollywood, fashion, clubs, you name it, and they forget the music. Cliff hasn't been like that. He has some expensive things but they've never taken him over.'

The Controller of Radio 1, Johnny Beerling, can span the years: 'I remember him once terribly nervous, early hits or not. He would gabble. Then I remember he had this problem with his weight. But that was twenty-six years or more ago! He's essentially niceness and goodness, his charm comes through, he's almost too good to be true. His achievement is spectacular. He's always locked into the general mainstream. He has this tremendous willpower, and he must be a terribly ambitious person, even if he has kept himself a pretty private person. About his records and if they will be played on Radio 1, well, what he does, what anyone does, has to be judged as a piece of music – if it fits, then fine.'

George Hoffman, a great friend of both Cliff and Bill, was director of Tear Fund through some great times. He knows well the amount of time Cliff has given, in a busy show-biz itinerary, to the charity, and he knows the money raised by Cliff passes the million-pound mark. 'He's someone who always wants to get it right. There is always a freshness about him, and at the same time he doesn't have airs and graces. He wants to know answers, and he has travelled to see what kind of work Tear Fund has done with the various monies over the years. He hasn't stood afar, merely a wealthy patron.' Hoffman says more: 'He has such infinite patience, unbelievable at times. I remember once being with him on a flight to India, a long haul, and there were people continually waking him up since we were in economy, yet he was always cheery. I learnt then why he needs isolation. I remember Cliff for the small arenas, and I mean a church youth fellowship! Some of the young people cautiously brought their guitars and when I arrived there he was with them, working things out, far from the "star" image that some people might have adopted. And even for his performance in this setting he still chalks where he will move, gets down to a fine art the space for walking, runs down the cues. I mean, he could have just turned up, sat on a stool, sang some songs, and people would have thought what a great honour it was! Do you know of any stars like him who do this sort of thing?'

Una Stubbs has told me, 'I can remember when the Beatles were around. I think Cliff admired them and he was friendly towards them. I think some people thought his innings was over with all these new groups. But here he is. When I think of Cliff and past times I can remember we laughed a lot, and we still do when we meet. I suppose it gets a bit boring saying positive things about Cliff but I have to say he is intelligent and a very responsible artist, and that's important in show business if you are going to stay around. You can have some wonderful conversations with him. I worked a lot with him at one time, in film and television, and all that we did was tightly scripted and he always got it right without as it were, being a trained actor. And there was panto-mime, and I can remember us being smuggled out because there were so many fans always waiting for him. He's the sort of person you instinctively keep in touch with. I remember the time when the Christian thing really got under way. I think he was floun-dering a bit, and wasn't too certain, there were so many pres-sures. But he has stayed with it and grown and grown. I recall the time when he wanted to be a teacher, and then he decided to stay in the business. I think show-biz was too much in his system. I've winced for him when I've seen people pick on him, use him unfairly, try and trap him and it's not usually in his nature to snap back. You know, he's kept on getting better. Maybe it's good not to have peaks but I suppose there are the special moments, and he's never lost out. All I can say is that I want to work with him again. But he has so much going for him, and I'm glad I've been in his success story.'

His Christian friend Garth Hewitt, who has been with him on gospel tours and keeps in close contact with him, has had his differences of opinion, especially at one time over Cliff's views on South Africa (though not on apartheid, which both abhor) but he has always been impressed. 'I think if you want to work with him then you have to have done your homework, you have to come up to scratch. He has lots of character and he demands. He hasn't any time for the sub-standard from people who ought to know more and do better. He is such a strong person in so many ways, and that's a major reason why he will continue. Really he has contributed so much to so many different areas. His Christian sentiments now feature even more strongly, they interweave more in all that he does. I suppose I would like to see him with a few raw edges (well, yes, he is a perfectionist), I mean be pushed creatively but in so many ways he's out there doing it.'

But there are so many people with things to say, some of whom may have done so elsewhere. Some have played important parts in his life. Among these are Alan Tarney and Malcolm Addey, who once sat at the controls in Studio 2 as 'Move It' was recorded. These people have countless memories of other recordings and meetings and for them Cliff is one of the greats. I suppose this postscript has become Adulation Corner. But so? There is always something to say about Cliff and there will be more to write if there is a new edition of this book in 2001 – now there's a date and a thought!

# FACTS

# DIARY OF EVENTS 1959-92

In no way is it promised that every single Cliff public event is recorded. All listings continue from the hardback edition of *Cliff* (1981) and not the ensuing paperback that saw an extra six months added. His post-1981 Christian activities have been incorporated into this section and no longer have a section of their own.

February 1959: elected Best New Singer by readers of *New Musical Express* in their annual poll (in those days the *NME* was pop and chart orientated).

February 1960: *NME* readers vote Cliff Top British Male Singer.

February 1961: Cliff continues where he left off in 1960. In the *NME* poll he is voted Top British Male Singer.

March 1961: Peter Gormley becomes Cliff's manager (and he still is!). A note in the diary for 1961 says the two met for talks in Peter's office on 20 January.

May 1961: Cliff's father dies.

11 May 1961: Cliff goes to the Variety Club Awards dinner at the Dorchester, London.

13 May 1961: with the Shadows Cliff attends a special event organized by the Variety Club at the Festival Gardens, Battersea, London.

26 May 1961: Cliff presents awards at the Methodist Association of Youth Clubs' annual national get-together at the Royal Albert Hall, London. He sings 'Living Doll'.

January 1962: the press report seventeen-year-old Valerie Stratford saying she is going to marry Cliff. Claim dismissed.

February 1962: *NME* readers again vote Cliff Top British Male Singer.

13 March 1962: Cliff receives award from Variety Club of Great Britain as Show Business Personality of the Year. Presentation is at the Savoy in London.

24 April 1962: Cliff dines with the head of EMI, Sir Joseph Lockwood.

11 December 1962: Cliff attends London Home Counties Cinematograph Exhibition's annual dinner.

10 January 1963: Cliff with the Shadows at *Summer Holiday* première, Warner Theatre, London.

11 February 1963: appears in a charity concert in Nairobi which is organized by Kenya leader Tom Mboya.

August 1963: top-selling US magazine *16* votes Cliff Most Promising Singer in annual poll.

19–21 August 1963: Cliff records in Nashville, backed by Elvis's Jordanaires.

27 September 1963: Cliff's rumoured romance with Jackie Irving hits the headlines.

20 October 1963: Cliff appears on the top-ranking US TV *Ed Sullivan Show*.

2 July 1964: attends premiere of *Wonderful Life* at Leicester Square Theatre, organized by the National Association of Youth Clubs. Princess Alexandra and Angus Ogilvy also attend.

November 1965: Cliff and the Shadows at the Royal Variety Show.

4 December 1965: Cliff in a show at his old school, Cheshunt Secondary Modern.

3 April 1966: appears in the Stars' Organization for Spastics concert at Wembley Empire Pool.

16 June 1966: on stage with Billy Graham at Earls Court, London.

3 July 1966: Cliff makes a radio appeal for Westminster Homes for Elderly People.

20 August 1966: news of Cliff purchasing

221

a house for his mother at Highfield Drive, Broxbourne. Two other houses also bought within easy distance of Highfield Drive for his two sisters and aunt.

24 October 1966: newspapers say Cliff is heading for concerts behind the Iron Curtain.

8 December 1966: attends première of *Finders Keepers* at Leicester Square, London.

12 December 1966: with the Shadows attends première of puppet film *Thunderbirds Are Go!* Cliff and the Shadows are the puppets!

14 February 1967: *Disc* votes Cliff Best-Dressed Male Star.

23 September 1967: *Melody Maker* readers vote Cliff Top Male Singer.

14 February 1968: Cliff at *Disc* Valentines Awards.

9 March 1968: sister Joan Webb marries and Cliff gives her away.

28 June 1968: Cliff lends aid to the National Society for the Prevention of Cruelty to Children projected Christmas card.

Late 1968: the Shadows split up.

10 December 1969: Cliff represents the pop world at a special gala midnight performance at the London Palladium in aid of the Royal Society for the Prevention of Cruelty to Animals.

14 February 1970: Cliff receives *Disc*'s Mr Valentine award. He is also voted Best-Dressed Male Star, comes second as Top British Singer, and third in the World Singer stakes.

3 May 1970: Cliff is voted second Top British Male Singer, Top British Vocal Personality, and third World Male Singer in the 1969 *NME* readers' poll. Cliff's personality award is presented by Malcolm Roberts at the *NME* Poll Concert.

5 July 1971: Antibes-Juan Les Pins. Eighth Festival of the Rose d'Or. Cliff receives Ivor Novello Award for outstanding service to British music from festival organizer Claude Tabel. With Olivia Newton-John, Cliff charms the music delegates. The duo sing together on each of the three festival nights and are filmed by the BBC. The festival is also filmed by French TV.

14 April 1972: *The Sun* presents Cliff with its award for Top Male Pop Personality for the third year running. He is out of London on a gospel tour at the time and receives the award in Liverpool,

the first location on the tour.

1974: Cliff is awarded a Silver Clef for outstanding services to the music industry at the second annual Music Therapy Committee luncheon. He receives his award from the Duchess of Gloucester.

3–11 April 1974: London Palladium season. Cliff falls ill with throat and chest problems. Rolf Harris deputizes for three nights.

9 July 1974: headlined as an 'All-time First', the International Cliff Richard Movement gathers members together at the United Reform Church, Crouch End, London, for a day of Cliff with material about Tear Fund, the film strip *Love Never Gives Up* (made during a visit by Cliff to Burundi), a 'Portrait of Cliff' competition, a short concert from Cliff, the chance to ask him questions, and a screening of the film *A Day in the Life of Cliff Richard*.

4 September 1974: Romsey Abbey Appeal. Cliff gives support and meets Lady Janet Mountbatten.

27 October 1974: Cliff at the London Palladium with the Shadows, who re-form to appear with him there in a charity concert for the widow of former BBC TV producer Colin Charman. The Shadows on this occasion are: Hank Marvin, Bruce Welch, Brian Bennett, with John Farrar replacing the late John Rostill who had died on 26 November 1973. Cliff sings 'Willie And The Hand Jive', 'Bachelor Boy', 'Don't Talk To Him', 'A Matter Of Moments', 'Power To All Our Friends'.

21 February 1975: lunch with the head of BBC religious programmes John Lang.

1 May 1975: at the offices of the World Record Club (affiliated to EMI) Cliff receives a presentation from Managing Director Derek Sinclair to mark the sale of 40,000 of the six-record boxed set, *The Cliff Richard Story*. A gold presentation soon follows, on 8 June, for double that amount.

5 June 1975: Cliff headlines a special charity concert at Manchester's Free Trade Hall promoted by Radio Piccadilly. Proceeds are for the families of Sergeant Williams and PC Rodgers, two Manchester policemen who had died on duty.

22 July 1975: attends Variety Club luncheon honouring Vera Lynn at the Savoy, London.

1976: A record deal is announced by EMI

for the release of Cliff recordings in the
USSR: *I'm Nearly Famous* and *The Best of
Cliff Richard*. Cliff is the third EMI artist
given record release in the Soviet
Union. The others are Wings and
Robert Young.

March 1976: Cliff's visit to the Soviet
Union is postponed. In the States,
'Miss You Nights' gives promise of the
long-awaited Cliff record triumph
across the Atlantic.

8 June 1976: Cliff is back at World Records
for a gold disc presentation for *The Cliff
Richard Story* six-record boxed set.

15 September 1976: Cliff begins his visit to
the Soviet Union via Copenhagen and
Stockholm, from where he proceeds to
Leningrad.

25 September 1976: reception at the
British Embassy, Moscow.

December 1976: Cliff in India, the country
of his birth. Meets Mother Teresa of
Calcutta and her Missionaries of
Charity. Cliff spends an hour singing
carols and visits the Home for the
Destitute and Dying. Two major
appearances at the Kalamandir
Auditorium, New Delhi, on 7 and 8
December. Visits Tear Fund projects in
Bangladesh.

10 February 1977: obviously appreciated
by World Records, Cliff is guest of
honour on its twenty-first anniversary.

6 June 1977: Cliff speaks at a Youth Rally,
part of the Queen's Silver Jubilee
celebrations, in Windsor Great Park.

5 September 1977: publication of Cliff's
book, written with Bill Latham, *Which
One's Cliff?*

18 October 1977: to celebrate the
coinciding events of the Queen's Silver
Jubilee and the centenary of the
gramophone, the British Phonographic
Institute in its Britannia Awards names
Cliff Best British Male Solo Artist.

28 October 1977: Cliff receives the Gold
Badge Award from the Songwriters'
Guild of Great Britain.

27 February 1978: appears at the London
Palladium reunited with the Shadows.
Season ends 11 March.

6 March 1978: special dinner with EMI at
Rags restaurant.

7 March 1978: dines with Elton John.

29 June 1978: Music Therapy Committee
luncheon.

1 September 1978: presents budgerigars
to pensioners in Weybridge.

6 November 1978: is photographed, with
others, for the front cover of the

*Guinness Book of Hit Singles*.

1 February 1979: EMI throw a special
luncheon at Claridges to celebrate their
twenty-one-year partnership with Cliff,
who receives a gold replica of the key to
EMI's Manchester Square offices, and a
gold clock.

13 February 1979: *Music Week* annual
awards. Cliff and the Shadows receive
an award for their twenty-one years as
major British recording artists.

27 February 1979: Cliff lunches at New
Scotland Yard.

1 May 1979: attends Local Radio Awards
at Grosvenor House Hotel, London,
organized by *Radio and Record News*,
*Radio Month*.

5 July 1979: Variety Club of Great Britain
lunch, Dorchester Hotel, London. Cliff
presents the Sunshine Coach, which
has been given by the organization to
children in the Club's homes. Cliff is
guest of honour in celebration of his
twenty-one years in show business.
The Shadows, Joan Collins, and the
Duke of Kent are some of the guests.

22 September 1979: Cliff takes part in an
anti-racist festival in Birmingham
– Hosannah '79.

4 October 1979: Cliff and Kate Bush with
the London Symphony Orchestra
appear in concert at the Royal Albert
Hall in aid of the LSO's Seventy-fifth
Birthday Appeal.

2 December 1979: Cliff takes part in a
concert in aid of the International Year
of the Child at Camberley, Surrey.

16 December 1979: Cliff leads a crowd
estimated at 30,000 in Carols for the
Queen outside Buckingham Palace,
part of the International Year of the
Child activities.

1980: Cliff voted number one in the Top
Pop Star category by listeners of BBC's
high-audience Saturday morning show
*Swapshop*. He wins the *TV Times* Award
for the Most Exciting Singer (male) on
television.

6 February 1980: Cliff tops the bill at a
special tribute concert at Fairfield Hall,
Croydon, to long-time musical mentor
Norrie Paramor who died in 1979. The
concert, in aid of the Stars'
Organization for Spastics, is attended
by the Duchess of Kent. Cliff,
accompanied by the Ron Goodwin
Orchestra with aid from Tony Rivers,
John Perry, and Stu Calver, sings six
numbers closely connected with
Norrie: 'Congratulations', 'Summer

Holiday', 'The Young Ones', 'Bachelor Boy' (Cliff on guitar), 'Constantly', and 'The Day I Met Marie'.

27 February 1980: *Nationwide, Daily Mirror* and *Radio 1* annual awards. Cliff receives the Nationwide Golden Award as Best Family Entertainer.

16 April 1980: mother-of-two Kim Kayne pays £1,400 for the privilege of lunching with Cliff. Capital Radio (London) listeners were invited to make a financial offer for this meeting with Cliff, with the winning total being donated to the charity Help a London Child. The menu: melon, fillet steak with Spanish sauce, green beans with ham, new potatoes, aubergines in batter, salad, strawberry shortcake, champagne, wine and coffee. The lunch was held at Cliff's office.

23 July 1980: at 10.10 a.m. Cliff arrives at Buckingham Palace with his mother to receive his OBE. Those watching break into 'Congratulations' as he drives through the Palace gates. At 12.30 Cliff leaves, weaving a Union Jack through an open car window and holding his OBE high. He then attends a champagne lunch.

2 October 1980: Cliff takes part in a long-lasting Telethon TV show organized to raise money for charity.

January 1981: promotional visit to the United States for March tour.

24 February 1981: at the Café Royal Cliff receives the *Daily Mirror* readers' award as Outstanding Music Personality of the Year, presented by Una Stubbs.

27 February 1981: at 12.30 Cliff leaves London's Heathrow Airport for the US and Canada for a tour which was originally planned to last a month but which extends to seven weeks. Cliff regards this as a most important tour. The locations were: 3 March, Seattle; 4th, Victoria (Canada); 5th, Vancouver; 6th, day off; 7th, Calgary; 8th, Edmonton; 9th, Saskatoon; 10th, Regina; 11th–12th, Winnipeg; 13th–14th, days off; 15th, Minneapolis; 16th, TV programme *Solid Gold*, Los Angeles; 17th, Grand Forks; 18th, day off; 19th, Thunder Bay; 20th, Sault St Marie; 21st, day off; 22nd, Sudbury; 23rd, Ottawa; 24th, Hamilton; 25th, day off; 26th, Kingston; 27th, Kitchener; 28th, London; 29th, day off; 30th, Toronto; 31st, Montreal; 1 April, Boston; 2nd New York; 3rd, Philadelphia; 4th, Baltimore; 5th, day off; 6th, Cleveland;

7th, Cincinnatti; 8th, Columbus; 9th, Chicago; 10th, Milwaukee; 11th, day off; 12th, Kansas City; 13th, day off; 14th, Denver; 15th, Salt Lake City; 16th, day off; 17th, San Francisco; 18th, Los Angeles.

1 May 1981: Cliff Richard Rock Special at Odeon Theatre, Hammersmith – one show, filmed by BBC producer Norman Stone. Audience in fifties-style gear.

Spring 1981: voted Top Pop Star in the *Sunday Telegraph* readers' poll of major personalities in British life.

3 May 1981: Cliff is filmed at London's Hard Rock Café. The press is invited. He relives the early rock 'n' roll days. He wears black leather drainpipes, lurex tour tie, crêpe-soled shoes, white jacket plus a wig combed into a greasy teddy boy quiff. He sings '"D" In Love' and is backed by the Fantoms. The next day the newspapers show pictures of the event. He has been filmed by the BBC for a forthcoming documentary on his life.

27 June 1981: poet and writer Steve Turner weds Mo MacAfferty. Cliff attends. The reception is held at Cliff's house.

24 July 1981: Milton Keynes: shoppers see Cliff being filmed for a video which is for promoting the single 'Wired For Sound' and the album of the same title.

Late July to August 1981: holiday in Portugal and some concerts in South Africa.

28 August 1981: along with Garth Hewitt and Network Three, at Youth for Christ concert organized by Kamperland Muziek Festival.

30 August 1981: at the Greenbelt festival.

1–2 September 1981: takes part in tenth anniversary of Arts Centre Group. Two special concerts at Wembley Conference Centre.

30 September 1981: begins two-week US promotional visit.

15 October 1981: hardback edition of *Cliff* is published by Sidgwick and Jackson.

2 November 1981: British tour opens at Glasgow and like all Cliff's locations, tickets sold out within hours of date being announced.

5 November 1981: begins Edinburgh booking.

11 November 1981: starts four nights at Manchester's Apollo Theatre.

16 November 1981: Tear Fund Gala Night at Royal Albert Hall, London. Cliff is surprise guest.

18 November 1981: commences concerts at The Centre, Brighton.

21–7 November 1981: appears on the front page of the *Radio Times* edition for this week.

23 November 1981: Cliff is one of the invited artists at the Royal Variety Command Performance.

25 November 1981: starts four nights at the Odeon, Birmingham.

2 December 1981: the London four-concert booking begins at the Odeon, Hammersmith.

10 December 1981: Cliff makes a public appearance at Woolco, Bournemouth. He signs 1,057 albums and books.

16 December 1981: Coliseum, St Austell, the last tour venue. Final night is 19 December.

23 December 1981: off to Florida for his Christmas holiday.

4 January 1982: returns from Florida.

12–13 February 1982: plays the Queen Elizabeth Hall, Hong Kong.

15–16 February 1982: at the Hua Mark Stadium, Bangkok, Thailand.

19 February 1982: in Singapore.

22 February 1982: a concert at the Entertainment Centre, Perth, Australia.

24–25 February 1982: concert at the Apollo Stadium, Adelaide, Australia.

27–28 February 1982: at the Festival Hall, Melbourne, Australia.

3 March 1982: appears at the Festival Hall, Brisbane, Australia.

5–6 March 1982: at the Horden Pavilion, Sydney, Australia.

9–10 March 1982: plays the Town Hall in Christchurch, New Zealand.

12–13 March 1982: at the Lagan Campbell Centre, Auckland, New Zealand.

25 March 1982: British papers carry story of possible romance between Cliff and tennis star Sue Barker.

31 March 1982: Cliff launches an appeal in London for children's hospitals.

1 April 1982: the *Daily Mail* quotes Cliff on his relationship with Sue Barker in a front-page article saying: 'Our relationship has only just started, but I have seen more of her than anyone else for quite a while.'

17 April 1982: interviewed at The Night Out, Birmingham.

5 June 1982: he is spotted at the Beckenham Tennis Tournament and watches Sue Barker with doubles partner Pam Shriver beat Billie Jean King and Ilana Kloss in the Doubles Final.

21 June 1982: at Wimbledon.

22 June 1982: sees Sue Barker beaten by Sharon Walsh in the first round.

10 July 1982: USA tour opens in San Francisco.

30 July 1982: ends USA tour where he started.

25 August 1982: Miss UK Contest. No, not Cliff! But Miss Belfast says she admires him more than any other man.

27 August 1982: back in Britain after holiday, jets in from Bermuda.

10 October 1982: begins European tour in Hanover.

14 October 1982: 42nd birthday spent in Aalborg, Denmark.

2 November 1982: ends his European tour in Münster, West Germany.

Early November: attends the British Wightman cup events at the Royal Albert Hall, in which Sue Barker is a participant.

23 November 1982: he is featured in a concert at the Royal Albert Hall, London, with the London Philharmonic Orchestra which is celebrating its 50th anniversary, filmed by the BBC and recorded by EMI.

25 November 1982: performs a private concert for pupils of St Brandon's School in the Avon area, where he is a governor.

Christmas: spends it in Bavaria with his mother.

13 January–19 February: Tear Fund: *The Road To Freedom* As part of the show, video of Cliff in Kenya is shown.

1 February 1983: arrives in Singapore, beginning his South East Asia tour.

5 February 1983: arrives in Bangkok.

8 February 1983: arrives in Hong Kong.

12 February 1983: in Manila.

9 March 1983: in Australia. Concerts attend by 8,000 plus.

2 April 1983: opens a new record shop, owned by Bernie Brown, in Terence Road, Walton-on-Thames.

August 1983: Host of events take place for this Silver Jubilee. Avalanche of Cliff music, comments, some interviews on media (*see* radio, television, and Chapter 15). Receives various awards, including one at the EMI Sales Conference.

26–29 August 1983: Greenbelt festival and Cliff takes part. So does Sheila Walsh. He appears on 27 August.

3 September 1983: promotional TV work in Germany for new album.

14 September 1983: in America, appears

on *Solid Gold* and other TV shows.

24 September 1983: Olivia Newton-John is with him when he returns from the US.

26 September 1983: launches his book, *You, Me and Jesus* (Hodder and Stoughton).

26 September 1983: begins rehearsing for Silver Jubilee tour.

5 October 1983: begins new UK tour at the Apollo Theatre, Oxford. Remains there until 8th.

11–12 October 1983: Apollo Theatre, Glasgow.

14–15 October 1983: the Playhouse, Edinburgh.

19–22 October 1983: Apollo Theatre, Manchester.

26–29 October 1983: Odeon Theatre, Birmingham.

3 November 1983: Apollo, Victoria, London. Remains there until finale on 3 December.

12 December 1983: plays in Pro-Celebrity Tennis Tournament at the Brighton Centre. It is his debut as a tennis player in the public arena.

25 March 1984: spotted at another Davis Cup event, watching Sue Barker.

April 1984: overseas, involved with Tear Fund projects.

13 May 1984: speaks at London's famous All Souls Church, Langham Place, London; queue commences 90 minutes before start.

2 June 1984: appears at Elmbridge Leisure Centre, to raise money for Princess Alice Hospital, Esher.

5 June 1984: on stage with evangelist Luis Palau at White City, along with Miss London.

13 June 1984: joins Sheila Walsh on stage with Luis Palau.

2–5 July 1984: appears with the Shadows at Wembley Arena, moving on to NEC, Birmingham.

August 1984: spends entire month in Portugal.

7 September 1984: begins another British gospel tour, opening at the Gaumont, Southampton

8 October 1984: begins six-night residency at Blazers.

20 October 1984: begins Australian tour at Amphi Theatre, Darwin. Takes a tennis coach with him for tour. Had been suffering from a bad back.

27–28 October: appears in Perth Channel 7 Telethon.

23 November 1984: in New Zealand and arrives in Auckland for his Thunder tour.

6 December 1984: his gold jacket is auctioned by Tyne Tees TV during a Telethon to aid Ethiopia.

15 December 1984: Pro-Celebrity Tennis Tournament at Brighton Centre.

16 December 1984: Arts Centre Group Christian event at Fairfield Hall, Croydon.

28–30 December 1984: in South Africa.

1 January, 1985: plays Sun City.

3–6 January 1985: Three Arts Centre, Cape Town.

9–11 January 1985: City Hall, Durban.

12 January 1985: Christian booking in Pretoria.

25 March 1985: attends special tribute service to David Watson, evangelist at City Temple, London.

April and May 1985: intensive recording schedules.

8 June 1985: appears with Luis Palau in Amsterdam.

1 July 1985: preview of video *It's A Small World*.

2 July 1985: Tells *Daily Mirror* that charity concerts may become a fad.

9 July 1985: begins UK Gospel tour in Conference Centre, Harrogate.

24–27 July 1985: cancels five gospel concerts because of laryngitis.

1 August 1985: performs with Sheila Walsh at Praise In The Rockies.

Much of August and September out of Britain, although ill while on holiday, and then promoting end of September British and European tour. Also appears at Christian Youth Conference in Warsaw.

8 August 1985: *Cliff Richard and the Shadows Around the World in Pictures* by Dezo Hoffman (the photographer who went everywhere with Cliff and whose pictures largely adorned 1981 edition of *Cliff*.

29 August 1985: Sotheby's auction some Cliff material, including his first acetate recording and his Ibanez Concord electric acoustic guitar.

4, 5 and 7 October 1985: laryngitis postpones three opening concerts of European tour.

6 October 1985: Cliff's name is removed from UN Anti-Apartheid list: Bill Latham follows with a statement.

21 December 1985: Pro-Celebrity Tennis Tournament in Brighton.

21 December 1985: sad death from heart attack of Graham Jarvis, age thirty-five, who had been the drummer with Thunder.

25 December 1985: spends quiet Christmas at home. Proposed early 1992 visit to the US cancelled for several weeks when he hears tragic news of 21 December.

10 January 1986: Cliff speaks at gathering of Graham Jarvis's friends after the cremation service. Members of Thunder were present. Cliff recalls how Graham had worked with him for ten years.

Mid-January: flies to America after postponing earlier booking.

26 February 1986: receives Top Singer award from *TV Times*.

2 March 1986: mayor's charity show, Secombe Centre, Sutton.

9 April 1986: *Time* has its première. Cast of thirty with eight principals.

19 April 1986: National Viewers' and Listeners' Association annual meeting. Cliff presents best TV show award to *Blue Peter*.

18 May 1986: another visit to All Souls Church, Langham Place, to talk of faith and answer questions.

28 August 1986: another rock 'n' roll memorabilia auction at Sotheby's. On offer and sold, 'Deep Purple', early 1960s acetate recording never issued. Also two others, 'Who's Gonna Take You Home?' and 'Let's Stick Together' with both late 1959 recordings. Also 10-inch acetate of 'Breathless', 'Lawdy Miss Clawdy', and 'We Had It Made'. Also offered, Cliff song, 'Sweet Loving Ways'.

7 September 1986: one of numerous artists recording during day at Abbey Road, EMI studio for charity record *Live-In-World*. Cliff arrives in fairly new green metallic Rolls with black interior upholstery.

No date but Cliff makes rare club appearance at Stringfellows, London's Leicester Square area. He is pictured with Paul Young.

29 October 1986: attends launch of Mike Read's book, *Old 2i's*. in Old Compton Street, Soho, although now a French restaurant. Book was intended for publication on 14 October. Entitled: *The Cliff Richard File*.

8 December 1986: attends Tearcraft sale at St Peter's Church, Vere Street.

21 December 1986: another year passes, another Pro-Am Celebrity Tournament.

27 December 1986: attends No To Drugs event at London's famous Hard Rock Café.

6 February 1987: presents prize to best optician's receptionist in Britain – Pamela Atwood.

11 April 1987: leaves *Time*.

14 April 1987: returns to *Time* for special matinée performance in honour of Laurence Olivier.

6 June 1987: signs new record contract with EMI, most sensible in view of the sales to come.

8 June 1987: plays a special concert at Wimbledon Theatre but not recognized as part of gospel tour. New-look band and singers.

10–27 June 1987: UK gospel tour opens at the Edinburgh Playhouse.

15 June 1987: at the Alton Towers leisure centre for BBC TV's *It's A Knockout*.

28 August 1987: Christie's auction. Cliff material is lot 97.

14 September 1987: release of album *Always Guaranteed*.

25 September 1987: performs three tour break-in dates at Wimbledon Theatre.

1 October 1987: begins extremely long tour at ICC, Berlin, with last date in Europe 1 December at Vejlby Risskov H., Aauhus, Denmark, before playing 7–12 December at NEC, Birmingham.

14 October: Mother joins him in Baden-Baden for his birthday.

2 November 1987: first-ever CD single with 'Remember Me'.

26 November 1987: Royal Variety Performance.

12 December 1987: learns that he has broken all NEC attendance records with 66,000 paying more than £500,000 to see him.

19 December 1987: another Pro-Celebrity event at Brighton. Partner Mike Read gets a 'plug' as his engagement is announced. Closes with carol singing and a double dose of 'O Come, All Ye Faithful'.

6 January 1988: arrives in Sydney with his mother and David Bryce.

10 January 1988: plays in a tennis celebrity tournament.

25 January 1988: performs at Australian Royal Command Performance attended by Prince Charles and Princess Diana. Part of the country's bicentennial celebrations.

27 January 1988: once more in New Zealand, at Auckland airport.

1 February 1988: British release of 99th solo single 'Two Hearts' comes with picture disc cut in the form of a Valentine.

2 February 1988: first of three Auckland concerts.

14 February 1988: New Zealand tour ends with his nine-piece band. Tour features for NZ audiences new version of 'Do You Wanna Dance?'

7 April 1988: another Sotheby's sale produces script for film *Take Me High*, a Russian poster from 1976 and seven 78 rpm singles.

14 April 1988: special performance of *Time* for Terrence Higgins Trust and Frontliners. Cliff returns for part of show, joined by Freddie Mercury.

16 April 1988: *Time* closes, due to legal problems.

21 April 1988: lends musical support to Israel's 40th birthday celebrations.

6 May 1988: launches £250,000 appeal for Dr Barnados in conjunction with Thompson Holidays. Held at Abbey Road studios.

8 May 1988: commences small tour of Europe, beginning with Oslo and ending in Kiel on 21 May.

1 June 1988: support for his Search For A Star tennis talent scheme, goes to Beckenham with major Cliff fan Eileen Edwards, a qualified LTA umpire, including Wimbledon, sometimes in the chair. Cliff presents SFAS scheme awards on Centre Court.

9 July 1988: tickets go on sale for all-important 30th Anniversary Tour with 8,000 tickets of 14,000 available in Bournemouth going first day but fans later disgruntled, saying tickets in hands of tour operators and theatre agencies.

9 August 1988: anniversary date of his thirty years in show business.

27 August 1988: appears at Greenbelt festival.

31 August 1988: Cliff signs *Single-minded* in Dillon's and Selfridge's in London's West End.

2 September 1988: signs book copies at Bentall's in Kingston.

18 September 1988: at Oakleigh School, North London.

Numerous 30th anniversary events: see Chapter 17.

5 October 1988: opens 30th Anniversary Tour at the Hammersmith Odeon, London.

8 October: records video for Christmas single 'Mistletoe And Wine', Albert Wharf Studio, London.

20 October 1988: Radio Forth, Edinburgh, produce competition winner who for charity offered £500 to meet him.

21 October 1988: at St Paul's and St George's Church, Edinburgh for Third World.

26 November 1988: Royal Variety Performance, performs 'Mistletoe and Wine'.

13 December 1988: at special charity concert for Great Ormond Street Hospital for Children.

17 December 1988: Brighton Centre. Tennis time once more with sixth Pro-Celebrity tournament. £150,000 raised for Cliff Richard Search for a Star scheme. Cliff partners Anne Hobbs.

21 January 1989: in Auckland for Tear Fund and Youth for Christ.

22 January 1989: in Wellington, New Zealand, same causes as previous day.

8 February 1989: honoured at 30th Anniversary Luncheon in aid of the Nordoff-Robbins Music Therapy Centre, at Mayfair Inter-Continental Hotel, Stratton Street, London W1. With the Shadows.

16 February 1989: receives Lifetime Achievement award from BPI.

3 April 1989: at Palladium where fans get taste of new album.

7 April 1989: in Budapest. (*See* Diary).

18–22 April 1989: once again at Caesar's Palace.

25–29 April 1989: returns to Savvas Club.

2–6 and 9–13 May 1989: at Blazer's, Windsor.

17 May 1989: Jet Harris and Tony Meehan have reunion with Cliff at Esher. All went well; doubts because of newspaper articles by wife of Jet Harris.

6 June 1989: Lord Olivier dies. Cliff among those who offer much praise. Says it was the biggest thrill in his career to be linked with the great actor (*Time* musical).

16–17 June 1989: The Event at Wembley Stadium.

16 June 1989: Jasper book, *Survivor*, loaded with big-name tributes from many walks of Cliff's life is launched to coincide with The Event concert.

23 June 1989: plays with Ilie Nastase for the Diners Club 35+ Tennis Legends Tournament in Mook, Holland.

26 June–1 July 1989: Billy Graham has religious campaign, Mission '89, at Earls Court, Cliff in support.

19 July 1989: another gospel tour with first date City Hall, Newcastle, and ending 5 August at the Mayflower, Southampton.

2 August 1989: at Guildford Civic Hall,

gospel tour concert, he introduces Paul Jones and actress wife Fiona Henley and remembers how back in 1966 the then-famed Manfred Mann singer was hostile to Christianity.

5 October 1989: photographic celebration of Cliff published, entitled *Cliff – A Celebration* by Theresa Wassif (Hodder and Stoughton).

9 October 1989: *Woman's Own* prints photographs of Cliff and dog at home.

Mid-October: spends a few days in Zagreb and Ljubljana, then Yugoslavia, and making plans for concerts with his friend Alexander John. Also a month which sees extensive promotional activity in Europe.

30 October 1989: *Stronger* is released. Album was launched at the Guinness World of Records at London's Trocadero Centre. During proceedings Cliff, weighing in at a little over 11 stone, is lifted high in the air by 27-stone Geoff Capes.

31 October 1989: arrives at Gothenburg Airport, Sweden.

6 November 1989: spends week in Japan for mainly promotional purposes.

20 November 1989: performs in front of 17,000 people at Diamond Awards Festival in Antwerp. Receives Lifetime Achievement Diamond Award.

27 November 1989: his surprise association with rock legend Van Morrison produces single on Polydor, 'Whenever God Shines His Light'.

3 December 1989: Cliff records his contribution for new charity Christmas single 'Do They Know It's Christmas?' Leaves 4 a.m. the next day for Sweden to record several TV shows.

7 December 1989: turns on Christmas lights of Weybridge Traders' Association at Bowman's Garage: Cliff expresses pleasure and calls himself a local boy; receives presents from two 'angels'.

9 December 1989: in Germany. More promotional activity.

16 December 1989: more Pro-Celebrity tennis at the Brighton Centre with tickets sold out within two days of the box office opening.

19 December 1989: appears at the Royal Albert Hall in *Joy to the World*.

1 January 1990: Mayfair tailor John Kent hears he will clothe Cliff in a naval style suit with white trousers, blue reefer jacket and gold epaulettes on forthcoming tour.

15 January 1990: appears with Rick Wakeman and Justin Hayward at Queen Elizabeth Hall, London, in charity occasion for leukaemia.

31 January: back in New Zealand, then Australia for 35-concert, 13th Australasia tour.

28 March 1990: supports United Church's Student of the Year (Australia) quest for disabled students.

3 April 1990: fans have preview of some *Stronger* tracks at London Palladium.

6 April 1990: at the Cottenham Park tennis courts in Merton, Surrey.

13 April 1990: one of rare Cliff 'social' spottings. Is seen arm in arm with Marietta Parfitt, ex-wife of Status Quo guitarist Rick. Romance denied, friendship and Christian sharing is stressed.

19 April 1990: opens brave new venture, First Floor Theatre. First director is Carole Henderson.

1 May–7 June 1990: European tour commences. Opens at Ice Hall, Helsinki, and concludes at the Zenith, Paris.

21 May 1990: *Woman* magazine runs a competition that promises winner chance to interview Cliff on British *TV-AM* show.

4 June 1990: tickets go on sale for pro-Celebrity Tennis Tournament in Brighton on 16 December.

20 June 1990: appears at St Nicholas Church, Sevenoaks, Kent.

30 June 1990 Cliff appears at the huge Knebworth Festival with the Shadows. Syndicated to ninety-five countries with claim that 90 per cent of world's population can view the happening.

5 July 1990: at *Rock On The Lock* (sub-titled *Gospel Music Summer Special*) at Picketts Lock Centre, Edmonton, London.

13 August 1990: Cliff single 'Silhouettes' is marketed in a package that takes the form of a picture frame.

5 September 1990: *Cliff Richard – The Complete Recording Sessions 1958–1990* is published (Blandford/Cassell). Put together by Peter Lewry and Nigel Goodall. Cliff appears on front cover from Hanne Jordan photograph.

17–22 September 1990: again at the Savvas Club in Usk, Wales.

October 1990: Hodder and Stoughton issue new edition in hardback and paperback of *Which One's Cliff?*

25 September 1990: Makes video of 'Saviour's Day' at Lulworth Cove.

Birthday celebrations, see Chapter 19.

29 September 1990: Bishop's Park, London, attends National Wheelchair Tennis Association Meeting, First National Tournament.

10 October 1990: at the Professional Sound and Light Exhibition, Olympia, London.

14 October 1990: fiftieth birthday.

18 October 1990: presented with the Cliff Richard Rose by Wendy Leftwich. Formerly a dream apparently, now come true, for fan club member Anne Dassie who in the early 1980s had thought this should happen. The rose has cerise pink petals with a pale creamy reverse suffused with a rose-pink blush, along with a delicate scent (*Cliff United* description). Now available early November to UK members with hopes that 1992 may see export licence granted.

7 November 1990: special birthday celebration at NEC, Birmingham.

31 August 1990: tickets go on sale for extra Cliff tour dates, such was the demand for first batch of bookings. Original venues had begun with NEC Birmingham, 1–15 November, minus 8th and 12th. Aberdeen Exhibition Centre, 17–21, but not 20th, and London's Wembley from 2–12 December but not 5th or 9th. New bookings mean two more Birmingham dates, one extra for Aberdeen and three additions for Wembley. Also dates in Dublin and Belfast. For the Wembley dates, 216,000 see him and he has 18 sell-out nights. He is presented with a plaque commemorating his record-breaking appearance at the stadium by Sir Brian Wolfson, Chairman of Wembley Stadium Ltd. Cliff receives special plaque that has a framed gold ticket, gold staff pass and company employees' handbook, making Cliff presumably an honorary member of staff, although no reported sightings of Cliff ushering people to their seats at other artist concerts.

12 December 1990: turns on the Christmas lights, London's Oxford Street.

12 December 1990: attends handicapped children's party at 11 Downing Street. For Handicapped Adventure Playgrounds Association. Wheelchair Championships (1st British open).

16 December 1990: Pro-Celebrity Tournament, Brighton.

23 December 1990: All Souls Church for Christmas celebrations. Songs, 'Saviour's Day' and 'From A Distance'.

9 January 1991: to Florida for a holiday.

Mid-January 1991: American fan Mary James of Cocoa, Florida, unexpectedly sees Cliff at Disney World in Orlando, Florida.

28–29 January 1991: Cliff is in Toronto promoting 'From A Distance'.

1 February 1991: attends Lorna Fogarty Trust Pro-Celebrity Tennis Day at Bramhall, Cheshire. Cliff flies to Manchester Airport, stays for five hours, presents prizes.

24 February 1991: Royal Shakespeare Theatre, Stratford-upon-Avon, talks about his faith, arranged with Saltmine Trust. Same month sees a private concert for Mildmay Mission Hospital.

14 March 1991: annoyed when bomb threat means cancellation of Christian concert at Sands Centre, Carlisle, the second concert on gospel tour that runs from 13–30 March.

26 March 1991: performs cancelled show of 14 March.

30 March 1991: Easter Sunday, ends gospel tour at the Royal Albert Hall, London.

15 April 1991: goes to his North Wales residence for some rest.

22 April 1991: sees off first sending of vital medicines and supplies for Chernobyl's suffering children. Sponsored by *Daily Express*, £300,000-worth of materials sent.

15 May 1991: Award ceremony in Monte Carlo.

12 June 1991: takes part in The Event In A Tent, Cobham. Gerald Coates introduces.

17 June 1991: pays one of his many visits to Jersey.

20 June 1991: 'An Evening with Cliff:' takes place in Tonbridge, Kent.

21 June 1991: umpires at Arrows, Pro-Celebrity Tennis Tournament, at the Royal Albert Hall.

21 July 1991: attends tennis Federation Cup meeting in Nottingham.

23 July 1991: plays an exhibition match with Sue Barker against Virginia Wade and Ross King.

2 September 1991: release of TV theme for new BBC series, *Trainer*.

16–21 September 1991: another season at Savvas Club.

12 October 1991: 29th big Cliff evening for one of the most flourishing of Cliff

clubs, that of Waterlooville, Portsmouth area.

14 October 1991: Logan Campbell Centre, Auckland, New Zealand, until 19th.

21 October 1991: opens at Michael Fowler Centre, Wellington, New Zealand, staying until 27th.

29 October 1991: plays the Town Hall, Wellington, until 3 November.

9 November 1991: opens Australian tour in Perth. Tour ends 30 November in Sydney. Fairly flexible timetable with latter dates, 23 (Canberra), 27 (Brisbane) and 30 (Sydney) Intended visit to Japan is cancelled.

12 December 1991: appears at Joy to the World, Royal Albert Hall.

3 January 1992: sings and is interviewed at the Flame, organized by the Saltmine Trust, at London's Royal Albert Hall.

14 January 1992: attends wedding of his niece, Clare Harrison, daughter of his sister Jacqueline.

28 January 1992: major press conference to push home his tennis mission to find a British star; promises he will attend special find-a-star meets all over Britain during 1992. Runs under heading of the Cliff Richard Tennis Trail. Turns up in his Mercedes 500SL. During this month: goes skiing in Europe. Also promotional work in France.

28 January 1992: attends première of Jack Good musical, *Good Rockin' Tonite*.

19 February 1992: Cliff is measured so he can be one of many lifesize replicas at London's Rock Circus. Unveiling set for July.

10 March 1992: attends a performance of the long-running musical *Carmen Jones* at the Old Vic, London.

11 March 1992: meets legendary guitarist James Burton, who inspired many a British guitar player, including the Shadows.

October to December: Access to All Areas tour centred at Birmingham NEC, Sheffield Arena and London, Wembley. March sees extra dates added to early 1992 tour details.

4 April 1992: goes to see *Good Rockin' Tonite*, and this time takes his family.

11 April 1992: Waterlooville fan club guided by Ruth Wylie hits its 30th year and regular Cliff Richard Evening.

25 April 1992: leaves for Uganda on Tear Fund matters.

1 May 1992: returns from Uganda.

12 June 1992: *Expresso Bongo* is re-issued by Virgin Vision in their Film Collection series.

August 1992: on holiday.

24–29 August 1992: Savvas Night Club, Usk, Gwent.

Autumn 1992: tour commences in October through to December.

19 December 1992: Pro-Celebrity Tennis National Indoor Arena, Birmingham.

# CHRISTIAN ACTIVITIES 1966–81

These, as with almost all categories for Cliff Richard, are considerable. This section lists some of the most interesting and important. The many gospel concert tours are not listed, nor are the endless meetings at which Cliff and Bill Latham engaged in dialogue in schools, colleges and churches, or the many charitable organizations helped by Cliff.

16 June 1966: Cliff proclaims from the stage of Earls Court, London, that he is a Christian. He takes part in the evening meeting of the Billy Graham crusade and sings 'It's No Secret'. 'The most exciting moment of my life,' Cliff says.

24 June 1966: an announcement is made that Cliff is closing down his 42,000-strong British fan club and will begin a three-year divinity course. The following month these retirement plans are denied. Cliff decides on a healthy mix of music and religion.

22 October 1966: Cliff joins the

Archbishop of York, Dr Coggan, and the Bishop of Coventry, Dr Bardsley, to mark the twenty-first anniversary of Lee Abbey evangelical training centre.

9 July 1967: Cliff appears on the ABC TV discussion programme *Looking For an Answer* with evangelist Dr Billy Graham.

16 July 1967: Cliff appears once more on *Looking For an Answer* and this time is in discussion with Paul Jones, lead singer of Manfred Mann.

6 December 1967: Cliff is confirmed and becomes a communicant of the Church of England. The event takes place at St

Paul's, Finchley, London. The Bishop of Willesden, Graham Leonard, presides.

13 June 1968: showing of *Two a Penny* for religious press.

22 September 1968: Cliff attends Coventry Call to Mission meeting.

1 December 1968: Cliff introduces *Songs of Praise* BBC television programme from Manchester.

4 December 1968: Cliff takes part in Christmas cake cutting for the Mental Health Trust at the Carlton Towers Hotel, London.

January 1969: Cliff begins filming a major religious series, *Life With Johnny*, for Tyne Tees Television.

11 June 1969: Cliff goes to the Holy Land where he films *Fire in Zion* for Worldwide Films, part of the Billy Graham organization. Later the film is re-titled *His Land*.

October 1970: EMI Columbia issue Cliff's *About That Man* album.

9 October 1970: Cliff is awarded the National Viewers and Listeners Association annual award for his outstanding contribution to religious broadcasting and light entertainment.

5 March 1971: records with Dora Bryan *Music for Sunday* series for BBC Radios 1 and 2. Producer is Jack Davies.

16 May 1971: presents prizes at the Methodist Association of Youth Clubs' yearly extravaganza at the Royal Albert Hall.

22 May 1971: opens a fête at St Anthony's Hospital, Cheam, Surrey.

24 June 1971: attends Arts Centre Open Day. The Arts Centre provides a meeting place for Christians professionally involved in the arts.

28 August–4 September 1971: attends the European Congress on Evangelism at Amsterdam.

8 September 1971: attends Festival of Light meeting, Westminster Central Hall, London.

26 October 1971: attends Christian Film Awards meeting.

1 November 1971: press conference to publicize Cliff's cassette series *Start the Day*.

25 November 1971: records another *Music for Sunday* series for BBC Radios 1 and 2.

11 December 1971: takes part in carol concert at the Royal Festival Hall and sings 'Yesterday, Today, Forever', 'Down To Earth', 'The First Noel'.

15 December 1971: goes to see *Godspell*.

11 March 1972: Cliff gives a religious concert for Tear Fund at New Century Hall, Manchester.

14–15 April 1972: appears in a special gospel concert at Philharmonic Hall, Liverpool, for charity. He leads a gospel session.

6 December 1972: a special Cliff concert with Dana, Gordon Giltrap, the Settlers, and Roy Castle is held to raise money for the Arts Centre Group.

February 1973: Cliff releases the song 'Jesus' as a single. The record is ignored by some radio stations and does not become a major hit. Cliff is disappointed.

25 February 1973: Cliff appears in the eight-week series of contemporary Christian and general music concerts being held at St Paul's Cathedral.

12 April–8 May 1973: Cliff aligns himself with an evangelistic crusade with the general title of Help, Hope and Hallelujah, and appears in concerts across Australia. Cliff is backed for his singing by the Strangers, a group reformed by John Farrar and including his wife Pat. The address is given by the Reverend David MacInnes, Precentor of Birmingham Cathedral. MacInnes asks Cliff questions about his faith. Among the songs Cliff sings are: 'Sing A Song Of Freedom', 'How Great Thou Art', 'Day By Day', 'Everything Is Beautiful', 'Silvery Rain', 'Jesus Loves You'.

27 August–1 September 1973: Spree (Spiritual Emphasis) gathering at Earls Court, London, for a gigantic teach-in. Johnny Cash, Parchment, Judy McKenzie, and Cliff are some of the musical contributors.

1 January 1974: at Southall Football Ground Cliff plays (for about ten minutes) in his first football game in about twenty years. The charity match is between the *Buzz* All Stars XI (*Buzz* being a British Christian youth monthly journal) and Choralerna (a Swedish Christian choir who had been at Spree the previous August). Cliff is sent off for fouling a player, though it looks like a theatrical foul to enable a cold Cliff to leave the pitch.

June 1974: release of the album *Help It Along* in aid of Tear Fund.

17 June 1974: speaks on BBC Radio 2 programme *Pause For Thought*.

28 August 1974: appears in a special

concert at the New Gallery, Regent Street, London, for Crusaders.

19 November 1974: opens Christian bookshop in Sutton.

1 January 1975: rehearses with Choralerna.

18 January 1975: appears with Choralerna in Newcastle.

22 January 1975: appears with Choralerna in De Montfort Hall, Leicester.

25 January 1975: appears in The Name of Jesus concert, Royal Albert Hall, with Malcolm and Alwyn, and Choralerna. Cliff sings 'Bless You', 'Help It Along', 'Jesus Is My Kind Of People', 'Why Me Lord', 'Power' (with Choralerna), 'Amazing Grace'. Cliff speaks of Tear Fund and of his faith.

19 April 1975: attends Way to Life rally, Empire Pool, Wembley, presided over by evangelist Dick Saunders. Bill Latham also sits on the platform. Cliff speaks of his Christian conversion and continuing faith. He sings 'Didn't He', 'Love Never Gives Up', 'Why Me Lord'. Part of this rally is broadcast the following weekend on *Sunday*, the BBC Radio 4 religious current affairs magazine programme.

30 April 1975: goes to see *Joseph and the Amazing Technicolour Dreamcoat*.

3 December 1975: records a Christmas Day Special for BBC Radio. Producer David Winter.

4 December 1975: begins recording for a series of *Gospel Road* for BBC Radios 1 and 2.

15 April 1976: Scope, a religious organization, presents two major charity concerts featuring Cliff and US artist Larry Norman at the Odeon Theatre, Birmingham. The concerts are in aid of Free – The National Institute for the Healing of Addictions. Eric Clapton was the first of several personalities to be cured by the treatment offered. Pete Townshend of The Who was the first person to give a donation.

6 March 1977: the International Cliff Richard Movement magazine *Dynamite* reports, in anticipation of Tear Fund Sunday, that in 1976 Cliff's concerts for Tear Fund raised over £37,000. The money provides six vehicles which go to Argentina, the Yemen Arab Republic, Nigeria, Haiti, and Burundi, a generator for a hospital in India, a rural development centre in Kenya, and a nutritional training centre in Zaire. The same issue carries a commentary on

Cliff's recent visit to India, his meeting with Mother Teresa and his visit to some of the Tear Fund projects in Bangladesh.

5 September 1977: Hodder and Stoughton publish Cliff's thoughts on his career, *Which One's Cliff?* in which he tells why he is a Christian and how he relates show business and his Christian convictions.

November 1977: EMI issue *Small Corners*, an album of Cliff's often-featured religious songs.

31 January 1978: Face to Face meeting organized as part of the Booksellers Convention at Wembley Conference Centre. Chuck Girard, Roy and Fiona Castle also take part. Cliff accompanies himself on guitar and among his songs are: 'Why Should The Devil Have All The Best Music', 'When I Survey The Wondrous Cross', 'Every Face Tells A Story'.

16 February 1978: Cliff joins Dana, Neil Reid, and Roy Castle at a special concert at Croydon for the Arts Centre Group. Graham Murray provides extra guitar to Cliff's.

April 1978: French single pairs 'Why Should The Devil Have All The Best Music' and 'Hey Watcha Say'.

27 June 1978: Cliff attends opening of new Arts Centre Group building, Short Street, London SE1.

2 September 1978: Cliff joins evangelist Dick Saunders on stage and sings, amongst other songs, 'Up In Canada', 'Lord I Love You', and 'When I Survey The Wondrous Cross'. He tells the Crusade audience that his faith daily grows stronger. In an interview prior to the event Cliff tells the magazine *Dynamite* that he thinks the Rolling Stones make great records but their song lyrics are ridiculous; he makes complimentary remarks about Elvis.

9–10 October 1978: Cliff gives two concerts to celebrate the tenth anniversary of Tear Fund. In the first half he sings 'World Of Difference' with Garth Hewitt and Dave Pope. In the second half he sings 'Such Is The Mystery', 'Song For Sarah', 'Yes He Lives!', 'Yesterday, Today, Forever', 'Up In Canada', 'Night Time Girl', 'When I Survey The Wondrous Cross', 'Leaving My Past Behind', 'You Can't Get To Heaven by Living Like Hell', and 'Why Should The Devil Have All The Best Music'.

January 1979: UK Scripture Union launches a series of cassettes which feature Cliff reading the Scriptures.

20 April 1979: Cliff takes part in a special Youth Festival at St Alban's Cathedral.

10 June 1979: Cliff takes part in a chat show at a theatre in Liverpool and speaks of his Christian faith.

12 June 1979: further Bible readings for cassette series recorded at Scripture Union.

28 June 1979: Cliff is involved with both providing entertainment and giving Christian witness at the European Baptist Congress at the Great Brighton Centre, Brighton. He talks of his work for Tear Fund, his visit to the Soviet Union and the Baptist church he visited while there. He sings nine songs – his total singing spot is fifty minutes. At the meeting's completion he leads, with Bryan Gilbert, the general singing of 'God Is So Good'.

Autumn 1979: Cliff launches his own gospel label, Patch Records, in association with EMI's export division. The first release is an album from Garth Hewitt with Cliff producing. The album is launched at the Greenbelt religious music festival. On this occasion Garth appears for the first time with a backing band.

26 August 1979: at the Greenbelt festival Cliff is interviewed by poet and writer Steve Turner about his music and faith. Wearing his 'Rock 'n' Roll Juvenile' jacket he sings for one and a half hours during one of the concert sessions.

18 September 1979: attends Filey Christian Holiday Crusade meeting. He participates in four sessions and signs books.

18 December 1979: sings at a special concert to raise money for the Arts Centre Group.

7 February 1980: attends Christians in Sport dinner in London.

10 February 1980: appears with Dr Billy Graham at an evangelist meeting in Cambridge. In the afternoon Cliff takes part in the meeting and in the evening he speaks at Great St Mary's, the university church.

27 March 1980: Cliff cuts short his American music business trip to appear on stage at London's Royal Albert Hall at the Sing Good News event honouring the top writers in a contest organized by the Bible Society. The audience numbers 5,500, the choir 300, and the orchestra 60 plus a rhythm group. Over 1,300 entrants were attracted by the competition. Cliff sings 'Why Should The Devil Have All The Best Music' and 'When I Survey The Wondrous Cross'.

15 April 1980: Cliff records for the popular Granada TV show *Pop Gospel* in Manchester.

1, 8 and 15 September 1980: Cliff contributes his thoughts to a BBC World Service radio series *Reflections* in which he chooses biblical texts that he says sustain his faith.

September 1980: a fun Yuletide volume, *Happy Christmas From Cliff*, is published by Hodder and Stoughton. The book has lavish colour illustrations, stories, poems, puzzles, information and Christmas readings, and looks at how the countries of the world take account of Christmas and the birth of Jesus.

Christmas 1980: Cliff is one of a number of major stars invited to design their own shop window at Selfridges, London. Cliff's window takes a traditional religious theme – Christmas through the eyes of a child.

16 January 1981: Cliff attends the twenty-fifth birthday celebrations of the major British evangelical magazine *Crusade*. Along with Dr Billy Graham, Cliff is interviewed by Ronald Allison. Cliff talks about his recent promotional tour in the States, his forthcoming concert programme, and his thoughts on the death of John Lennon.

# CHRISTIAN ORGANIZATIONS

**Tear Fund:** founded in 1968, its work has been much furthered by Cliff. Its full title is The Evangelical Alliance Relief Fund. It channels money which has been donated by individuals and groups into relief and development work around the world. Tear Fund has projects in sixty countries in the Third World – in Africa, South-East Asia, and Central and South America. The Fund aims to demonstrate the love of God to needy people all over the world. Apart from Cliff, Tear Fund has received tremendous financial support from the many member societies of the International Cliff Richard Movement, as well as meeting houses associated with the umbrella organization, and those with allegiance to Grapevine, the Cliff fan club movement. Tear Fund has its headquarters in the United Kingdom at 110 Church Road, Teddington, Middlesex TW11 8QE.

# DISCOGRAPHY

The information given below is record title(s), in the case of singles highest chart position position, record number, and release date.

In the early chart days if there was a demand in record retail outlets for both sides of a single then each was noted independently for chart statistics. If this had not been the practice, a number of Cliff's records would have obtained a higher position and would doubtless have increased the total number of his chart-toppers. Where both sides of a single were listed separately in the charts, the position of each is given in brackets after the title. In all other cases except one the number in brackets refers to the first (A-side) title. The exception is 'Move It', originally released as the B-side, which reached no. 2 in the charts.

## SINGLES

Schoolboy Crush/Move It (2). Columbia DB 4178. August 1958. Also 78 rpm release.

High Class Baby/My Feet Hit The Ground (7). Columbia DB 4203. November 1958. Also 78 rpm release.

Livin' Lovin' Doll/Steady With You (20). Columbia DB 4249. January 1959. Also 78 rpm release.

Mean Streak (10)/Never Mind (21). Columbia DB 4290. April 1959. Also 78 rpm release.

Living Doll/Apron Strings (1). Columbia DB 4306. July 1959. Re-entered charts December 1959 (26) and again January 1960 (28). Also 78 rpm release.

Travellin' Light (1)/Dynamite (16). Columbia DB 4351. October 1959. Also 78 rpm release.

Voice In The Wilderness/Don't Be Mad At Me (2). Columbia DB 4398. January 1960. Re-entered charts May 1960 (36). Also 78 rpm release.

Fall In Love With You/Willie And The Hand Jive (2). Columbia DB 4431. March 1960.

Please Don't Tease/Where Is My Heart (1). Columbia DB 4479. June 1960.

Nine Times Out Of Ten/Thinking Of Our Love (3). Columbia DB 4506. September 1960.

I Love You/'D' In Love (1). Columbia DB 4547. December 1960.

Theme For A Dream/Mumblin' Mosie (4). Columbia DB 4593. February 1961.

Gee Whizz It's You/I Cannot Find A True Love (export single) (4). Columbia DC 756. March 1961. Demand in the UK for this export single was such that it reached no. 4 in the UK charts.

A Girl Like You/Now's The Time To Fall In Love (3). Columbia DB 4667. June 1961.

When The Girl In Your Arms Is The Girl In Your Heart/Got A Funny Feeling (3). Columbia DB4716. October 1961.

The Young Ones/We Say Yeah (1). Columbia DB 4761. January 1962.

I'm Lookin' Out The Window/Do You Want To Dance (2). Columbia DB 4828. May 1962.

It'll Be Me/Since I Lost You (2). Columbia DB 4886. August 1962.

The Next Time/Bachelor Boy (1). Columbia DB 4950. February 1963.

Summer Holiday/Dancing Shoes (1). Columbia DB 4977. February 1963.

Lucky Lips/I Wonder (4). Columbia DB 7034. May 1963.

It's All In The Game/Your Eyes Tell On You (2). Columbia DB 7089. August 1963.

Don't Talk To Him/Say You're Mine (2). Columbia DB 7150. November 1963. Re-entered charts February 1964 (50).

I'm The Lonely One/Watch What You Do With My Baby (8). Columbia DB 7203. January 1964.

Constantly/True True Lovin' (4). Columbia DB 7272. April 1964.

On The Beach/A Matter Of Moments (7). Columbia DB 7305. June 1964.

The Twelfth Of Never/I'm Afraid To Go Home (8). Columbia DB 7372. October 1964.

I Could Easily Fall In Love With You/I'm

In Love With You (9). Columbia DB 7420. December 1964.

The Minute You're Gone/Just Another Guy (1). Columbia DB 7496. March 1965.

Angel/Razzle Dazzle (export single). Columbia DC 762. May 1965.

On My Word/Just A Little Bit Too Late (1). Columbia DB 7596. June 1965.

The Time In Between/Look Before You Love (22). Columbia DB 7660. August 1965.

Wind Me Up (Let Me Go)/The Night (2). Columbia DB 7745. November 1965.

Blue Turns To Grey/Somebody Loses (15). Columbia DB 7866. March 1966.

Visions/What Would I Do (For The Love Of A Girl) (7). Columbia DB 8968. July 1966.

Time Drags By/La La La Song (10). Columbia DB 8017. October 1966.

In The Country/Finders Keepers (6). Columbia DB 8094. December 1966.

It's All Over/Why Wasn't I Born Rich (9). Columbia DB 8150. March 1967.

I'll Come Running/I Get The Feelin' (26). Columbia DB 8210. June 1967.

The Day I Met Marie/Our Story Book (10). Columbia DB 8245. August 1967.

All My Love/Sweet Little Jesus Boy (6). Columbia DB 8293. November 1967.

Congratulations/High And Dry (1). Columbia DB 8376. March 1968.

I'll Love You Forever Today/Girl You'll Be A Woman Soon (27). Columbia DB 8437. June 1968.

Marianne/Mr Nice (22). Columbia DB 8476. September 1968.

Don't Forget To Catch Me/What's More (I Don't Need Her) (21). Columbia DB 8503. November 1968.

Good Times/Occasional Rain (12). Columbia DB 8548. February 1969.

Big Ship/She's Leaving You (8). Columbia DB 8581. May 1969.

Throw Down A Line/Reflections (with Hank Marvin) (7). Columbia DB 8615. September 1969.

With The Eyes Of A Child/So Long (20). Columbia DB 8641. December 1969.

Joy Of Living/Boogatoo, Leave My Woman Alone (25). Columbia DB 8687. February 1970.

Goodbye Sam, Hello Samantha/You Never Can Tell (6). Columbia DB 8685. June 1970.

Ain't Got Time Anymore/Monday Comes Too Soon (21). Columbia DB 8708. September 1970.

Sunny Honey Girl/Don't Move Away

(with Olivia Newton-John)/I Was Only Fooling Myself (19). Columbia DB 8747. January 1971.

Silvery Rain/Annabella Umberella/Time Flies (27). Columbia DB 8774. April 1971.

Flying Machine/Pigeon (37). Columbia DB 8797. July 1971.

Sing A Song Of Freedom/A Thousand Conversations (13). Columbia DB 8836. November 1971.

Jesus/Mr Cloud (35). Columbia DB 8864. March 1972.

Living In Harmony/Empty Chairs (12). Columbia DB 8917. August 1972.

Brand New Song/The Old Accordion. (No chart placing.) Columbia DB 8957. November 1972.

Power To All Our Friends/Come Back Billie Joe (4). EMI 2012. March 1973.

Help It Along/Tomorrow Rising/The Days Of Love/Ashes To Ashes (29). EMI 2022. May 1973.

Take Me High/Celestial Houses (27). EMI 2088. December 1973.

(You Keep Me) Hanging On/Love Is Here (13). EMI 2150. May 1974.

It's Only Me You've Left Behind/You're The One. (No chart placing.) EMI 2279. March 1975.

Honky Tonk Angel/Wouldn't You Know It. (No chart placing.) EMI 2344. September 1975.

Miss You Nights/Love Is Enough (15). EMI 2376. February 1976.

Devil Woman/Love On (9). EMI 2485. May 1976.

I Can't Ask For Anything More Than You Babe/Junior Cowboy (17). EMI 2499. August 1976.

Hey Mr Dream Maker/No One Waits (31). EMI 2559. December 1976.

My Kinda Life/Nothing Left For Me To Say (15). EMI 2584. March 1977.

When Two Worlds Drift Apart/That's Why I Love You (46). EMI 2663. June 1977.

Yes He Lives/Good On The Sally Army. (No chart placing.) EMI 2730. January 1978.

Please Remember Me/Please Don't Tease. (No chart placing.) EMI 2832. July 1978.

Can't Take The Hurt Anymore/Needing A Friend. (No chart placing.) EMI 2885. November 1978.

Green Light/Imagine Love (57). EMI 2920. March 1979.

We Don't Talk Anymore/Count Me Out (1). EMI 2975. July 1979.

Hot Shot/Walking In The Light (46). EMI 5003. November 1979.

Carrie/Moving In (4). EMI 5006. February 1980.
Dreamin'/Dynamite (8). EMI 5095. August 1980.
A Little In Love/Keep On Looking (15). EMI 5123. February 1981.

Many of Cliff's singles in the 1980s and 1990s were released in 7-inch and 12-inch form, and later in cassette and CD format. When there are additional tracks to those found on the basic 7-inch release, the single gains further entry in this listing, but it should be noted that these variances do not mean an extra Cliff single release nor are they computed separately for British Gallup chart statistics. This listing covers track titles and is not concerned with various marketing techniques that in certain instances have meant a picture disc, special bag, poster, and so on.

Wired For Sound/Hold On (4). EMI 5221. August 1981.
Daddy's Home/Shakin' All Over (2). EMI 5251. November 1981.
The Only Way Out/Under The Influence (10). EMI 5318. July 1982.
Where Do We Go From Here/Discovering (60). EMI 5341. September 1982.
Little Town/Love And A Helping Hand/ You, Me And Jesus (11). EMI 5348. November 1982.
True Love Ways/Galadriel (8). EMI 5385. April 1983.
Never Say Die/Lucille (15). EMI 5415. August 1983.
Please Don't Fall In Love/Too Close To Heaven (7). EMI 5437. November 1983.
Baby You're Dynamite/Ocean Deep (27). EMI 5457. March 1984.
Shooting From The Heart/Small World (51). Rich 1. October 1984.
Heart User/I Will Follow You (46). Rich 2. January 1985.
She's So Beautiful/She's So Beautiful (instrumental) (17). EMI 5531. September 1985.
It's In Every One Of Us/Alone (instrumental) (45). EMI 5537. November 1985.
Born To Born To Rock 'n' Roll/Law Of The Universe. (No chart placing.) EMI 5545. May 1986.
My Pretty One/Love Ya (6). EM4. June 1987.
Some People/One Time Lover Man (3). EM18. August 1987.
Remember Me/Another Christmas Day (35). EM31. October 1987.
Two Hearts/Yesterday, Today, Forever (34). EM42. February 1988.
Mistletoe And Wine/Marmaduke (1). EM78. November 1988.
The Best Of Me/Move It/Lindsay Jane (2). EM92. May 1989.
I Just Don't Have The Heart/Wide Open Space (3). EM101. August 1989.
Lean On You/Hey Mister (17). EM105. October 1989.
Stronger Than That/Joanna (14). EM129. February 1990.
Silhouettes/The Winner (10). EM152. August 1990.
From A Distance/Lindsay Jane (11). EM155. October 1990.
Saviour's Day/The 'Oh Boy' Medley (1). XMAS 90. November 1990.
More To Life/Mo's Theme (instrumental) (23). EM205. September 1991.
We Should Be Together/Miss You Nights (live) (10). EMI XMAS91 November 1991.
This New Year/Scarlet Ribbons (30). EMI 218. December 1991.

## EPs

*Serious Charge:* Living Doll/No Turning Back/Mad About You/Chinchilla (The Shadows). May 1959.
*Cliff No. 1:* Apron Strings/My Babe/Down The Line/I Gotta Feeling/Baby I Don't Care. June 1959.
*Cliff No. 2:* Donna/Move It/Ready Teddy/ Too Much/Don't Bug Me Baby. July 1959.
*Expresso Bongo:* Love/A Voice In The Wilderness/The Shrine On The Second Floor/Bongo Blues (The Shadows) (24). January 1960.
*Cliff Sings No. 1:* Here Comes Summer/ I Gotta Know/Blue Suede Shoes/The Snake And The Bookworm. February 1960.
*Cliff Sings No. 2:* Twenty Flight Rock/ Pointed Toe Shoes/Mean Woman Blues/I'm Walkin'. March 1960.
*Cliff Sings No. 3:* I'll String Along With You/Embraceable You/As Time Goes By/The Touch Of Your Lips. June 1960.
*Cliff Sings No. 4:* I Don't Know Why (I Just Do)/Little Things Mean A Lot/ Somewhere Along The Way/That's My Desire. September 1960.
*Cliff's Silver Discs:* Please Don't Tease/Fall In Love With You/Nine Times Out Of Ten/Travellin' Light. December 1960.
*Me And My Shadows No. 1:* I'm Gonna Get

You/You And I/I Cannot Find A True Love/Evergreen Tree/She's Gone. February 1961.

*Me And My Shadows No. 2:* Left Out Again/You're Just The One To Do It/Lamp Of Love/Choppin' 'n' Changin'/We Have Made It. March 1961.

*Me And My Shadows No. 3:* Tell Me/Gee Whizz It's You/I'm Willing To Learn/I Love You So/I Don't Know. April 1961.

*Listen To Cliff No. 1:* What'd I Say/True Love Will Come To You/Blue Moon/Lover. October 1961.

*Dream:* Dream/All I Do Is Dream Of You/I'll See You In My Dreams/When I Grow Too Old To Dream. November 1961.

*Listen To Cliff No. 2:* Unchained Melody/First Lesson In Love/Idle Gossip/Almost Like Being In Love/Beat Out Dat Rhythm On A Drum. December 1961.

*Cliff's Hit Parade:* I Love You/Theme For A Dream/A Girl Like You/When The Girl In Your Arms. February 1962.

*Cliff Richard No. 1:* Forty Days/Catch Me/How Wonderful To Know/Tough Enough. April 1962.

*Hits from The Young Ones:* The Young Ones/Got A Funny Feeling/Lessons In Love/We Say Yeah. May 1962.

*Cliff Richard No. 2:* Fifty Tears for Every Kiss/The Night Is So Lonely/Poor Boy/Y'Arriva. June 1962.

*Cliff's Hits:* It'll Be Me/Since I Lost You/Do You Want To Dance/I'm Looking Out The Window. November 1962.

*Time for Cliff and the Shadows:* So I've Been Told/I'm Walkin' The Blues/When My Dreamboat Comes Home/Blueberry Hill/You Don't Know. March 1963.

*Holiday Carnival:* Carnival/Moonlight Bay/Some Of These Days/For You, For Me. May 1963.

*Hits from Summer Holiday:* Summer Holiday/The Next Time/Dancing Shoes/Bachelor Boy. June 1963.

*More Hits from Summer Holiday:* Seven Days To A Holiday/Stranger In Town/Really Waltzing/All At Once. September 1963.

*Cliff's Lucky Lips:* It's All in the Game/Your Eyes Tell On You/Lucky Lips/I Wonder. October 1963.

*Love Songs:* I'm In The Mood For You/Secret Love/Love Letters/I Only Have Eyes For You. November 1963.

*When in France:* La Mer/Boum/J'attendrai/C'est Si Bon. February 1964.

*Cliff Sings Don't Talk To Him:* Don't Talk To Him/Say You're Mine/Spanish Harlem/Who Are We To Say/Falling In Love With Love. March 1964.

*Cliff's Palladium Success:* I'm The Lonely One/Watch What You Do With My Baby/Perhaps Perhaps Perhaps/Frenesi. May 1964.

*Wonderful Life:* Wonderful Life/Do You Remember/What've I Gotta Do/Walkin'. August 1964.

*A Forever Kind Of Love:* A Forever Kind Of Love/It's Wonderful To Be Young/Constantly/True True Lovin'. September 1964.

*Wonderful Life No. 2:* Matter Of Moments/Girl In Every Port/A Little Imagination/In The Stars. October 1964.

*Hits from Wonderful Life:* On the Beach/We Love A Movie/Home/All Kinds Of People. December 1964.

*Why Don't They Understand:* Why Don't They Understand/Where The Four Winds Blow/The Twelfth Of Never/I'm Afraid To Go Home. February 1965.

*Cliff's Hits From Aladdin And His Wonderful Lamp:* Havin' Fun/Evening Comes/Friends/I Could Easily Fall In Love With You. March.

*Look In My Eyes Maria:* Look In My Eyes Maria/Where Is Your Heart/Maria/If I Give My Heart To You. May 1965.

*Angel:* Angel/I Only Came To Say Goodbye/On My Word/The Minute You're Gone. September 1965.

*Take Four:* Boom Boom/My Heart Is An Open Book/Lies And Kisses/Sweet And Gentle. October 1965.

*Wind Me Up:* Wind Me Up/In The Night/The Time In Between/Look Before You Love. February 1966.

*Hits From When In Rome:* Come Prima (The First Time)/Nel Blu Dipinto, Di Blu (Volare)/Dicitencello Vuie (Just Say I Love Her)/Arrivederci Roma. April 1966.

*Love Is Forever:* My Colouring Book/Fly Me To The Moon/Someday/Everybody Needs Somebody To Love. June 1966.

*La La La La La:* La La La La La/Solitary Man/Things We Said Today/Never Knew What Love Could Do. December 1966.

*Cinderella:* Come Sunday/Peace And Quiet/She Needs Him More Than Me/Hey Doctor Man. May 1967.

*Carol Singers:* God Rest You Merry Gentlemen/In The Bleak Midwinter/Unto Us A Boy Is Born/While Shepherds Watched/Little Town Of Bethlehem. November 1967.

SINGLES RECORDED WITH OTHER
ARTISTS
*Aladdin:* cast members: 'This Was My
Special Day'/'I'm Feeling Oh So
Lonely'. Columbia DB 7435. November
1964. (Technically a single since it was
given a normal catalogue number, and
pressed as a single, but it was only
available in the foyer of the London
Palladium.)
Olivia Newton-John with Cliff Richard:
'Suddenly' (15). Jet 7002. October 1981.
Phil Everly with Cliff Richard: 'She Means
Nothing To Me' (9). Capitol CL 276.
January 1983.
Sheila Walsh with Cliff Richard: 'Drifting'
(64). DJM SHEIL. 1. May 1983.
Janet Jackson with Cliff Richard: 'Two To
The Power'. No chart listing. A&M 210.
September 1984.
The Young Ones with Cliff Richard:
'Living Doll' (1) WEA YZ65. March
1986.
Sarah Brightman with Cliff Richard: 'All I
Ask Of You' (3). Polydor POSP 802.
Elton John with Cliff Richard: 'Slow
Rivers' (44). Rocket EJS13. November
1986.
Van Morrison with Cliff Richard:
'Whenever God Shines His Light' (20).
Polydor VANS 2. December 1989.
Note: EMI flipped the single 'Baby You're
Dynamite' with 'Ocean Deep'
becoming the main promotional side,
and so gaining a fresh entry in the
*Guinness Book of Hit Singles and the Top
20: The British Record Charts.* The
catalogue number remained the same.
However, it did little good for in the
new form it reached only 72, 45 places
lower than the original coupling.

ALBUMS (all released by EMI)

*Cliff:* Apron Strings/My Babe/Down The
Line/I Got A Feeling/Jet Black (The
Drifters)/Baby I Don't Care/Donna/
Move It/Ready Teddy/Too Much/Don't
Bug Me Baby/Driftin' (The Drifters)/
That'll Be The Day/Be-Bop-A-Lula (The
Drifters)/Danny/Whole Lotta Shakin'
Goin' On. Mono SX 1147. April 1959.
*Cliff Sings:* Blue Suede Shoes/The Snake
And The Bookworm/I Gotta Know/
Here Comes Summer/I'll String Along
With You/Embraceable You/As Time
Goes By/The Touch Of Your Lips/
Twenty Flight Rock/Pointed Toe Shoes/
Mean Woman Blues/I'm Walkin'/I
Don't Know Why/Little Things Mean A

Lot/Somewhere Along The Way/That's
My Desire. Mono SX 1192. November
1959.
*Me and My Shadows:* I'm Gonna Get You/
You And I/I Cannot Find A True Love/
Evergreen Tree/She's Gone/Left Out
Again/You're Just The One To Do It/
Lamp Of Love/Choppin' 'n' Changin'/
We Have It Made/Tell Me/Gee Whizz
It's You/I Love You So/I'm Willing To
Learn/I Don't Know/Working After
School. Mono SX 1261, stereo SCX
3330, different takes. October 1960.
*Listen to Cliff:* What'd I Say/Blue Moon/
Trust Love Will Come To You Lover/
Unchained Melody/Idle Gossip/First
Lesson In Love/Almost Like Being In
Love/Beat Out Dat Rhythm On A
Drum/Memories Linger On/
Temptation/I Live For You/Sentimental
Journey/I Want You To Know/We Kiss In
A Shadow/It's You. Mono SX 1320, stereo
SCX 3375, different takes. May 1961.
*21 Today:* Happy Birthday To You/Forty
Days/Catch Me/How Wonderful To
Know/Tough Enough/Fifty Tears For
Every Kiss/The Night Is So Lonely/Poor
Boy/Y' Arriva/Outsider/Tea For Two/To
Prove My Love For You/Without You/A
Mighty Lonely Man/My Blue Heaven/
Shame On You. Mono SX 1368, stereo
SCX 3409. October 1961.
*The Young Ones:* Friday Night/Got A
Funny Feeling/Peace Pipe/Nothing's
Impossible/The Young Ones/All For
One/Lessons In Love/No One For Me
But Nicky/What D'You Know We've
Got A Show And Vaudeville Routine/
When The Girl In Your Arms Is The
Girl In Your Heart/Just Dance/Mood
Mambo/The Savage/We Say Yeah.
Mono SX 1384, stereo SCX 3397.
December 1961.
*32 Minutes and 17 Seconds With Cliff
Richard:* It'll Be Me/So I've Been Told/
How Long Is Forever/I'm Walkin' the
Blues/Turn Around/Blueberry Hill/Let's
Make A Memory/When My Dreamboat
Comes Home/I'm On My Way/Spanish
Harlem/You Don't Know/Falling In
Love With Love/Who Are We To Say/I
Wake Up Cryin'. Mono SX 1431, stereo
SCX 3436. October 1962.
*Summer Holiday:* Seven Days To A
Holiday/Summer Holiday/Let Us Take
You For A Ride/Les Girls/Round And
Round/Foot Tappers/Stranger In Town/
Orlando's Mime/Bachelor Boy/A
Swingin' Affair/Really Waltzing/All At
Once/Dancing Shoes/Jugoslav

239

Wedding/The Next Time/Big News.
Mono SX 1472, stereo SCX 3462.
January 1963.
*Cliff's Hit Album:* Move It/Living Doll/
Travellin' Light/A Voice In The
Wilderness/Fall In Love With You/
Please Don't Tease/ Nine Times Out Of
Ten/I Love You/Theme For A Dream/A
Girl Like You/When The Girl In Your
Arms Is The Girl In Your Heart/The
Young Ones/I'm Looking Out The
Window/Do You Want To Dance.
Mono SX 1512, stereo SCX 1512. July
1963.
*When in Spain:* Perfidia/Amor Amor
Amor/Frenesi/You Belong To My
Heart/Vaya Con Dios/Sweet And
Gentle/Maria No Mas/Kiss/Perhaps
Perhaps Perhaps/Magic Is The
Moonlight/Carnival/Sway. Mono SX
1541, stereo SCX 3488. September 1963.
*Wonderful Life:* Wonderful Life/A Girl In
Every Port/Walkin'/A Little
Imagination/Home/On The Beach/In
The Stars/We Love A Movie/Do You
Remember/What've I Gotta Do/Theme
For Young Lovers/All Kinds Of People/
A Matter Of Moments/Youth And
Experience. Mono SX 1628, SCX 3515.
July 1964.
*Aladdin and His Wonderful Lamp:* Emperor
Theme/Chinese Street Scene/Me Oh
My/I Could Easily Fall In Love With
You/There's Gotta Be A Way/Ballet
(Rubies, Emeralds, Sapphires,
Diamonds)/Dance Of The Warriors/
Friends/Dragon Dance/Genie With The
Light Brown Lamp/Make Ev'ry Day A
Carnival/Widow Twankey's Song/I'm
Feeling Oh So Lovely/I've Said Too
Many Things/Evening Comes/Havin'
Fun. Mono SX 1676, stereo SCX 3522.
December 1964.
*Cliff Richard:* Angel Sway/I Only Came To
Say Goodbye/Take Special Care/Magic
Is The Moonlight/House Without
Windows/Razzle Dazzle/I Don't Wanna
Love You/It's Not For Me To Say/You
Belong To My Heart/Again/Perfidia/
Kiss/Reelin' And Rockin'. Mono SC
1709, stereo SCX 3456. April 1965.
*More Hits – By Cliff:* It'll Be Me/The Next
Time/Bachelor Boy/Summer Holiday/
Dancing Shoes/Lucky Lips/It's All In
The Game/Don't Talk To Him/I'm The
Lonely One/Constantly/On The Beach/
A Matter Of Moments/The Twelfth Of
Never/I Could Easily Fall In Love With
You. Mono SX 1737, stereo SCX 3555.
July 1965.

*When in Rome:* Come Prima/Volare/
Autumn Concerta/The Questions/
Maria's Her Name/Don't Talk To Him/
Just Say I Love Her/Arrivederci Roma/
Carina/A Little Grain Of Sand/House
Without Windows/Che Cosa Del Farai
Mio Amore/Tell Me You're Mine. Mono
SX 1762, no stereo version. August
1965.
*Love Is Forever:* Everybody Needs
Someone To Love/Long Ago and Far
Away/All Of A Sudden My Heart
Sings/Have I Told You Lately That I
Love You/Fly Me To The Moon/A
Summer Place/I Found A Rose/My
Foolish Heart/Through The Eye Of A
Needle/My Colouring Book/I Walk
Alone/Someday You'll Want Me To
Want You/Paradise Lost/Look
Homeward Angel. Mono SX 1769,
stereo SCX 3569. November 1965.
*Kinda Latin:* Blame It On The Bossa Nova/
Blowing In The Wind/Quiet Night Of
Quiet Stars/Eso Beso/The Girl From
Ipanema/One Note Samba/Fly Me To
The Moon/Our Day Will Come/Quando
Quando Quando/Come Closer To Me/
Meditation/Concrete and Clay. Mono
SX 6039, stereo SCX 6039. May 1966.
*Finders Keepers:* Finders Keepers/Time
Drags By/Washerwoman/La La La
Song/My Way/Senorita/Spanish Music
– Fiesta/This Day/Paella/Medley
(Finders Keepers/My Way/Paella/
Fiesta)/Run To The Door/Where Did
The Summer Go/Into Each Life/Some
Rain Must Fall. Mono SX 6079, stereo
SCX 6079. December 1966.
*Cinderella:* Welcome To Stonybroke/Why
Wasn't I Born Rich/Peace And Quiet/
The Flyder And The Spy/Poverty/The
Hunt/In The Country/Come Sunday/
Dare I Love Him Like I Do (Jackie
Lee)/If Our Dreams Came True/
Autumn/The King's Place/She Needs
Him More Than Me/Hey Doctor Man.
Mono SX 6103, stereo SCX 6103.
January 1967.
*Don't Stop Me Now:* Shout/One Fine Day/
I'll Be Back/Heartbeat/I Saw Her
Standing There/Hang On To A Dream/
You Gotta Tell Me/Homeward Bound/
Good Golly Miss Molly/Don't Make
Promises/Move It/Don't/Dizzy Miss
Lizzy/Baby It's You/My Babe/Save The
Last Dance For Me. Mono SX 6133,
stereo SCX 6133. April 1967.
*Good News:* Good News/It Is No Secret/We
Shall Be Changed/Twenty-Third Psalm/
Go Where I Send Thee/What A Friend

We Have In Jesus/All Glory Laud and
Honour/Just A Closer Walk With Thee/
The King Of Love My Shepherd Is/
Mary What You Gonna Name That
Pretty Little Baby/When I Survey The
Wondrous Cross/Take My Hand
Precious Lord/Get On Board Little
Children/May The Good Lord Bless
And Keep You. Mono SX 6167, stereo
SCX 6167. October 1967.

*Cliff in Japan:* Shout/I'll Come Runnin'/The
Minute You're Gone/On The Beach/
Hang On To A Dream/Spanish Harlem/
Finders Keepers/Visions/Move It/
Living Doll/La La La La La/Twist And
Shout/Evergreen Tree/What I'd Say/
Dynamite/Medley (Let's Make a
Memory/The Young Ones/Lucky Lips/
Summer Holiday/We Say Yeah). Mono
SX 6244, stereo SCX 6244. May 1968.

*Two a Penny:* Two A Penny/I'll Love You
Forever Today/Questions/Long Is The
Night (Instrumental)/Lonely Girl/And
Me (I'm On The Outside Now)/
Daybreak/Twist And Shout/Celeste
(Instrumental)/Wake Up Wake Up/
Cloudy/Red Rubber Ball/Close To
Kathy/Rattler. Mono SX 6262, stereo
SCX 6262. August 1968.

*Established 1958:* Don't Forget To Catch
Me/Voyage To The Bottom Of The Bath
(The Shadows)/Not The Way That It
Should Be/Poem (The Shadows)/The
Dreams I Dream/The Average Life Of A
Daily Man (The Shadows)/Somewhere
By The Sea/Banana Man (The
Shadows)/Girl On The Bus/The Magical
Mrs Clamps (The Shadows)/Ooh La/
Here I Go Again Loving You (The
Shadows)/What's Behind The Eyes Of
Mary/Maggie's Samba (The Shadows).
Mono SX 6282, stereo SCX 6282.
September 1968.

*The Best of Cliff:* The Minute You're Gone/
Congratulations/Girl You'll Be A
Woman Soon/The Time In Between/
Time Drags By/In The Country/Blue
Turns To Grey/On My Word/Wind Me
Up/Visions/ It's All Over/I'll Come
Runnin'/The Day I Met Marie/All My
Love. Mono SX 6343, stereo SCX 6343.
June 1969.

*Sincerely Cliff:* Sam/London's Not Too Far/
Take Action/I'm Not Getting Married/
In The Past/Always/Will You Love Me
Tomorrow/ You'll Want Me/Time/For
Emily Whenever I May Find Her/Baby I
Could Be So Good At Loving You/Take
Good Care Of Her/When I Find You/
Punch And Judy. Mono SX 6357, stereo

SCX 6357. October 1969.

*Cliff 'Live' at The Talk of the Town:* Intro
(Congratulations)/Shout/All My Love/
Ain't Nothing But A House-Party/
Something Good/If Ever I Should Leave
You Girl/You'll Be A Woman Soon/
Hank's Medley/London's Not Too Far/
The Dreams I Dream/The Day I Met
Marie/La La La La La/A Taste Of Honey
(Guitar Solo)/The Lady Came From
Baltimore/When I'm Sixty-Four/What's
More (I Don't Need Her)/Bows And
Fanfare/Congratulations/Visions/Finale
(Congratulations). Regal SRS 5031. July
1970.

*About That Man:* Sweet Little Jesus Boy/
Where Is That Man/Can It Be True/
Reflections/ Cliff tells the story of Jesus
in the words of the Living Bible. SCX
6408. October 1970.

*Tracks 'n' Grooves:* Early In The Morning/
As I Walk Into The Morning Of Your
Life/Love, Truth and Emily Stone/My
Head Goes Around/Put My Mind At
Ease/Abraham Martin And John/The
Girl Can't Help It/Bang Bang My Baby
Shot Me Down/I'll Make It Up To
You/I'd Just Be Fool Enough/Don't Let
Tonight Ever End/What A Silly Thing
To Do/Your Heart's Not In Your Love/
Don't Ask Me To Be Friends/Are You
Only Fooling Me. SCX 6435. November
1970.

*His Land:* Ezekiel's Vision (Ralph
Carmichael Orchestra)/Dry Bones
(Ralph Carmichael Orchestra)/His
Land/Jerusalem, Jerusalem/The New
Twenty-Third/His Land/Hava Nagila
(Ralph Carmichael Orchestra)/Over In
Bethlehem (and Cliff Barrows)/Keep
Me Where Love Is/He's Everything To
Me (and Cliff Barrows)/Narration and
Hallelujah Chorus (Cliff Barrows). SCX
6443. November 1970.

*The Best of Cliff Volume 2:* Goodbye Sam,
Hello Samantha/Marianne/Throw
Down A Line/Jesus/Sunny Honey Girl/I
Ain't Got Time Anymore/Flying
Machine/Sing A Song Of Freedom/
With The Eyes Of A Child/Good Times
(Better Times)/I'll Love You Forever
Today/The Joy Of Living/Silvery Rain/
Big Ship. SCX 6519. November 1972.

*Take Me High:* It's Only Money/Midnight
Blue/Hover (Instrumental)/Why (And
Anthony Andrews)/Life/Driving/The
Game/Brumburger Duet (and Debbie
Watling)/Take Me High/The Anti-
Brotherhood Of Man/Winning/Driving
(Instrumental)/Join The Band/The

World Is Love/Brumburger (finale).
EMI EMC 3016. December 1973.

*Help It Along:* Day By Day/Celestial
Houses/ Jesus/Silvery Rain/Jesus Loves
You/Fire And Rain/Yesterday, Today,
Forever/Help It Along/Amazing Grace/
Higher Ground/Sing A Song Of
Freedom. EMI EMA 768. June 1974.

*The 31st of February Street:* 31st Of
February Street/Give Me Back That Old
Familiar Feeling/The Leaving/Travellin'
Light/There You Go Again/Nothing To
Remind Me/Our Love Could Be So
Real/No Matter What/Fireside Song/
Going Away/Long Long Time/You Will
Never Know/The Singers/31st Of
February Street Closing. EMI EMC
3048. November 1974.

*I'm Nearly Famous:* I Can't Ask For
Anymore Than You/It's No Use
Pretending/I'm Nearly Famous/Lovers/
Junior Cowboy/Miss You Nights/I Wish
You'd Change Your Mind/Devil
Woman/Such Is The Mystery/You've
Got To Give Me All Your Lovin'/If You
Walked Away/Alright, It's Alright. EMI
EMC 3122. May 1976.

*Every Face Tells a Story:* My Kinda Life/
Must Be Love/When Two Worlds Drift
Apart/ You Got Me Wondering/Every
Face Tells A Story (It Never Tells A
Lie)/Try A Smile/Hey Mr Dream Maker/
Give Me Love Your Way/Up In The
World/Don't Turn The Light Out/It'll
Be Me Babe/Spider Man. EMI EMC
3172. March 1977.

*Small Corners:* Why Should The Devil
Have All The Good Music/I Love/I've
Got News For You/Hey Watcha Say/I
Wish We'd All Been Ready/Joseph/
Good On The Sally Army/Goin' Home/
Up In Canada/Yes He Lives/When I
Survey The Wondrous Cross. EMI
EMC 3219. November 1977.

*Green Light:* Green Light/Under Lock and
Key/She's A Gipsy/Count Me Out/
Please Remember Me/Never Even
Thought/Free My Soul/Start All Over
Again/While She's Young/Can't Take
The Hurt Anymore/Ease Along. EMI
EMC 3231. October 1978.

*Thank You Very Much* (with The
Shadows): The Young Ones/Do You
Want To Dance/The Day I Met Marie/
Shadoogie (The Shadows)/Atlantis
(The Shadows)/Nivram (The Shadows)/
Apache (The Shadows)/Please Don't
Tease/Miss You Nights/Move It/Willie
And The Hand Jive/All Shook Up/
Devil Woman/Why Should The Devil

Have All The Good Music/End Of The
Show (Cliff plus Shadows). EMI EMTV
15. February 1979.

*Rock 'n' Roll Juvenile:* Monday Thru'
Friday/Doing Fine/Cities May Fall/You
Know That I Love You/My Luck Won't
Change/Rock 'n' Roll Juvenile/Sci-Fi/
Fallin' In Love/Carrie/Hot Shot/
Language Of Love/We Don't Talk
Anymore. EMI EMC 3307. September
1979.

*Cliff Richard's 40 Golden Greats:* Move It/
Living Doll/Travellin' Light/Fall In Love
With You/Please Don't Tease/Nine
Times Out Of Ten/Theme For A Dream/
Gee Whizz It's You/When The Girl In
Your Arms Is The Girl In Your Heart/A
Girl Like You/The Young Ones/Do You
Want To Dance/I'm Lookin' Out Of The
Window/It'll Be Me/Bachelor Boy/The
Next Time/Summer Holiday/Lucky
Lips/It's All In The Game/Don't Talk To
Him/Constantly/On The Beach/I Could
Easily Fall In Love With You/The
Minute You're Gone/Wind Me Up (Let
Me Go)/Visions/Blue Turns To Grey/In
The Country/The Day I Met Marie/All
My Love/Congratulations/Throw
Down A Line/Goodbye Sam, Hello
Samantha/Sing A Song Of Freedom/
Power To All Our Friends/(You Keep
Me) Hangin' On/Miss You Nights/Devil
Woman/I Can't Ask For Anything More
Than You/My Kinda Life. EMI EMTVS
6. October 1979.

*Cliff – The Early Years* (this album was
scheduled for release February 1980 but
its release was cancelled): Please Don't
Tease/Willie And The Hand Jive/'D' In
Love/High Class Baby/Mean Woman
Blues/Nine Times Out Of Ten/My Feet
Hit The Ground/Apron Strings/Livin'
Lovin' Doll/Never Mind/Schoolboy
Crush/It'll Be Me/Gee Whizz It's You/
Choppin' 'n' Changin'/Blue Suede
Shoes/Dynamite/Mean Streak/She's
Gone/I Cannot Find a True Love/Move
It.

*I'm No Hero:* Take Another Look/
Anything I Can Do/A Little in Love/
Here (So Doggone Blue)/Give A Little
Bit More/In The Night/I'm No Hero/
Dreamin'/A Heart Will Break/
Everyman. EMI EMA 796. August
1980.

*Cliff – Love Songs:* Miss You Nights/
Constantly/Up In The World/Carrie/A
Voice In The Wilderness/The Twelfth
Of Never/I Could Easily Fall/The Day I
Met Marie/Can't Take The Hurt

Anymore/A Little In Love/The Minute You're Gone/Visions/When Two Worlds Drift Apart/The Next Time/It's All In The Game/Don't Talk To Him/ When The Girl In Your Arms/Theme For A Dream/Fall In Love With You/We Don't Talk Anymore. EMTV 27. June 1981.

*Wired For Sound:* Wired For Sound/Once In A While/Better Than I Know Myself/ Oh No Don't Let Go/'Cos I Love That Rock 'n' Roll/Broken Doll/Lost In A Lonely World/Summer Rain/Young Love/Say You Don't Mind/Daddy's Home.

*Now You See Me . . . Now You Don't:* The Only Way Out/First Date/Thief In The Night/Where Do We Go From Here/ Son Of Thunder/Little Town/It Has To Be You It Has To Be Me/The Water Is Wide/Now You See Me Now You Don't/Be In My Heart/Discovering. EMC 3415/TCEMC 3415. August 1982.

*Dressed For The Occasion:* Green Light/We Don't Talk Anymore/True Love Ways/ Softly As I Leave You/Carrie/Miss You Nights/Galadriel/Maybe Someday/ Thief In The Night/Up In The World/ Treasure Of Love/Devil Woman. EMC 3432/TCEMC 3432. May 1983.

*Silver:* Silver's Home Tonight/Hold On/ Never Say Die (Give A Little Bit More)/ Front Page/Ocean Deep/Locked Inside Your Prison/Please Don't Fall In Love/ Baby You're Dynamite/The Golden Days Are Over/Love Stealer/Lean On You/I Just Don't Have The Heart/ Joanna/Everybody Knows/Share A Dream/Better Day/Forever You Will Be Mine. EMC 1077871. October 1983.

*Rock 'n' Roll Silver:* Makin' History/Move It/Donna/Teddy Bear/It'll Be Me/Little Bitty Pretty One/There'll Never Be Anyone Else But You/Be Bop A Lula/ Tutti Frutti.

*The Rock Connection:* Heart User/Willie And The Hand Jive/Lovers And Friends/Never Be Anyone Else But You/La Gonave/Over You/Shooting From The Heart/Learning How To Rock 'n' Roll/Lucille/Be Bop A Lula/Donna/ Dynamite/She Means Nothing To Me/ Makin' History. Clif2/TCCLIF 2. November 1984.

*Always Guaranteed:* One Night/Once Upon A Time/Some People/Forever/Two Hearts/Under Your Spell/This Time Now/My Pretty One/Remember Me/ Always Guaranteed. EMD 1004/ TCEMD 1004. September 1987.

*Private Collection:* Some People/Wired For Sound/All I Ask Of You/Carrie/ Remember Me/True Love Ways/ Dreamin'/Green Light/She Means Nothing To Me/Heart User/A Little In Love/Daddy's Home/We Don't Talk Anymore/Never Say Die/The Only Way Out/Suddenly/Slow Rivers/Please Don't Fall In Love/Little Town/My Pretty One/ Ocean Deep/She's So Beautiful/Two Hearts/Mistletoe And Wine. CRTV 30/ TCCRTV 30/CDCRTV 30. November 1988.

*Stronger:* Stronger Than That/Who's In Love/The Best Of Me/Clear Blue Skies/ Keep Me Warm/Lean On You/I Just Don't Have The Heart/Joanna/ Everybody Knows/Share A Dream/ Better Day/Forever You Will Be Mine. EMD 1012/TCEMD 1012/CDEMD 1012. October 1989.

*The EP Collection – Ballads and Love Songs:* Look In My Eyes Maria/If I Give My Heart To You/Maria/Secret Love/Love Letters/I Only Have Eyes For You/All I Do Is Dream Of You/When I Grow Too Old To Dream/My Heart Is An Open Book/Boom Boom (That's How My Heart Beats)/Moonlight Bay/A Forever Kind Of Love/La Mer/J' Attendrai/The Shrine On The Second Floor/Where The Four Winds Blow/Solitary Man/Things We Said Today/Carnival/Little Rag Doll. *See* 280/SEEK 280/SEECD 280. October 1989.

*From A Distance – The Event:* Oh Boy Medley/Zing Went The Strings Of My Heart (Dallas Boys)/Always/When (Kalin Twins)/The Glory Of Love/Hoots Mon (Oh Boy Band)/Don't Look Now (Vernon Girls)/The Girl Can't Help It/Sea Cruise/Oh Boy Medley/From A Distance/Some People/We Don't Talk Anymore/Shake Rattle And Roll/ Silhouettes/Move It/Summer Holiday/ The Young Ones/In The Country/Good Golly Miss Molly/Fighter/Thief In The Night/Share A Dream/All The Time You Need/Saviour's Day. CRTV 31/TCCRTV 31/CDRTV 31. November 1990.

*From A Distance – The Event:* Limited edition box set featuring the same tracks as the double album, includes 6 exclusive prints, giant poster-lyrics, plus engraved 7 inch single including a cappella version of 'Miss You Nights'. The Album Box Set/The Cassette Box Set/The CD Box Set. CRTVB 31/ TCCRTVB 31/CDCRTVB 31. December 1990.

*Together With Cliff*: Have Yourself A Merry Little Christmas/Venite (O Come, All Ye Faithful)/We Should Be Together/Mistletoe And Wine/Christmas Never Comes/Christmas Alphabet/Saviour's Day/The Christmas Song (Merry Christmas To You)/Little Town/Scarlet Ribbons/Silent Night/White Christmas/This New Year. EMI TCEMD 1028/CDEMTV 30/EMTV. November 1991.

## MISCELLANEOUS

*The Cliff Richard Story*: six-record boxed set with booklet featuring the Shadows, mail order from World Records.

*Cliff Richard*: tape-only compilation. TC EXE 1006.

*The Music and Life of Cliff Richard*: tape-only compilation, a de luxe set of six cassettes. Apart from music, it has Cliff giving an account of his life. He narrates his story from 'schoolboy crush' days to the second half of the seventies. In addition, there are comments about him from close associates. His Christian testimony is highlighted several times. There is also an inspiring and nostalgic live recording of Cliff's testimony delivered at the Billy Graham Crusade meeting, Earls Court, London, in 1966. TC EXSP 1601.

*Start the Day* (first series) Bible-reading cassettes: eighteen in the series, available separately. Each with an introduction by Cliff: 'Galatians', 'Exodus', 'Psalms', 'Proverbs', 'Acts', 'Isaiah', 'Matthew', 'Mark', 'Luke', 'John', 'Romans', 'Timothy', 'Job', 'James', 'Hebrews', 'Ephesians', 'Philippians', 'Colossians'. The second series has six cassettes covering the books of 'Job', 'Hebrews', Colossians', 'Philippians', 'James', and 'Ephesians'. Each contains twenty three-minute programmes made up of a reading by Cliff, a question, a prayer and general thought for the day. Cassettes are available from Scripture Union bookshops or Scripture Union, 130 City Road, London EC1V 2NJ.

Comments/Questions/Interview. A-side from the album *Two A Penny*, promo single issued to radio stations only on TAP, PRI-855W–4694 DH, plays at 33 rpm. Interview by Dick Strout. August 1968.

*All My Love*: Sway/I Only Came To Say Goodbye/Take Special Care/Magic In the Moonlight/House Without Windows/Razzle Dazzle/All My Love/I Don't Wanna Love You/You Belong To My Heart/Again/Perfidia/Reelin' 'n' Rockin'. Music For Pleasure MFP 1420. Late 1970.

*Everybody Needs Somebody* (originally *Love Is Forever*): Everyone Needs Someone To Love/Fly Me To The Moon/Have I Told You Lately That I Love You/Long Ago (And Far Away)/(All Of A Sudden) My Heart Sings/Theme From A Summer Place/I Found A Rose/My Foolish Heart/My Colouring Book/Look Homeward Angel/Paradise Lost/Through The Eye Of A Needle/I'll Walk Alone/Somebody. Sounds Superb SPR 90070.

*How Wonderful to Know*: same tracking as *21 Today* (see album list) minus Happy Birthday. World Records STP 643.

*Cliff Richard*: I'll String Along With You/The Touch Of Your Lips/Temptation/We Kiss In A Shadow/Long Ago (And Far Away)/I'll Walk Alone/Come Closer To Me/Maria/All I Do Is Dream Of You/I'll See You In My Dreams/When I Grow Too Old To Dream/Dream. World Records ST 1051.

*Cliff Richard* (Reader's Digest offer): as above.

'Nothing To Remind Me'/'The Leaving' from *The 31st of February Street* album, issued to radio stations on PSR 368 (EMI demo). October 1974.

*Cliff Live*: Music For Pleasure MFP 50307. October 1976.

*Rock On With Cliff*: Move It/High Class Baby/My Feet Hit The Ground/Mean Streak/Living Doll/Apron Strings/Travellin' Light/Dynamite/Willie And The Hand Jive/A Voice In The Wilderness/Please Don't Tease/Gee Whizz It's You/Theme For A Dream/It'll Be Me/We Say Yeah/Do You Want To Dance. Music For Pleasure MFP 50467. February 1980.

'Every Face Tells A Story'/'You Got Me Wondering'/'Spider Man', taken from *Every Face Tells A Story* album, demo single for radio stations only, EMI PSR. March 1977.

*Listen to Cliff* (double): same tracking as *Listen to Cliff* and *32 Minutes and 17 Seconds With Cliff Richard*. Music For Pleasure MFP 1011. July 1980.

Interview with Cliff by music writer and poet Steve Turner at Greenbelt, August 1979. Christian Audio Vision Services Ltd. Cassette, GBO 083.

Demo for trade purposes: 'Don't Forget to Catch Me' from *Established 1958*. Columbia PSR 316.

Sampler double EP on EMI demo (PSR 414/5) with glossy picture sleeve and distributed to retail shops.

Singles sampler: 14 track album entitled *Cliff*, released to retail shops only in 1982, to promote reissue of 12 singles form the period 1958–79, available in single or box set form. Most Cliff albums have been reissued through Music For Pleasure or in the EMI Price Attack series, and have been made available in cassette and CD format. Religious recordings have been reissued by Word, with tracks culled from various albums, and even an EP of old times, and include *Hymns and Inspirational Songs* (Word), *It's A Small World* and *Walking In The Light*, both on Myrrh.

Reader's Digest have released music by Cliff and the Shadows, spreading itself over eight albums.

*From The Heart* (Tellydisc) contains a selection of Cliff material chosen by the man himself.

*Music and Life of Cliff Richard* is a six album set.

## FLEXIS

These include 'A Personal Message To You' for *Serenade* magazine, 1960.

'The Sound of the Stars' for *Disc* magazine, 1967.

*Cliff and the Shadows* for Readers Digest. No date.

Excerpts from *The Cliff Richard Story* for World Records issuing of recorded material, 1973.

*Always Guaranteed* was issued in a special boxed set that contained a large colour poster, calendar, autographed colour prints, four colour postcards plus a 7-inch single of 'Another Christmas Day' with the B-side having an engraved message from Cliff.

*Cliff Richard Songbook:* 84 tracks. World Records. 1981.

*Cliff Richard* (box set). EMI Europe. 1983.

*Cliff In The 60's:* Music for Pleasure. 1984.

*An Hour Of Cliff Richard:* Hour Of Pleasure. 1986.

*Cliff Richard:* interview picture disc. Not well recorded. Baktabak. 1987.

EMI issued a special promo CD with excerpts from the 1991 Christmas album, *Together With Cliff Richard*. Over the top of the track 'Have Yourself A Merry Little Christmas' there was a seasonal message for listeners from Cliff.

## K-TEL COMPILATIONS

*The Summit:* Cliff track: 'Devil Woman'. NE 1067.

*The Love Album:* Cliff track: 'When Two Worlds Drift Apart'. NE 1092.

*Chart Explosion:* Cliff track: 'We Don't Talk Anymore'. NE 1103.

## OTHER ARTIST OR COMPILATION ALBUMS FEATURING CLIFF

*Oh Boy:* seven Cliff tracks: 'At the Hop', 'Rockin' Robin', 'High School Confidential', 'King Creole', 'I'll Try', 'Early in the Morning', 'Somebody Touched Me'. Recorded 19 October 1958. Reissued in EMI's Nut Gold series, 1978. Parlophone PMC 7072.

*Thunderbirds Are Go!* The Shadows, featuring one Cliff song, 'Shooting Star'. December 1966. SEG 8510.

*Spree 73:* gospel/religious convention album featuring one track from Cliff: 'Jesus Is My Kind Of People'. Key KL 021.

*Greenbelt:* album of the religious pop festival, held in 1979, with one track by Cliff, 'Yes He Lives'. Pilgrim MRT 1001.

*Xanadu:* film soundtrack album. Jet JETLX 526. Cliff sings 'Suddenly' with Olivia Newton-John, which was also released as a single (Jet 7002).

*Dick Saunders 10th Annual Rally:* album recorded live at Wembley Stadium. One Cliff track, 'Love Never Gives Up'. September 1975. Now only a cassette. Echo ECR 008.

*Alan Freeman's History of Pop:* one Cliff plus Shadows track, 'Living Doll'. Arcade.

*Best Shows of the Week:* one song from Cliff, 'The Day I Met Marie'. BBC Records BELP 002.

*The Eddy Go Round Show:* Cliff sings 'It's Only Me', 'You're Left Behind', 'Give Me Back That Old Familiar Feeling'. European release, EMI 5C062 25252X.

*Stars Sing a Rainbow:* Save the Children Fund compilation album, 1970. Cliff's song is 'Dancing Shoes'. Philips 6830 034.

*Supersonic:* TV show compilation, 1975. Cliff sings 'Take Me High'. SSM 001.

CLIFF

*Louise:* album by Phil Everly features two
Cliff duets with Everly, 'She Means
Nothing To Me', 'I'll Mend Your
Broken Heart'. Vinyl/CD respectively.
Magnum Force. 1987/8.
*Drifting:* album by Sheila Walsh features
Cliff on title track. DJM. 1983.
Anti-Heroin Project: Cliff featured among
artists. Track: 'Live-In World'. Cliff
sings title line three times. EMI 12-inch-
12AMPI.
*The Hunting Of The Snark:* Cliff reads part
of the Bellman. Cassette/CD
respectively. Epic. 1986/1988.
*The Young Ones:* single featuring Cliff
singing 'Living Doll' WEA YZ65. Also
album of the same title. 1986.
Elton John: album *Leather Jackets.* Cliff

joins with Elton on 'Slow Rivers'.
Rocket EJLP/EJMCI. Issued as a single
Rocket EJS 13, with picture disc version
having different cover from 7-inch.
1986.
*Mission England Volume 2:* features Cliff
singing 'I Will Follow You'. Word
WSTR9661. 1989.
*Songs For Life: Mission '89:* Cliff sings
'Where You Are'. Word. 1989.
*Kendrick Collection:* Cliff sings 'Burn On',
'Fighter' and 'Shine Jesus Shine'.
Langham/Word LANGR 003. 1989.
*Knebworth* Album: with artists at festival
event, Cliff, with the Shadows, sings
'On The Beach' and 'Do You Wanna
Dance' (video has other songs, see
video entries). Polydor. 1990.

# FILMS

Various Cliff films are available in the UK in part or in whole as Super 8 Home Movies.
They can be obtained from Derann Film Services Ltd, 99 High Street, Dudley, West
Midlands DY1 1QP, England.

*Serious Charge.* Stars: Anthony Quayle,
Sarah Churchill, Andrew Ray. Cliff
played the part of Curley Thompson.
Thompson was the brother of the
leader of a gang of youngsters who
were into speed and lived for the next
joy ride.
   Songs sung by Cliff were 'Mad', 'No
Turning Back', 'Living Doll'. He was
backed by the Drifters but they did not
appear on screen.
   Director: Terrence Young. Producer:
Michael Delamar.
*Expresso Bongo.* Stars: Laurence Harvey,
Yolande Donlan, Sylvia Syms. Cliff was
Bert Rudge, a young beat singer who
became world famous as Bongo
Herbert. Laurence Harvey played his
rather unscrupulous manager.
   Songs sung by Cliff were 'Love',
'Shrine on the Second Floor', 'A Voice
in the Wilderness'.
   Director and producer: Val Guest.
Story: Wolf Mankowitz.
*The Young Ones.* Stars: Robert Morley,
Carole Gray, Shadows. Cliff plays
Nicky, the leader of a youth club. Their
headquarters is a rundown hut in an
equally deteriorating London district.
A rich property owner wishes to buy
the land on which the club stands. A
many-variation fight follows between
developer and youth group.

   Songs sung by Cliff are on the album
*The Young Ones* (SCX 3397). Singles
from the film: When The Girl In Your
Arms/Got A Funny Feeling (DB 4716);
The Young Ones/We Say Yeah (DB
4761); The Savage/Peace Pipe (The
Shadows) (DB 4726).
   Director: Sidney J. Furie. Producer:
Kenneth Harper. Choreographer:
Herbert Ross. Original screenplay and
story: Peter Myers and Ronald Cass.
Background score, orchestrations and
musical direction: Stanley Black.
*Summer Holiday.* Stars: Ron Moody,
Melvyn Hayes, Lauri Peters, Shadows,
David Kossof, Jeremy Bulloch, Teddy
Green, Pamela Hart, Jacqueline Daryl,
Una Stubbs. Cliff is one of four London
Transport mechanics who form a band
named Don. They take an old bus and
travel through five countries. The film
depicts their adventures.
   Songs sung by Cliff are on the album
*Summer Holiday* (SCX 3462). Singles
from the film: Summer Holiday/
Dancing Shoes (DB 4977); The Next
Time/Bachelor Boy (DB 4950); Foot
Tapper/The Breeze and I (The Shadows
– only the A-side was in the film) (DB
4984). Two more Shadows songs were
in the film and these, together with
'Foot Tapper', are included on the EP.
*Foot Tapping With The Shadows* (SEG

246

8286). Cliff co-wrote two songs: 'Big News' with Mike Conlin; 'Bachelor Boy' with Bruce Welch.

Director: Peter Yates. Producer: Kenneth Harper. Choreographer: Herbert Ross. Original screenplay and story: Peter Myers and Ronald Cass. Release: through Warner-Pathé.

*Wonderful Life.* Stars: Susan Hampshire, Shadows, Walter Slezak, Una Stubbs, Richard O'Sullivan, Gerald Harper, Derek Bond. Cliff plays Johnnie. He and friends entertain passengers on a luxury Mediterranean cruise but lose their jobs. They find themselves put to sea on a raft by an irritated ship's Captain. They reach land, which just happens to be the Canary Islands, and there they find themselves causing more than a minor disturbance in the filming of *Daughter of a Sheikh*.

Songs sung by Cliff are on the album *Wonderful Life* (SCX 3515). Single from the film: On the Beach/Matter of Moments (DB 7305). 'Walkin'' by the Shadows is on the album *Those Brilliant Shadows* (SEG 8321) and 'Theme for Young Lovers', also by the Shadows, is on the album *More Hits* (SXC 3578).

Director: Sidney J. Furie. Producer: Kenneth Harper. Associate producer: Andrew Mitchell. Choreographer: Gillian Lynne. Original screenplay and story: Peter Myers and Ronald Cass. Background score, orchestrations, musical direction: Stanley Black. Elstree Distributors.

*Finders Keepers.* Stars: Robert Morley, Graham Stark, Viviane Ventura, Peggy Mount, Shadows. Cliff and the Shadows play a group who have been booked into a hotel for the season but find the management cannot pay them. They become friendly with local people and hear how the traditional fiesta which surrounds the blessing of fishing boats is threatened by possible repercussions from a clutch of bombs which has been dropped in error by an American aircraft. Cliff plays himself.

Songs sung by Cliff are on the album *Finders Keepers* (SCX 6079). Singles from the film: Time Drags By/La La La Song (DB 8017). 'Finders Keepers' was issued as the B-side of 'In the Country' (DB 8094). Tracks from the Shadows, other than 'Spanish Music', are on *The Shadows on Stage and Screen* (SEG 8528).

Director: Sidney Hayers. Producer: George H. Brown. Choreographer:

Malcolm Clare. Original story: George H. Brown. Screenplay: Michael Pertwee. Music and lyrics: The Shadows. Inter-State Films Production for United Artists.

*Two a Penny.* Stars: Dora Bryan, Avril Angers, Ann Holloway, Nigel Goodwin, and as himself Billy Graham. Cliff plays Jamie Hopkins, a young pedlar who encounters Christian faith thanks to his girlfriend Carol.

Songs sung by Cliff are on the album *Two A Penny* (SCX 6262). Cliff wrote three songs for the film: 'Two a Penny', 'Questions', and 'I'll Love You Forever Today', the latter two with J. F. Collier. Single from the film: I'll Love You Forever Today/Girl You'll Be A Woman Soon (only the A-side was in the film) (DB 8437).

Director: James F. Collier. Executive producer: Frank R. Jocobson. Screenplay and original story: Stella Linden. Music composed and conducted by Mike Leander, and also Cliff Richard. A Worldwide film.

*His Land.* A documentary film which Cliff made in Israel. It was an hour long and was shown in youth clubs and church halls. A soundtrack album, *His Land* (SCX 6443), contained: 'His Land', 'Jerusalem Jerusalem', 'The New 23rd', 'Over in Bethlehem', 'Keep Me Where Love Is', and 'He's Everything To Me'. The songs were written by American Ralph Carmichael.

*Take Me High.* Stars: Debbie Watling, Moyra Fraser, George Cole, Hugh Griffith, Anthony Andrews. Cliff plays Tim Matthews, a rich, somewhat ruthless and ambitious young city gent. He works for a London merchant bank and expects an assignment to New York. Instead, he finds himself sent to Birmingham. Later he finds himself involved with a French restaurant owner, Sarah. They open a brumburger establishment, brumburger being a new form of hamburger! The film was Cliff's first major screen work for seven years.

Songs sung by Cliff are on the album *Take Me High* (EMC 3016). 'Hover' is an instrumental, as is 'Driving', though there is a vocal version of this song. 'Brumburger' is a duet between Cliff and Debbie Watling. A poster with the album showed a portrait of Cliff on one side, and on the other, scenes from the film.

Director: David Askey. Producer: Kenneth Harper. Screenplay: Charles Penfold. Music: Tony Cole. Distribution: through Anglo-EMI.

*Why Should the Devil Have All the Good Music.* This was a 16mm Eastman colour film with a running time of 50 minutes. It was produced by Colin Rank of Abba Productions. Direction was by James Swackhammer. Cliff starred along with a number of well-known Jesus Music artists, including Larry Norman, Judy McKenzie and Dave Cooke, Malcolm and Alwyn, Graham Kendrick, the Arts Centre Group director and actor Nigel Goodwin, and pop singer Dana. It was a documentary of the 1972 London Festival for Jesus, basically a celebration of Christian beliefs.

*A World of Difference.* This was a 16mm colour documentary for Tear Fund centring on the Fund's director George Hoffman. Cliff contributed to the film.

*Loved into Life* and *Love Never Gives Up.* Two Tear Fund filmstrips about Cliff's visit to Bangladesh.

*Cliff: Flipside.* This was filmed at Cliff's Tear Fund concert at the Royal Albert Hall, 1979, and also at his home. He talks about his faith. The director and scriptwriter was Mike Pritchard. Intamedia produced the film for International Films. It runs for 30 minutes and is a 16mm colour presentation.

*A Day With Cliff.* As the title indicates, the film follows Cliff through a day. It was made by Dutch television in the early seventies and is available via International Films.

*Come Together.* A film of the popular religious musical by American Jimmy Owens. Cliff is interviewed by Pat Boone. The film is 16mm colour, from International Films.

*Let's Join Together.* Cliff plus Johnny Cash and Choralerna. The music and message of the Spree Festival, London 1973. International Films.

*Life With Johnny* series. Three films: *Johnny Up the Creek (The Good Samaritan); Johnny Faces Facts (The Mote and the Beam);* and *Johnny Come Home (The Prodigal Son).* These were made in 1969 when Cliff was invited by the religious department of Tyne Tees Television to present a series of contemporary religious programmes. Now available via Worldwide films, International Films. Each film places a New Testament parable in a musical modern setting.

*Greenbelt Live!* Some of the highlights of the major British religious festival held in 1979 where music is an important ingredient. Cliff gives a brief interview, is glimpsed from time to time, and has one stage song, 'Yes, He Lives'. Also in the film, among many, are Garth Hewitt, After the Fire, Randy Stonehill, and Larry Norman. A Tony Tew film for Grenville Film Productions in association with Marshalls Publishing.

*Judge for Yourself.* This Scripture Union filmstrip deals with basic religious questions like: Does it make sense? Does it work? Does it fit in with what I know! Can it be applied to God's message?

*London Crusade.* Documentary in which Cliff makes an appearance. 1966. Worldwide films.

*I'm Going to Ask You to Get Out of Your Seats.* Richard Causton's documentary on Billy Graham for BBC TV. Cliff makes an appearance.

*Rhythm 'n' Greens.* The Shadows starred in this 1964 32-minute film. There are those who swear the part of King Canute was played by Cliff! It was.

# VIDEO

The first UK Cliff video was issued in March 1981. This was of *The Young Ones* (EVH 20242) with a UK price of £28.30.

*The Kenny Everett Show* (EVH 36207). Cliff makes an appearance.

*Summer Holiday, Wonderful Life, Take High, Mine To Share* (double video and booklet), *His Land, Two A Penny, Private Collection, Rock In Australia, Thank You Very Much* (with the Shadows), *Cliff And The Shadows Together, Thunderbirds* (Cliff and the Shadows, puppets), *It's A Small World, Journey Into Life, Cliff And The Shadows Together, Always Guaranteed, The Event, Together, The Video Collection, The Rock That Doesn't Roll, Blue Suede Shoes* (90-minute film that includes Cliff), individual single videos. *Greenbelt* video 1988 (contains Cliff words, songs).

## STAGE APPEARANCES

December 1959: Cliff and the Shadows appear at Stockton Globe in *Babes in the Wood*.

June–December 1960: *Stars in Your Eyes* at the London Palladium. This starred Joan Regan, Russ Conway, Edmund Hockeridge, David Kossof, the Shadows and Cliff.

28 August and for six weeks, 1961: Blackpool Opera House.

June–September 1963: *Holiday Carnival* at the ABC Theatre, Blackpool. This starred Carole Gray, Dailey and Wayne, Arthur Worsley, Norman Collier, Ugo Garrido and Cliff.

December 1964–April 1965. *Aladdin and His Wonderful Lamp* at the London Palladium. This starred Arthur Askey, Una Stubbs, Charlie Cairoli and Company, and Cliff. The music and lyrics were by the Shadows. An album of the show was issued December 1964 (SCX 3522).

11 May 1970: *Five Finger Exercise* by Peter Schaeffer, Bromley New Theatre. Three-week run. Producer Patrick Tucker. Cliff plays Clive, a twenty-year-old university student.

10 May 1971: *The Potting Shed* at Bromley New Theatre. Cast included Patrick Barr, Margo Jenkins, Margot Thomas, Kathleen Harrison. Performance cancelled owing to fire.

17 May 1971: *The Potting Shed* opens at Sadlers Wells Theatre, London. Same cast as above. Cliff plays James Calliger, a thirty-year-old who is denied family love and attempts to find out why. The original production was twenty years previously when Sir John Gielgud played James Calliger. Press reviews for the play and for Cliff were good. Numerous friends of Cliff attended the first night.

3 July 1974: *A Midsummer Night's Dream* performed by the Riversmead School Dramatic Society. Cliff played Bottom. Actors were past and present pupils of his old school. Cliff took six weeks off normal show and business engagements to rehearse. The play ran until 12 July with a break on 9 and 10 July. It was performed at Riversmead School, College Road, Cheshunt. Mrs Jay Norris produced. The same day that Cliff opened at the school Olivia Newton-John opened a season at Las Vegas!

9 April 1986: *Time* at the Dominion Theatre, London. Cliff played a rock singer called Chris. He stayed in the show for one year and was replaced by David Cassidy. On 14 April 1988 he appeared in a charity performance of the production to raise funds for the fight against Aids.

## TELEVISION AND RADIO

Cliff has taken part in so many television and radio programmes throughout the world that it is impossible to trace them all. This section gives some of the most important television and radio broadcasts, with most of the information relating to the UK. His many appearances year by year on the long-running high-audience BBC TV show *Top of the Pops* are not listed save for early bookings. The same goes for other long-running television and radio shows.

13 September 1958: ABC TV, *Oh Boy*. Cliff makes his programme debut and becomes a resident. The *New Musical Express*, describing his regular appearances on the show, writes, 'the most crude exhibitionism ever seen on TV' and adds, 'If we are expected to believe that Cliff Richard was acting naturally then consideration for medical treatment before it's too late may be advisable.'

25 October 1958: Cliff makes his debut on the popular BBC Light Programme *Saturday Club*.

21 January 1960: *Pat Boone Show* (US TV). Cliff sings 'Forty Days', 'Dynamite', 'Voice In The Wilderness', 'Living Doll', and 'A Whole Lot Of Shakin''.

8 April 1961: Cliff appears on the panel of the BBC TV *Juke Box Jury* show where four panel members give their opinions on latest single releases. Chairman is David Jacobs.

26 April 1961: *Parade of the Pops*, BBC Light Programme.

20 May 1961: *Thank Your Lucky Stars*, ITV.

2 August 1961: records for *Easy Beat*, BBC Light Programme.

10 October 1961: records special material for Radio Luxembourg.

17 December 1961: records for ITV's *Thank Your Lucky Stars* Christmas Hit Parade for 1961.

17 January 1962: on *Parade of the Pops* Cliff sings 'The Young Ones' and 'WhoAre We To Say'.

11 April 1962: interviewed for Radio Free Europe.

28 August 1962: sings 'It'll Be Me' for the BBC1 *Billy Cotton Show*.

14 December 1962: for *Saturday Club* Cliff records 'Do You Want To Dance', 'Bachelor Boy', 'The Next Time' and 'It'll Be Me'.

18 December 1962: takes part in *Pop Inn* (BBC Light Programme).

21 January 1963: for the first time in the history of Radio Luxembourg's programme *ABC of the Stars* it devotes the whole show to one person – Cliff.

22 April 1963: BBC TV. Cliff records his own special.

3 November 1963: Cliff and the Shadows on ATV's *Sunday Night at the London Palladium*.

12 May 1964: Cliff in German TV show in Munich.

1 July 1964: ATV gives Cliff and the Shadows a one-hour special.

June 1965: Cliff and the Shadows record three one-hour specials for ATV.

10 August 1965: tenth anniversary edition of *Thank Your Lucky Stars*. Cliff receives a gold disc for 'Bachelor Boy' coupled with 'The Next Time'.

22 September 1965: Cliff records for US TV *Ed Sullivan Show*.

6 March 1966: Cliff stars in BBC 2's *Show of the Week*. It's his first BBC TV for three years.

9 October 1966: compères and takes top billing for the ATV show *Sunday Night at the London Palladium*.

7 December 1966: Granada TV show *Cinema*. Cliff talks about his films.

14 October 1967: in Tokyo for Japanese TV special.

19 December 1967: announcement made that Cliff will take a straight acting role in the play *A Matter of Diamonds*. Transmitted on ITV April 1968.

23 February 1968: Cliff is on *Dee Time* (BBC TV).

27 February 1968: *The Golden Shot*, German TV. Cliff sings 'Don't Forget To Catch Me' in German.

5 March 1968: BBC 1. Cliff sings the six short-listed titles for the Eurovision Song Contest.

31 March 1968: *Morecambe and Wise Show*, BBC TV.

April 1968: *A Matter of Diamonds* is transmitted on ITV. It is a thriller in which Cliff has a straight acting role. He plays a young man who has decided he will steal a girl's diamond necklace but when he meets her he falls in love with her.

6 April 1968: *Eurovision Song Contest*, BBC TV. Cliff comes second with 'Congratulations'.

17 May 1968: *Cliff's TV Show* (BBC). He sings 'My Babe', 'Congratulations' (backed by the Breakaways), 'It's All In The Game', 'Feeling Groovy' (with Hank Marvin), 'Perhaps I Had A Wicked Childhood', 'There Must Have Been A Moment Of Truth', 'The Minute You're Gone', 'The Day I Met Marie', 'Take A Bird Who Can Sing' (with help from Una Stubbs, Sheila White and Hank Marvin), 'Oh No John No' (Cliff and others), 'Passing Strangers' (with Cilla Black), 'Big Ship', and 'Visions'.

22 May 1968: BBC Light Programme. Cliff is a member of the panel for *Any Questions*.

23 June 1968: ITV *Big Show*. Cliff sings 'The Day I Met Marie', 'All My Love', and 'Shout'.

28 June 1968: *Talk of the Town*, relayed on ITV. He sings 'Shout', 'All My Love', 'Nothing But A House-Party', 'If Ever I Should Leave You', 'Girl', 'London's Not Too Far', 'The Dreams That I Dream', 'The Day I Met Marie', 'A Taste Of Honey', 'The Lady Came From Baltimore', 'When I'm Sixty-Four', 'The Young Ones', 'Lucky Lips', 'Living Doll', 'In The Country', 'Congratulations', and a brief snatch of 'Visions'. Vocal back-ups from the Breakaways.

17 July 1968: takes part in David Jacobs' BBC TV show *Juke Box Jury*.

2 October 1968: interviewed by Keith Skues for BBC Light Programme *Saturday Club*.

5 November 1968: records for BBC Light Programme *Off the Record*. Chooses eight favourite discs and talks about them.

4 December 1968: interviewed by Adrian Love for BBC World Service.

17 December 1968: records

'Congratulations' for BBC TV *Top of the Pops* Christmas show.

18 and 19 December 1968: records for Scottish TV.

19 February 1969: on the *Cilla Black Show* (BBC TV), sings 'Good Times' and 'Don't Forget'.

22 February 1969: BBC Radio, *Pete Murray Show*.

7 and 8 March 1969: records for *Rolf Harris Show*, BBC TV.

17 March 1969: takes part in *Sooty*, BBC TV show. Transmitted 12 May.

25 March 1969: *Dave Cash Show*, BBC Radio 1.

7 June 1969: *Dee Time*, BBC TV recording.

4 September 1969: interview on BBC Radio 1 *Scene and Heard*.

29 September 1969: BBC Radio, *Open House* with Pete Murray.

28 November 1969: French TV, Paris. Sings 'Throw Down A Line' and 'Eyes Of A Child'.

24 December 1969: BBC 1 *Cilla Black Show*.

3 January 1970: Cliff's own BBC TV show. The series showcased prospective British entries for the Eurovision Song Contest.

20 February 1970: *Dave Cash Show*, BBC Radio 1.

7 March 1970: *Children's Favourites*, BBC Radio 1.

13 April 1970: BBC Radios 1 and 3, *The Cliff Richard Story* with Robin Boyle.

19 May 1970: records contribution for Disney show, BBC TV.

31 August 1970: Cliff special, BBC TV Aretha Franklin is the guest, with others taking part, including Hank Marvin and Una Stubbs. The show lasts fifty minutes.

4 October 1970: *Sing a New Song*, BBC TV. First of three shows, with the Settlers, for the religious department. (The Settlers are also resident for six weeks from 20 September in the ATV Sunday programme *Beyond Belief*.)

2 January 1971: new BBC TV series *It's Cliff Richard* with Hank Marvin and Una Stubbs resident. Thirteen weeks.

24 January 1971: 'Lollipop Tree', BBC 2. Cliff provides the commentary for this section of *The World About Us*. The segment tells of a home for 800 children located at the foot of the Himalayas where for a time Cliff's aunt was a teacher.

27 March 1971: final screening of Cliff's TV series which began 2 January.

30 August 1971: BBC 1 *Getaway With Cliff* holiday special. Cliff joined by Olivia Newton-John, Hank Marvin, Bruce Welch and John Farrar. The show, which lasts fifty minutes, is filmed in various parts of Britain.

24 December 1971: BBC TV, Cliff's own Christmas Eve special.

1972: *It's Cliff Richard*. A thirteen-week BBC TV series beginning January. Resident guests were Olivia Newton-John and the Flirtations. The Breakaways provided the vocal backing and the Pamela Davis Dancers provided the dancing. Hank Marvin declined a residency for this series. Another familiar face, that of Una Stubbs, was prevented from appearing in the early programmes because she was expecting a baby. Dandy Nichols provided the early replacement. Also guesting in the series were the New Seekers. They sang the songs which were short-listed for Britain's entry to the 1972 Eurovision Song Contest. Among other series guests were Elton John and Labi Siffre. The series gained over two million viewers more than the one in 1971. It was scripted by Eric Donaldson and produced by Michael Hurll.

27 February 1972: last programme of the series in which Cliff presents *Music for Sunday* for BBC Radios 1 and 2. In this series he played records by other Christian artists and some of his own. Programme devised and produced by Jack Hywel Davies.

19 August 1972: Cliff makes a guest appearance on the *Lulu* show. He sings 'Reason To Believe' and his new single 'Living In Harmony".

2 September 1972: *The Case* is screened in the UK. This film was specially made for the BBC and Swedish, Norwegian and Finnish broadcasting companies. It starred Cliff, Tim Brooke-Taylor, Olivia Newton-John and two Scandinavians, Mathi Rannin and Pekka Laitho. The plot was scripted by Eric Donaldson. It was described as a musical comedy thriller. Some reviewers likened Tim Brooke-Taylor and Cliff to Bob Hope and Bing Crosby! The programme producer was Michael Hurll. It took ten days of filming.

2 January 1973: BRT TV, Belgium, shows Cliff in Scotland with the songs 'Hail Caledonia', 'Skye Boat Song', 'Courting In The Kitchen', 'Let's Have a Ceilidh', 'Bonnie Mary Of Argyll', and, among

others, 'Scotland The Brave'.

**10 January 1973:** Cliff appears on the *Cilla Black Show* and sings the six entries for the Eurovision Song Contest (he had been chosen for the second time to represent Britain at this event). The six songs are 'Come Back Billie Joe', 'Ashes to Ashes', 'Tomorrow's Rising', 'The Days Of Love', 'Power To All Our Friends', and 'Help It Along'. The song selected was 'Power To All Our Friends'.

**13 January 1973:** British Forces Broadcasting Service interview with Brian Cullingford.

**19 January 1973:** BBC 2 *They Sold a Million*.

**2 April 1973:** BBC Radio 1 *Top 12*. Cliff chooses his top twelve records. Compère Brian Matthew, producer Paul Williams.

**7 April 1973:** Cliff appears at the Eurovision Song Festival and sings the British entry 'Power To All Our Friends', which comes third. The song was written by Guy Fletcher and Doug Flett. An estimated 300 million in thirty-two countries saw the show. Cliff was very disappointed at not winning and told reporters he was getting too old. However, 'Power To All Our Friends' became a worldwide pop hit.

**4 May 1974:** BBC TV *Mike Yarwood Show*. When Cliff appears it is to find Mike impersonating Hughie Green, a well-known British TV presenter of new acts. Cliff sings his latest single '(You Keep Me) Hanging On'.

**9 May 1974:** *The Nana Mouskouri Show*. BBC TV Cliff sings 'Give Me Back That Old Familiar Feeling'. Later he sings 'Constantly', sporting a yellow jacket and multi-coloured tie, and with his fringe parted in the middle. With Nana he sings 'I Believe In Music'.

**24 August 1974:** the first of the 1974 *It's Cliff Richard* series is transmitted.

**9 April 1975:** *Shangalang*, Bay City Rollers' Granada TV show. Interview.

**19 April 1975:** Cliff is a special guest on London Weekend Television's *Saturday Scene*, compère Sally James. The original version of 'Travellin' Light' is played. Cliff remarks on another and better version which is on his new album *31st of February Street*. He says he has recently been in Vienna 'plugging my new record "It's Only Me You've Left Behind"'.

**9 July 1975:** *Jim'll Fix It*. Cliff fan Helen Moon of Cromer writes in to the BBC asking if she could meet her pop hero. The wish is granted. With the Shadows Cliff sings 'Run Billy Run'. After the show spot Helen Moon receives from Cliff an autographed copy of *31st of February Street*.

**6 September 1975:** first of a new series on BBC TV, *It's Cliff and Friends*. Major guests are Su Shiffron, David Copperfield and Alan Shiers. Musical director, Ronnie Hazelhurst; sound, Adrian Bishop-Laggett; lighting, Robbie Robinson; design, Chris Pemsel; producer, Phil Bishop. Cliff sings 'All You Need Is Love', 'Good On The Sally Army', 'With Su', 'All I Wanna Do', 'I've Got Time', 'Love Train'.

**20 September 1975:** *Supersonic*, ITV programme produced by Mike Mansfield. Cliff wears a blue denim suit. He sings 'Honky Tonk Angel', 'Let's Have A Party', and does a brief take-off of Elvis.

**3 October 1975:** *Pop Quest*, ITV. A clip of Cliff is shown.

**14 October 1975:** Noel Edmonds on his Radio 1 show at 07.40 welcomes 1940-born Cliff into the world and plays 'Please Don't Tease'.

**November 1975:** Cliff appears on Capital, the London radio station, for a nostalgia show which recalls February 1959, with compère Roger Scott. 'High Class Baby' is played.

**4 January 1976:** BBC Radios 1 and 2. New *Gospel Road* series. Cindy Kent, ex-Settlers, reviews new records while Cliff, as before, contributes material of his own and introduces songs by other people.

**14 February 1976:** ITV *Supersonic*. Wearing a white jacket and trousers with a green shirt Cliff sings 'Miss You Nights'.

**26 April 1976:** records TV special, Holland. *Eddy Go Round* show. Broadcast 15 June 1976.

**3 May 1976:** Radio Luxembourg. Cliff previews his new album *I'm Nearly Famous*.

**17 May 1976:** begins recording *Insight* with Tim Blackmore, Radio 1.

**19 and 26 June 1976:** *Supersonic*, ITV. On the 19th Cliff sings 'Honky Tonk Angel'; on the 26th 'Let's Have A Party'.

**6 September 1976:** interviewed on BBC TV *Nationwide* and on Thames TV.

**30 December 1976:** Belgian TV, *Adamo*

*Special*. Cliff sings 'Living Doll' (with Adamo), 'Power To All Our Friends', and 'Honky Tonk Angel'.

28 September 1977: *DLT Show*, Radio 1. DJ Dave Lee Travis talks with Cliff from 6 to 7 p.m. Producer Dave Atkey.

1 October 1977: *Michael Parkinson Show*, BBC TV Cliff is a guest along with Robert Morley, who was with Cliff in his films *The Young Ones* and *Finders Keepers*.

November 1977: *TisWas*, ATV. Cliff talks with compere Sally James and undergoes the usual rituals for programme participants – something squashy stuffed in the face and cold water to soothe a high temperature.

15 February 1978: BBC TV, *Pebble Mill*. On this lunchtime show Cliff speaks about his new album *Small Corners* and sings two songs from it.

21 September 1978: *Star Parade*, German TV. Cliff sings 'Please Remember Me' and 'Lucky Lips'.

1 October 1978: BBC Radio 1. *20 Golden Years*. First in a series which tells the Cliff show business story.

30 October 1978: Australian TV. *Australian Music to the World*. Cliff sings 'Devil Woman', an interview is shown which had been filmed at his English home and in which he talks of John Farrar and Olivia Newton-John.

1 January 1979: Korea. KBS TV shows *The Young Ones* in a New Year programme.

12 June 1979: Dutch TV *AVRO Gala Special*. Cliff records on 31 May and 1 June items for inclusion in this show, in aid of the fiftieth anniversary of the Dutch Youth Hostel Organization, NJHC. Cliff sings 'Miss You Nights', 'When Two Worlds Drift Apart'.

27 August 1979: BBC Radio 1 broadcast a special programme on the Greenbelt Jesus Music Festival in which Cliff is interviewed and heard on stage.

5 September 1979: Capital Radio, London. Cliff takes part in the top-rated *Roger Scott Show*. The two chat and a number of Cliff record tracks are played.

19 September 1979: Manchester's Radio Piccadilly. Cliff is the guest of well-known DJ Roger Day between 3 and 4 p.m. Several Cliff tracks are played and Cliff also talks about his new record label Patch and his first signing, Garth Hewitt.

23 December 1979: BBC Radio 1. *Star Special*. Cliff becomes a DJ for two

hours and plays his favourite records. He names 'Rock 'n' Roll Juvenile' as the recording of his own that he most likes.

26 December 1979: *Two Sides of Cliff*. BBC Radio 2. Cliff plays his own and Shadows' records.

7 January 1980: *Mike Douglas Show*, USA TV. Cliff is interviewed by the well-known chat-show personality. Douglas talks to Cliff about his OBE. He tells how a great chunk of his career could be labelled 'European' and that he doesn't need America for finance.

8 January 1980: *The Dinah Shore Show*, USA TV. Dinah tells of Cliff's current US hit 'We Don't Talk Anymore'. Cliff explains what an OBE is and shows the audience his Union Jack coloured socks. He talks of his childhood memories, explains why he is not married, and discusses the pros and cons of American girls.

March 1980: *Pop Gospel* ITV series begins. Cliff appears in two shows.

22 June 1980: BBC TV, *Greenbelt*. An edited version of the film which has Cliff in film shots, in interview and in concert, but for Cliff fans the live footage is meagre.

23 July 1980: BBC Radio 1. Cliff on his OBE day takes part in a telephone link-up with friend and Radio 1 DJ Mike Read on his breakfast show.

23 September 1980: BBC Radio 2, *The John Dunn Show*. A general chat and interview, one of many which Cliff has had over the years with this popular BBC presenter. Cliff defines himself on this programme as 'basically a pop-rock singer'.

27 September 1980: BBC *Swapshop*. Cliff appears on this high-audience younger listener programme and talks about himself and his music.

13 December 1980: BBC 1, *Michael Parkinson Show*. He sings 'Heartbreak Hotel'. In a finale with other programme guests Cliff joins in singing 'All The Way'. This programme was repeated 28 March 1981.

4 January 1981: US TV *The John Kelly Show*, Los Angeles.

5 January 1981: US TV *The John Davison Show*, Los Angeles.

6 January 1981: US TV *Dionne Warwick's Solid Gold Show*, Los Angeles.

7 January 1981: US TV *Merv Griffin Show*, Los Angeles.

20 March 1981: *Cliff in London*, BBC 1. Excerpts from Cliff's autumn concerts

at the Apollo. The first part of the programme has Cliff accompanying himself on acoustic guitar.

Autumn 1981: BBC 1. Four programmes on Cliff expected: a look at twenty-two years in show business; a Gospel concert, Cliff and his faith; Cliff on the road, particularly his 1981 US tour; his lifestyle, charity work and thoughts.

7 September 1981: Centre Radio, a new commercial station, opens in Leeds and commences sound transmission with Cliff's *Wired For Sound*.

30 September 1981: Cliff filming four TV shows in Hollywood, California.

23 November 1981: BBC 2 transmits the first of four consecutive programmes on Cliff's career in show business. Series is entitled *Cliff*, and is made by the BBC in co-operation with Lella Productions, produced and directed by Norman Stone. The first programme showed the Rock 'n' Roll Special concert which was recorded and filmed at Hammersmith, 1 May 1981. There are also film extracts from *Expresso Bongo* (Pendennis Pictures), *The Young Ones* (EMI Elstree) and *Oh Boy!* (EMI Pathé), with use of both Pathé and BBC newsreels. Numerous people from the time are interviewed. Most controversial is Neil Spencer of the *NME*.

27 November 1981: ATV has Cliff with Tony Jasper and Patrick Doncaster.

30 November 1981: second *Cliff* focuses on a gospel concert recorded at the Apollo, Manchester, 6 February 1981.

7 December 1981: third *Cliff* centres on American tour and a concert at New York's Savoy Theatre, 2 April 1981.

14 December 1981: *Cliff* features a birthday concert at Apollo Victoria, London in 1981.

27 December 1981: in *Everyman*, BBC 1, Cliff discusses his faith and beliefs.

27 November 1982: Noel Edmonds' *Late Late Show*, BBC1.

13, 14, 15 October 1983: Mercia Radio, Coventry, plays 75 Cliff Richard hits.

31 March 1983: *Wogan*, BBC 1.

21 April 1983: *TV Hour*, Finland.

7 September 1983: Roger Scott interview, Capital Radio, London.

25 March 1984: *Fiesta Continual*, Portuguese TV.

11 June 1984: *Rock Gospel* BBC 1.

22 December 1984: *A Celebration of Christmas*, Radio 2. ACG occasion with Cliff (repeated 25 December).

23 December 1984: *Rock Gospel*, BBC 1.

25 January 1985: goes hip on *The Tube*, Channel 4.

28, 29, 30 January 1985: extended interview with Simon Bates.

1 February 1985: Radio 2, Gloria Hunniford.

7 February 1985: *Good Morning Britain*, ITV.

9 February 1985: *Saturday Superstore*, BBC1.

26 August 1985: *Wogan*, sings 'She's So Beautiful'.

23 November 1985: *TX*, ITV.

3 December 1985: *Open to Question*, BBC2.

11 December 1985: *Pebble Mill*, BBC 1.

21 December 1985: *Saturday Superstore*.

21 December 1985: special *Pebble Mill. A Song for Christmas* is transmitted.

22 February 1986: Hong Kong major TV, Channel 2.

22 February 1986: breakfast TV.

29 August 1986: appears with Sarah Brightman on *Wogan*, singing 'All I Ask Of You'.

25 September 1986: Cliff interviewed by Simon Bates, Radio 1.

26 September 1986: once more on Radio 1 this time with Andy Peebles.

11 October 1986: *Superstore*, BBC, with Sarah Brightman.

27 December 1986: *Cliff from the Hip* (at London's Hippodrome), Channel 4.

26 March 1987: on TV-AM.

2 April 1987: appears on a keep-fit programme, *Don't Break Your Heart*.

19 June 1987: *It's A Knockout*.

20 June 1987: *It's Wicked*.

End of June 1987: on *Wogan*, BBC1.

1 August 1987: *Summertime Special* ITV sings 'Summer Holiday', 'Some People' and 'My Pretty One'. Makes numerous appearances promoting 'Some People', as often happens around single releases.

19 August 1987: pops in on *Hold Tight*, ITV. 1987.

12 September 1987: *Dame Edna Experience*. Asked who his favourite female might be, he answers Farrah Fawcett, Mary Whitehouse and Dame Edna.

1 January 1988: on *Wogan*, BBC1.

26 January 1988: Royal Command Performance.

11 May 1988: appears on programmes promoting appeal for Dr Barnado's.

16 July 1988: *Saturday Night*, ITV. Appears on radio and television celebrating 30 years in show-biz (*see* Chapter 17).

13 November 1988: *TV Calendar* (Yorkshire TV).

14 November 1988: *Des O'Connor Show*, ITV.

16 November 1988: more of Cliff on *Wogan*, BBC1.

19 November 1988: presents a Radio 1 show on EMI's 90th birthday.

26 November 1988: Royal Command Variety Performance. ??? TV.

27 November 1988: Live from the Palladium. ??? TV.

29 May 1989: Presents Sarah Greene with award on show hosted by Noel Edmonds.

9 September, 1989: *Saturday Matters* with Sue Lawley.

1 November 1989: records for *Wogan*, BBC1.

9 November 1989: *Wogan* transmission.

24 December 1989: *Sunday Sunday*.

6 February 1990: Radio 1, speaks to Simon Mayo while in New Zealand.

4 August 1990: special gala show from Royal Albert Hall marking Queen Mother's 90th birthday.

12 December 1990: interviewed by Jacki Brambles, Radio 1.

26 June 1991: *This Morning*.

12 July 1991: makes a surprise appearance on *Gardener's World*.

21 and 27 July 1991: appears on *Mike Read Show*, Radio 1.

11 December 1991: *Des O'Connor Show*, ITV.

13 December 1991: *This Morning 'Live'*. ITV.

16 December 1991: *Pebble Mill*, BBC 1.

31 January 1992: *Gloria Hunniford Show*, BBC TV.

28 February 1992: on *Wogan*, BBC TV.

1 March 1992: *Wired For Sound: Cliff Richard Story*, Radio 2. Six-programme series.

4 April 1992: gains front-cover TV weekly section of *Daily Mirror*.

10 April 1992: appears on new *Bruce Forsyth Guest Night* series: plays tennis with Pat Cash.

11 April 1992: appears on front cover of *TV Quick* listings magazine.

## BOOKS ON OR BY CLIFF

*Cliff Around the Clock* (Daily Mirror Publications, 1959).

*The Cliff Richard Story*, George Tremlett (Futura, 1975).

*DI*, Issues 1–63 (International Cliff Richard Movement).

*From Cliff to You*, Janet Johnson (International Cliff Richard Movement – for members only).

*Happy Xmas from Cliff*, Cliff Richard (Hodder and Stoughton, 1980).

*It's Great to Be Young*, Cliff Richard (Souvenir, 1960).

*Me and My Shadow*, Cliff Richard (*Daily Mirror* Publications, 1960).

*New Singer, New Song*, David Winter (Hodder and Stoughton, 1967).

*Questions*, Cliff answering reader and fan queries (Hodder and Stoughton).

*The Wonderful World of Cliff Richard*, Bob Ferrier (Peter Davies, 1960).

*Two a Penny*, film story by David Winter and Stella Linden (Hodder and Stoughton, 1978).

*Visions* (Cliff Richard Fan Club of London, 1980).

*The Way I See It*, Cliff Richard (Hodder and Stoughton, 1968).

*Which One's Cliff?*, Cliff Richard and Bill Latham (Hodder and Stoughton, 1978, re-issued and updated, 1990).

*Cliff*, Pat Doncaster and Tony Jasper (Sidgwick and Jackson, 1981).

*Silver Cliff*, Tony Jasper (Sidgwick and Jackson, 1982).

*Cliff In His Own Words*, Kevin St John (Omnibus, 1981 edition, revised 1992).

*25 Years of Cliff*, John Tobler (W. H. Smith, 1982).

*St Michael Biographies: Shout!* Philip Norman; *Frank Sinatra*, Tony Scaduto; *Cliff*, Patrick Doncaster and Tony Jasper, in one volume (Octopus, 1983).

*You, Me And Jesus*, Cliff Richard (Hodder and Stoughton, 1985).

*Mine Forever*, Cliff Richard (Hodder and Stoughton, 1989).

*Mine To Share* (booklet), Cliff Richard (Hodder and Stoughton, 1984).

*Happy Christmas from Cliff*, Cliff Richard (Hodder and Stoughton, 1980).

*Cliff Richard and The Shadows*, Dezo Hoffman (Virgin, 1985).

*The Cliff Richard File*, Mike Read (Roger Houghton, 1986).

*Single-minded*, Cliff Richard (Hodder and Stoughton, 1988).

*Jesus, Me and You*, Cliff Richard (Hodder and Stoughton, 1988).

*Survivor*, Tony Jasper (Marshall Pickering, 1989).

*Cliff – A Celebration*, Theresa Wassif (Hodder and Stoughton, 1989).

*Cliff* (in series Heroes of the Cross), Gale Barker (Marshall Pickering, 1992).

*Cliff Richard – The Complete Recording Sessions 1958–1990*, Peter Lewry and Nigel Goodall (Blandford/Cassell, 1991).

## BOOKLETS (about Cliff)

Over the years there have been flurries of booklets published, often coinciding with particular events.

Star Specials: No. 2. *Meet Cliff Richard*. No 24. *Meeting Cliff in Wonderful Life*.

*Life with Cliff* (Charles Buchan publications).

*Cliff Around The Clock* (*Daily Mirror* publications).

*Visions* (Cliff Richard Fan Club, yearly issues and extremely good).

*Cliff With The Kids In America* (Empire Records, Leicester).

*Congratulations Cliff – 30th Anniversary* (Starbitz).

*Cliff Richard – A 30th Anniversary Souvenir* (Lionbound).

*Cliff Special – Photo Mags* (ICRM).

*Cliff – Music Collector*, January–March 1991, three-part disc and career coverage, with extensive space.

*Cliff Richard: Hit-Maker*. William Hopper (ICRM).

*Cliff Richard Songbook – It's A Small World*.

## BOOK MENTIONS

(Where there is particular chapter treatment or major reference in a number of text areas.)

*Feel So Real*, Tony Jasper (Marshall Pickering, 1991).

*Rock Solid*, Tony Jasper (Word, 1986).

*Moments Of Truth*, Tony Jasper (Marshall Pickering, 1991).

*Rock 'n' Roll: I Gave You The Best Years Of My Life*, Bruce Welch (Viking).

*God Put A Fighter In Me*, Sheila Walsh (Hodder and Stoughton).

*My Faith*, Mary Elizabeth Callen (Hodder and Stoughton).

*The Story Of The Shadows*, Mike Read (Roger Houghton).

*Jesus In A Pop Culture*, Tony Jasper (Collins, 1975).

*Jesus and the Christian in a Pop Culture*, Tony Jasper (Robert Royce, 1984).

Numerous album and film songbooks and programmes are available. Enquiries as to the likely availability of these should be made to the Cliff United Fan Club, for the attention of Ms Christine Whitehead. Also available are numerous T-shirts and sweatshirts from the many tours, stickers, pens and photographs.

# FAN CLUBS

There is no official Cliff fan club, but the long-standing and efficiently run International Cliff Richard Movement (ICRM) has gained the co-operation of the Cliff Richard management.

The ICRM publishes a bi-monthly club paper *DI* (*Dynamite International*). Its headquarters is ICRM, Postbox 4164-1009AD, Amsterdam, Netherlands. The editor of *Dynamite* is Harry De Louw, Marco Pololaan 304, Utrecht, Holland. The secretary is Anton Husmann Jr. The ICRM supplies a wide range of information and material for members. There is a yearly subscription. Listed below are the worldwide locations of the ICRM as of spring 1981.

## CLIFF RICHARD FAN CLUBS IN THE UK

AVON & SOMERSET: Maureen Neathway, 22 Trent Close, Yeovil, Somerset BA21 5XQ ● BIRMINGHAM: Anthea Jansen, 1 Aldis Road, Walsall WS2 9AY ● DERBYSHIRE & NOTTS.: Pam Thorpe, 20 Kempton Drive, Arnold, Nottingham NG5 8EU ● DEVON & CORNWALL: Sonia Nield, 14 Meadway, Saltash, Cornwall ● DORSET: Freda Hector/Maureen Wakefield, 22 Benmoor Road, Creekmoor, Poole, Dorset BH17 7DS ● EDINBURGH: Susan Davie,

8 Neidpath Court, Craigievar Wynd, Edinburgh EH12 8UF ● GLASGOW: Elizabeth Daly, 15 Ryedale Place, Drumchapel, Glasgow G15 7HP ● GLOUCESTER & OXFORD: William Hooper, 17 Podsmead Road, Tuffley, Gloucester GL1 5PB ● HAMPSHIRE: Marion Cunningham, 67 Park Road, Freemantle, Southampton SO1 3DD ● HEREFORD AND WORCESTER: Nicky Piercey, 12 Monks Way, Peopleton, Pershore, Worcs. WR10 2EH ● HERTFORDSHIRE & BEDFORDSHIRE: Judy Brewin, 39 Caves Lane, Bedford MK40 3DW ● KENT: Jacquey Hartree, Walsingham Cottage, Manor Park, Chislehurst, Kent ● LANCASHIRE: Kathleen Fereday, 46 Rydal Road, Lancaster LA1 3HA ● LEICESTERSHIRE & NORTHAMPTONSHIRE: Mrs L. Mowe, 148 Roston Drive, Hinckley, Leics. LE10 0XP ● LINCOLNSHIRE & HUMBERSIDE: Mrs Julie Leighton, 3 Folkingham Road, Billingborough, Lincs NG34 0NT ● LONDON & SURREY: Bridget Bowles, PO Box 792, London SE9 4PT ● MANCHESTER: Sandra J. Hough, 4 Dawlish Avenue, Cheadle Hulme, Stockport, Greater Manchester ● MERSEYSIDE & CHESHIRE: Wendy Leftwich, Greystones Cottage, 85 Thingwall Road East, Thingwall, Wirral L61 3UZ ● MIDDLESEX & BUCKINGHAMSHIRE: PO Box 2BQ, London W1A 2BQ ● NORTHERN IRELAND: Ann Thompson, 409 Ballysillan Road, Belfast BT14 6RE ● NORTH-EAST ENGLAND: Maureen Winn, 29 Rodsley Avenue, Gateshead, Tyne and Wear NE8 4JY ● EAST ANGLIA: Sandy McGreish, 133 George Lambton Avenue, Newmarket, Suffolk CB8 0BN ● SUSSEX: Carole Davis, 8 Lansdowne Court, Landsdowne Road, West Worthing BN11 5HD ● WALES: Angela King, 7 The Broadway, Prestatyn, Clwyd LL19 8AU, N. Wales ● WARWICKSHIRE: Wendy Ashby, 51 Shenstone Avenue, Rugby CV22 5BL ● ISLE OF WIGHT: Dawn Nott, 5 Park

Road, King's Town Estate, PO36 0HU, I.o.W. PO36 0DN ● WILTSHIRE & BERKSHIRE: Sarah and Paul Mullins, St Teresa's Cottage, Church Street, Tisbury, Salisbury, Wilts. ● YORKSHIRE: Jennifer Chatten, 26 Wentworth Drive, Harrogate, Yorks. HG2 7LA.

## FAN CLUBS IN OTHER COUNTRIES

AUSTRALIA: CRM of Australia, Gwenda Hughes, 24 King Street, Waterford, Queensland 4133 ● AUSTRIA: CRFC of Austria, Christine Schauer, Robert Lachg. 42/43/14, 1210 Vienna ● BELGIUM: CRFC of Belgium, Marleen Suykerbuyk, Postbox 234, 2000 Antwerpen 1 ● CANADA: CRFC of Canada, Denise Magi, PO Box 124 – Station 'F', Toronto, Ontario M4Y 2L4 ● FRANCE: Les amis de CR & Shadows, Bernard Broche, 10 rue Edouard Rouviere, 38450 Vif ● GERMANY: CR Fans of Germany, Eva Opolka, Krahnenburgstrasse 23, 4000 Düsseldorf 30 ● NEW ZEALAND: CRM of New Zealand, Katrina Richards, 29 Cotton Street, St Johns, Auckland 6 ● NORWAY: CRFC of Norway, Helle Kjendlie, PO Box 57, 1351 Rud ● PHILIPPINES: CRFC of The Philippines, Edna Salva, 6514 Pastrana, Leyte ● SOUTH AFRICA: South African CRM, Robert Witchell, PO Box 3505, Pretoria 0001 ● SWEDEN: CRFC of Sweden, Marie Nilsson, Dukes Väg 28b, 575 36 Eksjö ● SWITZERLAND: CRFC SCHWEIZ, Stefanie Brühlmann, Am Pfisterhölzli 15, 8606 Griefensee ● USA: CRFC of America, Mary Posner, 8916 N. Skokie Blvd. #3, Skokie, IL 60077.

## ICRM REPRESENTATIVES

SCANDINAVIA: Bo Larsson, Förvalterv.20, 123 57 Farsta, Sweden ● JAPAN: Miyoko Watanabe, 853–24 Kuden-cho, Sakae-ku, Yokohama-shi, Kanagawa, 247.

## CLIFF RICHARD GRAPEVINE

Grapevine came into being in September 1978 and has a worldwide membership. It was started by a group of Colchester-based fans for the purpose of providing information about Cliff's concert tour dates and supporting his charitable activities. Grapevine issues a quarterly magazine-format illustrated newsletter. All profit realized from the sale of Grapevine items, photographs, stationery, sweatshirts, etc. is donated to Cliff's Charitable

Trust Fund. Grapevine also sponsors a little boy in India, through the Tear Fund Childcare Programme. UK membership costs £4.50 per year in the UK, £6 in Europe, and £7 outside Europe. English pounds, Eurocheques or International Money Orders in pounds sterling are accepted. The Grapevine address is PO Box 55, Colchester, Essex CO4 3XJ.

Grapevine is run by Veronica Owen, Diana Duffet, Judith Abbott and Gordon Donaldson, with additional help from Margaret Fox, Linda Lees, Jocelyn Leyland, Christine Godfrey and Celia McNeilly.

The Cliff United Fan Club is run by Christine Whitehead. It offers the best magazine. It also organizes many events. It emphasizes Cliff's Christian activities. The address is 28 Blenheim Road, Sutton, Surrey SM1 2PX.

## THE CLIFF RICHARD CHARITABLE TRUST

Clubs and meeting houses of the ICRM and those of the Grapevine movement make donations to Cliff's trust fund. The fund is a small one but was established so that Cliff had a convenient channel for his support of the many charities with which he sympathizes, but for which he is unable, owing to pressure on his time, to present special fund-raising concerts. The trust makes a series of donations each quarter – a maximum of £200 to any organization. All recipients have to be registered charities and appeals from individuals cannot be considered. Obviously, the trust makes no public appeal for funds and is essentially a channel for Cliff's own personal donations. If fans from time to time make a donation then this is included in the funds to be distributed at the next quarter.

## INTERNATIONAL CLIFF WEEK

This is held during the week of Cliff's birthday, 14 October. During this special week every single member of the ICRM writes to their local radio station telling them of the week and asking for Cliff records to be played.

## CLIFF AND THE SHADOWS ON TOUR

This section records the song programme by Cliff in gospel or secular concerts and is intended to offer a guide to the material he has used, but, of course, without listing each and every concert it cannot circumvent the occasional change that Cliff makes either in order or content of a minor or major tour.

24 January 1959: Rialto Theatre, York. Among his numbers Cliff sang: 'Move It', 'High Class Baby', 'Make Believe', 'King Creole', 'Whole Lot Of Shakin' Goin' On', 'Schoolboy Crush'. Also on the bill: Wee Willie Harris, Tony Crombie and His Rockets.

17 August 1961: Tivoli Gardens, Stockholm. The Shadows: 'Apache', 'Frightened City', 'F.B.I.'. Cliff Backed by the Shadows: 'Move It', 'Please Don't Tease', 'Living Doll', 'My Blue Heaven', 'A Girl Like You', 'What'd I Say'.

2 April 1964: ABC, Kingston. The Shadows: 'Chattanooga Choo Choo', 'Dance On', 'In The Mood', 'That's The Way It Goes', 'Theme For Young Lovers', 'Little Bitty Tear', 'Big B', 'Foot Tapper', 'F.B.I.'. Cliff backed by the Shadows, Bob Miller and His Millermen: 'I Wanna Know', 'Don't Talk To Him', '24 Hours From Tulsa', 'Da Doo Ron Ron', 'Moon River', 'It's All In The Game', 'Maria', 'I'm The Lonely One', 'Constantly', 'Whole Lot Of Shakin' Goin' On', 'What'd I Say', 'Bachelor Boy'.

7 and 9 September 1964: ABC, Great Yarmouth. The Shadows (Hank, Bruce, Brian and John): 'In The Mood', 'Dance On', 'Nivram', 'The Rise And Fall Of Flingel Bunt', 'Theme For Young Lovers', '500 Miles', 'Little Bitty Tear', 'Tonight', 'Big B', 'F.B.I.'.

16 February 1965: Pantomime Season, London Palladium, *Aladdin and His Wonderful Lamp*. The Shadows: 'Me Oh

My', 'Genie With The Light Brown Lamp'. Cliff backed by the Shadows and the Palladium Orchestra: 'I Could Easily Fall', 'This Was My Special Day', 'I'm In Love With You', 'There's Gotta Be A Way', 'Friends', 'Make Every Day A Carnival Day', 'I've Said Too Many Things', 'Evening Comes', 'Havin' Fun'.

8–14 June 1965: Hippodrome Theatre, Birmingham. The Shadows (Hank, Bruce, Brian and John): 'Brazil', 'In The Mood', 'Apache', 'Stingray', 'Mary Anne', 'Let It Be', 'Big B', 'The Rise And Fall Of Flingel Bunt', 'Tonight', 'F.B.I.'.

3 October 1965: Gaumont, Derby. The Shadows (Hank, Bruce, Brian and John): 'Brazil', 'Foot Tapper', 'Apache', 'Don't Make My Baby Blue', 'Let It Be Me', 'Stingray', 'Tonight', 'Big B', 'F.B.I.'. Cliff backed by the Shadows: 'Do You Want To Dance ', 'Angel', 'Don't Talk To Him', 'On The Beach', 'The Minute You're Gone', 'The Time In Between', 'The Twelfth Of Never', 'Long Tall Sally', 'It's All In The Game', 'Da Doo Ron Ron', 'I Could Easily Fall', 'The Young Ones', 'Living Doll', 'Lucky Lips', 'Bachelor Boy', 'Razzle Dazzle', 'What'd I Say'.

21 February 1966: Cabaret Season, Talk of the Town, London. The Shadows (Hank, Bruce, Brian and John): 'Brazil', 'Dance On', 'Nivram', '500 Miles', 'A Little Bitty Tear', 'Tonight', 'Little B', 'F.B.I.'. Cliff backed by the Shadows: 'I Could Easily Fall', 'The Minute You're Gone', 'Do You Want To Dance', 'Wind Me Up', 'My One And Only Love', '24 Hours From Tulsa', 'On The Beach', 'Girl From Ipanema', 'My Colouring Book', 'What'd I Say', 'The Young Ones', 'Living Doll', 'Bachelor Boy'.

3 April 1966: Empire Pool, Wembley, Record Star Show in aid of spastics. The Shadows (Hank, Bruce, Brian and John): 'The Rise and Fall of Flingel Bunt', 'Somewhere', 'Dance On'. Cliff backed by the Shadows: 'I Could Easily Fall', 'Wind Me Up', 'Blue Turns To Grey', 'The Young Ones', 'Living Doll', 'Lucky Lips', 'Bachelor Boy'.

3 July 1966: ABC, Great Yarmouth. The Shadows (Hank, Bruce, Brian and John): 'In The Mood', 'Dance On', 'Don't Make My Baby Blue', 'Nivram', 'Sloop John B', 'Let It Be', 'Will You Be There', 'Somewhere', 'Little B', 'The

Rise And Fall Of Flingel Bunt'.

10 March 1967: Pantomime Season, London Palladium, *Cinderella*. The Shadows (Hank, Bruce, Brian and John): 'The Flyder And The Spy', 'Autumn'. Cliff backed by the Shadows and the Palladium Orchestra: 'Why Wasn't I Born Rich', 'Peace And Quiet', 'In The Country', 'Come Sunday', 'If Our Dreams Come True' (with Pippa Steel), 'Poverty', 'Peace And Quiet' (reprise), 'The King's Palace', 'She Needs Him More Than Me', 'Hey Doctor Man'.

27 August 1967: Winter Gardens, Bournemouth. The Shadows (Hank, Brian, Bruce and John): 'In the Mood', 'Dance On', 'Don't Make My Baby Blue', 'Let It Be Me', 'Apache', 'Nivram', 'Bombay Duck', 'Foot Tapper', 'Little Bitty Tear' 'Death Of A Clown', 'San Francisco', 'The Rise And Fall Of Flingel Bunt', 'Somewhere', 'Little B', 'F.B.I.'.

15 and 18 January 1968: Cabaret Season, Talk of the Town, London. The Shadows (Hank, Brian, Bruce and John): 'Sleepwalk', 'In The Mood', 'Dance On', 'Don't Make My Baby Blue', 'Let It Be Me', 'Wonderful Land', 'Nivram', 'Apache', 'Foot Tapper', 'Cool Water', 'Little Bitty Tear', 'The Rise And Fall Of Flingel Bunt', 'Somewhere', 'Little B', 'F.B.I.'. On the 15th Hank, Bruce, Brian and Liquorice played. On the 18th, Hank, Bruce, John and Tony. 'Little B' was not played on the 18th. At the start of the season, John Roshill was unwell and was replaced by Brian 'Liquorice' Locking. Later in the season Brian Bennett was taken to hospital with appendicitis and was replaced by Tony Meehan, by which time John Rostill had recovered sufficiently to rejoin the group.

23 May 1968: The Tom Jones Season, London Palladium. The Shadows (Hank, Bruce, John and Brian): 'Dance On', 'Lara's Theme', 'Dear Old Mrs Bell', 'Nivram', 'Putting On The Style', 'Somewhere', 'Little B', 'F.B.I.'.

11 October 1968: season at the London Palladium. The Shadows (Hank, Bruce, Brian and John): 'In the Mood', 'Lara's Theme', 'Foot Tapper', 'For Emily', 'Putting On The Style', 'Somewhere', 'F.B.I.'. Cliff backed by the Breakaways and the Palladium Orchestra: 'Shout', 'Marianne', 'Bachelor Boy', 'Somewhere In My Youth Or

Childhood', 'If Ever I Should Leave You', 'The Day I Met Marie', 'La La La La La', 'The Young Ones', 'Lucky Lips', 'Living Doll', 'In The Country', 'Don't Forget To Catch Me', 'When I'm 64', 'Congratulations', 'Visions'.

7 October 1969: The Alaska, Tokyo. The Shadows appeared in the first half as part of the orchestra that accompanied Cliff. Cliff had the support of three Japanese girl singers. 'Shout', 'Move It', 'It's All In The Game', 'Something Good', 'If Ever I Should Leave You', 'Nothing But A House-Party', 'Throw Down A Line', 'The Day I Met Marie', 'La La La La La', 'Taste Of Honey', 'The Lady Came From Baltimore', 'Big Ship', Medley: 'The Young Ones', 'Living Doll', 'In The Country', 'Bachelor Boy', 'Early In The Morning', 'When I'm 64', 'Congratulations', 'Visions'.

7 November 1969: Astoria, Finsbury Park, London. The Shadows (Alan, Brian and John): 'Nivram', 'Exodus', 'Little B'. Cliff backed by the Brian Bennett Orchestra (including John Rostill, A. Hawkshaw, Marcie and the Cookies): 'Shout', 'Move It', 'It's All In The Game', 'Good Times', 'Somewhere In My Youth Or Childhood', 'If Ever I Should Leave You', 'Throw Down A Line', 'The Day I Met Marie', 'La La La La La', 'A Taste Of Honey' (instrumental with Cliff on guitar), 'The Lady Came From Baltimore', 'Big Ship', 'The Young Ones', 'Living Doll', 'In The Country', 'Bachelor Boy', 'With The Eyes Of A Child', 'When I'm 64', 'Congratulations', 'Visions'.

21 November 1970: Odeon, Golders Green, London. Hank Marvin, Bruce Welch and John Farrar: 'Hide Your Love Away', 'My Home Town', 'You're Burning Bridges', 'Silvery Rain', 'Throw Down A Line', 'Faithful', 'Keep The Customer Satisfied'. Cliff backed by the Cookies and the Brian Bennett Orchestra: 'La La La La La', 'Goodbye Sam, Hello Samantha', 'Words', 'The Young Ones', 'Living Doll', 'Move It', 'Travellin' Light', 'Bachelor Boy', 'Congratulations', 'The Day I Met Marie', 'Soul Deep', 'I Ain't Got Time Anymore', 'I Who Have Nothing', 'Proud Mary', 'Walk On By', 'The Look Of Love', 'The Girl Can't Help It', 'Great Balls Of Fire', 'Lucille', 'Jailhouse Rock', 'Good Old Rock 'n' Roll', 'Rock 'n' Roll Music', 'Do You Want To Dance', 'I Saw The Light'.

13 June 1971: A Night With the Stars, tribute to Dickie Valentine, London Palladium. Hank Marvin, Bruce Welch and John Farrar: 'Down On The Corner', 'Lady Of The Morning', 'My Home Town', 'Faithful', 'Apache', 'Keep The Customer Satisfied'. Cliff backed by the Cookies and the Jack Parnell Orchestra conducted by Norrie Paramor: 'Get Ready', 'Sunny Honey Girl', 'The Day I Met Marie', 'Fire And Rain', 'Today, Tomorrow, Forever', 'Congratulations', 'Silvery Rain', 'I Saw The Light', 'I Want To Hold Your Hand' (with Petula Clark).

25 October 1971: season at the London Palladium. Hank Marvin, Bruce Welch, and John Farrar: 'Lady Of The Morning', 'My Home Town', 'Faithful', 'Black Eyes', 'Keep The Customer Satisfied'. Cliff backed by the Flirtations and the Palladium Orchestra, leader Brian Bennett: 'We Can Work It Out', 'Flying Machine', 'Fire And Rain', 'Yesterday, Today, Forever', 'Congratulations', 'Silvery Rain', 'The Day I Met Marie', 'Walk On By' and 'The Look Of Love' (with Olivia Newton-John), 'The Girl Can't Help It', 'Great Balls Of Fire', 'Lucille', 'Jailhouse Rock', 'Good Old Rock 'n' Roll', 'Rock 'n' Roll Music', 'Do You Want To Dance', 'Sing A Song Of Freedom' (with Olivia Newton-John, Marvin, Welch and Farrar).

17 November 1972: Fairfield Hall, Croydon. Cliff backed by Bones and the Brian Bennett Band: 'I Can't Let You Go', 'Gonna Have A Little Talk With Myself', 'The Day I Met Marie', 'Make It Easy On Yourself', 'The Sun Ain't Gonna Shine Anymore', 'Jesus', 'Mr Business Man', 'What The World Needs Now', 'I've Got God', 'My Way', 'Reflections', 'Living In Harmony', 'Brand New Song', 'It's A Saturday Night At The World', 'Don't Move Away' and 'Love' (both with Olivia Newton-John), 'Congratulations', 'Whole Lot of Shakin' Goin' On', 'Keep A Knockin'', 'Tutti Frutti', 'Rave On', 'Long Tall Sally', 'Rip It Up', 'Dancing Shoes', 'Sing A Song Of Freedom'.

17 September 1973: in aid of John Grooms Association for the disabled, Royal Festival Hall. Cliff backed by Barry Guard and the Orchestra: 'The Day I Met Marie', 'The Next Time', 'Jesus', 'Jesus Loves You', 'Jesus Is My Kind Of People', 'Silvery Rain', 'Guitar Man',

'His Latest Flame', 'Chantilly Lace', 'Bony Moronie', 'Do You Want To Dance', 'Crocodile Rock', 'I Could Easily Fall', 'Higher Ground', 'Visions', 'Power To All Our Friends', 'Living In Harmony', 'Come Back Billy Jo', 'The Minute You're Gone', 'Goodbye Sam, Hello Samantha', 'You Will Never Know', 'Guitar Tango' (instrumental, Cliff on guitar), 'Fireside Song', 'Travellin' Light', 'Throw Down A Line', 'It's A Saturday Night At The World', 'Give All Your Love To The Lord', 'Got To Get You Into My Life', 'Congratulations', 'In The Country', 'Dancing Shoes', 'Sunny Honey Girl', 'On The Beach', 'Sing A Song Of Freedom'.

31 March 1974: Lakeside Country Club in Surrey. Hank Marvin and John Farrar backed by Cliff Hall (keyboards), Dave Ackley (bass), Andrew Steel (drums), Jean Hawker (vocals); 'Keep The Customer Satisfied', 'Lonesome Mole', 'Wonderful Land', 'Music Makes My Day', 'Marmaduke', 'Turn Around And Touch Me', 'The Rise And Fall Of Flingel Bunt', 'Lara's Theme', 'Tiny Robin', 'Time Drags By', 'Take Me Home, Country Roads', 'The Banks Of The Ohio', 'In The Country', 'The Day I Met Marie', 'Apache', 'F.B.I.', 'Lucille', 'Rip It Up', 'Blue Suede Shoes'.

17 April 1974: The Cliff Richard Show, London Palladium. Cliff backed by Barry Guard and the Orchestra: 'Dance The Night Away', 'Can't Help Myself', 'Do You Want To Dance', 'Constantly', 'Take Me High', 'You Got What It Takes' (with Pat Carroll), 'Summer Holiday', 'The Next Time', 'Amazing Grace', 'Jesus Is My Kind Of People', 'I've Just Realized', 'Living In Harmony', 'Give Me Back That Old Fashioned Feeling', 'Congratulations', 'In The Country', 'Dancing Shoes', 'The Day I Met Marie', 'On The Beach', 'Visions', 'Power To All Our Friends'.

27 October 1974: The Colin Charman Benefit Gala, London Palladium. Cliff backed by the Shadows (Hank, Bruce, Brian, John and Alan): 'Willie And The Hand Jive', 'Don't Talk To Him', 'Bachelor Boy', 'A Matter Of Moments', 'Power To All Our Friends'.

9 March 1975: The Shadows in Concert, Fairfield Hall, Croydon. Hank Marvin, Bruce Welch, Brian Bennett, John Farrar, Alan Tarney with John Piddy (keyboards): 'The Rise And Fall Of

Flingel Bunt', 'Man Of Mystery', 'Lady Of The Morning', 'Lonesome Music', 'Black Eyes', 'Turn Around And Touch Me', 'Guitar Tango', 'Faithful', 'Tiny Robin', 'Marmaduke', 'Foot Tapper', 'Apache', 'Dance On', 'Let Me Be The One', 'Nivram', 'Wonderful Land', 'Music Makes My Day', 'Silvery Rain', 'My Home Town', 'Frightened City', 'Honourable Puff Puff', 'Somewhere', 'Lucille', 'Rip It Up', 'Blue Suede Shoes', 'Sleepwalk', 'F.B.I.'.

12 May 1977: The Shadows in Concert, 20 Golden Dates, Royal Albert Hall. Hank Marvin, Bruce Welch and Brian Bennett with Alan Jones (bass guitar) and Francis Monkman (keyboards): 'Shazam', 'Man Of Mystery', 'Kon-Tiki', 'Marmaduke', 'Atlantis', 'Don't Throw It All Away', 'Shadoogie', 'Guitar Tango', 'Please Don't Tease', 'Summer Holiday', 'The Day I Met Marie', 'Bachelor Boy', 'I Could Easily Fall In Love With You', 'In The Country', 'Shindig', 'Apache', 'Foot Tapper', 'The Rise And Fall Of Flingel Bunt', 'Dance On', 'Nivram', 'Walk Don't Run', 'Don't Make My Baby Blue', 'Theme For Weekend Lovers', 'Frightened City', 'Peace Pipe', 'The Savage', 'Little B', 'Sleepwalk', 'Let Me Be The One', 'Wonderful Land', 'F.B.I.'.

8 March 1978: two-week season at the London Palladium. The Shadows comprised Hank Marvin, Bruce Welch, Brian Bennett, Cliff Hall, Alan Jones. The band credits read Terry Britten (lead guitar), Stu Calver (guitar), Clem Cattini (drums, percussion), Dave Christopher (guitar), Mo Foster (guitar), Graham Jarvis (drums, percussion), Graham Murray, John Perry and Tony Rivers (vocals), Graham Todd (keyboard). Cliff and the Shadows: 'The Young Ones', 'Do You Want To Dance', 'The Day I Met Marie'. The Shadows: 'Shadoogie', 'Atlantis', 'Apache', 'Nivram', 'Walk Don't Run', 'Little B', 'Let Me Be The One', 'Wonderful Land', 'F.B.I.'. Cliff and the band: 'Please Don't Tease', 'Yes He Lives', 'Every Face Tells A Story', 'Up In The World', 'Miss You Nights', 'Up In Canada', 'Melting Into One'. Cliff and the Shadows: 'Move It', 'Willie And The Hand Jive', 'The Minute You're Gone', 'Bachelor Boy'. Cliff, Hank and Bruce: 'All Shook Up'. Cliff and the band: 'Devil Woman', 'Why Should The Devil Have All The

Good Music'. Cliff, the Shadows and the band: 'We All Have Our Dreams'.

29 January 1979: Tear Fund Concert, Chichester Festival Theatre. Local group of boys and girls: 'Sons And Daughters'. Cliff: 'Rock 'n' Roll Juvenile', 'Night Time Girl', 'Up In Canada', 'Can't Take The Hurt Anymore', 'Why Should The Devil Have All The Good Music', 'Moving In', 'Why Me Lord', 'Reflections'.

1979: European Tour. Cliff plus Skyband. Skyband consisted of Terry Britten (lead guitar), George Ford (bass guitar), Mart Jenner (guitar), Graham Todd and Adrian Lee (keyboards), Graham Jarvis (drums), Stu Calver, John Perry and Tony Rivers (back-up vocals). The three vocalists joined Cliff up front for 'Theme For A Dream' and 'Spanish Harlem'. Cliff: 'Move It', 'Doing Fine', 'The Young Ones', 'Rock 'n' Roll Juvenile', 'If You Walked Away', 'Hot Shot', 'Visions' (with Graham Todd and Adrian Lee), 'Theme For A Dream', 'Spanish Harlem', 'Lucky Lips', 'Give Me Love Your Way', 'Did He Jump Or Was He Pushed', 'Why Should The Devil Have All The Good Music', 'Sci Fi', 'Carrie', 'Never Even Thought', 'My Luck Won't Change', 'Green Light', 'Miss You Nights', 'Do You Want To Dance', 'Monday Thru Friday', 'Devil Woman', 'We Don't Talk Anymore', 'Thank You Very Much'.

1–3 November 1979: Oxford. Cliff with Skyband and back-ups as on European tour: 'Move It', 'Doing Fine', 'The Young Ones', 'Rock 'n' Roll Juvenile', 'If You Walked Away', 'Hot Shot', 'Theme for a Dream', 'Spanish Harlem', 'The Shape I'm In Tonight', 'Under Lock And Key' (later titled 'I'm Nearly Famous'), 'Did He Jump Or Was He Pushed', 'Why Should The Devil Have All The Good Music', 'Sci Fi', 'Carrie', 'Never Even Thought', 'My Luck Won't Change', 'Green Light', 'Miss You Nights', 'Do You Want To Dance', 'Monday Thru Friday', 'Devil Woman', 'We Don't Talk Anymore', 'Living Doll', 'Summer Holiday'.

1980: Cliff in Germany. Cliff and band – Mike Moran (keyboards), Martin Jenner, Mark Griffiths (guitars), Graham Jarvis (drums), Dave McRea (synthesizers), Tony Rivers, John Perry and Stu Calver (back-up vocals). 'Living Doll', 'Lucky Lips', 'The Minute

You're Gone', 'I'm Nearly Famous', 'Take Another Look', 'The Twelfth Of Never', 'Hey Mr Dream Maker', 'Green Light', 'Learnin' To Rock 'n' Roll', 'Heartbreak Hotel', 'Move It', 'In The Night', 'Carrie', 'When Two Worlds Drift Apart', 'I'm No Hero', 'Dynamite', 'Give a Little Bit More', 'Devil Woman', 'Sci Fi', 'Miss You Nights', 'Everyman', 'The Rock That Doesn't Roll', 'A Heart Will Break', 'Dreamin'', 'We Don't Talk Anymore'.

1980: The Best of British Gospel Rock, South Africa. Gospel concerts with Nutshell (later known as RPM, then Network Three), Garth Hewitt. The concerts were before mixed audiences. Cliff: 'Sweet Little Jesus Boy', 'O Little Town Of Bethlehem', 'Silent Night', 'In the Bleak Midwinter', 'Away In A Manger', 'We're All One' (with Garth Hewitt and Nutshell). Garth Hewitt: 'Jesus Is A Friend Of Mine', 'Under the Influence', 'Did He Jump Or Was He Pushed' (with Cliff, vocal back-up and guitar). Nutshell:'You Can't Get To Heaven By Living Like Hell' (with Cliff). 'Lifeline', 'I Am Nothing Without You', 'Jesus Is the Answer' and 'Get Up And Dance' (both with Garth and Cliff). Cliff: 'Dreamin''. Garth Hewitt: 'Riding On The King's Highway', 'Come Out Fighting' (Cliff backing), 'May You Live To Dance On Your Grave'. Nutshell: 'Don't Let Me Fall', 'Like A Thief In The Night'. Cliff: 'Everyman', 'Song For Sarah', 'The Rock That Doesn't Roll', 'How Great Thou Art'.

14 October 1980: Cliff's birthday night. Five nights at the Apollo Theatre, London. The first night began with the audience singing 'Happy Birthday', and Cliff singing some lines of 'I'm 21 Today'. Cliff and band: 'Living Doll', 'The Young Ones', 'The Minute You're Gone', 'I'm Nearly Famous', 'Take Another Look', 'Twelfth Of Never', 'Hey Mr Dream Maker', 'Suddenly' (Olivia Newton-John's voice on backing track, face on screen), 'Green Light', 'Learning To Rock 'n' Roll', 'Heartbreak Hotel', 'Move It', 'In The Night' segueing into 'Carrie', 'When Two Worlds Drift Apart', 'I'm No Hero', 'A Little in Love', 'Give A Little Bit More', 'Devil Woman', 'Sci Fi', 'Miss You Nights', 'Everyman', 'The Rock That Doesn't Roll', 'A Heart Will Break', 'Dreamin'', 'We Don't Talk Anymore'.

1981: Tear Fund tour. Lasted two and a

half weeks and raised around £50,000 for the Fund. Network Three provided the support act and included in their set 'Long Train Home', 'Lifeline', 'Thief in the Night', 'Solo' and 'Keep Your Eyes on Jesus'. Cliff: 'Son of Thunder', 'Loving Me Lord Forever', 'Under The Influence', 'Better Than I Know Myself', 'You Can't Get To Heaven' (joined by Mo and Annie of Network Three), 'Summer Rain', 'Moving In', 'You And Me And Jesus', 'Fool's Wisdom' (Cliff guitar duet with Paul Field of Network Three), 'Take Me Where I Wanna Go', 'Lost In A Lonely World', 'I Wish We'd All Been Ready', 'Everyman', 'The Rock That Doesn't Roll', 'How Great Thou Art'.

1981: U.S. Tour. Cliff: 'Son Of Thunder', 'Monday Thru Friday', 'Dreamin'', 'When Two Worlds Drift Apart', 'Green Light', 'Move It', 'Heartbreak Hotel', 'Why Should the Devil Have All The Good Music', 'Hey Mr Dream Maker', 'Carrie', 'Miss You Nights', 'A Little in Love', 'Everyman', 'Sci Fi', 'Summer Rain', 'Devil Woman', 'The Rock That Doesn't Roll'. Encore: 'Give A Little Bit More', 'A Heart Will Break', 'We Don't Talk Anymore', 'Thank You Very Much'. Other titles substituted: 'Take Another Look', 'Do You Wanna Dance' and 'My Luck Won't Change'.

10 February 1982: Queen Elizabeth Stadium, Hong Kong. 'Son Of Thunder', 'Young Love', 'A Little In Love', 'Better Than I Know Myself', 'We Don't Talk Anymore', 'Broken Doll', 'Summer Rain', 'Dreamin'', 'Sci-Fi', 'Carrie', 'The Next Time', 'The Day I Met Marie', 'Miss You Nights', 'Lost In A Lonely World', 'Devil Woman', 'Thief In The Night' (during the Far East tour, he substituted 'Once In A While'), 'Daddy's Home', 'Blue Suede Shoes', 'Great Balls Of Fire', 'Long Tall Sally', 'Rip It Up', It'll Be Me'.

28 April 1983: gospel tour. Brussels. 'Why Should The Devil Have All The Good Music', 'Where Do We Go From Here', 'The Only Way Up', 'Song For Sarah', 'You Need A Light', 'Son Of God', 'Lord I Love You', 'True Love Ways', 'Yes He Lives', 'Up In Canada', 'Be In My Heart', 'Whispering My Love', 'I Wish We'd All Been Ready', 'The Rock That Does Not Roll', 'How Great Thou Art', 'Yes He Lives', 'When I Survey The Wondrous Cross'.

25 October 1984, Perth Entertainment Centre, Australia. 'Learning How To Rock 'n' Roll', 'The Young Ones', 'Dreamin'', 'Never Say Die', 'Donna', 'The Only Way Out', 'Love Stealer', 'Locked Inside Your Prison', 'Shooting From The Heart', 'Miss You Nights', 'Heart User', 'Galadriel', 'Devil Woman', 'Move It', 'Daddy's Home', 'Be Bop A Lula', 'Lucille', 'Under The Gun', 'Lovers and Friends', 'The Golden Days Are Over', 'Ocean Deep', 'Thief In The Night', 'Wired For Sound', 'Living Doll', 'Summer Holiday', 'Bachelor Boy', 'We Don't Talk Anymore'.

9 July 1985: gospel tour. Harrogate Conference Centre. 'Lord I Love You', 'Joseph', 'The Only Way Out', 'Good On The Sally Army', 'Take Me Back', 'La Gonave', 'A World Of Difference', 'Under The Gun', 'Year After Year', 'Yesterday, Today, Forever', 'Walking In The Light', 'Call Your Lambs' (duet with Sheila Walsh), 'His Love Covers Your Sin', 'When I Survey', 'Rock 'n' Roll Juvenile', 'The Rock That Doesn't Roll', chorus, 'Not By Might'.

2 October 1985: Stockholm, Sweden. 'Wired For Sound', 'Heart User', 'Move It', 'Please Don't Fall In Love', 'Never Say Die', 'A Heart Will Break', 'Yesterday, Today, Forever', 'Under The Gun', 'Free My Soul', 'Take Me Back', 'Miss You Nights', 'Dreamin'', 'Daddy's Home', 'Devil Woman', 'It's No Use Pretending', 'Sci-Fi', 'We Don't Talk Anymore', 'You Know That I Love You', 'Hey Mr Dream Maker', 'It Must Be Love', 'Carrie', 'Ease Along', 'Walking In The Light', 'She's So Beautiful', 'It's Every One Of Us'.

16 June 1987: gospel tour. Brighton Centre. 'I'm Alive', 'She's So Beautiful', 'Such is the Mystery', 'Under The Gun', 'Money', 'Mr Businessman', 'All I Want', 'A World Of Difference', 'All By Myself', 'Little Town', 'Another Christmas Day', 'Yesterday, Today, Forever', 'His Love Covers Our Sin', 'Wild Geese', 'When I Survey', 'Yes He Lives', 'Where Do We Go From Here', 'Reunion Of The Heart', 'I Will Follow You', 'My Pretty One', 'Walking In The Light', 'It's In Every One Of Us', 'Where Are You', 'I Wish We'd All Been Ready', 'Brave New World', 'Share A Dream With Me'.

24 September 1987: Wimbledon Theatre. 'I'm Alive', 'We Don't Talk Anymore', 'Daddy's Home', 'All The Time You

Need', 'Mr Businessman', 'Devil Woman', 'All By Myself', '(Wouldn't You Know It) Got Myself A Girl', 'Spanish Harlem', 'Living Doll', 'The Young Ones', 'Gee Whizz It's You', 'Move It', 'My Pretty One', 'Under Your Spell', 'This Time Now', 'Always Guaranteed', 'Two Hearts', 'Some People', 'Forever', 'One Night', 'Remember Me', 'Once Upon A Time', 'Miss You Nights', 'Thief In The Night', 'I Wish We'd All Been Ready', 'Share A Dream With Me', 'Little Town'. During the forthcoming European tour, Cliff sang 'Lucky Lips', ending the first half of the show with this song instead of 'Move It'. 'Once Upon A Time' was deleted from the *Always Guaranteed* tour.

5 October 1988: Odeon Hammersmith, London. 'Born To Rock 'n' Roll', 'Move It', 'Daddy's Home', 'All The Time You Need', 'Devil Woman', 'All By Myself', 'We Don't Talk Anymore', 'Another Tear Falls', 'Some People', 'Marmaduke', 'Under The Gun', 'Ocean Deep', 'Living Doll', 'The Young Ones', 'Bachelor Boy', 'In The Country', 'Visions', 'Fabulous', 'All Shook Up', 'The Minute You're Gone', 'I Wish You'd Change Your Mind', 'Carrie', 'True Love Ways', 'My Pretty One', 'Miss You Nights', 'Thief In The Night', 'U.F.O.', 'Get It Right Next Time', 'Blue Suede Shoes', 'Great Balls of Fire', 'Lucille', 'Long Tall Sally', 'Rip It Up', 'It'll Be Me', 'Mistletoe and Wine'.

16 June 1989: Wembley Stadium, London. With the Kalin Twins, 'The Glory of Love'. Conversations with Jimmy Henney, Cathy McGowan. With the Shadows: 'The Young Ones', 'In The Country', Bachelor Boy', 'Willie And The Hand Jive', 'Living Doll', 'Please Don't Tease', 'Dynamite', 'It'll Be Me'. Own spot: 'Wired for Sound', 'Dreamin'', 'Daddy's Home', 'I Could Easily Fall In Love With You', 'Some People', 'We Don't Talk Anymore', 'Two Hearts', 'Move It' (with Jet Harris and Tony Meehan), 'Shake Rattle and Roll', 'Joanna', 'Silhouettes', 'Good Golly Miss Molly', 'Miss You Nights', 'Summer Holiday', 'I Just Don't Have The Heart', 'God Put A Fighter In Me', 'Thief In The Night', 'The Best Of Me', 'From A Distance'.

8 February 1990: Fowler Centre, Wellington, New Zealand. 'The Best of

Me,' 'Green Light', 'Dreamin'', 'Please Don't Tease', 'Daddy's Home', 'Keep Me Warm', 'Lean On You', 'Sea Cruise', 'We Don't Talk Anymore', 'My Pretty One', 'Carrie', 'Shake Rattle And Roll', 'Silhouettes', 'I Just Don't Have The Heart', 'Stronger Than That', 'Joanna', 'Everybody Knows', 'Some People', 'It'll Be Me', 'Good Golly Miss Molly', 'The Young Ones', 'Summer Holiday', 'Living Doll', 'Anyone Who Had A Heart', 'Devil Woman', 'Miss You Nights', 'Fighter', 'Thief In The Night', 'Share A Dream', 'From A Distance'.

8 December 1990: Wembley Arena, London. 'Move It', 'Bird Dog', 'Let's Have A Party', 'Party Doll', 'It's My Party' (sung by Chantilly Lace), 'C'mon Everybody', 'Whole Lotta Shakin' Goin' On', 'Zing Went The Strings Of My Heart', 'Always', 'When', 'Shake Rattle And Roll', 'Why Do Fools Fall In Love', 'Willie And The Hand Jive', 'Hoots Mon' (Oh Boy Band), 'Don't Look Now' (Chantilly Lace), 'The Girl Can't Help It', 'Sea Cruise', 'Daddy's Home', 'The Book Of Love', 'Blue Moon', 'Do You Wanna Dance' (Chantilly Lace), 'At The Hop', 'Rock 'n' Roll Is Here To Stay', 'Living Doll', 'Travellin' Light', 'My Heart' (a few bars), 'A Voice In The Wilderness', 'I Love You' (with Cilla Black), 'Saviour's Day' (musical introduction to *Coronation Street*), 'Happy Birthday To You', 'Stronger Than That', 'Always Guaranteed', 'Some People', 'What's Love Go To Do With It' (short version), 'Carrie', 'I Just Don't Have The Heart', 'Miss You Nights', 'Devil Woman', 'We Don't Talk Anymore', 'God Put A Fighter In Me', 'Thief In The Night', 'The Rise And Fall Of Flingel Bunt', 'Mistletoe and Wine', 'Little Town', 'Saviour's Day', 'From A Distance'. During the show Cliff was linked with Cilla Black in Manchester as part of the birthday show celebrations for the long-lasting soap opera, *Coronation Street*. Due to technical problems an expected timed link proved difficult, and during this time Cliff calmed an excited and expectant audience with some of the songs mentioned – 'Travellin' Light', 'My Heart' (a brief snatch, since it didn't seem to work out), announced 'The Young Ones' but sang a brief snatch of 'A Voice In The Wilderness'.

30 March 1991: gospel tour. Royal Albert Hall, London. 'All Shook Up', 'Move It', 'Better Than I Know Myself', 'Saviour's Day', 'The Only Way Out', 'My Soul Is My Witness' (with Helen Shapiro), 'From A Distance', 'Where You Are', 'Discovering', 'Yesterday, Today, Forever', 'Lost In A Lonely World', 'When I Survey The Wondrous Cross', 'Flesh And Blood', 'Make Me New', 'Shine Jesus Shine' (with Helen Shapiro). Helen Shapiro did not appear at the other tour concerts and Cliff substituted with 'I Will Follow You' and 'Free'.

14 October 1991: City Hall, Auckland, New Zealand. 'Move It', 'Living Doll', 'I Could Easily Fall', 'The Young Ones', 'Summer Holiday', 'Bachelor Boy', 'Love On', 'It's All In The Game', 'Silhouettes', 'All Shook Up', 'That's Alright Mama', 'Lord I Love You', 'Free', 'Daddy's Home', 'Please Don't Tease', 'On The Beach', 'From A Distance', 'Wired For Sound', 'Scarlet Ribbons', 'Miss You Nights', 'Devil Woman', 'Silvery Rain', 'Joy Of Living', 'Some People', 'Stronger', 'The Best Of Me', 'We Don't Talk Anymore', 'Mistletone And Wine', 'Little Town', 'Saviour's Day' and with the audience, 'We Wish You A Merry Christmas'.

# CLIFF ON DISC

The following lists every song Cliff has recorded, and for the first time relates those titles to EMI released albums, but not compilation sets culled from these releases, unless issued by EMI. Odd tracks released elsewhere and not on an official Cliff album are also listed with source.

'A Brand New Song' Single release
'A Forever Kind of Love' *The EP Collection*
'A Girl In Every Port' *Wonderful Life* (parts 1–3)
'A Heart Will Break' *I'm No Hero*
'A Little Grain Of Sand' *When In Rome*
'A Little Imagination' *Wonderful Life*
'A Little In Love' *I'm No Hero, Love Songs, Private Collection*
'A Matter Of Moments' *Wonderful Life, More Hits By Cliff*
'A Mighty Lonely Man' *21 Today*
'A Sad Song With A Happy Soul' Not released
'A Spoonful Of Sugar' Not released
'A Summer Place' *Love Is Forever*
'A Swingin' Affair' *Summer Holiday*
'A Taste Of Honey' *Cliff 'Live' At The Talk Of The Town*
'A Teenager In Love' Not released
'A Thousand Conversations' B-side of 'Sing A Song Of Freedom'
'A Voice In The Wilderness' *Cliff's Hit Album, Cliff – Love Songs*
'Abraham, Martin And John' *Tracks 'n' Grooves*
'Again' *Cliff*
'Ain't Nothing But A House-party' *Cliff 'Live' At The Talk Of The Town*
'All At Once' *Summer Holiday*
'All For One' *The Young Ones*
'All Glory Laud And Honour' *Good News*
'All I Ask Of You' *Private Collection*
'All I Do Is Dream Of You' *The EP Collection*
'All In The April Evening' Not released
'All Kinds Of People' *Wonderful Life*
'All My Love' *The Best Of Cliff, Cliff 'Live' At The Talk Of The Town, 40 Golden Greats*

'All My Sorrows' Not released
'All Of A Sudden My Heart Sings' *Love Is Forever*
'All Shook Up' *Thank You Very Much*
'All The Time You Need' *From A Distance – The Event*
'Almost Like Being In Love' *Listen To Cliff*
'Alright, It's Alright' *I'm Nearly Famous*
'Always' *Sincerely Cliff Richard, From A Distance – The Event*
'Always Guaranteed' *Always Guaranteed*
'Amazing Grace' *Help It Along*
'Amor, Amor, Amor' *When In Spain*
'(And Me) I'm On The Outside Now' *Two A Penny*
'Angel' *Cliff Richard*
'Annabella Umbrella' German release
'Another Christmas Day' B-side of 'Remember Me'
'Anti-Brotherhood of Man' *Take Me High*
'Anything I Can Do' *I'm No Hero*
'Apron Strings' *Cliff*
'Are You Only Fooling Me' *Tracks 'n' Grooves*
'Arriverderci Roma' *When In Rome*
'As I Walk Into The Morning Of Your Life' *Tracks 'n' Grooves*
'As Time Goes By' *Cliff Sings*
'As Wonderful As You' not released
'Ashes To Ashes' No album tracking. B-side of 'Help It Along'
'At The Hop' *From A Distance*
'Autumn' *Cinderella*
'Autumn Concerto' *When In Rome*

'Baby Don't You Know Anymore' German release
'Baby I Could Be So Good At Loving You' *Sincerely Cliff Richard*
'Baby I Don't Care' *Cliff*

266

'Baby It's You' *Don't Stop Me Now*
'Baby You're Dynamite' *Silver*
'Bachelor Boy' *Live In Japan, Summer Holiday, More Hits By Cliff, 40 Golden Greats*
'Back In Vaudeville' No album tracking. Intended for B-side foreign single
'Ballet' (Parts 1–4) *Aladdin And His Wonderful Lamp*
'Bang Bang' *Tracks 'n' Grooves*
'Be Bop A Lula' *Cliff, Rock 'n' Roll – Rock Connection*
'Be In My Heart' *Now You See Me . . . Now You Don't*
'Beat Out Dat Rhythm On A Drum' *Listen To Cliff*
'Better Day' *Stronger*
'Better Than I Know Myself' *Wired for Sound*
'Big News' *Summer Holiday*
'Big Ship' *The Best Of Cliff, Volume 2*
'Bilder Von Dir' German release
'Bin Verliebt' German release
'Bird Dog' *From A Distance*
'Blame It On The Bossa Nova' *Kinda Latin*
'Blue Moon' *Listen To Cliff*
'Blue Suede Shoes' *Cliff Sings*
'Blue Turns To Grey' *The Best Of Cliff, 40 Golden Greats*
'Blueberry Hill' *32 Minutes And 17 Seconds With Cliff Richard*
'Bonie Moronie' *Live in Japan*
'Book Of Love' *From A Distance*
'Boom Boom' *The EP Collection*
'Born To Rock 'n' Roll' *Silver, Rock Connection, Time*
'Boum' *When In France* EP, *EP Collection*
'Bows and Fanfares' *Cliff 'Live' At The Talk Of The Town*
'Brave New World' 'Remember Me' single, 12-inch
'Breathless' Not released
'Broken Doll' *Wired For Sound*
'Brumburger Duet' *Take Me High*
'Brumburger Finale' *Take Me High*
'Burn On' *The Kendrick Collection*

'Can It Be True' *About That Man*
'Can't Let You Go' *Live In Japan*
'Can't Take The Hurt Anymore' *Green Light, Love Songs*
'Carina' *When In Rome*
'Carnival' *When In Spain, The EP Collection*
'Carrie' *Rock 'n' Roll, Love Songs, Dressed For The Occasion, Private Collection*
'Cas Senza Finestre' *When In Rome*
'Catch Me' *21 Today*
''Cause I Believe In Loving' Not released
'Celebrate' Not released (with the Settlers)
'Celeste' *Two A Penny*

'Celestial House' *Help It Along*
'C'est Si Bon' *When In France* EP
'Chantilly Lace' *From A Distance*
'Chaser' Not released
'Che Cosa Del Farai Mia Amour' *When In Rome*
'Chi Lo Sa' Italian B-side
'Chim Chim Cheree' Not released
'Choppin'' 'n' Changin'' *Me And My Shadows*
'Christmas Alphabet' *Together With Cliff*
'Christmas Never Comes' *Together With Cliff*
'Cities May Fall' *Rock 'n' Roll Juvenile*
'Clear Blue Skies' *Stronger*
'Close To Cathy' *Two A Penny*
'Closer To You' Not released
'Cloudy' *Two A Penny*
'C'mon Everybody' *From A Distance*
'Come Back Billie Joe' B-side of 'Power To All Our Friends'
'Come Closer To Me' *Kinda Latin*
'Come Prima' *When In Roma*
'Come Sunday' *Cinderella*
'Compassion Road' Not released
'Concerto D'Automno' *When In Rome*
'Concerto 94' German release
'Concrete And Clay' *Kinda Latin*
'Congratulations' *The Best Of Cliff, Cliff 'Live' At The Talk Of The Town, 40 Golden Greats, Live In Japan*
'Constantly' *More Hits By Cliff, 40 Golden Greats, Cliff – Love Songs*
''Cos I Love That Rock 'n' Roll' *Wired For Sound*
'Count Me Out' *Green Light*
'Crocodile Rock' Not released UK

' "D" In Love' B-side of 'I Love You'
'Daddy's Home' *Wired For Sound, Private Collection*
'Dancing Shoes' *Summer Holiday, Private Collection*
'Danny' *Cliff*
'Dare I Love Him Like I Do', *Cinderella*
'Das Girl Von Nebenan' German release
'Das Gluck Ist Rosarot' German release
'Das Ist Die Frage Aller Fragen' German release
'Day By Day' *Help It Along*
'Deep Purple' Emidisc acetate
'Deine Augen Traumen Mary' German release
'Der Mann Neben Dir' Not released UK
'Devil Woman' *I'm Nearly Famous, 40 Golden Greats, Thank You Very Much, Dressed For The Occasion*
'Dim Dim The Lights' Not released. Tapes – Radio Luxembourg
'Discovering' *Now You See Me . . . Now You Don't*

'Dizzy Miss Lizzy' *Don't Stop Me Now*
'Do They Know It's Christmas' Band Aid
recording: single
'Do What You Gotta Do' Not released
'Do You Remember' *Wonderful Life*
'Do You Want To Dance' *Cliff's Hit Album,
40 Golden Greats, Thank You Very Much,
Dressed For The Occasion*
'Doing Fine' *Rock 'n' Roll Juvenile*
'Donna' *Cliff, Rock 'n' Roll, Silver, The Rock
Connection*
'Don't' *Don't Stop Me Now*
'Don't Ask Me To Be Friends', *Tracks 'n'
Grooves*
'Don't Be Mad At Me' Not released
'Don't Blame Me' Not released
'Don't Bug Me Baby' *Cliff*
'Don't Forget To Catch Me' *Established
1958*
'Don't Let Tonite Ever End' *Tracks 'n'
Grooves*
'Don't Look Now' *From A Distance*
'Don't Make Promises' *Don't Stop Me Now*
'Don't Meet The Band' Not released UK
'Don't Move Away' B-side of 'Sunny
Honey Girl'
'Don't Talk To Him' *More Hits By Cliff,
When In Rome, 40 Golden Greats, Cliff –
Love Songs*
'Don't Turn The Light Out' *Every Face
Tells A Story*
'Down The Line' *Cliff*
'Dream' *Dream* EP
'Dreamin'' *I'm No Hero, Private Collection*
'Dreizehn Auf Ein Dutzend' German
release
'Driftin'' *Cliff*
'Driving' *Take Me High*
'Dry Bones' *His Land*
'Du Du Gefallst Mir' German release
'Du Fragst Mich Immer Wieder' German
release
'Dynamite' *Cliff In Japan, The Rock
Connection*

'Early In The Morning' *Tracks 'n' Grooves,
Oh Boy!, Cliff In Japan*
'Ease Along' *Green Light*
'Embraceable You' *Cliff Sings*
'Empty Chairs' Not released
'End Of The Show' *Thank You Very Much*
'Es Gehören Zwei Zum Glücklich Sein'
German release
'Es Ist Nicht Gut, Allein Zu Sein' German
release
'Es Könnte Schon Morgen Sein' German
release
'Es War Keine So Wunderbar Wie Du'
German release
'Eso Beso' *Kinda Latin*
'Evening Comes' *Aladdin And His*

*Wonderful Lamp*
'Evergreen Tree' *Me And My Shadows, Cliff
In Japan*
'Every Face Tells A Story' *Every Face Tells
A Story*
'Everybody Knows' *Stronger*
'Everybody Needs Someone To Love'
*Love Is Forever*
'Everyman' *I'm No Hero*
'Ezekiel's Vision' *His Land*

'Fall In Love With You' *Cliff's Hit Album,
40 Golden Greats, Cliff – Love Songs*
'Falling In Love' *Rock 'n' Roll Juvenile*
'Falling In Love With Love' *32 Minutes
And 17 Seconds With Cliff Richard*
'Fiesta' *Finders Keepers*
'Fifty Tears For Every Kiss' *21 Today*
'Fighter' *From A Distance – The Event,
Kendrick Collection* (different version)
'Finders Keepers' *Finders Keepers, Cliff In
Japan*
'Fire And Rain' *Help It Along*
'Fireside Song' *The 31st Of February Street*
'First Date' *Now You See Me . . . Now You
Don't*
'First Lesson In Love' *Listen To Cliff*
'Fly Me To The Moon' *Love Is Forever,
Kinda Latin*
'Flying Machine' *The Best Of Cliff, Volume
2, Cliff In Japan*
'For Emily Wherever I May Find Her'
*Sincerely Cliff Richard*
'For The First Time' *When In Rome*
'For You For Me' *Holiday Carnival* EP
'Forever' *Always Guaranteed*
'Forever You Will Be Mine' *Stronger*
'Forgive Me' Not released
'Forty Days' *21 Today*
'Free My Soul' *Green Light*
'Frenesi' *When In Spain*
'Friday Night' ('See You At The Dance')
*The Young Ones*
'Friends' *Aladdin And His Wonderful Lamp*
'From A Distance' *From A Distance*
'From This Day On' Not released
'Front Page' *Silver*

'Galadriel' *Dressed For The Occasion*
'Gee But It's Lonesome' Not released
'Gee Whizz It's You' *Me And My Shadows,
40 Golden Greats*
'Geh' Deinen Weg Nicht So Allein'
German release
'Get Back' *Cliff In Japan*
'Get On Board Little Children' *Good News*
'Gettin' The Feelin'' Not released
'Girl On The Bus' *Established 1958*
'Girl You'll Be A Woman Soon' *The Best Of
Cliff, Cliff 'Live' At The Talk Of The Town*
'Give A Little Bit More' *I'm No Hero*

268

'Give Me Back That Old Familiar Feeling'
   *The 31st Of February Street*
'Give Me Love Your Way' *Every Face Tells
   A Story*
'Glaub Nur Mir' German release
'Go Where I Send Thee' *Good News*
'God Put A Fighter In Me' (also under
   'Fighter') *From A Distance*
'God Rest Ye Merry Gentlemen' *Carol
   Singers* EP
'Going Away' *The 31st Of February Street*
'Going Home' *Small Corners*
'Good Golly Miss Molly' *Don't Stop Me
   Now, From A Distance*
'Good News' *Good News*
'Good Old Rock 'n' Roll' *Rock Medley (Cliff
   in Japan)*
'Good On The Sally Army' *Small Corners*
'Good Times' *The Best Of Cliff, Volume 2*
'Goodbye Sam, Hello Samantha' *The Best
   Of Cliff, Volume 2, 40 Golden Greats, Cliff
   In Japan*
'Goodbye Sam Das Ist Die Liebe' German
   release
'Got A Funny Feeling' *The Young Ones*
'Great Balls Of Fire' (Rock medley: *Cliff In
   Japan*)
'Green Green' German release
'Green Light' *Green Light, Dressed for the
   Occasion, Private Collection*
'Gretna Green' German release
'Gut Dass Es Freunde Gibt' German
   release

'Hang On To A Dream' *Don't Stop Me
   Now, Cliff In Japan*
'Hang Up My Rock And Roll Shoes' Not
   released. Tapes – Radio Luxembourg
'Hangin' On' *40 Golden Greats*
'Hank's Medley' *Cliff 'Live' At The Talk Of
   The Town*
'Happy Birthday' *21 Today*
'Happy World' Not released
'Hava Nagila' *His Land*
'Have A Little Talk With Myself' *Cliff In
   Japan*
'Have I Told You Lately That I Love You'
   *Love Is Forever*
'Have Yourself A Merry Little Christmas'
   *Together With Cliff*
'Havin' Fun' *Aladdin And His Wonderful
   Lamp*
'Heart User' *The Rock Connection, Private
   Collection*
'Heartbeat' *Don't Stop Me Now*
'Help' Not released
'Help It Along' *Help It Along*
'Here Comes Summer' *Cliff Sings*
'Here' ('So Doggone Blue') *I'm No Hero*
'He's Everything To Me' *His Land*
'Hey Doctor Man' *Cinderella*

'Hey Mister' B-side of 'Lean On You'
'Hey Mr Dream Maker' *Every Face Tells A
   Story*
'Hey Watcha Say' *Small Corners*
'High Class Baby' Main side single. CD:
   *The Best of Me*
'High 'n' Dry' B-side of 'Congratulations'
'High School Confidential' *Oh Boy*
'Higher Ground' *Help It Along*
'His Execution And His Death' *About That
   Man*
'His Land' *His Land*
'His Latest Flame' *Cliff in Japan*
'Hold On' *Silver*
'Home' *Wonderful Life*
'Homeward Bound' *Don't Stop Me Now*
'Honky Tonk Angel' A-side single
'Hot Shot' *Rock 'n' Roll*
'House Without Windows' *Cliff Richard,
   When In Rome*
'How Long Is Forever' *32 Minutes And 17
   Seconds With Cliff Richard*
'How Wonderful To Know' *21 Today*

'I Ain't Got Time Anymore' *Best Of Cliff,
   Volume 2*
'I Cannot Find A True Love' *Me And My
   Shadows*
'I Can't Ask For Anything More Than
   You' *I'm Nearly Famous, 40 Golden Greats*
'I Could Easily Fall In Love With You'
   *Aladdin And His Wonderful Lamp, More
   Hits By Cliff, 40 Golden Greats, Cliff –
   Love Songs*
'I Don't Know' *Me And My Shadows*
'I Don't Wanna Love You' *Cliff Richard*
'I Found A Rose' *Love Is Forever*
'I Get The Feeling' B-side of 'I'll Come
   Running'
'I Got A Feeling' *Cliff*
'I Got The Feeling' German release
'I Gotta Know' *Cliff Sings*
'I Gotta Woman' Not released
'I Just Don't Have The Heart' *Stronger*
'I Live For You' *Listen to Cliff*
'I Love' *Small Corners*
'I Love The Way You Are' Not released
'I Love You' *Cliff's Hit Album*
'I Love You So' *Me And My Shadows*
'I Only Came To Say Goodbye' *Cliff
   Richard*
'I Only Have Eyes For You' *The EP
   Collection*
'I Only Know I Love You' Not released
'I Only Live To Love You' Not released
'I Saw Her Standing There' *Don't Stop Me
   Now*
'I Still Send Her Flowers' Not released
'I Wake Up Cryin'' *32 Minutes And 17
   Seconds With Cliff Richard*
'I Walk Alone' *Love Is Forever*

'I Want You To Know' *Listen To Cliff*
'I Was Only Fooling Myself' Not released
'I Who Have Nothing' Not released
'I Will Arise And Go' Not released
'I Will Follow You' *Mission England, Volume 2*
'I Wish We'd All Been Ready' *Small Corners*
'I Wish You'd Change Your Mind' *I'm Nearly Famous*
'I Wonder' B-side of 'Lucky Lips'
'I'd Just Be Fool Enough' *Tracks 'n' Grooves*
'Idle Gossip' *Listen To Cliff*
'If Ever I Would Leave You' *Cliff 'Live' At The Talk Of The Town*
'If I Do' Not released
'If I Give My Heart To You' *The EP Collection*
'If Our Dreams Come True' *Cinderella*
'If You Walked Away' Not released
'Il Faut Chanter La Vie' French release
'Il Mondo Et Tondo' Italian release
'I'll Be Back' *Don't Stop Me Now*
'I'll Be Waiting' Not released
'I'll Come Running' *Cliff In Japan, The Best Of Cliff*
'I'll Love You Forever Today' *Two A Penny, The Best Of Cliff, Volume 2*
'I'll Make It All Up To You' *Tracks 'n' Grooves*
'I'll See You In My Dreams' *Dream* EP
'I'll String Along With You' *Cliff Sings*
'I'll Try' *Oh Boy*
'I'm Afraid To Go Home' B-side of 'The Twelfth of Never'
'I'm Feeling So Lonely' *Aladdin And His Wonderful Lamp*
'I'm Gonna Get You' *Me And My Shadows*
'I'm In Love With You' *Aladdin And His Wonderful Lamp*
'I'm In The Mood' *Love Songs*
'I'm Looking Out The Window' *Hit Album, 40 Golden Greats*
'I'm Nearly Famous' *I'm Nearly Famous*
'I'm No Hero' *I'm No Hero*
'I'm Not Getting Married' *Sincerely Cliff Richard*
'I'm On My Way' *32 Minutes And 17 Seconds With Cliff Richard*
'I'm The Lonely One' *More Hits By Cliff*
'I'm Walkin'' *Cliff Sings*
'I'm Walkin' The Blues' *Cliff Sings*
'I'm Willing To Learn' *Me And My Shadows*
'Imagine Love' B-side of 'Green Light'
'In Love Again' Not released. Tapes – Radio Luxembourg.
'In Other Words' Not released
'In The Bleak Midwinter' *Carol Singers* EP, *Cliff Richard Carols*
'In The Country' *Cinderella, The Best Of Cliff, 40 Golden Greats, From A Distance – The Event*
'In The Night' *I'm No Hero*
'In The Past' *Sincerely Cliff Richard*
'In The Stars' *Wonderful Life*
'Indifference' Not released
'Into Each Life Some Rain Must Fall' *Finders Keepers*
'Is There An Answer' Not released
'It Came Upon The Midnight Clear' Not released
'It Could Already Be Tomorrow' Not released
'It Has To Be You, It Has To Be Me' *Now You See Me . . . Now You Don't*
'It Is No Secret' *Good News*
'It'll Be Me' *32 Minutes And 17 Seconds With Cliff Richard, 40 Golden Greats, Rock 'n' Roll, Silver*
'It's All In The Game' *More Hits By Cliff, 40 Golden Greats, Love Songs*
'It's All Over' *The Best Of Cliff*
'It's In Every One Of Us' *Single, Time*
'It's My Party' *From A Distance*
'It's No Use Pretending' *I'm Nearly Famous*
'It's Not For Me To Say' *Cliff Richard*
'It's Only Make Believe' Not released
'It's Only Me You've Left Behind' Not released
'It's Only Money' *Take Me High*
'It's Wonderful To Be Young' Not released
'It's You' *Listen To Cliff*
'I've Got Confidence' Not released
'I've Got News For You' *Small Corners*
'I've Said Too Many Things' *Aladdin And His Wonderful Lamp*

'Jailhouse Rock' (Rock Medley: *Cliff in Japan*)
'J'attendrai' *The EP Collection*
'Je Suis Formidable' French release
'Jerusalem, Jerusalem' *His Land*
'Jesus' *The Best of Cliff, Volume 2, Help It Along*
'Jesus Addresses The Crowd' *About That Man*
'Jesus, Call Your Lambs' (with Sheila Walsh) *Portrait* (Sheila Walsh)
'Jesus Is Betrayed And Arrested' *About That Man*
'Jesus Is My Kind Of People' Not released
'Jesus Loves You' *Help It Along*
'Jesus Recruits His Helpers' *About That Man*
'Jet Black' *Cliff*
'Joanna' *Stronger*
'John The Baptist . . .' *About That Man*
'Johnny' Not released
'Johnny Wake Up To Reality' Not released
'Join The Band' *Take Me High*

'Joseph' *Small Corners*
'Junior Cowboy' *I'm Nearly Famous*
'Just A Closer Walk With Thee' *Good News*
'Just A Little Bit Too Late' B-side of 'On My Word'
'Just Another Guy' B-side of 'The Minute You're Gone'
'Just Dance' *The Young Ones*
'Just Say I Love Her' *When In Rome*

'Keep Me Warm' *Stronger*
'Keep Me Where Love Is' *His Land*
'Keep On Looking' B-side of 'A Little In Love'
'Kein Zug Nach Gretna Green' German Release
'King Creole' *Oh Boy!*
'Kiss' *When In Spain*
'Kisses Sweeter Than Wine' Not released
'Kleine Taube' German release
'La Ballade De Baltimore' French release
'La Gonave' *The Rock Connection*
'La La La La La' *Cliff 'Live' At The Talk Of The Town*, *The EP Collection*
'La La La Song' *Finders Keepers*
'La Mer' *The EP Collection*
'Lady Came From Baltimore' *Cliff 'Live' At The Talk Of The Town*
'L'Amandier Sauvage' French release
'Lamp Of Love' *Me And My Shadows*
'Lass Uns Schnell Vergessen' German release
'Law Of The Universe' B-side of 'Born To Rock 'n' Roll'
'Lawdy Miss Clawdy' Not released
'Lean On You' *Stronger*
'Learning How To Rock 'n' Roll' *The Rock Connection*
'Leave My Woman Alone' B-side of 'The Joy Of Loving'
'Left Out Again' *Me And My Shadows*
'Legata Ad Un Granello Di Sabbia' *When In Rome*
'Lessons In Love' *The Young Ones*
'Let Us Take You For A Ride' *Summer Holiday*
'Let's Have A Party' *From A Distance* (*Oh Boy* medley)
'Let's Make A Memory' *32 Minutes And 17 Seconds With Cliff Richard*
'Let's Stick Together' Not released save for 7-inch acetate
'Lies And Kisses' *Take Four* EP
'Life' *Take Me High*
'Lindsay Jane' B-side of 'The Best Of Me'
'Lindsay Jane II' B side of 'From A Distance'
'Little B' Unreleased Kingston 'Live' set
'Little Bitty Pretty One' *Rock 'n' Roll Silver*
'Little Rag Doll' *The EP Collection*
'Little Things Mean A Lot' *Cliff Sings*

'Little Town' *Now You See Me . . . Now You Don't*, *Together*, *Private Collection*
'Little Town Of Bethlehem' *Cliff Richard Carols* (see also 'O Little Town')
'Livin' Lovin' Doll' Single
'Living Doll' *Cliff's Hit Album*, *40 Golden Greats*, *Cliff In Japan*, *The Young Ones*
'Living In Harmony' *Cliff In Japan*
'Locked Inside Your Prison' *Silver*
'London Ist Nicht Weit' German release
'London's Not Too Far, *Sincerely Cliff*, *Cliff 'Live' At The Talk Of The Town*
'Lonely Girl' *Two A Penny*
'Long Ago' *Love Is Forever*
'Long Long Time' *The 31st Of February Street*
'Look Before You Love' B-side of 'The Time In Between'
'Look Don't Touch' Not released
'Look Homeward Angel' *Love Is Forever*
'Look In My Eyes Maria' *The EP Collection*
'Lost In A Lonely World' *Wired For Sound*
'Love' *Expresso Bongo*
'Love And A Helping Hand' B-side of 'Little Town'
'Love Is Enough' B-side of 'Miss You Nights'
'Love Is Here' B-side of 'Hangin' On'
'Love Is Like A Crescendo' Not released
'Love Is More Than Words' Not released
'Love Letters' *The EP Collection*
'Love Never Gives Up' Dick Saunders: 10th Anniversary Rally
'Love On' B-side of 'Devil Woman'
'Love Stealer' *Silver*
'Love, Truth And Emily Stone' *Tracks 'n' Grooves*
'Love Ya' B-side of 'My Pretty One'
'Lover' *Listen To Cliff*
'Lovers' *I'm Nearly Famous*
'Lovers And Friends' *The Rock Connection*
'Lucille' *Rock 'n' Roll Silver*, *The Rock Connection*, *Cliff In Japan* (rock medley)
'Lucky Lips' *More Hits By Cliff*, *Cliff in Japan*, *40 Golden Greats*

'Mad About You' *Serious Charge* EP
'Maggie's Saml.a' *Established 1958*
'Magic Is The Moonlight' *When In Spain*, *Cliff Richard*
'Make Ev'ry Day A Carnival Day' *Aladdin and His Wonderful Lamp*
'Make It Easy On Yourself' Unreleased in UK *Cliff in Japan*
'Makin' History' *Rock 'n' Roll*, *Silver*, *The Rock Collection*
'Mambo' *The Young Ones*
'Man Gratuliert' German release
'Maria' *Look Into My Eyes Maria* EP, *The EP Collection*
'Marianne' *The Best of Cliff, Volume 2*

271

'Maria's Her Name' *When In Rome*
'Marmaduke' B-side of 'Mistletoe and Wine'
'Mary What You Gonna Call That Pretty Little Baby' *Good News*
'May The Good Lord Bless You And Keep You' *Good News*
'Maybe Someday' *Dressed For The Occasion*
'Me Lo Dijo Adela' *When In Spain*
'Mean Streak' A-side single
'Mean Woman Blues' *Cliff Sings*
'Meditation' *Kinda Latin*
'Memories Linger On' *Listen To Cliff*
'Michelle' Not released
'Midnight Blue' *Take Me High*
'Miss You Nights' *I'm Nearly Famous, 40 Golden Greats, Thank You Very Much, Cliff – Love Songs, Dressed For The Occasion, From A Distance – Box Set*
'Mistletoe And Wine' *Private Collection, Together*
'Mobile Alabama School Leaving Hullabaloo' Not released
'Monday Comes Too Soon' B-side of 'I Ain't Got Time Anymore'
'Monday Thru Friday' *Rock 'n' Roll Juvenile*
'Mood Mambo' *The Young Ones*
'Moonlight Bay' *The EP Collection*
'Move It' *Cliff, Cliff's Hit Album, Don't Stop Me Now, 40 Golden Greats, Thank You Very Much, Rock 'n' Roll Silver, From A Distance – The Event, Cliff In Japan*
'Moving In' B-side of 'Carrie'
'Mr Businessman' *Help It Along*
'Mr Cloud' B-side of 'Jesus'
'Mr Nice' B-side of 'Marianne'
'Mrs Emily Jones' German release
'Muddy Water' Not released
'Mumblin' Mosie' Not released
'Must Be Love' *Every Face Tells A Story*
'My Babe' *Cliff, Don't Stop Me Now*
'My Blue Heaven' *21 Today*
'My Colouring Book' *Love Is Forever*
'My Feet Hit The Ground' B-side of 'High Class Baby'
'My Foolish Heart' *Love Is Forever*
'My Head Goes Around' *Tracks 'n' Grooves*
'My Heart Is An Open Book' *The EP Collection, Take Four EP*
'My Kinda Life' *Every Face Tells A Story, 40 Golden Greats*
'My Luck Won't Change' *Rock 'n' Roll Juvenile*
'My Pretty One' *Always Guaranteed, Private Collection*
'My Way' *Finders Keepers, Cliff In Japan*

'Neben Dir Wird's Keine Geben' German release
'Needing A Friend' B-side of 'Can't Take

The Hurt Anymore'
'Never Be Anyone Else But You' *Rock 'n' Roll, Silver, The Rock Connection*
'Never Even Thought' *Green Light*
'Never Knew What Love Could Do' *La La La La La EP*
'Never Mind' B-side of 'Mean Streak'
'Never Say Die' ('Give A Little Bit More') *Silver, Private Collection*
'News For You' *Small Corners*
'Nine Times Out Of Ten' *Cliff's Hit Album, 40 Golden Greats*
'Nivram' *Thank You Very Much*
'No Matter What' *The 31st Of February Streeet*
'No Name No Fame' Not released
'No One For Me But Nicki' *The Young Ones*
'No One Seems To Care' Not released
'No One Waits' B-side of 'Hey Mr Dream Maker'
'No Turning Back' *Serious Charge* EP
'Non Dimenticare Chi Ti Ama' Italian release
'Non L'Ascoltare' *When In Rome*
'Not The Way It Should Be' *Established 1958*
'Note In A Bottle' Not released
'Nothing Is Impossible' *The Young Ones*
'Nothing Left For Me To Say' Single
'Nothing To Remind Me' *The 31st Of February Street*
'Now I've Done It' Not released
'Now That You Know Me' Not released
'Now You See Me, Now You Don't' *Now You See Me . . . Now You Don't*
'Nowhere Man' Not released
'Now's The Time To Fall In Love' Single
'Nur Bei Dir Bin Ich Zu Haus' German release
'Nur Mit Dir' German release

'O Little Town of Bethlehem' *Carol Singers* EP
'O Mio Signore' *When In Rome*
'Occasional Rain' B-side of 'Good Times'
'Ocean Deep' *Silver, Private Collection*
'Oh Boy' See Parlophone released album
'Oh Boy Medley' *From A Distance – The Event*
'Oh No, Don't Let Go' *Wired For Sound*
'Oh Señorita' Not released
'On My Word' *The Best of Cliff*
'On The Beach' *Wonderful Life, More Hits By Cliff, Cliff In Japan, 40 Golden Greats*
'Once In A While' *Wired For Sound*
'Once Upon A Time' *Always Guaranteed*
'One Fine Day' *Don't Stop Me Now*
'One Night' *Always Guaranteed*
'One Note Samba' *Kinda Latin*
'One Time Lover Man' B-side of 'Some

People'
'Only You' B-side of 'All I Ask Of You' –
   12 inch
'Ooh La La' *Established 1958*
'Our Day Will Come' *Kinda Latin*
'Our Love Could Be So Real' *The 31st Of*
   *February Street*
'Our Storybook' B-side of 'The Day I Met
   Marie'
'Outsider' *21 Today*
'Over In Bethlehem' *His Land*
'Over You' *The Rock Connection*

'Paella' *Finders Keepers*
'Paradise Lost' *Love Is Forever*
'Part Of Me' Not released
'Peace And Quiet' *Cinderella*
'Pentecost' Not released
'Per Un Bacio D'Amor' *When In Rome*
'Perfidia' *When In Spain, Cliff Richard*
'Perhaps Perhaps Perhaps' *When In Spain*
'Pigeon' B-side of 'Flying Machine'
'Please Don't Fall In Love' *Silver, Private*
   *Collection*
'Please Don't Tease' *Cliff's Hot Album,*
   *40 Golden Greats, Thank You*
'Please Remember Me' *Green Light*
'Poem' *Established 1958*
'Pointed Toe Shoes' *Cliff Sings*
'Poor Boy' *21 Today*
'Postmark Heaven' Not released
'Poverty' *Cinderella*
'Power To All Our Friends' *40 Golden*
   *Greats*
'Praise My Soul' Not released
'Punch And Judy' *Sincerely Cliff Richard*
'Put My Mind At Ease' *Tracks 'n' Grooves*

'Quando, Quando, Quando' *Kinda Latin*
'Que Buena Suerte' Spanish release
'Quelle Histoire Je Suis Millionaire'
   French release
'Questions' *Two A Penny*
'Quien Sera' Not released in UK
'Quiet Night Of Quiet Stars' *Kinda Latin*
'Quizas, Quizas, Quizas' *When In Spain*

'Rain Cloud' Not released
'Rattler' *Two A Penny*
'Razzle Dazzle' *Cliff Richard*
'Ready Teddy' *Cliff*
'Really Waltzing' *Summer Holiday*
'Red Rubber Ball' *Two A Penny*
'Reelin' And Rockin'' *Cliff Richard*
'Reflections' *About That Man*
'Relève Mon Defi' French release
'Remember Me' *Always Guaranteed,*
   *Private Collection*
'Rock 'n' Roll Is Here To Stay' *From A*
   *Distance*
'Rock 'n' Roll Juvenile' *Rock 'n' Roll*

*Juvenile*
'Rockin' Robin' *Oh Boy*
'Rosalie' Not released. Tapes – Radio
   Luxembourg.
'Rote Lippen Soll Man Küssen' German
   release
'Round And Round' *Summer Holiday*
'Roving Gambler' Not released
'Run For Shelter' Not released
'Run To The Door' *Finders Keepers*

'Sag 'No' Zu Ihm' German release
'Sally Sunshine' German release
'Sam' *Sincerely Cliff Richard*
'Saturday Night At The Whirl' Not
   released
'Save My Soul' Not released
'Save The Last Dance For Me' *Don't Stop*
   *Me Now*
'Saviour's Day' *From A Distance, Together*
   *With Cliff Richard*
'Say You Don't Mind' *Wired For Sound*
'Say You're Mine' B-side of 'Don't Talk To
   Him'
'Scarlet Ribbons' *Together With Cliff*
   *Richard*
'Schon Wie Ein Traum' German release
'Schoolboy Crush' B-side of 'Move It'
'Sci-Fi' *Rock 'n' Roll Juvenile*
'Sea Cruise' *From A Distance*
'Secret Love' *The EP Collection*
'Seeing Is Believing' Not released
'Sentimental Journey' *Listen to Cliff*
'Seven Days To Our Holiday' *Summer*
   *Holiday*
'Shadoogie' *Thank You Very Much*
'Shake, Rattle And Roll' *From A Distance*
'Shakin' All Over' B-side of 'Daddy's
   Home'
'Shame On You' *21 Today*
'Share A Dream' *Stronger, From A Distance*
'She Means Nothing To Me' *The Rock*
   *Connection, Private Collection*
'She Needs Him More Than Me'
   *Cinderella*
'She's A Gypsy' *Green Light*
'She's Gone' *Me And My Shadows*
'She's Leaving You' B-side of 'Big Ship'
'She's So Beautiful' *Private Collection, Time*
'Shine Jesus Shine' *The Kendrick Collection*
'Ships That Pass In The Night' Not
   released
'Shoom Llamma Boom Boom' German
   recording
'Shooting From The Heart' *The Rock*
   *Connection*
'Shooting Star' *Thunderbirds Are Go* EP
'Shout' *Don't Stop Me Now, Cliff In Japan,*
   *Cliff 'Live' At The Talk Of The Town*
'Silent Night' *Together*
'Silhouettes' *From A Distance*

273

'Silver's Home Tonight' *Silver*

'Silvery Rain' *The Best Of Cliff, Volume 2, Help It Along, Cliff In Japan*

'Since I Lost You' B-side of 'It'll Be Me'

'Sing A Song Of Freedom' *The Best Of Cliff, Volume 2, Help It Along, 40 Golden Greats, Live In Japan*

'Slow Rivers' *Private Collection*

'Small World' B-side of 'Shooting From The Heart'

'So I've Been Told' *32 Minutes and 17 Seconds With Cliff Richard*

'Solamente Una Vez' *When In Spain*

'Solitary Man' *The EP Collection*

'Some Of These Days' 'Holiday Carnival' EP

'Some People' *Always Guaranteed, Private Collection, From A Distance*

'Somebody Loses' B-side of 'Blue Turns To Grey'

'Somebody Touched Me' *Oh Boy!*

'Someday You'll Want Me To Love You' *Love Is Forever*

'Something Good' *Cliff 'Live' At The Talk Of The Town*

'Somewhere' Not released

'Somewhere Along The Way' *Cliff Sings*

'Somewhere By The Sea' *Established 1958*

'Son Of Thunder' *Now You See Me . . . Now You Don't*

'Sooner Or Later' Not released

'Spanish Harlem' *32 Minutes And 17 Seconds With Cliff Richard, Cliff In Japan*

'Spider Man' *Every Face Tells A Story*

'Star Of Hope' Not released

'Start All Over Again' *Green Light*

'Steady With You' B-side of 'Livin' Lovin' Doll'

'Stell Mich Deinen Eltern Vor' German release

'Sternegold' German release

'Story Ohne Happy End' German release

'Stranger In Town' *Summer Holiday*

'Street Scene' *Aladdin And His Wonderful Lamp*

'Streets Of London' Not released

'Stronger Than That' *Stronger*

'Such Is The Mystery' *I'm Nearly Famous*

'Suddenly' *Private Collection, Xanadu*

'Summer Holiday' *More Hits By Cliff, Cliff In Japan, 40 Golden Greats, From A Distance – The Event*

'Summer Rain' *Wired For Sound*

'Sunny Honey Girl' *The Best Of Cliff, Volume 2, Cliff In Japan*

'Sway' *When In Spain, Cliff Richard*

'Sweet And Gentle' *When In Spain*

'Sweet Dreams' Not released

'Sweet Little Jesus Boy' *About That Man*

'Sweet Loving Ways' Not released

'Swingin' Affair' *Summer Holiday*

'Take A Look Around' Not released

'Take Action' *Sincerely Cliff Richard*

'Take Another Look' *I'm No Hero*

'Take Good Care Of Her' *Sincerely Cliff Richard*

'Take Me High' *Take Me High*

'Take Me To The Leader' Not released

'Take Me Where I Wanna Go' Not released

'Take My Hand, Precious Lord' *Good News*

'Take Special Care' *Cliff Richard*

'Take You For A Ride' *Summer Holiday*

'Te Quiro Dijeste' *When In Spain*

'Tea For Two' *21 Today*

'Teddy Bear' *Rock 'n' Roll, Silver*

'Tell Me You're Mine' *When In Rome*

'Temptation' *Listen To Cliff*

'That'll Be The Day' *Cliff Sings*

'That's What Love Is' Not released

'That's Why I Love You' B-side of 'When Two Worlds Drift Apart'

'The Bellman's Speech' *The Hunting Of The Snark*

'The Best Of Me' *Stronger*

'The Birth Of John The Baptist' *About That Man*

'The Carnival's Just For Me' Not released

'The Christmas Song' *Together*

'The Day I Met Marie' *The Best Of Cliff, Cliff 'Live' At The Talk Of The Town, 40 Golden Greats, Thank You, Cliff – Love Songs, Cliff In Japan*

'The Days Of Love' Not released

'The Dreams I Dream' *Established 1958, Cliff 'Live' At The Talk Of The Town*

'The Evergreen Tree' *Cabaret Night In London*

'The Fellow Next To Me' Not released

'The First Easter' *About That Man*

'The Girl Can't Help It' *Tracks 'n' Grooves, From A Distance – The Event*

'The Girl From Ipanema' *Kinda Latin*

'The Glory Of Love' *From A Distance*

'The Golden Days Are Over' *Silver*

'The Holly And The Ivy' Not released

'The Hunt' *Cinderella*

'The Joy Of Loving' *The Best Of Cliff, Volume 2*

'The King Of Love My Shepherd Is' *Good News*

'The King's Place' *Cinderella*

'The Lady Came From Baltimore' *Cliff 'Live' At The Talk Of The Town*

'The Leaving' *The 31st Of February Street*

'The Letter' Not released

'The Long Way Home' Not released

'The Lord's My Shepherd' *Hymns And Inspirational Songs*

'The Minute You're Gone' *Cliff In Japan, The Best Of Cliff, Cliff – Love Songs*
'The New 23rd Psalm' *His Land*
'The Next Time' *More Hits By Cliff, 40 Golden Greats, Cliff – Love Songs*
'The Night' B-side of 'Wind Me Up'
'The Night Is So Lonely' *21 Today*
'The Old Accordion' B-side of 'A Brand New Song'
'The Only Way Out' *Now You See Me . . . Now You Don't*
'The Questions' *When In Rome*
'The Rock That Doesn't Roll' Not released
'The Shrine On The Second Floor' *The EP Collection*
'The Singer' *The 31st Of February Street*
'The Snake And The Bookworm' *Cliff Sings*
'The Song From Moulin Rouge' Not released
'The Sound Of The Candyman's Trumpet' 'Congratulations' EP
'The Sun Ain't Gonna Shine Anymore' Japanese released album
'The 31st Of February Street' *The 31st Of February Street*
'The Time In Between' *The Best of Cliff*
'The Touch Of Your Lips' *Cliff Sings*
'The Trial Of Jesus' *About That Man*
'The Twelfth Of Never' *More Hits By Cliff, Cliff – Love Songs*
'The Twelve Days Of Christmas' B-side of 'We Should Be Together' (Continental release)
'The Visit Of The Wise Men' *About That Man*
'The Water Is Wide' *Now You See Me . . . Now You Don't*
'The Winner' B-side of 'Silhouettes'
'The Winter Follows Spring' Not released
'The Word Is Love' *Take Me High*
'The Young Ones' *The Young Ones, Cliff Hit Album, Cliff In Japan, 40 Golden Greats, From A Distance – The Event, Cliff In Japan*
'Theme For A Dream' *Cliff's Hit Album, 40 Golden Greats, Cliff – Love Songs*
'There Is A Green Hill' Not released
'There You Go Again' *The 31st Of February Street*
'Thief In The Night' *Now You See Me . . . Now You Don't, Dressed For The Occasion, From A Distance – The Event*
'Things We Said Today' *The EP Collection*
'Thinking Of Our Love' B-side of 'Nine Times Out Of Ten'
'This Day' *Finders Keepers*
'This Is My Kind Of Love' Not released
'This New Year' *Together With Cliff*
'This Time Now' *Always Guaranteed*
'This Was My Special Day' *Aladdin And His Wonderful Lamp*

'Through The Eye Of A Needle' *Love Is Forever*
'Throw Down The Line' *The Best Of Cliff, Volume 2, 40 Golden Greats*
'Time' *Sincerely Cliff Richard*
'Time Drags By' *Finders Keepers, The Best Of Cliff*
'Time Flies' B-side of 'Silvery Rain'
'Tiny Planet' *It's A Small World*
'To Prove My Love For You' *21 Today*
'Todo El Poder A Los Amigos' Spanish release
'Tomorrow Rising' B-side of 'Help It Along'
'Too Close To Heaven' B-side of 'Please Don't Fall In Love'
'Too Late To Say Goodbye' Not released
'Too Much' *Cliff*
'Tough Enough' *21 Today*
'Travellin' Light' *Cliff's Hit Album, The 31st of February Street, 40 Golden Greats*
'Treasure Of Love' *Dressed For The Occasion*
'True Love Ways' *Dressed For The Occasion, Private Collection*
'True Love Will Come To You' *Listen To Cliff*
'True True Lovin'' B-side of 'Constantly'
'Try A Smile' *Every Face Tells A Story*
'Turn Around' *32 Minutes And 17 Seconds With Cliff Richard*
'Turn It Into Cash' Not released
'Tus Besos' *When In Spain*
'Tutti Frutti' *Rock 'n' Roll, Silver*
'TV Hop' *Oh Boy!*
'Twelve Days Of Christmas' Not released
'Twenty Flight Rock' *Cliff Sings*
'23rd Psalm' *Good News*
'Twist And Shout' *Two A Penny*
'Twist In Blut' German release
'Two A Penny' *Two A Penny*
'Two Hearts' *Always Guaranteed, Private Collection*
'Two To The Power' (with Janet Jackson) A-side of single

'Umbarella' German release
'Unchained Melody' *Listen To Cliff*
'Under Lock And Key' *Green Light*
'Under The Gun' B-side 12 inch of 'My Pretty One'
'Under The Influence' B-side of 'The Only Way Out'
'Under Your Spell' *Always Guaranteed*
'Until The Right One Comes Along' Not released
'Unto Us A Boy Is Born' *Carol Singers* EP
'Unto Us A Child Is Born' *Cliff Richard Carols*
'Up In Canada' *Small Corners*

'Up In The World' *Love Songs, Dressed For The Occasion*

'Vaudeville Routine' *The Young Ones*
'Vaya Con Dios' *When In Spain*
'Venite' *Together With Cliff*
'Visions' *Cliff In Japan, The Best Of Cliff, Cliff 'Live' At The Talk Of The Town, 40 Golden Greats, Love Songs*
'Volare' *When In Rome*
'Vrenli' German release

'Wake Up, Wake Up' *Two A Penny, Walk On By, The Look Of Love, Cliff In Japan*
'Walk Right In' Not released. Tapes – Radio Luxembourg
'Walking In The Light' B-side of 'Hot Shot'
'Walking The Blues' *32 Minutes And 17 Seconds With Cliff Richard*
'Was Ist Dabei' German release
'Washerwoman' *Finders Keepers*
'Watch What You Do With My Baby' B-side of 'I'm The Lonely One'
'We Don't Talk Anymore' *Rock 'n' Roll, Cliff – Love Songs, Dressed For The Occasion, Private Collection, From A Distance – The Event*
'We Had It Made' Not released
'We Have It Made' *Me And My Shadows*
'We Kiss In The Shadow' *Listen To Cliff*
'We Love A Movie' *Wonderful Life*
'We Say Yeah' *The Young Ones, Cliff In Japan*
'We Shall Be Changed' *Good News*
'We Should Be Together' *Together With Cliff*
'Welcome To Stoneybroke' *Cinderella*
'Wenn Du Lachst, Lacht Das Gluck' German release
'Were You There' Not released
'What A Friend We Have In Jesus' *Good News, Hymns And Inspirational Songs*
'What A Silly Thing' *Tracks 'n' Grooves*
'What Would I Do For The Love Of A Girl' B-side of 'Visions'
'Whatcha Gonna Do About It' Not released
'What'd I Say' *Listen To Cliff, Cliff In Japan*
'What's Behind The Eyes Of Mary' *Established 1958*
'What's More I Don't Need Her' *Cliff Live*
'What've I Gotta Do' *Wonderful Life*
'When' (duet with Kalin Twins) *From A Distance – The Event*
'When I Find You' *Sincerely Cliff Richard*
'When I Grow Too Old' *The EP Collection*
'When I Survey The Wondrous Cross' *Good News, Small Corners*
'When I'm 64' *Cliff Live*
'When My Dreamboat Comes Home' *32 Minutes And 17 Seconds With Cliff Richard*

'When The Girl In Your Arms' *The Young Ones, Cliff's Hit Album, 40 Golden Greats, Cliff – Love Songs*
'When Two Worlds Drift Apart' *Every Face Tells A Story, Cliff – Love Songs*
'When You Are There' Not released
'Where Did The Summer Go' *Finders Keepers*
'Where Do We Go From Here' *Now You See Me . . . Now You Don't*
'Where Is My Heart' B-side of 'Please Don't Tease'
'Where Is That Man' *About That Man*
'Where Is Your Heart' *Look In My Eyes Maria* EP
'Where The Four Winds Blow' *The EP Collection*
'Where You Are' *Songs For Life, Mission '89*
'While Shepherds Watched' *Carol Singers* EP, *Cliff Richard Carols*
'While She's Young' *Green Light*
'White Christmas' *Together With Cliff*
'Who Are We To Say' *32 Minutes And 17 Seconds With Cliff Richard*
'Who Is There To Say' Not released
'Whole Lotta Shakin' Goin' On' *Cliff*
'Who's Gonna Take You Home' 7-inch acetate in circulation
'Who's In Love' *Stronger*
'Why' *Take Me High*
'Why Don't They Understand' *Why Don't They Understand* EP
'Why Me Lord?' *Small Corners*
'Why Should The Devil Have All The Good Music?' *Small Corners, Thank You*
'Why Wasn't I Born Rich' *Cinderella*
'Wide Open Space' B-side of 'I Just Don't Have The Heart'
'Wild Geese' 'Two Hearts', 12-inch version
'Will You Love Me Tomorrow' *Sincerely Cliff Richard*
'Willie And The Hand Jive' *Thank You, The Rock Connection*
'Wind Me Up' *The Best Of Cliff, 40 Golden Greats*
'Winning' *Take Me High*
'Wired For Sound' *Wired For Sound, Private Collection*
'With The Eyes Of A Child' *Best of Cliff Volume 2*
'Without You' *21 Today*
'Wonderful Life' Not released
'Wonderful To Be Young' Canadian single release
'Wonderful World' *Congratulations* EP
'Words' Not released
'Working After School' *Me And My*

*Shadows*
'Wouldn't You Know It' B-side of 'Honky Tonk Angel'

'Y'Arriva' *21 Today*
'Yes He Lives' *Small Corners, Greenbelt 1979*
'Yesterday, Today, Forever' *Help It Along*
'You' Not released
'You And I' *Me And My Shadows*
'You And Me' Not released
'You Belong To My Heart' *When In Spain, Cliff Richard*
'You Can't Get To Heaven' Not released
'You Can Never Tell' B-side of 'Goodbye Sam, Hello Samantha'
'You Don't Know' *32 Minutes And 17 Seconds With Cliff Richard*
'You Got Me Wondering' *Every Face Tells A Story*
'You Gotta Tell Me' *Don't Stop Now*
'You Held My Hand' Not released
'You Know That I Love You' *Rock 'n' Roll Juvenile*
'You, Me And Jesus' 12-inch B-side of 'Little Town'
'You Will Never Know' *The 31st Of February Street*
'You'll Want Me' *Sincerely Cliff Richard* EP
'Young Love' Not released. Tapes – Radio Luxembourg
'Young Love' *Wired For Sound*
'Your Eyes Tell On You' B-side of 'It's All In The Game'
'Your Heart's Not In Your Love' *Tracks 'n' Grooves*
'You're Just The One To Do It' *Me And My Shadows*
'You're The One' B-side of 'It's Only Me You've Left Behind'
'Yours' German release
'Youth And Experience' *Wonderful Life*
'You've Got To Give Me All Your Lovin'' *I'm Nearly Famous*
'You've Lost That Lovin' Feelin'' *Live in Japan*
'Yugoslav Wedding' *Summer Holiday*

'Zartliche Sekunden' German release
'Zing Went The Strings Of My Heart' *From A Distance*
'Zip-A-Dee-Doo-Dah' Not released
'Zum Heiraten Bin Ich Kein Typ' German release
'Zuviel Allein' German release